22-7

AN OUTLINE HISTORY OF AMERICAN DRAMA

by Walter J. Meserve

About the Book

Written for students, teachers, and all readers of plays, this book describes the major trends in American drama from its beginnings to the present day. Each chapter is introduced by an essay which suggests the development of the drama, and all movements are illustrated by critical evaluations of the contributions of both major and minor dramatists and analyses of their plays.

Patterned on the developing cultural history of America, this volume emphasizes a critical history of the drama as literature but also traces a history of the American theater and the development of dramatic criticism in America.

Carefully designed section introductions, pertinent biographical information, and numerous plot summaries make this study valuable as a reference book as well as a new approach to a much neglected aspect of American literature. Additional features include selected bibliographies after each chapter and an extensive index.

About the Author

Dr. Meserve is a member of the English Department of the University of Kansas where he teaches, in addition to courses in American literature and American drama, a two semester graduate seminar in American Drama and Theater with a member of the Speech and Drama Department.

An Associate Editor of *Modern Drama,* he has published a number of articles in academic journals. His edition of *The Complete Plays of W. D. Howells* appeared in 1960. He has also edited and contributed to a *Discussions of Modern American Drama* which D. C. Heath has scheduled for publication in 1965. The present volume is viewed as a necessary pilot study for a multi-volume critical history of American drama.

LITTLEFIELD, ADAMS & CO.

TOTOWA, NEW JERSEY

AN OUTLINE HISTORY

OF

AMERICAN DRAMA

by

Walter J. Meserve

University of Kansas

1965

LITTLEFIELD, ADAMS & CO.

Totowa, New Jersey

Copyright © 1965
by Littlefield, Adams & Co.

FOR: Gayle

Peter

Jo

David

CONTENTS

ACKNOWLEDGMENTS

I wish to express my sincere gratitude to the University of Kansas for its continued support of my research in American drama. Without Research Grant #3554-5038 this outline would be far from complete. I would also like to thank the American Philosophical Society for a 1959 grant from its Penrose Fund which helped me to study the reception of nineteenth-century American drama in England. One always uses one's friends, consciously or unconsciously, and I am particularly indebted to Professor A. C. Edwards, Department of English, and Professor William R. Reardon, Department of Speech and Drama, at the University of Kansas, and to Rev. M. C. Allen, my research assistant, for generous amounts of information, insight, and inspiration. My numerous student research assistants and typists I shall always remember and appreciate.

WJM

PREFACE

American drama is a most neglected part of the study of American literature. Nearly a third of a century has passed since anyone has attempted an historical assessment of American drama, and no scholar has discussed the developing movements of American drama or tried to impose any critical order upon the three hundred years which separate contemporary drama from the first play written by a Colonist in English and performed in America. No one need argue that the literary value of American drama during its first two hundred years is very slight. That goes without saying. But as an index to an active society, as a background for modern American drama, and for the literary value of many plays, a study of American drama has its value as well as being a more significant and closely related part of American letters than is usually imagined. It is the purpose of this outline to present the many developing trends in American drama with the supporting detail and critical observations which will make this material meaningful to the student, the scholar, and the casual reader of American plays.

To make this material meaningful I have discussed each topic in terms of its historical development, the achievements of particular dramatists, and the contribution of particular plays. In all instances the plots of important plays are summarized and the titles of relatively significant plays are listed. Because most plays and playwrights suggest more than a single point of view, however, authors and their plays are frequently treated or mentioned under more than one heading. To show the closeness and the interdependence of American drama, theater, and criticism, each chapter relates the progress of dramatic criticism and the achievements of the theater to a developing American drama. Using information that has not been available to previous historians of American drama (the product of recent research and scholarship) and approaching the subject from the point of view of trends, ideas, and the contributions of particular plays rather than from a chronological discussion of important dramatists, this outline history provides a new and basic approach for a more appreciative understanding of American drama.

WJM

CHAPTER I

The Beginnings of American Drama

"The first efforts at dramatic literature in this country were wild," wrote William Dunlap in *A History of the American Theatre* (1832). American plays were "the essays of youth, not sufficiently instructed in anything, and deficient in literary education, and though received favorably . . . both the dramatist and the people they addressed had not yet sufficiently matured their notions of the result of the great political changes which had taken place to know how far to assert independence in literature or government or how far to imitate their European ancestors." Paralleling social and political attitudes which divided not only Patriots and Loyalists but also social classes, literature, particularly dramatic literature, developed two divergent characteristics which lasted more than half a century: the imitation of English and European literature, and the presentation of distinctive American qualities.

If early attempts at dramatic literature were wild, one could surely describe the beginnings of an American theater as stormy. Performances of plays were opposed by local and colonial governments and by certain religious groups. Bankruptcy was a common hazard for theater managers. Playwrights were constantly subjected to abuse by theater managers, actors, and the public.

It was not strange that good native drama before 1800 was rare. The middle-class popular tastes which dominated the theater did not appeal to an artistic temperament; and the lack of the protection of a copyright law discouraged many would-be playwrights. Plays, therefore, were written mainly by opportunists, political or theatrical. The results—propaganda plays, poetic tragedies, and comedies imitative of the English—were produced occasionally with the major theater fare of pirated English and European plays, adaptations, and translations. In healthy contrast, American originality appeared in the stage Yankee and in plays with native themes. By 1800, although conditions in the theater remained chaotic, a drama which could be called American was slowly forming.

I. COLONIAL THEATER AND DRAMA

For theater before the appearance of the white settlers, one must look at the celebrations or ceremonies of the American Indians. Primitive man has always enjoyed celebrating the changes in nature as they affected him and the cycle of life as he lived it. The settlers, however, needed their own form of amusement; and the raw material for their theater was the life they led. They fought with the Indians for their lives, strove for fortune in the new plantations of the South, or argued with their neighbors about religion in New England or politics in New York. Their experiences provided materials for some plays, or they turned to the familiar themes of English and European drama. Whichever impulse excited him, man in America early felt the need of drama in his world, and he soon began to satisfy that need.

A. Drama in the Colonies: First Performances

Early drama in the Colonies may be called "American" only because the term is a convenience. The land belonged to the French, the Spanish, the English, and the Indians. The people were as varied as could be imagined—in language, politics, economics, religion, customs, and so on—and could be related only by the fact that they shared the same New World. But the Colonies of England became the United States of America, and therefore the following information describes the beginnings of American drama and theater.

1. THE FIRST AMERICAN PLAY

Selection of the first play produced in America presents a problem. If plays not written in English are to be included, one can consider either a *comedia* by a Spanish captain, Marcos Farfán de los Godos, or a masque written by Marc Lescarbot, a Frenchman. The Spanish play, performed early in 1598 near what is now the city of El Paso, Texas, by the first white men to settle north of the Rio Grande, depicted the progress of that group and good-naturedly spoofed their adventures. Lescarbot's play, *Le Theatre de Neptune en La Nouvelle-France*, celebrated the return, on November 14, 1606, of the Sieur de Poutrincourt, who had brought a band of Frenchmen, including Lescarbot, to settle at Port Royal, Acadia. A third possibility, this one in English, arises from some evidence that Sir William Berkeley, Governor of Virginia, wrote a play in 1641 entitled *The Lost Lady*. Perhaps there were other "American" plays performed during this period, but the historian of drama has little information at his disposal. Few of the plays produced were written in America.

2. EARLY AMERICAN PLAYS ON STAGE

(a) *Ye Bare and Ye Cubb*, by William Darby, 1665

One of the earliest plays performed and perhaps the first one in English was *Ye Bare and Ye Cubb*. With the help of Cornelius Watkinson and Philip Howard, Darby produced his play on August 27, 1665, in Accomac County, Virginia, and was promptly sued for his troubles by the King's attorney—the implication being that such activity was either immoral or illegal and perhaps both. After inspecting the play, however, the court found the playwright and his players "not guilty of fault." The play, unfortunately, has been lost.

(b) Other Plays Written and Performed

About the turn of the century, Richard Hunter successfully petitioned the Acting Governor of New York for permission to present plays in New York City. Indicative of theater activity in the South was a recital in 1702 by students of William and Mary College of a "pastoral colloquy." The following year Anthony Aston, an English actor, wrote in his journal: "We arrived in Charles-Town, full of Lice, Shame, Poverty, Nakedness and Hunger. I turned Player and Poet and wrote one Play on the Subject of the Country." Whatever its merits, Aston's play was not preserved.

3. FIRST PLAY PRINTED IN AMERICA: *ANDROBORUS*, BY ROBERT HUNTER, 1714

(*Plot*) The play opens in the Senate where the Senators are portrayed as a ridiculous group who praise Androborus (whose name means man-eater) for courage and prudence he has not shown and rail violently against the Keeper, Governor Hunter. In Act II the Senate dissolves itself to become a Consistory, and the play becomes a bitter attack on the clergy. The farcical hero, Androborus, is the object of blatant satire in Act III. Stupidly believing in his own deification, he is shown to be so ethereal that some cannot see and others cannot hear him although most people can smell him. The play ends as all, including Androborus, who is hardly a man-eater, are trapped by the Keeper.

(*Discussion*) *Androborus*, by Robert Hunter, governor of the Province of New York from 1710 to 1719, is now preserved in the Huntington Library in California. From its formal dedication through its three acts—The Senate, The Consistory, The Apotheosis—the play is an occasionally witty but rowdy attack on the Provincial Council, the church government, and Lieutenant Governor Nicholson as Androborus. Called a "Biographical Farce," the play has no literary value and is connected both logically and theatrically by only the slightest of dramatic threads.

B. Actors and Acting Companies in the Colonies

During much of the eighteenth century, the actor in England experienced hard times. The drama of the Restoration (1660–1700) had been witty and brilliant but a bit too vulgar for the tastes of the rising middle class. Jeremy Collier's attack on the theater, *Short View of the Immorality and Profaneness of the English Stage* (1698), clearly indicated the change that was coming. Playwrights like Congreve left the stage. Moralists, humanitarians, and sentimentalists took their places, with the result that theater attendance dropped sharply. Probably the Colonies suggested to some actors an opportunity. At any rate, a number of them, though certainly not the best of England's performers, came individually and in companies to the New World and found both opportunity and adversity.

1. PROBLEMS OF THE ACTORS IN AMERICA

Had the actors thought to consider the kinds of people who had come to America—a large majority of whom were of the same middle class which was changing the English theater—they might have foreseen some of their problems. But actors are traditionally optimistic, and in a special prologue introducing the first performance of the first professional company to come to America (Williamsburg, Virginia, September 15, 1752), their faith was expressed:

> Haste, to Virginia's Plains, my sons, repair,
> The Goddess said, Go confident to find
> An audience sensible, polite and kind.

The players were soon to find, however, limited quantities of all three desirable qualities in the attitudes of some of the Colonial fathers and the people.

(a) Opposition by Religious Groups

One problem that has bothered actors since Tertullian (*ca.* 200 A.D.) and that became crucial for the actor in Colonial America was the antagonism of the small but strict religious sects. New England, and Boston in particular, long retained a reputation for severity toward the theater, and Pennsylvania was little better. In the Penn Colony (1681), three groups—the Quakers, the Germans, and the Scotch-Irish—opposed theaters and helped pass laws prohibiting their activity.

(b) Opposition by Governments

Reflecting the attitude of the people, governing officers and legislatures opposed theatrical ventures. On May 6, 1709, the Governor's Council of New York passed a law forbidding "play-acting and prize fighting." Following a minor riot caused by a 1750 performance in Boston, the Council and Legislature acted to prohibit all stage plays which, it was felt, tended "to increase immorality, impiety, and a contempt for religion." Not until 1791, after the Selectmen of Boston had thoroughly considered the matter, was the law repealed. A Pennsylvania act of 1778 (repealed in 1789) declared all theatrical performances illegal.

As war with England became imminent, the Continental Congress decided that amusements were not in keeping with the spirit of solemnity enveloping the Colonies, and on October 20, 1774, issued an interdict against "exhibitions of shews, plays, and other expensive diversions and entertainments." On October 16, 1778, a more severe interdict declared that government employees "who shall act, promote, encourage, or attend such plays" would lose their jobs.

(c) Actors' Response to Opposition

Such discouraging opposition taxed the inventive resources and finesse of the Colonial actors and acting companies. Lewis Hallam, manager of the first theater company in Virginia, brought to New York a certificate from Virginia's Governor Dinwiddie recommending his players. Occasionally, actors defended their art in prologues to plays:

> Much has been said at this censorious time,
> To prove the treading of the stage a crime.
>
> . . . .
>
> Yet wise men own a play well chose may teach
> Such useful moral truths as churchmen preach;

At other times an actor might hide behind a subterfuge of evasive words, by proposing a "Histrionic Academy," or naming a theater The Boston Museum, or performing *Othello* as a "Series of Moral Dialogues in five parts depicting the evil effects of Jealousy and other Bad Passions and Proving that Happiness can only Spring from the Pursuit of Virtue." Mainly, the actors in the Colonies met their problems with fortitude, ingenuity, and some success.

2. EARLY THEATERS AND ACTING COMPANIES IN THE COLONIES

Information about early theaters in the Colonies is very sketchy, but it is quite clear that the first theater was contracted for on July 11, 1716, in Williamsburg, Virginia. In 1723, a band of players visited Philadelphia, bowed to Quaker resentment of plays, and performed outside the city limits. The next theater came to Philadelphia when the "New Booth on Society Hill" announced a performance of acrobats and comedians. In New York, the New Theatre opened on December 6, 1732, with a performance of George Farquhar's *The Recruiting Officer* (1706). In 1735, at Charleston, South Carolina, Thomas Otway's *The Orphan* (1680) was performed in a courtroom before an enthusiastic audience, and on February 12, 1736, the "New Theatre in Dock Street" was opened. Plays were also produced occasionally in Williamsburg during the next several years, and theaters continued to be built throughout the century.

(a) Murray and Kean Acting Company: Professional Theater

Not until August, 1749, when a company of actors headed by Walter Murray and Thomas Kean acted plays in a warehouse on Water Street, Philadelphia, did America at last have the beginnings of professional theater. From March 5, 1750, until July 8, 1751, the Murray and Kean company performed once or twice a week in New York in a Nassau Street building. Their next stop was Williamsburg, where in October of 1751 they opened a new theater with Shakespeare's *Richard III*.

3. A COMPANY OF COMEDIANS FROM LONDON: LEWIS HALLAM

Records show that Murray and Kean's "Virginia Company" continued playing for nearly twenty years. Most significantly, however, it had stimulated an interest in the theater, thus creating an advantage for Lewis Hallam's Company of Comedians which opened at Williamsburg on September 15, 1752, with *The Merchant of Venice*. Newly arrived from London, experienced and competent, the company's opening bill was performed "before a numerous and polite audience with great applause" (*Virginia Gazette*, September 22, 1752). In June, 1753, Hallam left Williamsburg and after periodic difficulties with church and government groups, produced plays in New York, Philadelphia, and South Carolina. His next stop was Jamaica—perhaps to avoid the plague, perhaps to recoup losses in a colony that boasted some wealth. There, Lewis Hallam died and the company was disbanded, but a tradition of theater in America had been well started.

4. THE AMERICAN COMPANY: DAVID DOUGLASS

In 1758, David Douglass, a successful actor and manager of a company then active in the West Indies, married Lewis Hallam's widow, reorganized the Hallam company with Mrs. Douglass as the star, and her son, young Lewis Hallam, as the leading man, and went to New York. Faced with opposition from the authorities, Douglass, with typical resourcefulness, disassociated himself with plays, declaring his interest solely in "Dissertations on Subjects, *Moral, Instructive, and Entertaining*," and was allowed to open with Nicholas Rowe's *Jane Shore* (1713) on December 28, 1758. He played in a temporary theater on Cruger's Wharf until February 7, 1759, when his permit expired and the company left for Philadelphia where, in spite of opposition by religious groups, he was allowed to open in a new theater on Society Hill. After a successful season there and some time in Maryland and Williamsburg, Douglass invaded New England during the late summer of 1761. Never without some religious or government opposition, Douglass became sufficiently encouraged during the early 1760's to build temporary theaters in Annapolis, Maryland; Newport, Rhode Island; and New York City. During these years, anti-British feeling persuaded him to call his players the "American Company."

No figure in the American theater before the Revolution compares with David Douglass. His company enjoyed notable seasons; his success in overcoming objections to plays was remarkable; as a performer, he was always well received; as a builder of theaters, he had no equal during his lifetime. He should also be remembered for his Southwark Theatre in Philadelphia—the first permanent theater in America—where, in 1767, he produced the first play written by an American and presented on an American stage by professional actors—*The Prince of Parthia*.

C. Drama in the Colonies

While theaters were being built and acting companies were performing in many Colonial towns, plays written by Americans were disappointing and few. Beginning a tradition which lasted over a hundred years in America, players and managers took their repertory from the popular successes of England and the Continent. Doubtless both actors or managers wrote plays before 1767, but these plays seem to have been inconsequential farces, imitative curtain-raisers, or so poor that they never saw the professional stage. It was, therefore, a rather momentous occasion when David Douglass chose an American play for production in 1767.

1. THE PRINCE OF PARTHIA BY THOMAS GODFREY, (1759 ?): FIRST PLAY WRITTEN BY AN AMERICAN AND PERFORMED IN AMERICA BY PROFESSIONAL ACTORS

Thomas Godfrey (1736–1763) is described by John Galt (*The Life and Studies of Benjamin West, Esq.*) as "having given the most promising indications of an elegant genius for pathetic and descriptive poetry." The promise never materialized, however, and except for one venture in heroic tragedy, he is inconsequential in a history of literature. *The Prince of Parthia*, a tragedy in five acts, probably written in 1759, was published in 1765 by Nathaniel Evans, a friend of the poet. Douglass' production on April 24, 1767, was not repeated. Not until March 26, 1915, when the tragedy was given by the Zelosophic Society of the University of Pennsylvania, was the play revived.

(*Plot*) The play tells the story of a good but weak king, Artabanus, and his three sons—Arsaces, in whom "ev'ry virtue meets"; Vardanes, a man of pride, ambition, and "canker'd heart"; and Gotarzes, the youngest son, a "glorious youth." Returning victorious from battle, Arsaces brings Evanthe, whose beauty excites Vardanes to jealousy, and Bethas, who is discovered to be Evanthe's father. Not realizing that King Artabanus also loves Evanthe, Arsaces chooses her as his reward for victory; meanwhile Vardanes, plotting to overthrow the Empire, utilizes Arsaces' love for Evanthe and his sympathy for Bethas as indications of treachery. Angry and jealous, the king orders the arrest of Arsaces but is himself killed by Vardanes' henchmen to avenge personal insults. When the queen, Artabanus' second wife, tries to kill Arsaces to avenge her traitorous son whom Arsaces had previously killed in heroic action, her hand is stopped by the ghost of the king. Meanwhile, Vardanes has attacked the city and is defeated only after Arsaces, freed by

Gotarzes, turns the tide of the battle. Mistakenly told of Arsaces' death, Evanthe takes poison, living only long enough to bid good-by to Arsaces, who then kills himself, leaving Gotarzes to bring order to the city.

(*Discussion*) Unfortunately, *The Prince of Parthia,* the first American play, is imitative in both style and theme of English models. Shakespeare is a rich source: the rescue of a man from drowning, dreams of destruction, (*Julius Caesar*); the king's wish to retire, numerous storms (*King Lear*); the ghost (*Hamlet*); the heroine's self-administered poison and the hero's subsequent suicide (*Romeo and Juliet*). A number of these examples of indebtedness to Shakespeare, however, were also conventions of Tudor and Stuart drama.

Imitation of heroic tragedy and the excessive sentiment and rhetoric of the early eighteenth century are also clearly discernible. In the classical tradition of the heroic, Godfrey made frequent mention of the gods and the fates; the heroine's confidant watches the battle action and erroneously describes the death of the hero. The hero is a superhuman, an impossibly heroic character in the Marlovian tradition. Major themes of love and honor are exploited in the heroic fashion, complementing the almost unbearably excessive language of the hero.

The Prince of Parthia has some creditable qualities: a theme of love and honor, a relatively simple plot, some emotions suggesting a true sense of humanity, clearly accomplished exposition, and action frequently motivated by the characters and structured toward a logical and unified conclusion. Unfortunately, the modern reader, bored by excessively displayed emotions and exhausted by the unity of action, is also dulled by the moral and political themes forced upon playwrights of the era. Effectively used, the theme of love and honor was meaningful in middle-class philosophy, and politics as a theme was significant in a country already concerned with democracy, freedom, and tyrannical attitudes. The most difficult part of the play to enjoy—the poetry—remains, except in a few passages, uninspired.

2. OTHER EARLY NATIVE DRAMA

Few plays exist, and even fewer deserve comment. *The Disappointment* is interesting for the situation it caused, and

Ponteach has some dramatic value as well as an American theme. Worth only brief mention is *The Conquest of Canada; or, The Siege of Quebec*, written by George Cockings, an English Colonist living in Boston, and acted before the Revolution (1773) by Douglass' company at the Southwark Theatre in Philadelphia. A weak play, it describes the historic battle of Quebec in a peculiar mixture of prose and verse.

(a) *The Disappointment; or, The Force of Credulity,* by Thomas Forrest, 1767

(*Plot*) As they discuss hidden treasures, Hum, Parchment, and Quadrant discover that they have lost some valuable papers. A fourth man, Raccoon, finds the papers, demands and is given a part interest in the treasure. But later, when the treasure chest is discovered and opened, it turns out to be filled with stones. The whole affair has been a hoax. Songs and a moral discourse enlivened the entertainment, along with numerous coarse suggestions, particularly in Act II. In 1796, a second edition included satirical references to the President and Congress.

(*Discussion*) Only by chance was the first play written by an American and produced in America a tragedy rather than a comedy. Early in 1767—the same year *The Prince of Parthia* was produced—the American Company had put into rehearsal *The Disappointment*, a comic opera in three acts by Colonel Thomas Forrest (published in New York, 1767, under the pseudonym of Andrew Barton). Based on a trick Forrest had played on an old Dutchman who was searching for buried treasure, the play ridiculed the idea that Blackbeard the Pirate had buried any of his treasures on the banks of the Delaware River. Despite some interesting Scottish and Irish elements, the play is both crude in dramatic structure and coarse in matter. The discovery of "personal reflections" which made the play "unfit for the stage" brought an abrupt halt to rehearsals and the hasty substitution of *The Prince of Parthia*.

(b) *Ponteach; or, The Savages of America,* by Robert Rogers, 1766

(*Plot*) Cheated frequently by the trappers and the English soldiers, Ponteach and his sons, Philip and Chekitan plot their revenge. As Ponteach tries to rally the other Indian chiefs, however, he finds the Mohawk chief, Hendrick, difficult to persuade.

In council it is determined that Philip will convince Hendrick that he must fight the English. Ambitious and unscrupulous, Philip plans to provoke Hendrick by killing his daughter, Monelia (whom his brother Chekitan loves) and blaming the British for the deed. But Chekitan discovers that Philip murdered Monelia, kills him, and then takes his own life. As Ponteach sorrows for his dead sons, a French priest spreads lies about him, and the other Indian chiefs decide to revolt. At the end, the British are victorious, but Ponteach retains his pride:

> British may boast, the Gods may have their will,
> Ponteach I am, and shall be Ponteach still.

(*Discussion*) The first play to treat a native subject at all seriously was Major Robert Rogers' *Ponteach*, published in London in 1766 but not acted in America before the Revolution. Allan Nevins, in his 1914 edition of *Ponteach*, questions Rogers' authorship, but Rogers seems to have been mainly responsible for the play if not its sole author. London critics in 1766 accepted the play as Rogers' work but had little good to say for it. Concentrating on the cruel treatment of the Indians by the white man, the play is called a tragedy, and boasts an heroic-tragic figure in Ponteach. Some picturesque nature images and a few strong and dignified speeches by Ponteach distinguish the play, but like many early plays, it suffers from stilted language, amateurish polemics, a mixed style (mainly prose, with short passages in blank verse), and too numerous and confusing changes of scene.

3. COLLEGE DRAMA IN THE COLONIES

Although in the cities the drama suffered frequent attacks by religious groups and political parties, among the colleges of Colonial America it found some security. Writing of a production of *The Masque of Alfred*, produced at the College of Philadelphia in 1756–57, Provost William Smith noted that the students had "from Time to Time delivered proper Speeches and acted Parts of our best dramatic Pieces before large Audiences with great Applause" (*Pennsylvania Gazette*, January 20, 27; February 3, 10, 1757). In 1771, students at the College of New Jersey produced "The Rising Glory of America," a dialogue by Philip Freneau, America's best-known poet of the Revolution, and H. H. Brackenridge, playwright and author of *Modern Chivalry*, one of America's earliest novels. Perhaps a nonsectarian background for a college made it easier for students to produce plays, whereas the denominational affiliations of other colleges such as Harvard, Yale, Brown, and Dartmouth discouraged plays and play-acting.

II. DRAMA DURING THE REVOLUTION AND THE POST-REVOLUTIONARY PERIOD TO 1800

Almost as soon as the theater in America had become reasonably well established, a crisis occurred—the War for Independence. Anticipating the serious situation, the Continental Congress in 1774 recommended that all public entertainments be suppressed. Thus began an eight-year period in the history of American theater during which the stage was mainly controlled by the British military who performed some of the best plays of England and the Continent and entertained not just soldiers but great numbers of Colonists. Mainly, the actors were British soldiers and women who had, as Arthur Hornblow, historian of the American stage, wrote, "followed the drum," but some were members of Douglass' disbanded American Company.

American drama, on the other hand, was perhaps given additional impetus by the war years. With the spirit of nationalism, Americans found a new *raison d'être* for the drama. Plays became a prominent part of the "War of the Belles-Lettres," so aptly described by Vernon L. Parrington in *Main Currents in American Thought*. By the time the theaters were reopened after the war, American drama had launched a modest but definite beginning. A variety of aspects of American life appeared— moral lessons and dramatized political issues, social farces which often featured the native Yankee character or the Negro and commented on society in America, national plays by the score, plays imitative of English drama—in general, a reflection of the times. And by the turn of the century, America had a serious dramatist and student of the theater in William Dunlap, and its first effective writer of comedy in Royall Tyler.

A. Plays Reflecting Patriot Views during the Revolution

Long before the Battles of Lexington and Bunker Hill, the contest between Whig and Tory, Patriot and Loyalist, was being waged in literary circles. In the drama, the mode was satiric farce, and what the playwrights lacked in dramatic talent they made up for with partisan fervor. Frank and even libelous, only a few of these frequently anonymous satires have been preserved. Written in haste and for a particular purpose by men and women of little dramatic talent, the plays are now quite forgotten except to illustrate the drama of the Revolution.

1. MRS. MERCY OTIS WARREN: PARTISAN SATIRIST

Sister of James Otis, the patriot statesman, wife of James Warren, once President of the Provincial Congress, and close friend of John and Abigail Adams, Mrs. Warren (1728–1814) was well equipped to satirize the social as well as the political issues of her day. In her best plays, however, she was essentially a gadfly of the war, harassing the enemy with bitter satire and poignant observations on liberty and patriotism. A lady of culture, a wit, and a member of the literati, she inserted in her plays the conventional sentiment and moral strictures of her day along with interesting biographical, social, and political comment. Quite in spite of occasional dramatic effectiveness, she was clearly amateurish and lacked any real dramatic talent. Her published poems are also undistinguished, but her three-volume *History of the Rise, Progress, and Termination of the American Revolution* (1805) has some value for historians. It is, however, ironic that she remains best known for the political farces, which she doubtless wrote more for amusement than literary acclaim.

(a) *The Adulateur*, by Mercy Warren, 1773

(*Plot*) The scene is Servia: Brutus and Cassius are attempting to inspire the people to patriotic action. It is then reported that the soldiers of Rapatio have attacked the citizens in "promiscuous slaughter." Immediately, Brutus urges a revolution, and angry citizens appear before Rapatio, who alternately blames the Patriots for whatever wrongs exist and threatens economic revenge. The climax shows a pathetic picture of a frightened Rapatio but a distinct hope for national freedom as Brutus weeps for his country.

(*Discussion*) In weak blank verse, this "tragedy" in five acts is a bitter comment on conditions in New England during the immediate pre-revolution days. Servia is New England; the "promiscuous slaughter," the Boston Massacre; the "great hall," Boston's Faneuil Hall. As usual in the satires of Mrs. Warren and other writers of this period, the characters in *The Adulateur* are real people thinly disguised: Brutus (James Otis), Rapatio (Governor Thomas Hutchinson, the last royal governor of Massachusetts), Cassius (Samuel Adams), Hazelrod (Peter Oliver, Chief Justice of Massachusetts).

(b) *The Group*, by Mercy Warren, 1775

(*Plot*) As the play begins, the audience sees a swarm of Harpies led by Massachusettensis (Daniel Leonard, a Tory) in the form of a basilisk: "The whole supported by a mighty army and navy, from Blunderland [England] for the laudable purpose of enslaving its best friends." One by one, members of the Group comment on their acts of villainy and rationalize their betrayal of the Patriot cause. After only momentary concern for Hell and retribution, the Group decide that for fame and personal gain they can forego conscience and moral living.

(*Discussion*) The most incisive and perhaps the most important of Mrs. Warren's plays, this polemical farce in two acts enjoyed a patriot theme which made it quite popular. The Loyalist Group—a Council appointed by the King rather than elected by the Assembly, thus abrogating the Charter of Massachusetts —is composed of "selfish venal men," as their names suggest— Hateall (Timothy Ruggles), Humbug (John Erving), Spendall (William Pepperell). Obviously, the play is meaningless without an understanding of the situation in Massachusetts at the time when England's actions (the Stamp Act, the Intolerable Acts, the Sugar Act, the Townshend Acts) toward the American Colonists were felt to be unbearable by the Sons of Liberty and other patriots.

(c) Mrs. Warren's Poetic Dramas

In 1790, Mrs. Warren published two dull and didactic tragedies in verse: *The Sack of Rome* and *The Ladies of Castile.* "Debilitated by the habits of every species of luxury," she wrote in the Preface to *The Sack of Rome,* "man has sunk to his lowest depravity and wants a lesson in morality, valour, and virtue." In luxurious Rome, the Emperor's passion for another man's wife drives him to rape her before he is killed when an invading army sacks Rome. Innocent victims of the battle are the Emperor's daughter and the young soldier whom she loves. *The Ladies of Castile* describes Spain's last heroic struggle for liberty before the establishment of despotism by the family of Ferdinand. Both plays show Mrs. Warren's concern for freedom —from England's social as well as political control.

(d) Plays Attributed to Mrs. Warren
(i) The Blockheads; or, The Affrighted Officers, 1776
This three-act farce is frequently attributed to Mrs. Warren, although A. H. Quinn, quite correctly, denies her authorship on the basis of the play's crudity in thought and language. As a satire, however, it uses some of the characters that have appeared in her plays. The play is concerned with General Howe's unsuccessful attempt to subdue the Americans at Dorchester Heights during the Revolution, and satirizes the quarrels among the English, their doubts about their own cause, and their cowardice. Subtlety is completely lacking, and coarseness dominates many scenes. The play ends with a popular flag-waving technique which was not used by Mrs. Warren: "And let's conclude with huzzahs for America."

An interesting note to this play is the situation which supposedly stimulated its composition. During a performance in Boston (January 8, 1776) of General Burgoyne's play, *The Blockade of Boston,* an English soldier dashed on stage to shout that the rebels were attacking Bunker Hill. It was a moment before the audience realized that this was not part of the play. Hence *The Blockheads* was written in response to Burgoyne's farce lampooning the efforts of the Patriots.

(ii) The Motley Assembly, 1779
This one-act farce ridicules the Massachusetts Assembly, or legislative body. Once a simple diversion and entertainment for young ladies, the Assembly has a new significance; and politically vacillating fathers now refuse to allow their daughters to attend a Whig assembly for fear the British may return to Boston. The play shows Mrs. Warren's disdain for those who felt that they could not maintain their social standing and also sup-

port the Revolution. Awkward and slight, with some rude language, the play has wit, and in its best lines can be favorably compared to Royall Tyler's *The Contrast*.

2. HUGH HENRY BRACKENRIDGE: WAR OF THE BELLE-LETTRES

Although his reputation in the history of American literature rests quite appropriately on his authorship of the early picaresque and satirical novel *Modern Chivalry*, Brackenridge (1748–1816) also contributed two plays in the Whig-Tory "War of the Belles-Lettres." "The subject is not love," he wrote of his plays, "but valour. I meddle not with any of the effeminating passions, but consecrate my muse to the great themes of patriotic virtue, bravery and heroism." With the combination of sentiment and nationalism which these words suggest, he did not create a drama of great dignity. Only in comparison with contemporaries, who lacked his literary facility, was he outstanding. Although not a poet of consequence, his plays display passages of dignified blank verse and a sense of humanity which make his work significant at this early time. Like *The Rising Glory of America* (written with Philip Freneau), the plot of *The Battle of Bunkers-Hill* is carried on largely by conversation which could rarely be considered dramatic. Essentially, there is too much exposition and exhortation and too little action and attention to dramatic convention. *The Death of General Montgomery* is generally more effective as drama and as a pointed attempt to help the Colonial cause. Presumably, neither play was acted professionally.

(a) *The Battle of Bunkers-Hill*, by H. H. Brackenridge, 1776

In five short acts and a series of epilogues, this play in blank verse praises the courage of the American leaders and their men. The English generals (Gage, Howe, Burgoyne) and the American generals (Warren, Putnam, Gardiner) simply explain their positions in the battle and exhort their men to greater efforts before the battle in which the British are repulsed, Warren killed, and Gardiner wounded. With the final American retreat, the English honor their enemies. An epilogue, "Who fights for freedom fights for the cause of Heaven"—is followed by an ode on the "Battle of Bunkers-Hill," a speech by George Washington, and a song in praise of American efforts that day.

(b) *The Death of General Montgomery*, by H. H. Brackenridge, 1777

Mainly a patriotic play built around a recognized hero, *The Death of General Montgomery* dramatizes the attack on the fortress of Quebec. Disaster is foreshadowed throughout, but the death of General Montgomery is shown only by a tribute from Aaron Burr, thus weakening the dramatic structure. Ever a patriot, Brackenridge managed to reproach the King and the English Parliament as well as the English general Carleton.

3. POLITICAL FARCE-MELODRAMA: *THE FALL OF BRITISH TYRANNY*, 1776

Suggestive of other partisan dramas and in itself an ambitious attempt to dramatize the beginning war years is John (or Joseph) Leacock's *The Fall of British Tyranny, or American Liberty Triumphant, The First Campaign. A Tragi-Comedy of Five Acts as lately planned at the Royal Theatrum Pandemonium, at St. James's. The Principal Place of Action is America.* Although the language of the Whig-Tory argument is occasionally quite realistic and the plot idea of a scope to suggest something more than the usual nationalistic propaganda, the characters are caricatures, though identifiable, and the action is episodic and farcical.

(*Plot*) Emphasizing the idea that the American Revolution began in England's House of Parliament, the play begins with a vigorous speech by Lord Paramount (England's Earl of Bute) proposing to impoverish America by taxes, punitive legislative acts, and even military force. Opposed to Lord Paramount are Lord Wisdom, Lord Religion, and Lord Justice (William Pitt, the Bishop of St. Asaph, and the Earl of Camden). In Boston, the English tyranny is deeply resented; and as the Whigs and Tories argue, the British regulars are routed at Lexington and Concord by American militia. After the Battle of Bunker Hill, the English argue among themselves in a Council of War. Act V shows American prisoners of war joyous because they consider themselves victorious in battle, as Generals Washington, Putnam, and Charles Lee pledge their support to the cause of liberty and their country.

B. Plays Reflecting Loyalist Views during the Revolution

The bitter, satirical, and condemnatory views in the Patriot plays were no more acrimonious than those presented in Loyalist plays. The intensity of the partisan views is, in fact, a major characteristic of these satires and farces. Extant Loyalist plays indicate that few opportunities were overlooked to belittle the motives and abilities of the Colonists. Slanderous remarks concerning the Patriot leaders were not uncommon. Truth was not important; propaganda for the cause was.

1. *THE AMERICANS ROUSED IN A CURE FOR THE SPLEEN, OR AMUSEMENT FOR A WINTER'S EVENING. BEING THE SUBSTANCE OF A CONVERSATION ON THE TIMES OVER A FRIENDLY TANKARD AND PIPE BETWEEN SHARP, A COUNTRY PARSON, BUMPER, A COUNTRY JUSTICE, FILLPOT, AN INNKEEPER, GRAVEAIRS, A DEACON, TRIM, A BARBER, BRIM, A QUAKER, PUFF, A LATE REPRESENTATIVE. TAKEN IN SHORTHAND BY SIR ROGER DE COVERLY,* ATTRIBUTED TO JONATHAN SEWALL, 1775*

This is an obvious Tory tract in which the arguments from the British point of view are presented with wit and intelligence in contrast to the confusion and ignorance of those who espoused the Whig philosophy. When the Patriots were unsure of themselves, their vacillations became, as this simple conversational play indicates, good material for the Tory propagandist. Jonathan Sewall (1728–1796) was a notorious Tory.

2. *THE BATTLE OF BROOKLYN, A FARCE IN TWO ACTS. AS IT WAS PERFORMED ON LONG ISLAND, ON TUESDAY, THE 27th DAY OF AUGUST, 1776. BY THE REPRESENTATIVES OF THE TYRANTS OF AMERICA, ASSEMBLED AT PHILADELPHIA,* AUTHOR UNKNOWN, 1776*

(*Plot*) Mainly the action is episodic and libelous: the American General Stirling, badly frightened at the prospect of battle, tries to bolster his courage by drink; a young prostitute tells of her experiences with Washington and Harrison; the Patriot chiefs, Washington and Putnam, are presented as great cowards. After the battle and the retreat of the rebels, servants of Generals Stirling and Sullivan, obviously preaching the author's sentiments, decide to "renew our allegiance to the most amiable and virtuous Prince, that ever snag'd a sceptre."

(*Discussion*) History has shown that the Revolutionary leaders were unwise in that battle, but the harshness of the attack on the conduct of the Continental soldiers and the villification heaped upon Washington and his officers are unparalleled in extant drama of that time. Sketchy, irresponsible, and indicative of little dramatic talent, the play concludes with a partisan argument which the author tries to pass off as a moral.

C. Nonpartisan Drama: "Both Your Houses"

Most of the satires of the Revolution were strictly partisan, but one of the few playwrights who showed any detachment was Colonel Robert Munford (*c*. 1730–1784), who fought in the Revolution. Presenting quite accurately the feelings of the majority of the people who did not know what to do during the days of uncertainty early in the Revolution, Colonel Munford wrote *The Candidates* and *The Patriots*, published together in 1798.

The Candidates, probably written shortly before the Revolution, ineffectively satirizes the methods used to elect members to the Assembly. In *The Patriots*, Munford attacks the half-hearted and the professed Patriots. But both Patriots and Loyalists felt his barb. "I detest the opprobrious epithet of Tory, as much as I do the inflammatory distinction of Whig," says Trueman, Munford's spokesman.

D. Royall Tyler: The Beginnings of American Comedy

The first comedy and the first play on a native subject written by an American and produced by a professional company was *The Contrast*, by Royall Tyler (1757–1826). A Harvard College graduate, 1776, and a major in the Continental Army, he was admitted to the bar in 1780. Returning to military duty during Shay's Rebellion (1787), he visited New York City, and met Thomas Wignell, the leading comedian of the Old American Company. That same year, on April 16, Wignell acted with some personal success in *The Contrast* at the John Street Theatre in New York. Tyler also wrote a novel, *The Algerine Captive* (1797), many essays and verses, and at least seven more plays, only four of which have survived. His main career, however, was not literature but law, and he eventually became Chief Justice of the Supreme Court of Vermont (1807–13) and Professor of Jurisprudence at the University of Vermont (1811–14).

1. *THE CONTRAST*, BY ROYALL TYLER, 1787

(*Plot*) With an intricate plot involving love, filial obligation, intrigue, and the follies of fashion, this play abounds in contrasts between ideas, lovers, servants, fashions, and so on. As the scene opens, Charlotte and Letitia comment cleverly on men, themselves, and their society, while in the Van Rough household, Maria, the daughter, is being told that she must marry Dimple, whom she despises as a man "whose only virtue is a polished exterior." Then Colonel Manly, Charlotte's brother, appears and is cleverly contrasted by both Charlotte and Letitia with the fashionable beaux of their acquaintance, particularly Dimple, whose servant, Jessamy, meanwhile proceeds to give Manly's servant, Jonathan, advice on courting—which he follows with embarrassing consequences.

The main action of the play evolves around Dimple's personal problem; he loves the person of Charlotte and the fortune of Letitia, while he is engaged to Maria. To complicate the problem, Manly has met, impressed, and been impressed by Maria; Dimple has been unintentionally forced into making identical secret appointments with both Charlotte and Letitia; and Van Rough has discovered that Dimple is seriously in debt —he has not "minded the main chance." In the final act, Dimple is exposed in all of his duplicity; Manly will marry Maria; and Letitia and Charlotte have learned a moral lesson.

(*Discussion*) *The Contrast* has been revived occasionally, generally in university theaters; but in 1787, it played only five performances. A contemporary critic thought that the dialogue of the play wanted pruning, that the soliloquies were not probable, and that ridicule of Lord Chesterfield's letters was imprudent. Another reviewer who signed himself "Candour" in the *Daily Advertiser*, April 18, 1787, was impressed: "It was certainly the production of a man of genius, and nothing can be more praiseworthy than the sentiments of the play throughout. They are the effusions of an honest patriot heart expressed with energy and eloquence." Although the modern reader probably cannot approach this play in the spirit of "Candour" ("the contrast drawn between a gentleman, who has read Chesterfield and received the polish of Europe, and an unpolished, untraveled American"), he will find it sprightly, witty, and still very funny.

In descriptive terms *The Contrast* is more a caricature of society than a social comedy. There is much farcical action. Jessamy is the traditional intriguer; Jonathan is the shrewd but naïve country-bumpkin Yankee who became a major figure in American farce-comedy by the middle of the nineteenth century; Colonel Manly is the serious defender of honor and country—a startling contrast to Charlotte, the witty and indelicate flirt whose "head runs so upon beaux." Although a caricature, Charlotte establishes the pace of the drama with her wit, while her lines contain most of the play's satire upon fashion.

The wit and humor of *The Contrast* were unmatched in American drama until Mrs. Anna C. Mowatt Ritchie's *Fashion* in 1845. What is scandal, says Charlotte, "but amusing ourselves with the faults, foibles, follies, and reputations of our friends." Among the most humorous scenes are Jonathan's attendance at a play, *The School for Scandalization*; Jessamy's lessons to Jonathan on how to court a girl with an object of "cherubim consequences"; and his later instructions on how "to laugh by rule."

The Contrast also has a liberal amount of sentiment, moralizing, and nationalism—necessary ingredients of the successful American play. The patriotism that the Prologue proclaims,

> EXULT each patriot heart!—this night is shewn
> A piece, which we may fairly call our own;

Colonel Manly exemplifies in every action. And the outcome of the play is a national triumph. The necessary moral sentiment of the play is clear in Maria's "filial obligation." There are particular morals to be drawn, too, in the actions of both Charlotte and Colonel Manly. That moralizing was required for Tyler's audience is evidenced by a Boston performance of the play in 1792 advertised as "A Moral Lecture in Five Parts."

2. OTHER PLAYS BY ROYALL TYLER

A month after *The Contrast* opened in 1787, another play by Tyler, a comic opera called *May-Day in Town; or, New York in an Uproar*, was performed at the John Street Theatre. Not now extant, the play failed, perhaps because, as a contemporary critic suggested, the main female character was a scold whom the New York women may have resented.

Of the four plays by Tyler that are reprinted in *America's Lost Plays*, Vol. 15, three are sacred dramas in blank verse: *The Origin of the Feast of Purim, Joseph and His Brethren*, and *The Judgment of Solomon*. The fourth, *The Island of Barrataria*, is an amusing, satirical play based on parts of *Don Quixote*.

E. William Dunlap: Father of American Drama

William Dunlap (1766–1839) was the first professional dramatist in America. Although he must now be considered only a second- or third-rate playwright, his contribution of fifty-three plays (twenty-nine either wholly or partly original with him), his tireless and honorable work as a theater manager and producer, and his reputation as the author of the first history of the American theater, make him a significant figure in the history of American drama. In 1833, a critic of the New York *Mirror* (X, 266) wrote: "His numerous pieces were almost invariably performed with applause; and free as they are from false taste and extravagance, show the power of fixing attention and exciting interest by legitimate means—of touching the true springs of mirth and pity and terror." Later critics have pointed out that in large part he gained his reputation by catering to popular tastes with his melodramas, although he did show great skill in these plays. Dunlap also brought respectability to the theater, badly in need of this quality. A pioneer in an unproven field, with remarkable industry and abilities superior to his contemporaries, his uneven but occasionally superior dramatic creations, and his abiding interest in drama and theater, make his place as "Father of American Drama" secure. The Dunlap Society (established in 1885) has published his plays and promoted criticism of his works, and facilitated research in the whole field of early American drama.

Born in Perth Amboy, New Jersey, of staunch Loyalist parents, William Dunlap enjoyed a fair education. After his family moved to New York City in 1777, he found great delight in watching the plays given by the British soldiers at the John Street Theatre. Ten years later, he wrote his first long play, *The Modest Soldier; or, Love in New York,* inspired by Royall Tyler's *The Contrast,* which appeared that year, 1787. The play was not produced, but Dunlap had begun his career as a dramatist.

1. AS THEATER MANAGER

In the spring of 1796, Lewis Hallam and John Hodgkinson, partners and actors of the Old American Company performing in the John Street Theatre in New York, persuaded Dunlap to buy into the management. According to the agreement, Dunlap became the manager and had the freedom to produce his own plays. Jealousy between Hallam and Hodgkinson, however, spoiled the bright future Dunlap imagined.

During the spring of 1797, Hodgkinson and Hallam split: Hallam left the management; Hodgkinson took the company to Boston; and Dunlap stayed in New York to supervise the building of the new Park Theatre—a stone construction three stories high with a well-equipped stage, excellent scenery, and three tiers of boxes, a gallery, and a pit all colored in pink and gold—which, opening late in January, 1798, was in almost constant financial trouble. On April 27, 1798, Hodgkinson withdrew, and Dunlap took over the company. That he felt inadequate is clear from his comment in his *History* (II, 38):

> The opinion of the writer is . . . that he was not fitted for the arduous task. Had it been his lot to direct a theatre patronized by an enlightened government, having no care but that of selecting dramas and such performers as would best promote the great end of human happiness, he might perhaps have been entitled to the grateful remembrance of his fellow-men.

Surely a government-subsidized theater would have helped, but instead, an act of God further harassed Dunlap as a yellow fever epidemic hit New York and delayed his opening until December of that year.

On December 10, 1798, a week after the opening, Dunlap produced with startling success his own adaptation of an English version of August von Kotzebue's *The Stranger*. Dunlap's hopes revived, as Kotzebue (1761–1819), the most popular German dramatist of the eighteenth century, proved to have tremendous appeal for American middle-class audiences. By the end of the 1800 season, Dunlap had produced nineteen of Kotzebue's plays which had allowed him to star Hodgkinson and Thomas A Cooper. This season and that of 1801 were his most successful. Then a series of incidents occurred: Cooper left for England; dramatic critics started writing, particularly "Jonathan Oldstyle" (Washington Irving), whose very first letter called attention to the absurdities and inadequacies of the Park Theatre productions; Mrs. Hodgkinson, one of the female mainstays of the company, died; and Hodgkinson left New York. The losses were too severe, and in February, 1804, the theater was put up for auction. One year later Dunlap declared bankruptcy and closed the theater. It should be noted, however, that he left the theater materially well furnished and well supplied with play manuscripts and that his tour as theater manager was not as dismal as the dramatic ending sounds.

A year later Dunlap tried theater management once more, this time as assistant to Cooper, who reopened the Park. But Cooper was not successful. After other managerial duties, including a stint as traveling companion to the colorful and impressive but alcoholic English tragedian George Frederick Cooke, Dunlap gave up theater management for good in 1812.

2. AS PLAYWRIGHT

In productivity Dunlap was the major dramatist of his times. Realizing that a dramatist of his day had no chance for success without some claim on a theater, he became a manager. His versatility also deserves consideration. Partially as a practical measure to facilitate success, and partially in consequence of his pioneering nature, Dunlap wrote sentimental comedy, patriotic drama, the ballad-opera, Gothic melodrama, romantic tragedy, historic tragedy, farce, melodrama, adaptations, and translations. Compared even with Europe, where Kotzebue was being hailed as the German Shakespeare, and with England, where Richard Brinsley Sheridan was contenting himself with adaptations, Dunlap's activities suggest historical importance. Like Sheridan and others, Dunlap recognized his numerous adaptations as a matter of expediency, and he was not fooled by Kotzebue's popularity. His best plays, certainly, were those mainly original with him; and on these plays—*André, The Father, Leicester, The Italian Father*—his reputation as a playwright rests.

Dunlap was a sensitive artist with imaginative ideas which he did not always follow, an interest in literature which was not unswerving, a feeling for dramatic character and language, and a love of the theater. Perhaps his years in theater management hurt him as a playwright, for after 1812 his plays are not effective; and except for his *History* he did little of note after the turn of the century. Yet for his time he was a major dramatist, and in any history he becomes the principal figure in the establishment of an American drama.

(a) Comedy: *The Father; or, American Shandyism,* 1788

(Plot) After a Prologue praising the moral tendency of the stage in the New World, the action centers on Mrs. Racket. Tired of an indifferent and dissipating husband, she tries to excite him by pretending an affection for Captain Ranter, a man with all the marks of a scoundrel. Her sister, Caroline, grieving for her fiancé, Henry, whom she thinks dead, is consoled by a Colonel Duncan. The device to connect the hero, heroine, and villain is a ring—given by the Colonel to his son, described by Caroline as belonging to Henry, and worn by Ranter. It remains only for Henry to identify Ranter as the thief who has stolen the ring, thus bringing indescribable joy to his sweetheart and his father. Of course, the Rackets are reconciled in the fifth act.

(Discussion) The second comedy by a native American author to be performed on the professional stage (John Street Theatre, New York, September 7, 1789) *The Father*, was, according to its author, "received with great applause by the citizens." Its run of four performances was considered a favorable reception. Generally modeled on Laurence Sterne's novel *Tristram Shandy*, proposing to teach and amuse, *The Father* had

reasonably drawn characters and a "terseness and unstudied ease" in the dialogue, which a critic of the contemporary *American Quarterly Review* found indispensable to genuine comedy. Printed in a revised version in 1806, the play now presented more carefully developed characters and scenes and more moralizing.

(b) Romantic Tragedy: *The Fatal Deception; or, The Progress of Guilt*, 1790

(*Plot*) Returning after a long absence at war, Lord Leicester rescues Dudley Cecil from robbers before reaching Kenilworth, where Matilda, his bride, has been living in adultery with Henry, Dudley's younger brother. Frantic at Leicester's return, Matilda urges Henry to kill her husband, but in the dark of Leicester's room, Henry mistakes his victim and kills Dudley. Meanwhile Leicester, learning of Matilda's infidelity, vows revenge, and Matilda goes mad, tries to poison Leicester, and stabs herself when she fails. Finally, Henry, feeling himself "marked for destruction," refuses combat with the wronged husband and dies willingly on the sword of Leicester, who forgives the dying sinners.

(*Discussion*) Based on the story of Lord Leicester and Amy Robsart, the play was produced in 1794 and later published in 1806 as *Leicester*. Although having a certain intensity and force, *Leicester* is marred by loose construction, unrelieved tragedy, and weakly motivated action. Dunlap, however, deserves credit for seeing the dramatic potential of the Kenilworth story, which provided the necessary sentiment as well as the revenge theme and mad scene.

(c) Historical Tragedy: *André*, 1798

(*Plot*) André, in prison awaiting execution, asks only that he be shot rather than hanged. His friend, Captain Bland of the American army, pleads with General Washington for André's life. Refused, Bland tears the cockade from his helmet. (This action was hissed by the first-night audience, and Dunlap cut the scene.) When Bland's mother asks that André be exchanged for her husband, Colonel Bland, who is being held by the British as a hostage for André, her plea is also refused by Washington because Colonel Bland has told Washington in a letter to do "his duty." Again, young Bland is incensed and insults his superior officers. Finally, Honora, André's fiancée, arrives from England to plead for her lover—again in vain. In the final act, Captain Bland, made to understand reality, apologizes for his insubordination; Honora becomes insane; and André goes to his execution bravely.

(*Discussion*) *André*, first performed at the Park Theatre, New York, March 30, 1798, is based on the capture and execution of Major John André, the British messenger who, after meeting with Benedict Arnold, was captured and hanged by the Americans in 1780. Possibly because the event was too close, the play, Dunlap's best, was not a popular success, lasting only five performances. In 1803, however, Dunlap bowed to the popular demand for patriotic spectacles and rewrote *André* as *The Glory of Columbia—Her Yeomanry*. Essentially, the play was destroyed, but the spectacle was quite successful on the stage.

In spite of excessive romanticism, sentiment, and the artificialities of language and action which were characteristic of the drama of that time, this play has much that suggests excellence. It is not, however, André's courageous preparation for the kind of death that he must face (hanging) which is the central dramatic issue of the play.

The major conflict lies within a country which must assert its rights at the same time that it maintains a strong sense of humanity. Facing the problem is Washington. Opposing him is Bland, a romantic brash young man, fiercely loyal to André for once saving his life; a mother and her children; and André's sweetheart. But a country's honor must be triumphant, and as one might expect, nationalistic sentiment predominates. Within these two themes—a country's maturity, and the courage of a man facing death—*André* is well unified and includes effective exposition and change of pace. Except for the women, the main characters are real and well drawn. Although weak in language and poetry, it is a meaningful play that can still be read with pleasure.

(d) Translations and Adaptations

Almost from the time he got into theater management, Dunlap began to adapt and translate English and European plays. By the turn of the century, he was putting most of his energies into this work, particularly in the translation of German and French plays.

(i) Plays of Kotzebue

After his success with *The Stranger,* Dunlap continued this interest in Kotzebue, translating and adapting, among others, *False Shame* (1799). Dunlap's version, *False Shame; or, The American Orphan in Germany,* was extremely successful and supported the theater during the season in which it was produced. The plot unfolds a conventional farce of lost daughters, lost sisters, confused lovers, and mistaken identities. The source of false shame of one character is a physical deformity; of another, poverty. At the final curtain, however, everyone is happy: married or reconciled, they join in singing "Joy, brightest spark from Heaven."

Concerning *The Stranger* one critic wrote (*The New York Drama,* Vol. I, 1876, footnote to the play): "That interpretation of human passion cannot be wholly false, which awakens so many responses. The sentiment cannot be wholly mawkish or sickly, which, among various people and at various times, touches the deepest sensibilities of an audience." Critical opinions have changed, but nineteenth-century audiences invariably enjoyed the play and did not question either the sentiment or the interpretation of life.

(ii) French Plays

Mainly interested in French melodramas, Dunlap borrowed widely: *The Voice of Nature* (1803), based on L. C. Caigniez's *Le Jugement de Salomon; The Wife of Two Husbands* (1804), from Pixerécourt's popular melodrama *La Femme à deux Maris*; and *Thirty Years; or, The Life of a Gamester* (1828), from *Trente Ans; ou, La Vie d'un joueur* by Prosper Goubaux and Victor Ducange.

Produced first at the Bowery Theatre in New York, February 22, 1828, *Thirty Years* proved to be one of Dunlap's most successful melodramas. George St. Germain, a compulsive gambler controlled by a villain, steals, abuses his patient wife, and finally commits a murder before a spectacular but moral plot makes Germain a victim of his unhappy fate.

(e) Nationalistic Drama: *Yankee Chronology; or, Huzza for the Constitution,* 1812

In this combination sketch and monologue celebrating the beginning of the War of 1812, Ben Bundle, an American sailor, describes the battle between the *Constitution* and the English *Guerrière* and sings a song, "Yankee Chronology," tracing the

Revolution from Lexington to Yorktown. The great popularity of this patriotic but artless work suggests the low standards of the public.

3. AS THEATER HISTORIAN

A History of the American Theatre (1832), Dunlap's single most significant contribution to both American theater and drama, consists mainly of an interesting narrative of personal observations of a growing theater. Recent theater historians have deplored its errors and misleading statements, but they still regard it as an invaluable history written in a frequently delightful fashion. Dunlap also wrote prefaces to his published plays and *Memoirs of the Life of George Frederick Cooke* (1813). Many of his ideas, such as federal support for the theater and curtailment of the star system, are currently meaningful.

F. Post-Revolutionary Drama: Varied Directions

When the Revolution was over and the war satires had disappeared, the theater continued its role as a means of propaganda, entertainment, and moral instruction. Numerous playwrights discussed social and political issues. Other playwrights, inspired by the work of Tyler and Dunlap, wrote farce comedies and kept alive native character types. At the same time, the theaters continued to depend upon European dramatists. Translations and adaptations were constantly on the American stage, along with the pirated versions of current English successes and, of course, Shakespeare and the best of England's older plays. Along with these popular trends, the practicing moralists were at work, and the colleges were showing an increasing interest in drama.

1. NATIONALISTIC AND POLITICAL PLAYS

The tendency of playwrights during the Revolution to dramatize national issues and various attitudes toward political problems continued to be popular. Proud of their freedom, dramatists inserted nationalistic comments in almost everything they wrote. The democratic spirit of the new country became a common theme.

(a) Nationalistic Spirit

Numerous plays, from farce to poetic tragedy, gained some popularity through their patriotic sentiment. *The Better Sort; or, A Girl of Spirit,* an anonymous farce written in 1789, satirizes the American fashion of naively accepting foreign ideas and develops a true champion of America as its hero. *Americana; or, A New Tale of the Genii,* a patriotic spectacle dramatizing the bringing of the Genius of Liberty from England to America, was probably written during the Revolution, but not performed until 1798. Nationalistic feeling is strong in David Everett's *Daranzel; or, The Persian Patriot* (1800) in which Daranzel successfully leads a fight for freedom similar to the American Revolution.

(b) Political Issues

Plays also emphasized, or made passing comment on, a variety of domestic problems which were also political issues—the Constitution, money and speculation, taxation, the Whiskey Rebellion, education, and other such subjects. *The Politican Outwitted* (1788), by Samuel Low, is an interesting defense of the Constitution. John Murdock's *The Politicians; or, The State of Things* (1798) makes a strong plea for nationalism: "I trust the people will know how to prize their singular happy situation among the nations of the earth, and join heart and hand, in supporting the tired patriot who is at the head of their national affairs." John Beete's *The Man of the Times; or, A Scarcity of Cash* (1797) combines sentiment with a satire on the tactics of moneylenders during the Revolution.

(c) Patriot Leadership

Complementing those plays which commented on some aspect of the new nation or its policies were the plays which praised its leaders and suggested broader influences. Two of the best plays celebrating heroes or events were William Brown's *West Point Preserved* (1797) and John Daly Burk's *Bunker Hill; or, The Death of General Warren* (1797). According to A. H. Quinn (*History of American Drama*), Burk's play was frequently revived as a Fourth of July spectacle, having, as it did, a rather realistic attack on the Hill in the last act. Another play, *Columbia and Britannia* (1787), by a citizen of the United States, celebrates the international prestige of a country now reconciled with Britannia and accepted as an equal by both Britannia and Gallia.

(d) A National Affair: Barbary Coast Pirates

Before the turn of the century, America had enough problems to satisfy most of its politicians and playwrights. Plays that mentioned foreign powers usually had harsh words for England and a sympathy—sometimes reluctant, especially from the Federalists—for the French. The one external affair, however, which provided material for playwrights was the war with the Barbary Coast pirates. Although the fighting did not occur until 1801 when our infant navy was sent to Tripoli, for a long time before that date the North African states—Morocco, Algeria, Tunis, and Tripoli—had been making an effective income by plundering merchantmen that sailed into the Mediterranean. David Everett's *Slaves in Barbary* (1797) is concerned with that persecution, which aroused Americans to anger and indignation.

The most important American play dealing with the pirates is *Slaves in Algiers; or, A Struggle for Freedom* (1794) by Susanna H. Rowson, best known for her amazingly successful sentimental novel, *Charlotte Temple* (1791). Concerning the rescue of some Americans held prisoner by the pirates, the play, Mrs. Rowson's only extant drama, mixes an abundance of sentiment with the melodrama of captures, disguises, and escapes.

2. SOCIAL FARCE AND EARLY CHARACTER TYPES

Of her aims as a playwright, Mrs. Rowson wrote: "It has been my endeavor to place social virtues in the fairest point of view, and hold up, to merited contempt and ridicule, their [the people's] vices." Her objectives, shown also in *The Female Patriot* (1795) and *Americans in England* (1797), were shared by many: the stage became a place to improve the manners and morals and to castigate social foibles and vices; satire, the acceptable technique; sentiment, the means to please the middle-class taste; and farce-comedy, the usual genre. Consequently, plays were frequently a hodge-podge of social and political comment—well illustrated by *The Contrast*.

(a) Social and Political Themes

A good illustration of the fusion of socio-political ideas is John Murdock's *The Triumphs of Love; or, Happy Reconciliation* (1795), which includes comment on various aspects of the times: Quakers, the Whiskey Rebellion, a foreign-born character who loves America as a place of freedom and opportunity, the problem of the Barbary pirates, and Negro slavery. A contemporary critic described the play as having "sentiments that do honor to the writer's heart, both as man and citizen."

(b) Varied Satire

Topics for comment or satire suggest social biases of the day. Catholic attitudes were expressed in the anonymous play, *The French Revolution* (1790), and in Joseph Croswell's *A New World Planted* (1802). Jews were generally treated with disdain. Professional men were sometimes satirized—physicians, lawyers, and the clergy. Before the Revolution, lawyers were generally treated as troublemakers. (An early Connecticut law classed them with drunkards and brothel-keepers.) One anonymous and rather risqué play, *The Trial of Atticus Before Justice Beau for a Rape* (1771), generally satirized the legal profession.

(c) Character Types

Before 1800, the principal character types—the Yankee, the Indian, the Negro, and the Irishman—had been successfully introduced to the stage. Although the Yankee was once thought original with Tyler in *The Contrast* (1787), a humorous New England Yankee named Jonathan had previously appeared in *The Downfall of Justice*, (1777). Samuel Low's *The Politician Outwitted* (1788) included a clownish Yankee named Humphrey Cubb; and *The Better Sort* (anonymous, 1789) had a Yankee named Yorick. The least popular character was the Indian, first presented on the stage in Robert Roger's *Ponteach* (1766). The comic Negro appeared in a number of plays, usually as a servant, talking in dialect—for example, in *The Candidates* (1798), *The Fall of British Tyranny* (1776), *The Downfall of Justice* (1777), and *Sans Souci* (1785). John

Murdock, however, created a more individual Negro in *The Triumphs of Love* (1795) with Sambo, a simple, warmhearted, generous person. The stage Irishman, an adopted rather than a native son, appeared in *The Triumphs of Love* and in John Minshull's *Rural Felicity* (1801). These forged the models for the four character types which were to be enormously popular during the next fifty years.

3. ROMANTIC TRAGEDY

The trend toward poetic tragedy, started by Thomas Godfrey and followed by William Dunlap, continued through the eighteenth century and later became the mark of the serious dramatist. Unfortunately, the writing of poetic dramas at this time was not reserved for poets only, or even for those with dramatic talent. Illustrative of early poetic tragedies are Peter Markoe's *The Patriot Chief* (1784), and *The Mercenary Match* (1784) by Barnabas Bidwell. A more interesting but less successful play in the theater was John Daly Burk's *Female Patriotism; or, The Death of Joan d'Arc* (1798). A. H. Quinn called this play one of the "bright spots that reward the reader of our early drama." Generally unrelieved in their tragedy, frequently dull in plot, and written in quite ordinary verse, the romantic tragedies are of interest to the drama historian but are the least exciting to the general reader.

4. STRICTLY MORAL LESSONS

Playwrights well knew that the moral lesson in a play was extremely important not only for the audiences of New England but throughout the New World. The anonymous author of *The Better Sort* (1789) clearly stated that the playwright's task was to improve morals:

> For this the comick muse first trod the stage;
> And scourg'd the vice and folly of the age,
> Manners and sometimes principles she mended,
> Took her task up where the preacher ended.

When Dunlap rewrote *The Father* and increased the moralizing in the play, he acted in direct response to the desires of his audiences. The romantic tragedies of the time, the sentimental comedies, even the satires—all were written to point a moral effect. Sometimes the didacticism was so dominant that plot disappeared and only dialogue remained. One of the largest collections of published dialogues was Charles Stearns' 540 pages of *Dramatic Dialogues for the Use of Schools* (1798).

5. COLLEGE DRAMA

After the Revolution, college students continued to write and produce plays such as *The Mercenary Match* by Barnabas Bidwell, performed by Yale College students in 1784, and *The French Revolution*, written and produced by a student at Dartmouth College in 1790. Such activity was indicative of an interest which was to lie relatively fallow for over a hundred years before it became a meaningful part of our theater productivity.

III. THEATER DURING THE REVOLUTION AND THE POST-REVOLUTIONARY PERIOD TO 1800

During the last quarter of the eighteenth century, the American theater renewed its struggle for acceptance. Seriously hampered during the war years, it now made distinct advances in building theaters and developing companies of actors. Theater management continued to be a risky business. Theater people, however, were optimistic even as the slackening opposition of church and state seemed offset by the growing harassment of the theater critics.

A. Theater during the Revolution

Theater during the Revolution was largely controlled by the British. General Burgoyne opened a Boston theater in 1775; General Howe's so-called "strolling company" opened its season in Philadelphia on January 19, 1778. The center of English theater activity, however, was New York, where each season until 1782 a number of the best plays of that time were produced—including the first American performance of Sheridan's

The Rivals. During these years, Congress did everything it could to discourage the acting of plays, but neither American soldiers nor citizens were cut off completely from the theater. Soldiers at Valley Forge presented plays in the spring of 1778, and American forces opened the Southwark Theatre in Philadelphia later that year. Pennsylvania, Massachusetts, and New York were reasonably severe in their enforcement of the law against enacting plays; but Maryland as a state did not abide by the Congressional interdicts concerning entertainment, and both Baltimore and Annapolis enjoyed plays during the late years of the war.

B. Theater from the Revolution to 1800

After the Revolution, the members of the American Company who had gone to Jamaica began to return, but without David Douglass, who had retired from the company and become a British judge in Jamaica. In 1782, John Henry was the first to use the theaters built by the Old American Company; the young Lewis Hallam arrived in 1784. By 1785, they had joined forces and settled in New York's John Street Theatre where, with Thomas Wignell, they began to dominate American theater circles for the next several years. In 1791, Wignell left to form his own company, and John Hodgkinson took his place in the Old American Company. Not until Wignell returned from England with a larger and more talented company was the monopoly of the Old American Company broken. As the number of theater companies increased, so did the need for theaters. Charleston began to build a theater in 1792. Two years later, two famous theaters were opened: the Chestnut Street Theatre in Philadelphia and the Federal Street Theatre in Boston.

During these years, many new and talented actors and actresses gained eminence in the American theater: Mrs. Oldmixon, Eliza Kemble Whitlock, Thomas A. Cooper, and Joseph Jefferson I. The theater also provided its usual abundance of exciting and sometimes scandalous events. There was an extended feud between the management and the gallery hoodlums in Boston's Federal Street Theatre in which "apples, stones or other missiles" were nightly hurled into the orchestra. The rebellion of actors from conditions in John L. Solee's French Theatre in Charleston was colorfully reported in the newspapers.

Although this kind of news made the headlines, far more significant was the establishment of permanent theaters and the development of large companies of actors and actresses in America.

SUMMARY: BEGINNINGS OF AMERICAN DRAMA

Although it was a policy of theater managers during this time and for many years to come to laud foreign plays and to discourage American playwrights, plays before the turn of the century reveal the distinct beginnings of an American drama. Many, of course, indicate rather little dramatic talent and were written more to criticize or propagandize than to create a work of art, but the passion of some of these plays often strikes a spark of real life.

Because the Whig and Tory playwrights were much more interested in propaganda than in art, they became special pleaders, whose characters said only what the author demanded. The play was a weapon; it had a distinct purpose and an episodic structure determined by that purpose. Today, such plays are mainly interesting as partisan social history and as caricature or panegyric—having objectives similar to the satiric poetry of Philip Freneau and the essays of Thomas Paine. Although dramatically weak, many plays show enough passion, wit, and ingenuity to make them quite readable.

In *The Contrast* of Royall Tyler lie the faint beginnings of social comedy in America. The plays of William Dunlap show the serious dramatist experimenting in the drama as his talent excites him and as expediency demands, and creating both in amount and in qualified excellence a noteworthy beginning for American drama. The creation of American character types was another step forward, while the numerous plays commenting on social foibles and political issues indicate the vitality of a growing drama.

Essentially, this was a weak period for English and European drama, and America adulterated her natural force by adapting and translating and imitating the romantic tragedies of

England and the sentimental melodramas of France and Germany. But such was the fashion! It is with extreme care, certainly, that one commends the literary merit of more than a couple of these plays. Journalistic critics of the drama were just appearing before the turn of the century, but they wrote primarily in terms of the plot, the production, and the accomplishments of the actors. More recent critics would perceive that in the drama before 1800 the foundations for the development of an American drama were becoming established.

SELECTED BIBLIOGRAPHY

Anderson, John, *The American Theater in New York.* New York: Dial Press, 1938.

Austin, Mary, "Spanish Drama in Colonial America," *Theatre Arts,* XIX (September, 1935), 705.

Brown, Alice, *Mercy Warren.* New York: C. Scribner's Sons, 1896.

Brown, Herbert, "Sensibility in Eighteenth-Century American Drama," *American Literature,* IV (March, 1932), 49–60.

Brown, T. A., *A History of the New York Stage from the First Performance in 1732 to 1901.* 3 Vols. New York: Dodd, Mead, and Company, 1903.

Coad, Oral S., *William Dunlap: A Study of His Life and Works.* New York: The Dunlap Society, 1917.

Dunlap, William, *A History of the American Theatre.* New York: J. & J. Harper, 1832.

Elfenbein, Aaron, *American Drama 1782–1812 as an Index to Social Political Thought.* New York University, unpublished Ph.D. dissertation, 1951.

Ford, Paul L., "The Beginnings of American Dramatic Literature," *New England Magazine,* N.S. IX (February, 1894), 673–87.

Gay, F. L., "The First American Play," *Nation,* LXXXVIII (February 11, 1909), 136.

Hartman, John Geoffrey, *The Development of American Social Comedy from 1787 to 1936.* Philadelphia: University of Pennsylvania Press, 1939.

Hewitt, Barnard, *Theatre U.S.A., 1665 to 1957.* New York: McGraw-Hill Book Company, 1959.

Hornblow, Arthur, *A History of the Theatre in America,* Vol. I. Philadelphia: J. B. Lippincott Company, 1919.

Hughes, Glenn, *A History of the American Theatre, 1700–1950.* New York: S. French, 1951.

Ireland, Joseph N., *Records of the New York Stage from 1750 to 1860.* 2 Vols. New York: T. H. Morrell, 1866–1867.

Mayorga, Margaret G., *A Short History of the American Drama.* New York: Dodd, Mead & Company, 1932.

Menelly, John H., *A Study of American Drama Prior to 1801*. New York University, unpublished Ph.D. dissertation, 1911.

Moses, Montrose J., *The American Dramatist*. Boston: Little, Brown, and Company, 1925.

Odell, George C. D., *Annals of the New York Stage*. 15 Vols. New York: Columbia University Press, 1927–1949.

Pollock, Thomas C., *The Philadelphia Theatre in the Eighteenth Century*. Philadelphia: University of Pennsylvania Press, 1933.

Quinn, Arthur Hobson, *A History of the American Drama from the Beginning to the Civil War*. New York: Appleton-Century-Crofts, Inc., 1943.

Seldon, Samuel, *Man in His Theater*. Chapel Hill, N.C.: University of North Carolina Press, 1957.

Seilhamer, George O., *History of the American Theatre*. 3 Vols. Philadelphia: Globe Printing House, 1888–1891.

CHAPTER II

Drama of a New Nation, 1800-1865
A Period of Experimentation and Imitation

From the beginning of the century through the period of the Civil War, the progress of American drama was steady but generally unimpressive. The theater continued to expand amid difficulties, and various actors and actresses achieved reputations which gained them applause in America and even in England, but such appreciation was that due to youthful exuberance rather than to mature excellence. Certainly the most remembered theatrical events of this period resulted more from the pains of growth than from superiority of performance. Between the actor or the manager and the playwright there was little sympathy and even less co-operation. On only a very few occasions did a high point in the history of American theater and a significant play in the history of American drama occur simultaneously.

The power and influence of the actor (and particularly the actor-manager) was supreme; the tastes of American audiences were no higher than usual; and the dramatist was an insignificant person. With his eye on his fortune, the actor or actor-manager tried to provide the theater-goer with both the sentiment he enjoyed and the English plays he thought it fashionable to applaud. At the same time, the actor claimed the privilege of giving full vent to the declamatory style of acting then popular, although a few actors specialized in a single character such as the stage Yankee.

The American dramatist, meanwhile, was forced either

to imitate the style of successful foreign plays or to write a play for a particular actor. In either instance his work was likely to become unintentionally philanthropic. With very little professional status and without the protection of a copyright law—not to mention the pirating techniques of that day—the playwright could gain very little. In theater programs his name was frequently omitted, and his financial return was embarrassingly slight. The American dramatist was truly at the mercy of managers whose reasoning, if unethical, was at least understandable: Why pay Americans to write plays when we can get [steal] new plays from England for nothing?

In a Preface to his play *Thérèse, the Orphan of Geneva*—which was taken down in shorthand from the theater pit and thus stolen by theater managers in London—John Howard Payne complained about the situation of the dramatist and the subsequent poor plight of dramatic literature in America. No doubt, he expressed the opinions of many. J. S. Jones, a prolific writer of farce comedies, stated bluntly that there was no Standard American Drama because nobody would pay for it. Robert Montgomery Bird, a poet-dramatist, found it most disagreeable "to write for and be admired by groundlings! villains that will clap when you are most nonsensical and applaud you most heartily when you are most vulgar. . . ." Perhaps the time was not ripe for serious and creative dramatists. Certainly, with few exceptions—and these failures—men with reputations in literature did not write for the stage. And it was a long time before theater managers lamented this condition.

From 1800 to 1865, only a handful of dramatists achieved anything approaching literary quality. And these dramatists were not frequently encouraged, nor was the literary value of their work appreciated. Dramatic criticism had just started before the turn of the century, and of the few attempts to establish purely theatrical magazines, none lasted more than a year or two. Washington Irving was an outstanding and delightful critic, and with tongue in cheek his reviews suggest a perceptive attitude toward critics: "The critics, my dear Jonathan," Andrew Quoz explained to Jonathan Oldstyle, "are the very pests of society; they rob the actor of his reputation, the public of their amusement; they open the eyes of their readers to a full perception of the faults of our performers; they reduce our feelings to a state of miserable refinement, and destroy entirely all the enjoyments in which our coarser sensations delighted."

Generally, critics throughout the century were notorious for their ignorance of drama as literature as well as of drama as a scenic and declamatory production. In America as in England, criticisms of the theater were published in the "Sporting and Theatrical" journals such as the New York *Clipper* and the New York *Illustrated Times.* The earliest theatrical newspaper was the New York *Dramatic News and Society Journal,* established in 1874.

Before the Civil War, the greatest opportunity for the person interested in writing plays lay in becoming an actor or actor-manager-dramatist. Some did, of course—such as John Howard Payne, Dion Boucicault, and John Brougham. Others wrote plays, became disenchanted with conditions, and then left the theater—such as Robert Montgomery Bird. Still more wrote the innumerable lesser plays for their own or another's acting. It seems to have been neither a very happy time for the serious American dramatist nor a very productive period for good American drama. Yet there were some plays of merit being written in America. Among these are Payne's *Brutus* and *Charles the Second,* James N. Barker's *Superstition,* Robert M. Bird's *The Broker of Bogota,* Anna C. Mowatt Ritchie's *Fashion.* George H. Boker's *Francesca da Rimini* is considered by many to be superior to any play written on either side of the Atlantic Ocean during this time. But, quite generally, drama in America was diverse and superficial.

At the end of the eighteenth century in America, the drama had become established as a source of entertainment, as a political weapon, as well as a means of glorifying the nation and as a teacher of moral behavior. These trends continued as the playwright experimented further with his material. As wars were fought and a self-conscious new nation became aware of the necessity of tradition, various aspects of America's past appeared on the stage—all patriotically glorified. Those playwrights who wanted to write serious drama imitated the romantic verse plays of England and with a few notable exceptions remained simply imitators. Native characters soon proved an effective source of comedy, and while the Negro became a minstrel as well as a serious character in plays, the stage Yankee as a comic character was expanded into an evening's entertainment. As cities grew and social classes became distinguishable, the particular characteristics of these classes provided the object of ridicule in plays, and comedies of social caricature gained popular acclaim. In essence, American drama developed constantly, though slowly, and with significance in some areas, but it still showed the divided interests of a country (1) struggling for existence and experimenting with its material, and (2) attempting to gain status by imitating the drama of England and Europe.

I. PLAYS FROM THE TOWN CRIER: NATIONALISM ON THE STAGE

In his *History* (I, 163–4) William Dunlap quoted James Kirke Paulding, American novelist and dramatist, on national drama:

> By a national drama, we mean, not merely a class of dramatic productions, written by Americans, but one appealing directly to the national feeling—founded upon domestic incidents—illustrating or satirizing domestic manners, and, above all, displaying a generous chivalry in the maintenance and vindication of those great and illustrious peculiarities of situation and character by which we are distinguished from all other nations.

If followed seriously, Paulding's definition might include most of the plays discussed in this chapter, for the majority of the dramas written during these years included some aspect of the manners, politics, character, or particular glory of the nation. Here, however, national drama is limited to political incidents and historical events. Not only in the "coonskin" New Democracy of Andrew Jackson but also in the ultranationalistic ideas of John Quincy Adams' puritan New England, the "feelings of national glory" and "love of country" were prominent. The drama, always dependent upon popular tastes, followed the nationalistic trend. Like the town crier who heralded the news concerning the welfare of the town and the nation, these plays commented on political events and sounded the glory of the new nation.

A. Political Events and Issues

The inclination of post-Revolutionary playwrights to comment on political events continued—as it continues today. After the heated presidential campaign of 1800, for example, Thomas Jefferson defeated the Federalist incumbent, John Adams, and ended twelve years of Federalist rule. The following year, a play by J. H. Nichols celebrated Jefferson's inauguration: *Jefferson and Liberty; or, Celebration of the Fourth of March* (1801). Adams is ridiculed as the Duke of Braintree, and all is portrayed as corruption until Jefferson gives his inaugural speech promising freedom and justice.

1. REACTION TO PARTICULAR EVENTS

The purchase of Louisiana in 1803 inspired James Workman to write a farce-comedy called *Liberty in Louisiana* (1804). James Nelson Barker's *The Embargo; or, What News?* (1808) supports Jefferson's highly controversial Embargo Act of 1807, which forbade the export of all goods from America. *Removing the Deposits* (1835) by Henry J. Finn referred to Andrew Jackson's decision in 1833 to deposit no more funds with Nicholas Biddle's Bank of the United States.

2. BORDER DISPUTES

N. H. Bannister's *The Maine Question* (1839) was concerned with the boundary dispute involving some 12,000 square miles of wilderness claimed by both Maine and Canada. The Oregon Controversy of 1846 was dramatized that same year by Joseph M. Field in *Oregon; or, The Disputed Territory*, a kind of masque with Oregon, Texas, and California—three territories wanted by President James K. Polk—acting parts.

3. THE POLITICIAN

Politicians appeared in many plays. In the early 1820's, Seba Smith of the Portland, Maine, *Courier* created Major Jack Downing, a Yankee comic-critic of political issues and politicians, who dressed in the clothes we now give to Uncle Sam. In 1834, an anonymous playwright put this Downeast Yankee's political arguments into a play, *Major Jack Downing; or, The Retired Politician. Whigs and Democrats; or, Love of No Politics* (1839), attributed to J. E. Heath, and *The Politicians* (1840) by Cornelius Mathews, satirized methods used in a rural election in Virginia and the evils of the local campaign, respectively. Neither play is effective, and dramatists of distinctive talent seldom concerned themselves with political issues.

B. Reflected Glory: America's Past

As a young country still not completely certain of the distinctive values of originality or imitation, America was cautiously impressed by the importance of traditions and the past in England. On the other hand, strong feelings of nationalism prompted dramatists to exploit the few past events and the people of whom America could boast. The Revolution, of course, immediately offered itself as material, as did other military engagements, such as the battles with the Barbary Coast pirates, the War of 1812, and the Mexican War. Various activities of the Colonial Period were also dramatized. Generally, however, national plays are not among the best of this period, and only a relatively few plays have survived.

1. PLAYS ABOUT THE COLONIAL PERIOD

The best play based on a Colonial theme is, without question, James Nelson Barker's *Superstition* (1824), which dramatizes New England intolerance and the incident of a Puritan leading the people against the Indians. (Refer to the section on poetic drama with a native theme.) Most of the plays with Indian characters—which numbered, according to

Quinn, more than fifty plays in the 1825–1860 period—also are set in Colonial times. (Refer to the section on Indian characters.)

Only a handful of other plays exist which treated Colonial history. Richard Penn Smith's historical melodrama *William Penn* (1829) dramatizes William Penn's activities in saving the life of the Indian chief, Tammany. George H. Miles' *De Soto, the Hero of the Mississippi* (1852) combines an exploration theme with a Colonial setting. Cornelius Mathews, editor and playwright, wrote two plays with Colonial themes: *Jacob Leisler* (1848), based on events in the life of a Governor of New York, and *Witchcraft; or, The Martyrs of Salem* (1846).

2. PLAYS ABOUT THE REVOLUTION

By far the most stimulating period for early nineteenth century American playwrights was the period of the Revolution. Heroes, battles, fashions of the time—all appeared on the stage either as original plays or as adaptations from historical novels. Washington was most frequently used as a hero, but the traitorous act of Benedict Arnold was depicted in several plays in which Major André figured prominently. Generally, the plays were unpretentious farce-melodramas.

(a) *Putnam, The Iron Son of '76* by N. H. Bannister, 1844

General Israel Putnam is the subject of this three-act "National Military Drama." Opening with a "Vision," a chorus, and various tableaux, the play's hero, Putnam, rushes here and there—rescuing a maiden from the Indians, saving Washington and his staff from a renegade's betrayal, and escaping himself from General Cornwallis. One remembers, perhaps, the frantic energy of Putnam, the pseudo-literary quality of the Indians' speech, and the poorly motivated action.

(b) *Franklin* by John Brougham, 1856

In the main plot of this "historical drama" in five acts, Franklin (1) arrives in Philadelphia with his bread under his arm and starts work as a printer, (2) as an older, married man gives money to a man with the advice that he help another, (3) is reunited with his mother in Boston, (4) in England outwits Lord Hillsborough and William Pitt and wins a game of chess with Mrs. Howe before escaping to France, where (5) he buys a wig amidst great comedy and signs a treaty with Louis XVI, who toasts America: "Long live the Confederation of the United States." Throughout, the nationalistic flavor is unmistakable.

(c) Plays about Battles of the Revolution
Numerous other plays treated particular battles of the Revolution and reflected the general atmosphere of the times—such as, *The Boston Tea Party of 1774*, anon. (1843); *The Cradle of Liberty; or, Boston in 1775* by S. E. Glover (1832); and *A Tale of Lexington* by Samuel B. Judah (1822).

(d) Historical Novels of the Revolution Dramatized
Several contemporary historical novels were very successfully adapted to the stage. In 1856, Clifton W. Tayleure dramatized John P. Kennedy's popular novel, *Horseshoe Robinson*. Charles P. Clinch's *The Spy, A Tale of the Neutral Ground* (1822) was one of several adaptations of James Fenimore Cooper's novels.

(e) A Romance of the Revolution: *Love in '76* by Oliver Bell Bunce, 1857
Called the best of the Revolutionary plays by A. H. Quinn, the plot treats the love of a Captain Armstrong of the American army for Rose Elsworth, the daughter of a loyalist and sister of an officer in the English army. But the play is lively comedy, and the story dramatizes a series of clashes of wit in which a clever woman gets the man she loves. With the help of disguises, the plot is effectively worked out, and the dialogue is humorous, witty, and less stilted than other plays of this period.

3. PLAYS ABOUT THE WAR WITH THE BARBARY STATES

For some reason the romance of pirates and the Mediterranean did not interest many playwrights. The best play dealing with the Barbary pirates, Mrs. S. H. Rowson's *Slaves in Algiers* (1794), was written before the fighting began—at least, before Jefferson dispatched the Navy in 1801. [See Chapter I] One of the better plays was James Ellison's *The American Captive; or, The Siege of Tripoli* (1811), revised by J. S. Jones under the title *The Usurper; or, Americans in Tripoli* (1841). The play tells a story of romantic adventure, but nationalistic sentiment prevails as the playwright urges America to negotiate its problems and asks for the freedom of the brave sons of America. Other Barbary States War plays include M. Pinchney's colorful *The Young Carolinians; or, Americans in Algiers* (1818), *The Siege of Tripoli* (1820) by Mordecai Noah, and Jonathan S. Smith's extravagant work *The Siege of Algiers; or, The Downfall of Hadgi-Ali-Bashaw, a Political, Historical and Sentimental Tragi-Comedy* (1823).

4. PLAYS ABOUT THE WAR OF 1812

According to W. W. Clapp, Jr. (*A Record of the Boston Stage*, Boston, 1853, p. 134), "In the early days of the theatre, every public event of sufficient importance was immediately dramatized, and during the progress of the war [1812], the spirit was kept up by the frequent productions of pieces in honor of our naval victories." Spectacles on stage, of course, were well appreciated. Consequently, the capture of the *Macedonia* by the *United States* was celebrated in *The Return from a Cruise* (anonymous, 1812), and the victory of the *Constitution* over the *Guerrière* in Dunlap's *Yankee Chronology* (1812).

(a) Plays by Richard Penn Smith

The most significant of those playwrights who chose to dramatize the War of 1812 is Richard Penn Smith—a member of the so-called Philadelphia school of dramatists. A lawyer by profession, Smith became a competent craftsman of the theater. His play, *The Eighth of January*, produced in Philadelphia on January 8, 1829, and celebrating the election of Andrew Jackson as President, dramatizes Jackson's victory over the British at New Orleans on January 8, 1815. Although poorly written, the play was successful—obviously due to a well-timed production. The momentous victory at Platts-burg when General McDonough's fleet defeated the English on September 1, 1814, was the basis of *The Triumph at Plattsburg* (1830). Smith, however, sacrificed historical action in this play for the melodrama of fictional disguise, escape, and pursuit.

(b) Battles of the War of 1812

Mordecai Noah dramatized the Battle of Chippewa, July 5, 1814, in a play called *She Would Be a Soldier; or, The Plains of Chippewa* (1819). More romance than history, the play tells the story of Christine, who, to avoid an unwanted marriage and to find Lenox whom she loves, disguises herself as a man and enlists as a soldier, only to be discovered and condemned as a spy before she is finally saved—by Lenox, of course. Other plays on the war include C. E. Grice's *The Battle of New Orleans* (1815), G. W. P. Custis' *The Eighth of January* (1831) and *North Point; or, Baltimore Defended* (1833), and Richard Emmons' *Tecumseh; or, The Battle of the Thames* (1836).

5. PLAYS ABOUT THE MEXICAN WAR

William Gilmore Simms' *Michael Bonham; or, The Fall of Bexar* (1852) dramatizes the life of a Charleston soldier who fought through the Texas skirmishes to the battle of the Alamo. According to A. H. Quinn, the only surviving play on the Mexican War is *The Battle of Buena Vista* (1858); other titles include *The Siege of Monterey, Our Flag Is Nailed to the Mast*, and *Victory upon Victory*.

II. POETIC DRAMA: THE SERIOUS DRAMATIST AT WORK

If serious and high dramatic purpose existed in American plays before the Civil War, it found expression in the poetic dramas. From Godfrey's *Prince of Parthia* (1765) to Boker's *Francesca da Rimini* (1855), one can trace the development of poetic drama—from its most imitative beginnings to the greatest height in romantic tragedy ever reached by an

American in the nineteenth century. Having literary aspirations, poetic dramatists followed the dictum of Horace—to teach and to delight—and if they stressed the first precept, they were only obeying the impulse of the age. Their names— James Nelson Barker, John Howard Payne, Nathaniel Parker Willis, Robert Montgomery Bird, George Henry Boker— identify some of the most significant figures in American drama before the Civil War. Their plays are among the best that America can offer for this century.

That period before the Civil War was a period of poetry and of romantic themes. An American literature was being created by Irving, Hawthorne, Emerson, Longfellow, Cooper, Poe, and Melville, among others. Unlike other literary forms which stressed independence from England, the drama accepted English leadership as the standard which theater managers and actors demanded. Attempting to follow the mood of the times, as well as to reach a meaningful success in their art, the serious dramatists wrote poetic drama.

Considering all of the drama of this time, one finds that, by and large, poetic plays show the influence of foreign drama, while the prose plays exploit more of the qualities that are distinctly American. There are, however, several poetic dramas with native themes. The two major historians of American drama, Montrose Moses and A. H. Quinn, did not agree as to the value of poetic drama: Quinn organized a third of his *A History of American Drama from the Beginning to the Civil War* around the poetic dramatists; Moses, in *The American Dramatist*, seemed to feel that these men were overrated. Given a realistic perspective of American drama and its accomplishments during the first sixty or more years of the nineteenth century, one finds that the poetic plays fit into a relatively significant niche.

In the entire history of American drama, poetic plays have had a cyclical popularity. Prevalent during the early half of the nineteenth century, they nearly disappeared during the realistic movement in literature of the last part of the century. In the early years of the twentieth century, a half-dozen poet-dramatists produced some effective plays, only to be overwhelmed by World War I. Since then, only a few have attempted to write poetic drama, but the number is increasing.

A. The Pattern of Poetic Drama[1]

More than other dramatists, the writer of poetic plays was limited in what he could do. The audience, the actor, and the theater manager—all made certain demands. According to dramatic critic William Winter, the verse dramatist had to entertain and instruct a dull multitude that "never felt anything 'til it was hit with a club." Hence the subtleties of verse had little effect on the audience, and dramatic ironies were not appreciated. The actor, in turn, demanded bombastic speeches which would best adapt to a flamboyant delivery. Consequently, there emerged in America a poetic drama that, with foreign or native inspiration, followed certain patterns in plot, purpose, theme, setting, and characters. The best plays, of course, in some ways defied the pattern and thereby gained, in part, their excellence.

1. PLOT

Although a few poetic comedies were written (the best example is N. P. Willis' *Tortesa the Usurer*, 1839), most of the poet-dramatists had pretensions toward tragedy and were influenced by: (1) the melodramatic romances of the French (Alexandre Dumas and Victor Hugo, particularly the latter's Preface to *Cromwell*, 1827); (2) the sentimental and humanitarian dramas of the German Kotzebue; (3) the plays of Elizabethan England; and (4) the dramas of sensibility and the domestic tragedy of eighteenth-century England. Plots varied, of course, some writers bowing more to one model than to another. The general tragic plot, however, became sufficiently familiar that *Portfolio* magazine in 1803, with some facetiousness and some truth, gave the following instructions to the writer of tragedy:

> In order to make a striking and poetic plot, the author must collect as many black-looking tragedies as his industry can discover; the older they are the better; interweaving and jumbling them together, so that it will be

[1] See John Reardon, *Verse Drama in America from 1765 to the Civil War*, University of Kansas, unpublished Ph.D. dissertation, 1957.

impossible to develop or understand them. After arranging
the plot, the time must be laid in a century long since
gone by, and the place in a remote kingdom and among
grandees never heard of. Then for the sentiments; these
you will find in the Bible, in moral treatises, in Addison's
Cato, in Darwin's *Botanic Garden*, in a thousand well-
known books and common-place works, where no one
can suppose he has had the impudence to pick them up.

It is not surprising that Montrose Moses, with reference to
poetic plays, could write of the "second hand spirit" that pervaded American drama.

2. THE SETTING

The historical setting of the poetic dramas provided the
audiences with the pageantry and grandeur that they enjoyed
and with the moral instruction they demanded. In a prologue
to James McHenry's *The Usurper* (1827), J. N. Barker wrote:

> Our poet's pencil paints the moral scene
> Teaching what ought to be by what has been.

The majority of these verse plays employed an ancient setting.
Rome was a particular favorite (Payne's *Brutus*, Bird's *The
Gladiator*); as a republic with a history of rebellion, war, and
tyranny, it could support a political theme in which the American attitude toward democracy and freedom would be prominent
and readily understood. A medieval background was employed
for similar reasons. By writing of distant places in olden times,
the dramatists believed that they could infuse greater issues and
more universal themes into their works. Some dramatists, of
course, used native themes to great advantage, but the setting
was always from a past that could suggest grandeur as well as
instruction.

3. THE CHARACTERS

The best dramatists created characters of human dimen-
sions, such as Ravensworth in Barker's *Superstition* and Lan-

ciotto in Boker's *Francesca da Rimini*. More frequently, however, the characters were not individuals but social types. Lacking a sense of greatness and showing little psychological insight on the part of the dramatist, these characters were more a part of melodrama than tragedy. The heroes were simply virtuous—lovers, leaders, honorable men. Having no internal conflict, they had only to love the heroine, defeat the villain, and speak moral platitudes. The villain was the hero's opposite—evil, vicious, a scoffer at democracy, a man of unscrupulous ambition, sometimes ugly and physically deformed. Frequently, however, because of his greater imagination, he was the most interesting person in the play.

The women in these plays were of two distinct types. There was the angelic woman—virtuous, modest, obedient, faithful, truthful, beautiful, but emotionally cold. She was to be worshipped, not loved. Frequently, this woman was driven insane by the cruelties of a man's world. The more interesting and the more realistic woman was the sinner, a woman destroyed by her own passions.

4. THE THEME

A major interest of plays early in the century and of poetic drama in particular, because it was the serious drama of the time, was moral instruction. In varying degrees, plays became moral lectures; the poetry became sermonic, the characters personifications of vice and virtue to be punished and rewarded. Partially in response to demands for moral drama and in part following the traditions of English tragedy, the verse dramatist dealt almost exclusively with themes that he believed universal: (1) freedom and patriotism, (2) romantic love, (3) marital infidelity, or (4) parental tyranny and filial duty. A popular theme which combined public and domestic issues was the struggle of love with honor or duty.

5. THE POETRY

The demands of the theater upon the poet-dramatist had a distinct effect upon the kind of poetry he wrote. Also, with the exception of a few, those who wrote poetic plays were not good poets. Speeches in regular, stilted, and lifeless blank verse became rhetorical sermons rather than real speech. To most dramatists and, seemingly, to critics and managers, poetic speech meant exaggerated poetic diction with excessive use of abstract terms. Verbosity was common; imagery concerned with animals and mythology was elaborate. In *Caridorf* (1827), Bird exposed the common technique:

> Make thou no stops, no commas, no colons, nor periods; but between sentences draw thou a long dash, for this is significant of passion. Let there be breaks in the sentiment and style, the moderate complaining suddenly jumping into piteous ejaculations, with many an *O* and *Ah, Alas* and *Ah, me*. Then let the conclusion die away into a melancholy oath. . . .

There is, unfortunately, little to commend in the poetry of many of these plays. Few dramatists were capable of writing good poetic plays, but from these few there are surprising rewards for the interested reader.

B. Foreign Influences on Poetic Drama

As the patterns of poetic drama indicated, foreign influences on theme and technique were dominant in America. Of the many who wrote almost entirely of foreign scenes, three dramatists present sustained achievements—John Howard Payne, Robert Montgomery Bird, and George Henry Boker. In general, plays of lesser dramatists are not enjoyable for the modern reader, and the dramatists' reputations are of historical rather than literary interest.

1. JOHN HOWARD PAYNE (1791–1852)

As an actor and later as a dramatist, Payne was associated with the theater most of his life. Successful as a young actor in America, Payne went to England in 1813; but failing to impress the English audiences, he left the stage and began a new career as a playwright. In February, 1816, he started translating and adapting plays for the management at Drury Lane. Not satisfied with adaptations, however, he decided to write a tragedy for the great English actor, Edmund

Kean. The resulting play, *Brutus; or, The Fall of Tarquin,* was produced with wonderful success in December, 1818— success for everyone, that is, but Payne. Accused of plagiarism and abused by a grasping Drury Lane management, Payne also suffered a disastrous season as manager of Sadler's Wells Theatre. Sent to a debtor's prison, he wrote *Thérèse, the Orphan of Geneva* (1821), whose success brought him freedom.

Before returning to America in 1832, Payne wrote several popular plays. Among these are *Clari; or, The Maid of Milan* (1823), which includes "Home, Sweet Home," the poetry for which Payne is best remembered, and *Charles the Second* (1824), the successful comedy which he wrote in collaboration with Washington Irving. Back in America, Payne was treated to benefit performances of his plays and toasted by a literary group in New York: "Our distinguished countryman—John Howard Payne. The family of literature welcomes him to the home whose praises he has so sweetly sung." Although his plays were widely produced, he received little recompense for his work; and after an unsuccessful attempt to found a magazine and some bitter comments on the plight of the dramatist, he left the theater. When he died in 1851, he was the United States Consul at Tunis.

Payne's place in the history of American drama is significant. He was the first American dramatist to enjoy a substantial reputation abroad, and of the sixty or more plays attributed to him, several held the stage for many years, while his best efforts at comedy and tragedy are still worth considering. In each of the following types of drama, he presented a contemporary achievement—comedy, melodrama, opera— and in *Brutus*, he established a trend in romantic tragedy. His genius was not for creating the original play, but he did have remarkable talent for recognizing dramatic material and extracting theatrical success from his sources. Although he resorted to French drama for much of his inspiration, it must be remembered that at this time it was a great advertisement for a play to be the first English version of the latest French success. Because of his reputation abroad, his skillful use of dramatic materials, and his two or three major achievements in drama, he carried on the spirit of American drama where William Dunlap, the "Father," left off.

(a) *Brutus; or, The Fall of Tarquin,* 1818

(*Plot*) In Rome, Sextus Tarquin has seized the throne by murdering the father and brother of Lucius Junius, who now lives with the victors and feigns the "fool." Upset by a prophecy that "The race of Tarquin shall be kings, till a fool drive them hence, and set Rome free!" Tullia, Sextus' queen, suspects Lucius Junius and names him Brutus. Meanwhile, Titus, Brutus' son, not recognizing the tyranny, has decided to marry Sextus' daughter, Tarquinia, and is warned by Brutus that he must renounce either his father or his love. That night Sextus, having heard Collatinus boast of Lucretia's faithfulness as a wife, rapes her and describes his feat to Brutus, who drops his mask of idiocy and uses Sextus' action and Lucretia's suicide to rally the Romans to fight. Tullia dies; Sextus Tarquin is stoned to death; and Titus, controlled by those who conspired against Brutus, must be condemned. Passing this sentence, Brutus cries, "Justice is satisfied, and Rome is free!" before he falls, a final victim.

(*Discussion*) First performed at London's Drury Lane Theatre on December 3, 1818, the play was indebted, Payne noted in his Preface, to "seven plays upon the subject of Brutus." Its two major themes, however, came from myth and history: (1) Brutus' use of Sextus Tarquin's rape of Lucrece to expel the Tarquins, and (2) Brutus' dramatic condemnation of his own son. The success of the play was immediate and lasting. Written for Edmund Kean, the play also appealed to Edwin Forrest, who was attracted by the strong role of Brutus and the artificial elegance, which occasionally became dignity and power, in the blank verse.

2. ROBERT MONTGOMERY BIRD, 1806–1854

A very scholarly and versatile man but naïve and impractical in money matters, Bird started a trend in American drama parallel with that developing in French drama and became the foremost writer of American romantic tragedy in the first half of the nineteenth century. Beginning his mature life as a physician, he found more satisfaction in a career of playwriting until his association with Edwin Forrest, the actor, proved unbearable. He then turned to politics, journalism, and the writing of novels: *The Hawks of Hawk-Hollow* (1835) and *Nick of the Woods* (1837), among others.

When Bird began his literary career, the Romantic influence was being felt in American literature. Romanticism, a convenient term to describe some changes in literature that occurred particularly in the early nineteenth century, meant many things. It was the untamed and emotional attitude toward nature that distinguished Wordsworth's poetry. It was the emphasis on idealism and imagination that sparked the writing of Emerson and Thoreau; the interest in the Gothic that inspired Poe and Hawthorne; the sense of freedom, idealized individuals, and a realistic attitude toward background and scene that marked the historical romances of James Fenimore Cooper, John P. Kennedy, James Kirke Paulding, and William Gilmore Simms. Bird was a major force in bringing Romanticism to American drama.

Bird's relationship with Edwin Forrest was both his inspiration and his nemesis. In 1828, Forrest announced the first of nine playwriting contests through which he hoped to get new plays for himself and to inspire native dramatists. Four of the nine prize plays were written by Bird, and two of these—*The Gladiator* and *The Broker of Bogota*—were permanent plays in Forrest's repertoire. Having written plays from which Forrest reaped a fortune, Bird received only $1,000 for each play. Arrangements were poor, misunderstandings grew, and Bird stopped writing for the stage. An actor's greed and the lack of copyright laws in America cut short the creation of plays that in dramatic skill marked a high point in American drama.

Bird's particular skill in writing plays is not difficult to discover. The fact that he was able to write successfully for Forrest suggests three things: (1) that he had a keen instinct for the dramatic situation; (2) that he could create a well-developed hero; and (3) that he could write the kind of rhetorical and exclamatory poetic speech that fitted Forrest's robust style of acting. In describing his theory of dramatic composition, Bird noted that everything must lead toward the climax and stimulate interest in the hero—the power of the story, the passion of the characters, the strength of their speech, and the interest in the events. Unlike Payne, Bird found his dramatic incidents and inspiration in history, to which he applied a dramatic imagination and his novelist's ability to tell an interesting story. *The Broker of Bogota* and *The Gladiator* are his best plays, both tragedies, the former better as literature. In all his plays the Romantic attitude is prominent.

(a) *The Gladiator*, 1831

(*Plot*) Spartacus, a well-known Thracian gladiator captured by the Romans, refuses to fight until he is promised freedom for himself and his family if he fights another Thracian named Pharsarius. Just before the fight, Spartacus and Pharsarius discover that they are brothers; the gladiators' plot to rebel is revealed, and they rush the Roman guards, winning a great battle. Spartacus then rescues his wife and child and captures the Roman praetor's niece, whom he later decides to return over the objections of Pharsarius who wants the girl. The brothers split. Spartacus wants to go to Sicily and get reinforcements; Pharsarius takes most of the army, attacks Rome, and is defeated. Pompey's legions arrive; and when Spartacus' wife and child are killed, he rushes into battle to die like a gladiator.

(*Discussion*) This prize play was immediately successful on the stage and a favorite of Edwin Forrest, who performed the part of Spartacus for his debut in London on October 17, 1836. The critic of the London *Courier* was impressed: "America has at length vindicated her capability of producing a dramatist of the highest order, whose claims should be unequivocably acknowledged by the Mother Country."

According to his custom, Bird took freely from history and added conflicts and the touch of humanity which makes Spartacus a meaningful symbol of freedom. Into the most powerful tyranny the world has known, Bird brought Spartacus, a gladiator, who represents the value of individual man struggling against overwhelming force. The nobility of the theme is matched by Spartacus' deeds; witness the powerful emotional climax of his call for the gladiators' revolt at the end of Act II:

> Death to the Roman fiends, that make their mirth
> Out of the groans of bleeding misery!
> Ho, slaves, arise! it is your hour to kill!
> Kill and spare not—for wrath and liberty!
> Freedom for bondmen—freedom and revenge!

(b) *The Broker of Bogota,* 1834

(*Plot*) Led into dissolute ways by Caberero, Ramon has been disinherited by his father, Febro the broker, and refused by the father of Juana, his betrothed, because he has no inheritance. Now desperate for money, Ramon is easy prey for Caberero. Meanwhile, Febro tries to bribe Caberero to leave the city and would forgive Ramon, who now only rebukes him. When Febro is robbed by Caberero, circumstantial evidence that he stole from himself for his own advantage is very convincing, and Ramon will say nothing in his father's defense. Then Ramon, overwhelmed by remorse and persuaded by Juana, confesses his own and Caberero's guilt to the Viceroy, who frees Febro. Febro then learns that the Viceroy's son is in love with his daughter, and all seems well until Ramon jumps to his death and Febro falls lifeless to the floor.

(*Discussion*) True to his views on dramatic composition, Bird makes all speeches, scenes, and characters contribute to the interest in the main character. Baptista Febro, a good and noble man whose love goes beyond his middle-class morality, is both hero and victim: "Villains have entrapped him!" But because he is in no way responsible for such circumstantial misfortunes, the play is more melodramatic pathos than domestic tragedy. Opposing him is Caberero, a "devil-born destroyer of men's sons," whose greed, born of indifference to moral values in society, provides the basic plot. The Viceroy gives the theme and moral of the play: "the rigid sire and disobedient son."

3. GEORGE HENRY BOKER, 1823–1890

Of the poetic dramatists of this period, Boker is the only one with any substantial reputation as a poet. Although some of his plays were written after the Civil War, his best work, *Francesca da Rimini,* appeared in 1855 and is not only the best romantic tragedy of the century but the last one of any consequence in this period when poetic drama was popular and serious dramatists used it consistently. With the appearance of local color fiction and the beginnings of realism in literature, poetic drama was generally rejected by theater managers as not in the public taste. Although Boker's lyric and narrative poetry concerned with the Civil War (*Poems of the War*, 1891) are some of the best of that period, his work did not reflect prevailing social, economic, or literary changes. His romantic dramas written after the Civil War were seldom acted, and he remains a second-rate poet and a poetic dramatist whose work might as well have stopped in 1855. But not before! From Payne through Bird to Boker, one progresses from skillful fusion and imitation through the creation of human characters in theatrically effective plays to a work of literary as well as dramatic merit.

Boker wrote poetic comedy as well as tragedy, but he is distinguished among American dramatists only for his tragedies. His particular forte was his ability to create effective blank verse and to write witty as well as impassioned dialogue. Unlike Bird, who emphasized a single hero in each play, Boker built several characters into strong, forceful individuals with inner conflicts. His climaxes, too, were not climaxes of spectacle and bombast but of power and beauty. Although he wrote several plays—*Calaynos* (1848), *Leonor de Guzman* (1853), *Glaucus* (1886)—he remains recognized today mainly for a single masterpiece: *Francesca da Rimini*.

(a) *Francesca da Rimini* (1855)

(*Plot*) To cement relations between Ravenna and Rimini a marriage of state has been arranged between Francesca, daughter of Guido da Polenta of Ravenna, and Lanciotto, the hunchback son of Malatesta da Verruchio of Rimini. Aware of his ugliness, Lanciotto reluctantly agrees and sends his brother, Paolo, to Ravenna for Francesca who, romantic and unknowing, assumes that Paolo is Lanciotto and falls in love with him. Paolo finally confesses his identity, but not until Francesca arrives in Rimini does she know of Lanciotto's appearance. Hopeful of love, Lanciotto learns otherwise with his wedding kiss and rushes off to war. Thrust together, Paolo and Francesca find that they can contain their emotions no longer. When Pepe, the evil and vengeful court fool, overhears the lovers, he steals Paolo's dagger, and happily goes to Lanciotto with the lie that he was sent by Paolo to kill him. Unbelieving but enraged, Lanciotto kills Pepe, and rushes back to the palace where he finds both Paolo and Francesca, who readily admit their love and their sin. Compelled by his honor to kill them, Lanciotto ends his life regretting his act and his destiny, knowing that he loved Paolo more than honor.

(*Discussion*) Although early productions of this play were not successful, performances after 1882 with Lawrence Barrett as Lanciotto were received enthusiastically by critics. E. S. Bradley (*George Henry Boker: Poet and Patriot*, 1927) described it as "the greatest American romantic tragedy, and one of the greatest poetical tragedies in the language." In both scene and theme this play is representative of romantic tragedy. Rimini and Ravenna were both thirteenth-century city-states caught up in the struggle for power between the emperor and the pope. Into this scene Boker brought the traditional themes of love and honor, filial loyalty, and the evil consequences of sin, whether born of political greed or individual passion. The story of Paolo and Francesca has been treated many times in literature, but Boker was the first to write a play in English on the subject.

In addition to its poetry, the most distinguished of any poetic drama of nineteenth-century America, the play derives considerable power from the insight which Boker brings to his characters. Dramatically, he centers thoughtful attention on Lanciotto, whose physical ugliness is contrasted with the beauty and sensitivity of his soul. Francesca is always a living and vital person whose experiences in love are reflected in the maturing of her attitude toward the world. In Pepe, Boker found the ideal character whose warped humanity promotes the idea of a fateful as well as a personal tragedy. A clever fool who hides behind the coxcomb, an evil intriguer who enjoys inflicting unhappiness and lives for cruel revenge upon Lanciotto, Pepe foreshadows action.

In pleasing contrast to most tragedies of this period, *Francesca da Rimini*, with its humor, ironies, and diversified scenes, enjoys effective change of pace and relief from the overwhelming tragedy. The beginning scene with the minstrel has a light and charming touch. And there is broad humor in Guido's teasing of his servant girl and Pepe's witty and ironic songs.

4. THE PHILADELPHIA GROUP

Although in early times Philadelphia had been a difficult place for actors and dramatists, before 1800 the Chestnut

Street Theatre had been built and Thomas Wignell's acting company had been called the best in the country. Considering, too, the production of *The Contrast*, it is perhaps not surprising that Philadelphia should be the home of some of the better-known dramatists of the period. Richard Penn Smith, Robert Montgomery Bird, and John Augustus Stone have been mentioned. Others who wrote poetic plays were Mordecai Noah; James McHenry with his tragedy, *The Usurper* (1827), drawn from the Druidical times; David Paul Brown who wrote *Sertorius; or, The Roman Patriot* (1830), a play laid in Spain and dealing with the power of Sertorius in Spain, his victory over Pompey, and his eventual death; and Robert T. Conrad whose *Jack Cade* (1835), based on Wat Tyler's insurrection in England and the Kentish rebellion of 1450, was, according to *The Dramatic Authors of America* (1845), "undoubtedly destined to rank among the very highest dramatic productions of our language."

5. THE NEW YORK–NEW ENGLAND GROUP

Although by the late 1820's, the Tremont Theatre and the Federal Theatre were bringing good plays to Boston, the city was still not a strong center of theater activity. New Englanders who were serious in their work, such as Epes Sargent and Nathaniel Parker Willis, went to New York. But there were others. Henry W. Longfellow, poet and teacher, wrote several poetic dramas; but only *The Spanish Student* (1843), concerned with the love of a student for a gypsy girl, was not "closet" drama (for reading rather than the stage); and it was not acted. Julia Ward Howe wrote two poetic tragedies: *Leonora; or, The World's Own* (1857), which tells the story of Leonora's revenge upon the married Italian nobleman who seduced her; and *Hippolytus* (1864). Frances Wright came to New York to produce her tragedy *Altorf* (1819) named for William Tell's home and dramatizing in romantic fashion the activities of Tell.

(a) Nathaniel Parker Willis

An essayist, poet, editor, playwright, Willis (1806-1867) contributed in several ways to the growth of American literature: in sketches, *Pencillings by the Way* (1835), and in poetry. It is as a playwright, however, that he was most effective. His first play, a blank-verse tragedy entitled *Bianca Visconti* (1837), set in Milan, involves intrigues of love and politics.

Tortesa the Usurer (1839) is one of the few acceptable verse comedies of the time. Edgar Allan Poe wrote in *Burton's Gentleman's Magazine* of August, 1839, that its "merits are naturalness, truthfulness, and appropriateness upon all occasions of sentiment and language; a manly vigor and breadth in the conception of character." Owing debts to Shakespeare and the romantic traditions, the comedy depends for its interest on character and on various well-contrived scenes of sharp humor. Tortesa himself is a strange hero—an object of laughter and sympathy who is responsible for making a contrived situation comedy into a romantic comedy.

(*Plot*) In Florence, Tortesa arranges to give certain lands to Count Falcone in return for his daughter, Isabella, in marriage. But Tortesa really loves Zippa, a spirited lass, who loves Angelo, a painter; and Angelo and Isabella are deeply and secretly in love. Finally, Tortesa understands the situation, gives Isabella his blessing as well as the Count's land, and finds that Zippa will be happy to marry him.

(b) Epes Sargent

A Boston journalist, Epes Sargent (1814–1880), was responsible for two romantic tragedies in verse. Both illustrate very well the romantic theme of love versus honor or duty. *The Bride of Genoa* (1837, later published in *The New World*, 1842, as *The Genoese*) tells of a romantic hero who must free his future father-in-law from his problems, revenge his own father's murder, break the yoke of tyranny in Genoa, and win the heroine. *Velasco* (1837), laid in eleventh-century Spain, also emphasizes honor before love.

6. THE CHARLESTON GROUP AND THE SOUTH

Since pre-Revolution days the theater in Charleston, South Carolina, had been active, and during the first part of the nineteenth century, a group of playwrights provided it with some interesting, though not outstanding, plays. Two of the most effective of these dramatists were John Blake

White (1781–1859) with *Modern Honor* (1812) and *Foscari; or, The Venetian Exile* (1806), and Isaac Harby (1788–1828) with *The Gordian Knot* (1807) and *Alberti* (1819).

In other parts of the South active playwrights existed but usually came North to produce their plays. *Irma; or, The Prediction* (1830), written by James M. Kennicott of New Orleans, presents a girl whose life is ruined by the prediction that she will be a murderess. Baltimore produced Nathaniel H. Bannister, an actor who wrote many plays, including *Putnam* (which has been discussed) and a verse tragedy, *Gaulantus* (1836), which goes back to the time of the Roman seizure of Gaul for its setting.

C. Native Themes in Poetic Drama

Although poetic drama in America mainly exhibited a foreign scene, several poetic plays emphasized nationalistic theses. (For some of these see the first section of this chapter: "Nationalism on the Stage"; other plays about Indians are discussed later.) The best illustration of a romantic tragedy written on a native theme is J. N. Barker's *Superstition*.

1. JAMES NELSON BARKER, 1784–1858

Barker's biographer, Paul H. Musser (*James Nelson Barker*, Philadelphia, 1929) mentions eleven plays, the best of which are *Tears and Smiles* (1807) and *How to Try a Lover* (1817), two comedies; a romantic tragedy in poetry, *Marmion; or, The Battle of Flodden Field* (1812); and the tragedy of *Superstition; or, The Fanatic Father* (1824). Writing only as an avocation, Barker's seriousness is evident in his eleven critical articles on "The Drama" (appearing in the *Democratic Press*, Philadelphia, December 18, 1816, to February 19, 1817) as well as in his own account of his work in William Dunlap's *History*, pp. 308–316. His main career, however, was in government administration, either local or federal.

From his writings it is clear that Barker was interested in America. Like Irving, Bryant, Cooper, and Emerson, he regretted [in his Introduction to *Marmion*, 1812] the American "provincial sense of inferiority which still lingers among some, even of our highest-minded, with regard to the arts and refinements of society." His first completed play was *Amer-ica*, a one-act masque (1805), "consisting of poetic dialogue, and sung by the genius of America, Science, Liberty, and attendant spirits." *The Indian Princess; or, La Belle Sauvage* (1808) was the earliest play to treat the Pocahontas story, and the first Indian play to be acted in America. More than his contemporaries, he represented the truly American dramatist.

(a) *Superstition; or, The Fanatic Father,* 1824

(*Plot*) Recently come to New England are Isabella and her son, Charles, who, returning to the village from college, encounters The Unknown, really Isabella's father and one of the judges of Charles I. Charles also meets his sweetheart, Mary, the daughter of Ravensworth, the village clergyman, and protects her from the advances of George, light-hearted nephew of Sir Reginald Egerton, who was sent by Charles II to find the regicide. In the village the Indians attack and are repulsed when The Unknown appears briefly before the villagers as a leader. Immediately, however, Ravensworth turns the villagers against Charles because of his familiarity with The Unknown, charges Charles and Isabella with sorcery, and accuses Charles of murdering George and attempting to rape Mary. Protecting Mary's sensitivity, Charles refuses to plead and, at the frenzied insistence of Ravensworth, is executed. Then The Unknown enters and is reunited with his daughter, Isabella, before she dies of shock. Mary, too, breathes her last, raving of her love for Charles. Too late, Sir Reginald enters with a pardon for the regicide, The Unknown, and a message revealing Charles as the King's son.

(*Discussion*) The major theme revolves about New England intolerance activated by the superstitious mind. To this, Barker fused the incident of the Puritan refugee Goff leading the people against the Indians. Years later, Cooper was to employ the same story of the regicides of Charles I in *The Wept of Wish-Ton-Wish*, and Hawthorne would use the story of the Unknown in "The Gray Champion."

The characterization in the play gives it distinction—

particularly that of the villain Ravensworth. The hero and
the heroine are more traditional characters of romantic
tragedy. It is Ravensworth's personality, together with the
widespread belief in witchcraft, which makes the ending inevitable. A clergyman, he mistakes his own passions for the
voice of God and enjoys a powerful influence over his people
through his relentless revenge upon those who refuse to bow
to his authority. Showing fiendish glee at the hero's destruction, Ravensworth, like Chillingworth in Hawthorne's *Scarlet Letter*, is consumed by his own desire for revenge. A
villain-hero, his intelligence, his eloquence, his beliefs and
passions make him clearly the most interesting person in the
play.

In structure, the play shows the swift action and change
of pace of the better romantic tragedies. Incidents vary from
the meeting with The Unknown to the duel, to the Indian attack, to the trial, the execution, and the pardon that came
too late. There is some wit and humor in the speeches of
Sir Reginald and his nephew George, and the poetry in the
play generally aids its dramatic effectiveness.

III. NATIVE AMERICAN CHARACTER TYPES: JONATHAN, SAMBO, AND METAMORA

That spirit of the American Revolution which had fos-
tered feelings of personal and national independence was intensified by the so-called "Second War of Independence," the
War of 1812. At no time during the nineteenth century in
America was the feeling of nationalism higher than in the
period following that war. As the common man found his
voice more powerful in politics through the election of men
like Andrew Jackson and saw a measure of his individual
accomplishments in building a new country, his pride became
sensitive. He assumed an anti-foreign attitude, particularly toward the Irish immigrants who came by the tens of thousands
in the 1840's, and a few years later, he created an "American Party" with the slogan "Americans must rule America."
This strong sense of Nationalism made itself felt—significantly—in literature and in the theater.

It was in 1820 that the British critic Sydney Smith assured himself a place in histories of American literature with his rhetorical question: "In the four quarters of the globe who reads an American book or goes to an American play?" Unfortunately, the barb contained a bit of truth—felt more poignantly in America than in Europe. Some in America tried to encourage the arts; others scornfully condemned them. One of the latter, John Neal, a Maine novelist with more rancor than humor in this instance, wrote in *Blackwood's Magazine*, XVI, 427 (Oct., 1824); 567 (Nov., 1824); XVII, 48 (Jan., 1825):

> *Comedies*—See *Drama*. No such thing in America. One Mr. White has written two or three; but we have never seen or read them. They are spoken well of—in America. *Drama*—Mr. Noah . . . has written some tolerable farces, and some intolerable popular entertainments. . . . The writers of America have no encouragement, whatever, to venture upon the drama. *Farces*—About a dozen or twenty sober, childish, or disagreeable "entertainments" have been produced, in the United States of America— by the natives—within the memory of man, we believe— under this title. . . .

More constructive critics, such as Washington Irving and Robert Montgomery Bird, wrote essays suggesting the independence of American literature and arts from European models and describing values that would make American creations distinctive. Nationalistic drama, already mentioned, pointed to an obvious instance of American creativity. The historical novels of Cooper and James Kirke Paulding provided another. But Sydney Smith's question was, perhaps, more stimulating then he realized. Intense nationalism in politics spilled over into literature until, in 1837, Ralph Waldo Emerson's address, "The American Scholar," became recognized as America's Declaration of Intellectual Independence. Individualism and self-reliance were important for a nation as well as for an individual—for literature and the arts as well as for politics. But the people had to be provided with a representative American man—a symbol of their distinctive qualities—and Royall Tyler's Jonathan from *The Contrast* presented one solution for this problem.

American literature became identifiable only after writers had recognized the potential of American scenery, custom, character, and ideas. In the drama, both custom and character met in the Jonathan caricature, who was aided in his representation of America by other characters—the Negro and the Indian. All enjoyed a certain similarity. Each was introduced into the drama before 1800, and each developed irregularly during the nineteenth century. And in a sense, they were bound together by a similar desire for freedom: the Yankee from the English, the Indian from the Yankees, and the Negro from his bondage.

Each of the three characters—the Yankee, the Negro, and the Indian—reached a high point of popularity during the mid-nineteenth century and later became absorbed into the various social themes of modern drama. Jonathan of *The Contrast* developed from a greenhorn, whose credulity and prejudices made him an object of ridicule, to a shrewd hero, a witty storyteller whose clothes and language made him even more picturesque. The Negro, who had been a clownish servant, became both a minstrel character and a dramatic hero by mid-century. The Indian, primarily exploited as a major character from the beginning, continued in a primary role until John Brougham burlesqued him out of existence. It is perhaps significant that when the Indian left the stage his place was almost immediately taken by the backwoodsman, who became a new symbol of Nature's nobleman and America's individual prowess.

A. The Yankee Character

The origins of the stage Yankee, the character that so impressed England that Punch cartoonists soon referred to America as "Master Jonathan," are not clear. He appeared in Tyler's *The Contrast*, but he had been seen on the stage before this play. In part, his popularity resulted from the 1822–23 visit to America of the English actor Charles Mathews, who, after his return to England, collaborated with Richard B. Peake to write *Jonathan in England* (1824). This play's success was so great that it inspired numerous actors in America to write or request Yankee plays. About the same time, the Yankee began to appear in humorous essays and poems. Seba Smith, publishing the stories of Major Jack Downing in the Portland, Maine, *Courier*, was the first. Judge Haliburton's *Sam Slick* and James Russell Lowell's *Hosea Biglow Papers* soon followed.

Even before Mathews' visit, certain characteristics of the Yankee had been established. The preface to the 1815 edition of David Humphreys' *The Yankey in England* includes this comment:

> The Yankey is . . . made up of contrarieties—simplicity and cunning; inquisitive from nature and excessive curiosity, confirmed by habit; credulous, from inexperience and want of knowledge of the world; believing himself to be perfectly acquainted with whatever he partially knows; tenacious of prejudice; docile, when rightly managed; when otherwise treated, independent to obstinacy; easily betrayed into ridiculous mistakes; incapable of being overawed by external circumstances; suspicious, vigilant, and quick of perception, he is ever ready to parry or repel the attacks of raillery by retorts of rustic and sarcastic, if not of original and refined, wit and humour.

The beginnings had been made, and now patterns were being established. *The Contrast* produced the first widely imitated Yankee; Mathews interested the actors; Seba Smith suggested the costume the actors were to wear (very close to the traditional costume of our modern Uncle Sam); and the humorous stories provided some of the personality quirks.

1. THE YANKEE, 1800 to 1820

Imitation of Tyler's Jonathan continued in a variety of plays; and as the century progressed, the Yankee became a chief character in plays, and his personality became more fully developed. With the helpful and kindhearted hero of *Jonathan Postfree; or, The Honest Yankee* (1807) by L. Beach and the New England peddler who likes the girls and sings "Yankee Doodle" in A. B. Lindsley's *Love and Friendship; or, Yankee Notions* (1809), the Yankee achieved more important billing in a single play. The most significant

step, however, in the saga of the Yankee was David Humphreys' *Yankey in England* (1815), which included a seven-
page glossary "of words used in a peculiar sense in this
Drama; pronounced with an accent or emphasis in certain
districts; different from the modes generally followed by the
inhabitants of the United States."

2. THE POPULAR YANKEE AND HIS CREATORS

With *The Forest Rose* by Samuel Woodworth in 1825,
the Yankee became a very successful stock character in
comedy and farce. By the 1840's, he had attained a certain
stability as well as his greatest height in popularity, although
Yankee actors and plays were still applauded with enthusiasm into the '60's. As the years passed, this romantic, homespun philosopher and honest purveyor of his own tastes and
desires was occasionally joined by a Yankee girl. A total of
more than a hundred Yankee plays were written during this
period.

(a) Samuel Woodworth: *The Forest Rose; or, American Farmers*, 1825

Although Woodworth wrote other plays, his place in
American drama is judged mainly by *The Forest Rose,* which
not only helped establish the Yankee character but also
achieved great popular success, playing on the American
stage for forty years. Called a comedy with musical accompaniment, the play showed pretentions to literature in the
introduction to Act I, which begins, "The overture expresses
the various sounds which are heard at early dawn in the
country, . . ." Although Jonathan Ploughboy is not the main
character, much of the humor of the play comes from his
shrewd talk, his inability to woo, and his simplicity.

(*Plot*) On an American farm everyone is in love: Harriet and William, Lydia and Blandford, Jonathan Ploughboy
and Sallie. Into this network of love comes Bellamy, an Englishman and a cad, who wants Harriet. He displays his lust
when he attempts to abduct the wrong girl and is then tricked
by his own lechery. The veiled girl whom Bellamy has paid
to have delivered to his sloop in the harbor turns out to
be the Negro servant Rose, "the forest Rose." Finally, all are

happy but Bellamy, who warns that he will get revenge when he publishes his *Three Months in America.*

(b) Joseph S. Jones: *The People's Lawyer,* 1839

Although by profession a medical doctor, Jones was active in Boston theater circles as playwright, stage manager, and actor during the 1830's and early 1840's. The author of more Yankee plays than any other playwright, he wrote perhaps as many as one hundred and fifty plays, mainly farce comedies and melodramas, but, aware of the lack of copyright protection for the dramatist, objected to publishing his works. His published plays include *The Green Mountain Boy* (1833); *The Surgeon of Paris* (1838); and *The Carpenter of Rouen* (1837). *The People's Lawyer,* a comedy in two acts (1839), became popular because of the Yankee character Solon Shingle, who provides atmosphere, wit, humor, and a Yankee twang but has little connection with the plot. Revised several times, even billed as *Solon Shingle,* the play is unexceptional in all but the character of the Yankee.

(*Plot*) Charles Otis, a clerk, is fired because he will not be dishonest. When the boss leaves, Solon Shingle enters, mischievously puts flour and lampblack on himself, and accidentally fires a pistol he finds. At his home Charles tries to help John, another clerk, who has stolen a watch; he even writes a confession for him, only to be arrested by the police who find both watch and confession on his person. In court, Solon Shingle is sworn in as a witness by mistake and talks on and on about his "apple sarse" being stolen. Then Robert Howard, the People's Lawyer, enters, makes John confess, and wins an acquittal for Charles. Having previously rescued Charles' sister, Grace Otis, from a drunken man and Charles' lecherous boss, he is a true hero. Solon Shingle simply talks on and on.

(c) Cornelius A. Logan: *The Vermont Wool Dealer,* 1840

Logan seems not to have been very prolific, but the plays he wrote emphasize the Yankee character. An actor and a theater manager, he probably wrote plays to help the box office. *Yankee Land,* written about 1834, is a melodrama with a delightful Yankee character, Lot Sap Sago. Logan's most popular play was a one-act farce entitled *The Vermont*

Wool Dealer (1840). With its Yankee character, Deuteronomy Dutiful, its Irish chore boy, and its Negro serving girl, it included most of the typical American comedy characters. Here the Yankee, a blunt, easygoing fellow, is the main character, and amid the usual physical action of farce, his humor dominates.

(d) *The Yankee Pedler; or, Old Times in Virginia,* 1841

This play existed in several versions, but it was always a favorite of the actor specializing in Yankee characters. Plots differ slightly, but the main character is always Hiram Dodge, the Yankee pedler of "Fancyware," a brash wit and an impatient lover. Minstrel humor garnishes his speech, and his language sounds as colorful as his actions prove impertinent. The play tells of his call at the Fuller plantation in Virginia and his many problems in winning the love of Jerusha.

(e) **Other Yankee Plays**

The list of Yankee plays is a long one—E. H. Thompson's *Sam Patch* (1836); O. E. Durivage's *The Stage Struck Yankee* (1840); H. J. Conway's *Hiram Hireout* (1851); and *Major Jack Downing; or, The Retired Politician* (anon. 1834). Actually, the Yankee went everywhere and did many things. He was also much imitated by the English playwrights. In the late 1860's, Odell's *Annals of the New York Stage* lists the following plays at that time being produced: *The Yankee Jailor, The Yankee Inventor, Yankee Courtship, The Yankee in Cuba, Yankee Duelist, Yankee Tars in Scotland, The Fighting Yankee.* One must admit that playwrights were reluctant to leave a stageworthy character.

(f) **The Yankee Gal**

Several plays had Yankee gals—Jedidah in *The Stage Struck Yankee,* Jerusha in *The Yankee Pedler*—but they were minor characters. Other plays emphasized this female Yankee. *The Yankee Housekeeper* was supposedly written particularly for William Florence and his wife, an American acting team. Mrs. Florence played Peg Ann Mehitable Higginfluter, a maid-of-all-work from Maine who got involved in all manner of love affairs and intrigues. Her language, sauciness, and vigor supplied the evening's entertainment. Mr.

and Mrs. Barney Williams also acted plays in which Williams frequently played an Irishman and his wife a Yankee gal. Although never as successful as the Yankee plays, these works add their peculiar charm to the American Yankee caricature.

3. THE YANKEE ACTORS

A cult of Yankee actors, those who specialized in Yankee characters and even offered prizes for Yankee plays, started in the 1820's, undoubtedly stimulated by the success of Charles Mathews. One of the first was James H. Hackett, who in 1828 adapted George Colman's *Who Wants a Guinea?*, changed the name of a character from Solomon Gundy to Solomon Swap, a Yankee, and retitled the piece *Jonathan in England*, after Mathews' successful play. George Handel Hill, known also as "Yankee" Hill, was failing as an actor until he started performing Yankee characters, becoming probably the best of the Yankee impersonators. Others included John E. Owens and Dan Marble who, according to Joe Jefferson, (*Autobiography*, p. 20) dressed "much after the present caricature of Uncle Sam, minus the stars but glorying in the stripes." While he lasted, the Yankee specialist was a strange combination of actor, storyteller, and musical comedy star.

B. The Negro Character

During the first quarter of the century, the Negro continued as a clownish servant; then as the Yankee became popular, the Negro character underwent a curious split and was exploited in two ways: in the minstrel show, and in the farce or social comedy. The servant Sambo became both Uncle Tom and Bones. By the time of the Civil War, he had become a major character in drama.

1. THE NEGRO AMONG THE YANKEES AND IN SOCIAL COMEDY

One is struck by the number of Yankee plays of this period that have Negro characters and by the manner in which the Negro was treated. As a servant, a Negro was easily slipped into Yankee plays, but his social inferiority was frequently exploited by the Yankee. The "Forest Rose" is simply used to play a trick on Bellamy, who is shocked to discover that the veiled girl with him is a Negro rather than the beautiful Harriet. The same trick was used by Logan in *The Vermont Wool Dealer.* One made jokes about Negroes and used them to play jokes upon others.

In the few social comedies of this period, the Negro enjoyed higher social status and more character development, and was exploited for his comic possibilities. Aunt Chloe in Mrs. Sidney Bateman's *Self* (1856), although she has little to say, is a more serious interpretation of the Negro. Zeke, from Mrs. A. C. Mowatt Ritchie's *Fashion* (1845) also illustrates this different attitude toward the Negro. Zeke's language indicates an acquaintance, though inadequate, with literate people, and he is not a stupid servant; in fact, he fulfills his part in the intrigue of the play very well. It is interesting that the only person who treats him with great disrespect is Adam Trueman, the Yankee.

2. THE NEGRO AS MINSTREL

The Negro minstrel show was begun through the talent and imagination of one man, Thomas Dartmouth Rice, in 1828, and expanded into a business in which, from 1850 through 1870, there were hundreds of minstrel companies. Twenty-five years later, the tenor of the minstrel show had changed: the extravagant spectacle had become more important than the Negro, and the minstrel show gradually disappeared from the professional stage. (See section on "Yankee Originality.")

3. THE NEGRO AS HERO

There can be no question as to which American play best illustrates the Negro as hero—*Uncle Tom's Cabin* (1852). (See section entitled "Yankee Originality.") Harriet Beecher Stowe's other novel concerned with the Negro in the South, *Dred,* was presented in three different dramatizations, but none was successful on the American stage.

Plays about the Civil War and slavery, however, were numerous: *Ossawattomie Brown* (1859) by J. C. Swayze; James McCabe's *The Guerrillas* (1862), which first dramatized the difficulties of the freed slave and his frequent unwillingness to go North. Few of the main characters of these plays, however, were Negroes. After *Uncle Tom's Cabin,* the most successful play with a Negro theme was Boucicault's *The Octoroon.*

(a) Dion Boucicault: *The Octoroon; or, Life in Louisiana,* 1859

A tremendously prolific playwright, adapting or writing 124 plays, Boucicault was born in Ireland, and spent a fair portion of his life in England, but dominated the stage during his time in America (1853–1860, 1872–1890). His plays are mainly melodramas (see section on "The Appeal of Melodrama before the Civil War"), and *The Octoroon* has the sentiment and the exciting action which are typical of Boucicault's melodramas. Based on Mayne Reid's novel *The Quadroon* (1856) and using the photography device from the English novel, *The Filibuster* (1859) by Albany Fonblanque, the play also contains much of Boucicault's original thought, and, appealing to all popular trends, includes an Indian, a Yankee, an Irishman, and various Negroes. Although the theme of a white man falling in love with an octoroon in Louisiana might have aroused some sectional passions in 1859, the play was discreetly noncommittal.

(*Plot*) George Peyton returns to the Plantation Terrebonne which he has inherited from his uncle, complete with at least nine mortgages. But George is interested in the octooon Zoe, his uncle's illegitimate daughter, and so is the villain M'Closky, who finds that the judge never legalized Zoe's freedom. Creditors cause the plantation to be put up for sale, and the family anxiously awaits a letter from a firm in Liverpool which owed the estate a great sum of money. When the letter arrives, however, M'Closky intercepts it and kills the Negro messenger, unknowingly having his picture taken in the act. At the auction, amid great drama, M'Closky buys Zoe. Later, through the exposed photographic plate, M'Closky is revealed as the murderer, the Liverpool letter is found, and M'Closky is pursued to his death. Unaware of the change in

events and having heard George say that he would rather
have her dead than owned by M'Closky, Zoe takes poison
and dies.

C. The Indian Character

The first Indian play written by an American was *Ponteach; or, The Savages of America* (1776) by Robert Rogers. But this play was not acted, and it was not until 1808,
when James N. Barker's *Indian Princess* was performed,
that an American play on an Indian theme saw the stage.
From that time until mid-century, more than fifty plays on
Indian themes were performed. Of these many plays, *Pocahontas* (1830) by George Washington Parke Custis, is the
best illustration of the use of the Pocahontas theme, and
Metamora (1829) by John Augustus Stone, the most successful on the stage. Romanticized and idealized, the Indian
reached the height of his popularity in the 1830's and 1840's.
Then, quite suddenly, initiated by the clever burlesques of
John Brougham, the Indian play lost its appeal. One result
was the growth of the American backwoodsman plays—
James Kirke Paulding's *The Lion of the West* (1831) and
the dramatization of novels by Cooper and Simms—which
were extremely popular after the Civil War. Such were the
changing romantic tastes of the American public.

1. JAMES NELSON BARKER: *THE INDIAN PRINCESS; OR, LA BELLE SAUVAGE*, 1808

The subject matter of the play came from John
Smith's *General History of Virginia* (1624), but the play
is not documentary. With its main interest in romantic love,
it becomes not so much a plea for the noble Indians as praise
for the hardy explorers. This strong patriotic note is typical
of Barker's writing. Neither in structure nor language, however, is this play as well written as Barker's *Superstition,*
and with the exception of Pocahontas the characters are conventional and weakly developed.

(*Plot*) Captain Smith lands in Virginia, while at an Indian camp preparations are in progress for the marriage of

Pocahontas, daughter of the chief Powhatan, and Miami. The wedding plans are interrupted, however, when Smith is captured and Pocahontas saves him from being killed. Her friendship with Rolfe, one of Smith's men, so angers Miami that he makes war on Powhatan's tribe, which is helped to victory by the English. The guileful Miami then arranges to kill Smith and Rolfe at a banquet, but Pocahontas thwarts his plans and leads the English to Smith's rescue. At the climax, Rolfe and Pocahontas are engaged, and Powhatan has become an ally of the English.

2. GEORGE WASHINGTON PARKE CUSTIS: *POCAHONTAS; OR, THE SETTLERS OF VIRGINIA*, 1830

Raised at Mount Vernon under the care of President and Mrs. Washington (his father's step-father) and a landowner of some consequence, Custis was more than a dabbler in literature, writing prose (largely recollections), verse, and a half-dozen dramas. His first play, *The Indian Prophecy* (1827), was based on an event in George Washington's life. In *Pocahontas; or, The Settlers of Virginia* (1830) Custis was more effective, but the play is still weak, with stiff and excessively long speeches and generally undeveloped characters. Both Pocahontas and Matacoran, the villain, are hobbled by impossible rhetoric, but he manages to be the most interesting individual in the play with his hatred, bravery, and treachery.

(*Plot*) With John Smith as he returns to Virginia is Rolfe, who falls in love with Pocahontas, daughter of Powhatan and promised in marriage to Matacoran. In the name of the Queen, Smith crowns Powhatan, who still fears his guns and is easily influenced by Matacoran. Discovering the watchword of the English guard on the chosen night—"Pocahontas, the friend of the English"—the Indians, led by Matacoran, prepare for battle, but are foiled by Pocahontas, who naturally says the watchword as she comes to warn Smith of the Indians' treachery. In the battle, both Smith and Matacoran are captured, and Smith is finally saved from the executioner's axe by Pocahontas. The noble Smith allows Matacoran to escape, while Powhatan pledges his friendship to the English and his daughter to Rolfe.

3. JOHN AUGUSTUS STONE: *METAMORA; OR, THE LAST OF THE WAMPANOAGS*, 1829

Rather little is known of the author of *Metamora*. Two years after he started playing character parts in Boston theaters, his plays began to appear: *Restoration; or, The Diamond Cross* (1825); *Tancred; or, The Siege of Antioch* (1827); and others. His talents ran to romance and melodrama, but he was not financially successful. His share from *Metamora* was very slight, and in despair he committed suicide in 1834.

On November 22, 1828, *The Critic* printed a proposal by Edwin Forrest, the actor: "To the author of the best tragedy, in five acts, of which the hero or principal character shall be an aboriginal of this country, the sum of five hundred dollars, and half of the proceeds of the third representation, with my own gratuitous services on that occasion." Of the fourteen plays which the advertisement elicited, *Metamora* was considered the best. Produced by Forrest the following year, it earned him more money during the next thirty-five years than any other play. The language, the action, the suspense—every part of the play gave Forrest the kind of part that best fitted his bombastic style.

Termed an Indian tragedy, the play might be more accurately described as romantic melodrama, with all of the violence, the action, the love, and the sentiment that melodrama of this time required. The character Metamora was modeled on the famous New England Chief, King Philip, whose attacks upon the English in 1675–76 became known as "King Philip's War." Metamora's valiant but unsuccessful attempts to keep the white man from overrunning his lands provide the main thesis of the play. Metamora is also cleverly involved in the secondary theme, a more conventional love episode among the English.

(*Plot*) The two plot lines in the play are held together by a feather—one that Metamora gives Oceana as a symbol of his protection. As the play begins, Mordaunt explains to Oceana, his daughter, that rather than marry Walter, her intended, she must accept Lord Fitzarnold because he can identify Mordaunt as one of the regicides. At an English council meeting, Metamora, accused of a murder, recognizes his Indian betrayer, kills him, and escapes to lead an attack on the English. The attack interrupts Oceana's wedding to Fitzarnold, but the feather protects the house of Mordaunt. Walter, however, is captured by the Indians, while Metamora's wife, Nahmeokee, is taken by the English, until threats and negotiations by Metamora bring her release. In the subplot, Fitzarnold is killed by Metamora, and Walter is found to be the son of Sir Arthur Vaughan and therefore a suitable mate for Oceana. Defiant to the last, Metamora is beaten but not defeated—"yet we are forever!" His Indians scattered, his child killed, he stabs Nahmeokee and curses the white men before he is shot down by the English.

4. A VARIETY OF INDIAN PLAYS

The Indian appeared in numerous plays as both a major and a minor character. Mordecai Noah's *She Would Be A Soldier* (1819) had a minor Indian character; so did Boucicault's *Octoroon*. A majority of the plays, however, were about particular Indians: *Logan, the Last of the Race of Shikellemus, Chief of the Cayuga Nation* (1821), a dull but historically accurate play by Joseph Doddridge; *Carabasset* (1831), based on the life of the Jesuit missionary Rallé and his friendship with the Indians, by Nathaniel Deering; *Tecumseh; or, The Battle of the Thames* (1836), concerning the Indian chief who fought for the British in 1812, by Richard Emmons. The single character which appealed to the most playwrights, however, was Pocahontas. Among these plays, Robert Dale Owen's *Pocahontas* (1837) attempts a more complete picture than usual.

5. THE INDIAN RIDICULED: JOHN BROUGHAM'S BURLESQUES

The exaggerated characterization and interpretation of the noble Redskin by dramatists and actors finally brought about his fall from popularity. The man most responsible for helping change public tastes was John Brougham, a good actor and productive playwright, who was called the "Aristophanes" of the American stage by Laurence Hutton (*Curiosities of the American Stage*, New York, 1891, p. 164). And in no plays was he more deserving of this title than in his burlesques of the Indians.

Brougham's *Metamora; or, The Last of the Pollywogs* (1847) was an obvious satire on the Stone-Forrest success. The plot follows Stone's play, but at the end, as the English pepper Metamora with popguns, Metamora refuses to die. It is occasionally effective but generally crude and forced in its humor—a very broad burlesque. A better burlesque was Brougham's 1855 production of his "Original, Aboriginal, Erratic, Operatic, Semi-Civilized, and Demi-Savage Extravaganza of *Pocahontas*," *Po-Ca-Hon-Tas; or, The Gentle Savage.* Captain Smith's description of the court of "Pow-Ha-Tan I, King of the Tuscaroras—a Crotchety Monarch, in fact a semibrave" suggests the humor of the play:

> I visited his Majesty's abode,
> A portly savage, plump and pigeon-toed;
> Like Metamora, both in feet and feature,
> I never met-a-more-a-musing creature.

6. THE INDIAN REPLACED: APPEARANCE OF THE BACKWOODSMAN

About the time the Indian became popular on the American stage, the backwoodsman, another native American character, appeared as Nimrod Wildfire in James Kirke Paulding's *The Lion of the West* (1831). The Indian, however, held the stage through the mid-1840's, while the backwoodsman appeared only occasionally. Not until after the Civil War did the backwoodsman achieve popularity on the stage—long after the Indians had ceased to be "noble savages" and had become "varmint Redskins."

In the forty years between 1830 and 1870, there were, of course, a scattering of plays about frontier men or backwoodsmen. In *The Lion of the West,* Nimrod Wildfire—"half horse, half alligator, and a touch of the airthquake"—was the attraction. Another popular backwoodsman play was Louisa H. Medina's dramatization of Robert M. Bird's *Nick of the Woods* (1838). Other plays include dramatizations of some of Cooper's novels; Mordecai Noah's *The Frontier Maid*

(1840), and W. R. Derr's *Kit Carson, The Hero of the Prairie* (1850).

In the 1830's, Kentucky was the West. Twenty years later, the frontier had changed; the frontiersmen considered the Indian more of a menace that a "noble savage"; the Homestead Act of 1862 opened more land; wars were fought; and legends grew—legends of the backwoodsman's powers. Soon plays appeared with a new hero! And lo, the poor Indian vanished—at least, the theatrical Indian, who fits well Mark Twain's description of the literary Indian: a member of "an extinct race which never existed."

IV. A MIRROR OF THE TIMES

The theater is always a mirror of the times; it is history, sociology, and philosophy, as well as literature, theater art, and simple entertainment. To a greater or lesser degree, the theater reflects the interests of a people, the views of social critics, and the culture of a period. Although as a mirror of America, this study is limited by the fact that it includes only plays written by Americans, in two specific ways this aspect of the early American theater was a mirror of its time: various influences of the time are clear in the kinds of plays written, and the cultural tastes of the time are evident in the reactions of both audiences and critics to the plays produced.

The years reflected in this mirror—from Jefferson to Lincoln—are marked by growth and change, war and confusion, opportunity and idealism. A new nation was trying to establish itself; a new social culture was starting to develop while problems appeared: war and border disputes, economic panics, political arguments, population increases, expansion and transportation difficulties. By mid-century, America was becoming a vast and rapidly developing country, whose changes were reflected in its people and society. It had become known as a nation of hustlers, "dollar grabbers"—optimistic and boastful, rough-and-tumble individuals who practiced Ralph Waldo Emerson's doctrine of self-reliance and worked for their future, "Root, hog, or die." The East became distinct from the West, and people throughout expressed an individuality—anti-foreignism, the American Temperance Society in

1826, the Mormon trek to Utah in 1846–47, the Gold Rush in California, agitation for women's rights, political and social difficulties that led to the Civil War—which stimulated social problems. Strictly speaking, of course, there was no established society in the first half of the nineteenth century, but Tidewater Virginia, Back Bay Boston, and the Patroons of New York were the main pretenders. The playwright may have lacked the material for comedy of manners, but he had much material for drama; and mainly in farce and melodrama, he provided many caricatures of society and dramatized numerous social, political, and civil problems.

Frequently, the accepted criterion for the success of a work of art is the reception of this work by established literary critics in America and by the audiences and critics in England and Europe. Completely disregarding the validity of this approach, one may apply it to the drama of this early period when, if anything, it would be more meaningful. The major literary figures in America had little to say about the drama; but that it had an appeal for them, there is no question. Irving, Paulding, Bird, Poe, Longfellow—all wrote plays. Perhaps they hoped to improve the drama by improving the literary quality of American theater fare, but they were unsuccessful in their efforts, as were Shelley, Browning, and Byron in England. Toward the contributions of American playwrights, the English attitude ranged from abuse to amused toleration to enthusiasm. Generally, the effect of American drama was theatrical rather than literary, and perhaps that distinction suggests a major characteristic of the times. It was a time of idealism, individualism, and romance, when the open, frank movement of life was apt to be sensational and spectacular. Thus the drama, a mirror image of society, truthfully reflects the more theatrical than literary quality which was the spirit of the times.

A. The Comedy of America

In a strict sense, the comedy of this period in America was farce, or to be quite liberal, farce-comedy. The witty portrayal of some aspect of society with well-drawn characters who were logically motivated in both speech and action and whose thoughts and struggles directed the plot of the play—these characteristics of drama were largely lacking. Plays with a foreign setting came nearest to comedy; American people and society were caricatured. Fashionable life, of course, was a favorite target. As America's economy flourished, self-reliance sometimes became self-indulgence; and the natural social ego of an enterprising and successful nation more than once found itself in a ridiculous situation, ready-made for the satirical writer of farce-comedy, who doubled in nationalistic sentiment while emphasizing a romantic realism which was becoming popular in fiction. Comedy in America in the first half of the nineteenth century, then, variously emphasized three important aspects of American drama at that time: a dependence upon foreign setting; a reflection of American attitude toward the American people, society, and morals; and a concern for realistic touches.

1. THE COMIC IDEA WITH A FOREIGN SETTING

For the most part, America's playwrights seemed concerned either to express opinions about social or political issues or to exploit a currently popular phase in the theater. Although many had talent, very few were creative artists. They wrote to moralize, to satirize, to inform, and to entertain. They were not interested in objective views or detached attitudes. Consequently, the writer of pure comedy was rare and so were American plays which deserve to be called comedies. Only a few plays could boast some of the characteristics of comedy: detachment on the part of the author, well-developed characters, and witty and clever lines commenting on society. Invariably, the writer of anything approaching comedy either adapted a foreign play and kept the foreign scene because it was too difficult to change it to American circumstance or wrote of a foreign scene because somehow it facilitated a certain detachment in a playwright's works. The following are among the best that American dramatists could offer.

(a) James Nelson Barker, *How to Try a Lover*, 1817

(*Plot*) The scene is Catalonia in medieval Spain. Into the castle grounds of Count Almeyda, father of Eugenia, the object of their search, come Carlos and his servant Pacomo, both accomplished lovers. The fathers of Carlos and Eugenia are the intriguers. Believing that true love must conquer something, they plot to "try the lover," to put obstacles in his path. Finally, when, after much confusion, Carlos reaches Eugenia and declares his love, he is arrested. At the Court of Love, prepared by the fathers, Eugenia presides and, having secretly discovered the fathers' intrigue, amazes and horrifies them by seeming to condemn Carlos. But she finally relents. His punishment is, of course, that he must marry Eugenia, and everyone is happy.

(*Discussion*) Indebted in both plot and characterization to Pigault-Lebrun's picaresque novel *La Folie Espagnole*, Barker's *How to Try a Lover* is a well-wrought farce-comedy, complete with interesting dialogue and fast-moving intrigues. Theater audiences demanded the dramatic conventions of that time. There appear, therefore, secret letters and disguises and stock characters, such as the pure and innocent girl, the heroic young nobleman, and the servants who imitate their masters. But it is all very well done.

(b) John Howard Payne and Washington Irving, *Charles the Second; or, The Merry Monarch*, 1824

(*Plot*) As the play opens, Lady Clara proposes a bargain with her lover, Rochester, "the king's prime companion in all his excesses": she will consent to marry him if he will disgust the King with his "nocturnal rambles and bring him back to reason." Mulling over his task, Rochester meets Edward, his page and protégé, who in disguise is wooing a barmaid named Mary. Rochester decides to see Mary immediately and at the same time teach the King his "first lesson in morals." Disguised as common seamen, Rochester and the King visit the tavern of Captain Copp, Mary's uncle, who, it turns out, hates Rochester intensely because Mary's mother, Rochester's sister, ill-treated her husband. Rochester then leaves the King to pay a bill for which he has no money. Suspected and locked in a room when he offers his diamond-studded watch to Copp, the King bribes his way to freedom, only to be greeted at the palace the next morning by Copp and Mary who, in returning the watch to its owner, recognize the King and Rochester. But they can keep a secret, and all ends happily: Rochester will become a "rational and submissive husband"; Mary will marry Edward; and Charles swears that he will henceforth abjure nightly frolics.

(*Discussion*) Although the play contains more than a fair amount of farce, *Charles the Second* is the best comedy of this period, and, doubtless because of Washington Irving's part in its composition, one of the most readable. A quite free adaptation of Alexandre Duval's *La Jeunesse de Henri V*, the play owed its great success in part to Payne's creation of Captain Copp and to Irving's humorous touch in the dialogue, although Irving's work was kept secret for many years. A fine comic character, Captain Copp has a suggestion of humanity about him—a sentimental heart, an honest mind, the language and temper of a sailor, and a sense of humor. Equally significant are the comic dialogue and the language of this play, which set it apart from contemporary comedies.

2. FASHIONABLE LIFE

Various aspects of social life in America were caricatured in a number of farce-comedies, but few plays attempted to portray fashionable life. As the century progressed, however, social structures were becoming recognizable in major cities from Boston to Charleston, and both a genuine and an imitated sophistication became evident. The break with England and Europe was widening, although more slowly in fashion than in politics or literature. At the same time that one part of American society was reacting to nationalistic pressures, however, another part (the *nouveau riche*) was attempting to gain social standing by obvious adulation and imitation of foreign manners and customs. It was an awkward but interesting period for a developing society, but for a playwright with nationalistic bias or an inclination toward satire, America provided incomparable opportunity.

Plays about fashionable life were part satire, part farce, with a strain of melodrama, a pretension toward social comedy, and a liberal amount of frank nationalism. All of these ingredients had appeared on the American stage for many years, but the recent, more serious interest in social commentary plus the more witty satire provided some distinction for these forthcoming plays.

Using Royall Tyler's *The Contrast* as a model, playwrights wrote numerous satiric caricatures of American fashionable society. James N. Barker's *Tears and Smiles* (1807) contrasted the falseness of French fashions with America's more sterling national traits; Joseph Hutton's *Fashionable Follies* (1815) stressed the folly and stupidity of fashion-minded people; J. H. Hackett's *Moderns; or, A Trip to the Springs* (1831) ridiculed the absurdities and idiosyncracies of life in a summer colony. James K. Paulding's *The Bucktails; or, Americans in England* (1815, 1847) contrasted, quite favorably of course, an American girl with the Englishman who wanted to marry her.

(a) Anna Cora Mowatt Ritchie and *Fashion; or, Life in New York*, 1845

(*Plot*) Once a milliner, now the fashion-minded, social-climbing wife of a rich man, Mrs. Tiffany explains to her daughter, Seraphina, how she must catch Count Jolimaitre, a fashionable fraud who finds "but one redeeming charm in America—the superlative loveliness of the feminine portion of creation—and the wealth of their obliging papas." In contrast to Mrs. Tiffany, who worships all that is foreign, Adam Trueman personifies American independence. He is shocked to find that his old friend, Tiffany, has committed a forgery and is being blackmailed by Snobson, his clerk, who wants to marry Seraphina. When Millinette, the French maid, recognizes the Count as an imposter, Gertrude, the wholesome and lovable governess, overhears their talk, and puts herself in a very compromising position when she tries to trick the Count into confessing his true identity. So great is her shame that she is turned out of Tiffany's house but not before she writes an explanatory letter, which Trueman reads and discovers that Gertrude is his granddaughter and heir. Trueman then frees Tiffany by explaining that Snobson is as much as fault as he, and the Count is exposed as a fraud. But all ends happily: Millinette and the fake Count, who is really a nice fellow, will marry; Gertrude and Colonel Howard, a stuffy but true American, will marry with the blessings of Trueman, who will rescue the Tiffanys from their financial difficulties if they learn "to prize at its just value—Fashion."

(*Discussion*) In her *Autobiography of An Actress*

(1854), Mrs. Ritchie (1819–1870) tells of her early prejudices against the theater, which "melted" away as she grew.
After writing her first "positive attempt as a dramatist," *The
Gypsy Wanderer; or, The Stolen Child*, at seventeen, circumstances and desire started her on a career in the theater.
When her husband lost his fortune, she reluctantly accepted
a suggestion that she give public readings, and her success
soon brought her an offer to appear on the legitimate state—
an offer she most indignantly refused because people of her
social station did not act on the stage. Later, however, she
wrote *Fashion,* and its success on the New York stage
changed her views: she now "determined to fulfill the destiny
which seemed visibly pointed out by the unerring finger of
Providence. . . . I would become an actress." And in this
career she was also successful. When she retired from the
stage in 1854 for reasons of poor health, she had by her
presence on it raised the reputation of theater in America
and through her written plays had added to the stature of
American drama.

Fashion was her major contribution to the drama and
has since become a landmark for the development of social
comedy in the history of American drama, providing as it
does, a halfway point between Royall Tyler's *The Contrast*
and the transitional social comedies of Bronson Howard,
W. D. Howells, and Clyde Fitch. Mrs. Ritchie's Preface to
the London edition of her play, 1850, shows her objectives:

> The Comedy of *Fashion* was intended as a good-natured
> satire upon some of the follies incident to a new country,
> where foreign dross sometimes passes for gold, while
> native gold is cast aside as dross; where vanities rather
> than the virtues of other lands are too often imitated, and
> where the stamp of *fashion* gives currency even to the
> coinage of vice.

In spite of obvious inadequacies, *Fashion* illustrates better
than any American play of its time the characteristics of social comedy. Its theme is the relationship of the individual
to society, and its characters, though mainly caricatures, suggest a variety of social levels. The manner in which society
is satirized, the wit, and the epigrammatic quality of the

lines also add to the comedy: "A woman of fashion *never* grows old! Age is always out of fashion"; fashion is "an agreement between certain persons to live without using their souls! to substitute etiquette for virtue—decorum for purity— manners for morals!" Mixed with this comic caricature, and frequently dominating it, are aspects of farce and melodrama. The gestures, the exaggerated actions of Mrs. Tiffany, the cudgel waving by Trueman—all are farce actions. Disguises, letters, a forgery theme, a dastardly villain—these are the hallmarks of melodrama. There is still, however, a great deal of charm and brilliance in *Fashion*; Mrs. Ritchie understood her society well, and she was a clever writer.

(b) Mrs. Sidney F. Bateman and *Self*, 1856–57

(*Plot*) Extravagant and irresponsible, Mrs. Apex has ruined her husband with her excesses. When her stepdaughter, Mary, refuses to lend her legacy of $15,000, Mrs. Apex persuades her equally extravagant son, Charles, to forge a check for that amount. But Mary has written a check for $15,000 to help save her father's business, and when this check is returned, "without funds," Mr. Apex turns Mary out of the house as a worthless person. It is now up to John Unit, a Yankee who has been disgusted with the excesses of the Apex family from the beginning, to put things in order. Thanks to Mary's persuasion, he will supply the needed money if the extravagant buying stops. Everyone forgives anyone who needs forgiveness, and all are finally happy.

(*Discussion*) The wife and daughter of actors, Mrs. Bateman wrote several plays, but her methods and talent are limited. Generally a play of local allusions modeled on *Fashion, Self* is elevated by its thesis that "our labors are prompted by that great motive power of human nature— Self!" The parallels with *Fashion* include the characters (John Unit—Adam Trueman; Mrs. Apex—Mrs. Tiffany), the satire, and the theme of forgery, but *Self* lacks the artistic finesse of *Fashion*.

(c) G. P. Wilkins and *Young New York*, 1856

(*Plot*) Mr. Ten-per-cent, a retired and wealthy merchant, is very pleased with his accomplishments and is persuaded to run for Congress. Self-satisfied and society conscious, all the Ten-per-cents but Rose are disagreeable people. Rose is sweet but independent, and when she marries her music teacher, Skibberini, she is ostracized by the family. Later Mr. Ten-per-cent, having been defeated in his political campaign and having somehow lost his fortune, discovers that Rose is giving a concert. He attends, and is so overwhelmed with the beauty of her singing that he forgives Rose and her husband. All are happy at the final curtain, and, as Rose says, "every man and woman is to be tried by the standard of their acts alone, and upon them is to stand or fall. How do you like Young New York?"

(*Discussion*) Hardly a social comedy, *Young New York* is typical of a rather large number of farces which contain some satiric comment on various social conditions and conventions. Although the plot of *Young New York* is conventional, the dialogue weak, and the characters farcical in name and action, the idealized independence of the heroine, who reads Emerson, and the satirical comments in the play give it some distinction.

3. THE B'HOYS OF NEW YORK: THE MOSE PLAYS

Of the variety of plays which attempted to capitalize on the peculiarities of New York City, none achieved a more popular success than those built around the character of Mose, the New York fire b'hoy. Sketchy, episodic, with no finesse and little plot, these plays probably had dramatic ancestors in *The Fireman's Frolic* (1831), written by a fireman of Philadelphia, and *Beulah Spa; or, Two of the B'hoys* (1834). Whatever the background, Mose made his first full-length appearance in B. A. Baker's *A Glance at New York* (1848), with F. S. Chanfrau dressed in red shirt, plug hat, and the turned-up trousers of the New York fireman, playing the part of Mose. A roughneck who enjoyed physical action and practical jokes and who would fight a fire, sing a song, or love a girl with equal zest, Mose as a character enjoyed a brief but spectacular success. Baker featured him again in 1848 in *New York As It Is*. Then the imitations began: *Mose in California, A Glance at Philadelphia, Philadelphia As It Is, Mose in China, Mose in France*. Baker deserves the credit with *A Glance at New York*, which, flimsy, stilted in language, verbose, and farcical, is nevertheless interesting as characteristic of a brief trend in American drama.

(*Plot*) Called a "Local Drama," this fast-moving play has numerous and episodic short scenes. The play opens with a song on the steamship pier, as George, the country green-horn, arrives at the city to visit Harry. Immediately Jake and Mike, two city shysters, sell George an old watch for $10. After Mose arrives, the men dress as women and go to a woman's bowling alley, where Mary and Jane tease them. Next they go to Loafer's Paradise, where Mose hankers for a fight and finally manages to create one, in which, of course, poor George gets the worst of it. The second act is filled with similar incidents, and the ending can only be manipu-lated. About to run off to help a friend in a fight, Mose ex-plains to the audience: "And if you don't say no, why I'll scare up this crowd again tomorrow night, and then you can take another GLANCE AT NEW YORK."

4. COMEDY AND ROMANTIC REALISM: *RIP VAN WINKLE*

For purposes of classification, *Rip Van Winkle* remains an anomaly. Its history as a play covers nearly three-quarters of the nineteenth century. Although it is romantic in theme, its interpretation, particularly by Joseph Jefferson, shows realistic detail as well as some valid psychological insights into character. Moreover, the play plot was made consider-ably more melodramatic than Irving's story. More than any other play of the period, however, *Rip Van Winkle* deserves to be called a domestic comedy.

(a) History of *Rip Van Winkle* as a Play

Within a dozen years after Washington Irving pub-lished "Rip Van Winkle" in *The Sketch Book* (1819), at least five versions were produced on the stage. Basic to all later versions and the earliest surviving version, is John Kerr's *Rip Van Winkle; or, The Demons of the Catskill Mountains!!! A National Drama*, produced in Philadelphia in 1829. Kerr, an English actor, was responsible for the plot changes which others varied if only slightly: he invented a

love subplot between Rip's daughter Alice and Knickerbocker, an ex-schoolteacher; and he turned a romantic story
into a melodrama by bringing in a contract through which
a greedy slob named Derrick Van Slous hoped to get the
better of Rip. Charles Burke's version of *Rip Van Winkle*
(1850), although based on the Kerr play, softened the patriotic touches, added local color in the form of Dutch dialect, and included several songs. Called *Rip Van Winkle, A
Legend of the Catskills*, a romantic drama in two acts, the
play begins with a song and makes Rip a jolly, fun-loving
person loved by all except his wife, who berates his friends
and beats Rip when she finds him drinking. An English version by Thomas H. Lacy draws from both the Kerr and
Burke plays. Unlike the Kerr version it contains dialect, but
different from the Burke dialect. A major distinction is that
Dame Van Winkle is alive in the second act and married
to Nicholas Vedder; a good ironic effect is produced by having Vedder abuse her as she once abused Rip.

(b) Joseph Jefferson III and *Rip Van Winkle*

Today in American drama Joseph Jefferson means Rip
Van Winkle. In 1881, he wrote to a friend: "I think I have
played 'Rip Van Winkle' about twenty-five hundred times,"
and he continued playing the part until his death in 1905.
Reviews were generally excellent, and in Odell's *Annals of
the New York Stage* (VIII, p. 279) Jefferson is called a
"one-part actor *par excellence*." Although Rip had had a
long stage history, Jefferson first became interested in him
during the summer of 1859, and fashioned a three-act play
from the three printed versions of the play and Irving's
story. Dissatisfied with this play, however, six years later he
persuaded Dion Boucicault to rewrite his work. The result,
which Jefferson played throughout his life, bears some re-
semblance to Burke's play and, as in Lacy's version, keeps
Dame Van Winkle alive for all three acts (which, according
to Quinn, Jefferson later made into four by dividing Act I).

(*Plot*) In the village of Falling Waters, Gretchen Van
Winkle complains of Rip's foolishness and of the villainy of
Derrick, whom she might have married, who takes mortgages
on Rip's land and gives him money for drink. To protect
the houses he has built on Rip's land, however, Derrick must

own the property, and to this end he gives Rip a contract, actually a bill of sale, which he explains as an acknowledgment for a loan. But Rip, a bit drunk and a bit suspicious, puts the paper in his pocket unsigned. Time passes, and one stormy evening Rip comes home drunk, with an empty game bag, having shot nothing but their bull. Furious, Gretchen orders him out of the house, and Rip wanders off to meet the little men. In Act IV, Rip awakes from his sleep and returns to the village, where he is saved from abusive treatment from the people by Hendrich, who as a young boy had playfully promised to marry Rip's favorite little girl, Meenie. Then Gretchen enters; married to Derrick, browbeaten, and changed, she invites Rip to sit by her fire. In a dramatic scene, Gretchen faces Derrick and refuses to have Meenie marry his nephew; Meenie recognizes Rip, who produces the paper showing that Derrick does not own the house and land. As Derrick leaves, Gretchen gives a cup to Rip, who ends the play with a toast: "Unt ladies and gents, here is your goot health and your fortune and your future families; and may you all live long and prosper!"

B. An Active and Growing Society

Changes in American society were clearly reflected in its drama. Significant social movements, important events, and particular social problems provided subject matter for those playwrights and theater managers who were ever eager to please a fickle public. From 1830 to about 1865, the new nation developed a very active and growing society, and the drama reflected this activity.

Of these changes in social structure, a most obvious one stemmed from population increases and shifts. From 1830 to 1860, the population jumped 150 per cent and a major reason for this growth was the mass immigration of Europeans, particularly the Irish and Germans. Along with their native cultures, however, the immigrants brought social problems which were immediately recognized by outbursts of antiforeignism among the "natives." Because of their individuality in language and their striking personal characteristics, the Irish were ready-made characters for the theater, and were exploited in plays just as Jonathan and Mose had been popularized. Plays about the Germans—or "Dutchmen," as they were usually called—were less popular, possibly because the Germans were less exuberant than the Irish.

The social problems created frequently became theater fare. Temperance movements grew in response to the drinking habits of the Irish and Germans—and temperance plays multiplied. Americans also perceived a threat to their freedom of worship in the Roman Catholicism of the Irish and Germans. The Mormon trek westward was motivated mainly by a desire for religious freedom, but it was also part of the geographical expansion in which the immigrants became involved even before the discovery of gold in California sent the wagons rolling westward.

In this period of 1830 to 1860, the seeds of the Civil War were planted. The problems of Negro slavery—the abolitionists' arguments, the underground railroad, the Compromise of 1850, "Bleeding Kansas," the Dred Scott decision, John Brown—became material for the playwrights. If the dramatic growth of the country brought new characters and examples of romantic individuality to the American theater, the social, political, and religious upheaval that spread through the country provided an abundance of dramatic conflict.

1. RACIAL GROUPS: IRISH

If Paddy the Irishman cannot be placed with Jonathan the Yankee, Sambo the Negro, and Metamora the Indian, as a native American character, he can most certainly be called the most popular adopted son of nineteenth-century American drama. Beginning about the turn of the nineteenth century with John Murdock's *The Triumphs of Love* (1795) and John Minshull's *Rural Felicity* (1801), the Irishman reached his greatest popularity about mid-century. By then, his heroic actions and comic traits had made him a popular hero, recognized by speciality actors and playwrights. The most popular writers of Irish-American drama were James Pilgrim, John Brougham, and Dion Boucicault; and like the Yankee, the Irishman went many places and tried his hand at a number of things, as play titles suggest: *The Irish Attorney, The Irish Outlaw, The Irish Porter, The Irish*

Schoolmaster, The Irishman in Cuba, The Irishman in Greece.

(a) James Pilgrim

Along with Samuel D. Johnson, whose *Brian O'Linn* (produced 1851) well exemplifies his contribution to Irish plays, James Pilgrim wrote a good percentage of the popular Irish-American farces. Although he wrote a serious tragedy laid in Ireland, *Robert Emmett* (1853), he was more successful with plays like *Paddy the Piper* (n.d.) and *Shandy Maguire; or, The Bould Boy of the Mountains* (1851). Shandy was the typical Irishman of the farces—quick with his wits, his fists, and a joke, but in reality a softhearted hero who protected widows, saved the heroine from the villain, and beat up all the ruffians.

(b) John Brougham

An actor-manager-playwright, Brougham was born in Dublin and had some success in the London theater before coming to America in 1842. In New York, he achieved considerable success as a comedian, particularly in Irish roles, and displayed both wit and talent as a writer of farces and burlesques. Among his best Irish plays were *The Irish Fortune Hunter* (1850) and *Temptation; or, The Irish Immigrant* (1856). During his fifty years upon the stage, Brougham wrote seventy-five plays and, according to Montrose Moses in *The American Dramatist,* was second to none in the 1850's as an actor-manager-author.

(c) Dion Boucicault

Boucicault claimed to have "invented the Irish drama," but his plays were concerned with Ireland rather than with the Irish in America and really do not reflect the American scene. As "sensational dramas" (his own phrase), his Irish plays—*The Colleen Bawn* (1860), *Arrah-na-Pogue* (1864), *The O'Dowd* (1872), and *The Shaughraun* (1874)—were excellent and very successful melodramas. Before *The Colleen Bawn,* Boucicault had used the "faith-an-begorra" Irishman in such plays as *West End* (1842) and *Andy Blake* (1854). With *The Colleen,* however, Boucicault changed, and his Irish plays began to emphasize qualities of character rather than relying solely on amusing speech and antics.

(d) **Popular Irish play:** *Handy Andy*—**versions by T. D. English, 1844; H. Montgomery, 1860; and W. A. Floyd, 1862**

As the play opens, Squire Egan tells young Edward O'Connor that marriage to Fanny Dawson is impossible until O'Connor gets a deed for some property "given by Scatterbrain to your father." Enlivening this serious situation is Andy, "filius nullius" (son of nobody), an orphan found twenty years ago, whose blunders and witty comments are a major part of the action. For mystery, there is Mad Nance, who raves about a son who is heir to "his father's title and the broad lands" and about Squire O'Grady, "man of fraud and wrong," who has a certain deed. After a drunk scene, a pistol and knife scene, a switched bundle scene, and numerous incidents, Mad Nance visits O'Grady and gets the deed along with her marriage certificate as Ann Fitzgerald and the record of her son's birth. With the deed, Edward and Fanny can be happily married, and Andy obviously is Mad Nance's son, the Earl of Scatterbrain.

2. RACIAL GROUPS: GERMAN

No other racial group offered the dramatic possibilities of the Irish. Although German immigrants rivaled the Irish immigrants in number, they were a poor second in theater appeal. Misunderstood and disliked, the "Dutchmen" most frequently reached the stage as objects of ridicule, although sometimes they were treated with sympathy. Two plays featuring "John Schmidt" type Germans written by S. Barry—*The Persecuted Dutchman* (1845) and *The Dutchman's Ghost* (1857)—are, perhaps, typical of similar and more abundant theater fare.

The Persecuted Dutchman; or, The Original John Schmidt may not have been written originally by S. Barry, but he successfully acted the leading role in an 1857 New York production. As the play opens, the Honorable Augustus Clearstarch arrives at Mrs. Plentiful's Hotel with Miss Arabella Blowhard, whom he has taken from boarding school to marry so that he may get her father's fortune. Discovering that she has no money, he decides to send her back to school. Then the hero enters, John Schmidt, a tightfisted and tired businessman, who wants only a bed and sleep. He is immediately disturbed, however, by Arabella's father, who arrives, whip in hand, and mistakes Schmidt for the villain who took his daughter. "Oh, I am a persecuted Dutchman. Mine Cot in Hemmel!" moans Schmidt. Soon Arabella straightens everything out, apologies are made, and Schmidt will visit the Blowhards in New York if he can bring his friends—the audience.

3. PLAYS ABOUT MORMONS

Led by Brigham Young, the Mormons made their famous trek to Utah in 1846–48. During the 1850's, numerous Mormons and immigrants from Europe made the arduous trip, until several thousand had homes in the valley of the Great Salt Lake. Soon the Mormon adventure appeared in the theater: the anonymous *Deseret Deserted; or, The Last Days of Brigham Young* (1858); *Life of the Mormons at Salt Lake* (1858) by C. W. Taylor (?); and *The Mormons; or, Life at Salt Lake City* (1858) by Dr. Thomas Dunn English.

Using the common melodramatic devices of escapes, rescues, disguises, and a revenge theme in the subplot, *The Mormons* is obviously anti-Mormon as it dramatizes the activities of a new group of arrivals at Salt Lake City. Besides Noggs, a crooked New York civil official turned Mormon to escape the law, and the new Mormon converts, the Woodvilles, there is Mary, wooed by Pratt, an unscrupulous Mormon elder, and Eagle Eye, a mysterious fellow who is really trying to find his sister's murderer. When Mary decides to marry Pratt, however, Eagle Eye feels that he must save her. Later, with the Woodvilles, who have become disenchanted with Mormonism, Eagle Eye escapes to the mountains with Mary, chased by the Mormon military. After several incidents, Mary is threatened by a Mormon named Blair, whom Eagle Eye, really Walter Markham, recognizes as his sister's murderer. Overcome by his own guilt, however, Blair kills himself before a U.S. Army scouting party rescues the group.

4. PLAYS ABOUT THE MOVEMENT WESTWARD

The movement westward is reflected in numerous plays before and after the Civil War. (Plays dealing with the backwoodsman have been discussed.) A number of plays described the trip to California and the brand of society found there. Early in January of 1849, Charles Burke acted in an anonymous play called *A Trip to the California Gold Mines*. Other plays are *A Live Woman in the Mines* (1857), an anonymous work showing some of the admirable and fearless characteristics of Western people, and *Fast Folks; or, Early Days of California*, by Joseph A. Nunes, presumably acted during the 1858–59 theater season in Philadelphia. These plays presented a miscellany of social history, local color, and folk drama.

5. TEMPERANCE PLAYS

Within a few years after the American Temperance Society was formed at Boston in 1826, a thousand-odd local groups sprang up along with temperance crusades employing pictures, pamphlets, and reformed drunkards as lecturers. As the century progressed, the fervor of temperance supporters grew, but the best temperance plays were written about the middle of the century: Clifton Tayleure, *The Drunkard's Warning* (1856); H. Seymour, *Temperance Doctor* (n.d.); and the two minor classics, W. H. Smith's *The Drunkard; or, The Fallen Saved* (1844) and William W. Pratt's dramatization of the novel by Timothy S. Arthur, *Ten Nights in a Bar Room and What I Saw There*, which was presented on the New York stage in 1858. Both plays had long original runs and are still occasionally produced.

The Drunkard tells of the weak but well-meaning Edward Middleton, who is tempted to drink by the villain Cribbs and goes from bad to worse until, urged by Mr. Rencelow, he takes the pledge. He is then reformed and becomes successful while the villain is punished. In *Ten Nights in a Bar Room* John Morgan is made the slave of drink sold to him by Simon Slade, who in turn, victimized by his own greed, is finally killed by his son in a drunken quarrel. Other men are slain, good men; mothers and daughters die or go insane. Finally, when Morgan's little daughter ("Father, dear father, come home with me now. The clock in the belfry strikes one. . . .") is accidentally killed, Morgan reforms and leads a movement to close the tavern.

6. SLAVERY AND THE SOUTH

There had been slaves in all thirteen colonies before the Revolution, but after Congressional action in 1808, the importation of slaves to America was illegal. This, however, did not solve the social or moral problem, the question of the "fortunate" slave vs. black bondage. The argument continued, and plays reflected the turbulent events that immediately preceded the war—such as the Fugitive Slave Law of 1850, publication of *Uncle Tom's Cabin* in 1852, The Kansas-Nebraska Act of 1854, John Brown's Pottawatomie Massacre in 1856, the Dred Scott decision of 1857, the Harpers Ferry incident of 1859, and the subsequent hanging of John Brown.

The most famous of all these plays, of course, was *Uncle Tom's Cabin*, billed as "The World's Greatest Hit." Another very popular melodrama about Southern slave life was Dion Boucicault's *The Octoroon*. Mrs. Stowe's second novel of slavery, *Dred: A Tale of the Great Dismal Swamp* (1856) was dramatized several times but never successfully. Another play concerned with the tragedy of mixed blood was J. T. Trowbridge's dramatization of his own novel, *Neighbor Jackwood* (1857), which, showing the chase, capture, and rescue of an octoroon slave, dramatizes the bitter Northern attitude toward the Fugitive Slave Law. "Bloody Kansas" and John Brown's fanatical activity appear in several plays, but J. C. Swayze in *Ossawattomie Brown; or, The Insurrection at Harpers Ferry* (1859) tries to foreshadow martyrdom through the scenes of Brown's fanatical battle at Harpers Ferry.

C. The Appeal of Melodrama before the Civil War

Melodrama appealed to the majority of those who attended the theater—this is perhaps the only undebatable statement that one could make about American drama be-

fore the Civil War. Since the theater of the time was controlled by a manager who wanted to make money and an
actor who desired popularity, it is not surprising that a high
percentage of the plays written or adapted during that period
were melodrama. From Dunlap, who made a career of Kotzebue, to Boucicault, a master of melodrama, whether the
play was written in poetry or prose or was concerned with
political issues, native characters, or social problems, the
techniques of melodrama were prominent. (Farce, of course,
was also relished by the people who came at eight and can
be linked with melodrama as popular theater entertainment.)
Although melodramatic techniques in plays have been mentioned throughout this chapter, the following plays may
help intensify the desired impression. Nor was this interest
in melodrama a passing fad; many plays of the later nineteenth century became more violently and purposefully
melodramatic.

1. *MAZEPPA; OR, THE WILD HORSE OF TARTARY,* 1825

(*Plot*) Grandson of a Tartar chieftain, Mazeppa
(called "Casimir" in the Polish kingdom where he has been
raised) loves Olinska, who is being forced to marry the
Count Premislas. In anger Casimir tries to fight the Count,
is caught and sentenced to be tied to a wild horse and let
loose in the desert. Later, at the entrance of a cavern where
Korella, the prophetess of the Tartars, speaks of the return
of a leader, Mazeppa rides in on the back of the horse.
Fulfilling Korella's prophecy, Mazeppa persuades the Tartars to get Olinska for him. As the Tartars attack, Olinska,
fearing for her life and virtue, tries to stab herself, but is
prevented by Korella who also enlightens her. All ends happily, as the marriage of Mazeppa and Olinska brings peace
for the Poles and the Tartars.

(*Discussion*) *Mazeppa* is a spectacular melodrama
which, either in a version by John Howard Payne or—more
likely—an anonymous revision of it, achieved considerable
success on the American stage. (There is some doubt that
Payne's play was ever produced.) Whatever the version, the
daring historical ride of Mazeppa, Cossack leader and ally
of Peter the Great, provided all of the excitement and pag-

eantry necessary for melodrama. During the early 1860's, in an amazing, novelty performance, the exuberant actress, Adah Isaacs Menken, thrilled all as she played the male part of Mazeppa strapped "naked" (in flesh tights) to the back of a "wild" horse.

2. THE SENTINELS; OR, THE TWO SERGEANTS, by RICHARD PENN SMITH, 1829

(*Plot*) At a military prison, Sergeants Felix and Robert are on trial for allowing a woman and her child to pass the border and thereby increase the danger of a yellow fever contact. Arrested by Major Morazzi, who vies with Robert for the love of Laurette, the sergeants undergo swift trial. The sentence: death for either Felix or Robert! The dice are thrown and Robert wins. Secretly, Felix tells Robert that he is really Captain Derville, once wrongly thought guilty of stealing. Anxious to see his wife on the Isle of Roses, Felix is granted leave on the condition that if he fails to return Robert will be executed in his stead. Morazzi then persuades a man to keep Felix away—thus assuring Robert's execution and the hand of Laurette for himself. On the Isle of Roses, Felix meets his wife and has news that his name is cleared and his army grade raised to Chief of the Battalion. At the prison, Morazzi prepares for Robert's execution although he yields to the urgent pleas of Laurette's aunt and allows Robert to marry Laurette first. As the firing squad readies itself and Robert faces death, Felix, having realized the situation, returns just in time. His rank now gives him privileges, while the trial and the marriage papers free Robert and Laurette. And as usual in the world of melodrama, the villain Morazzi gets his just deserts.

(*Discussion*) The list of melodramas which Richard Penn Smith wrote is long and includes the best of his plays. The above play is adapted from *Les deux Sergents,* a French melodrama by D'Aubigny.

3. THE SENSATIONALISM OF DION BOUCICAULT: *THE POOR OF NEW YORK,* 1857

The name of Dion Boucicault must appear frequently in a review of American drama. His reputation rests on

(1) a few comedies; (2) his successful efforts to secure in America a copyright law giving the author of a play "the sole right to print and publish the said composition, the sole right also to act, perform, or represent the same" (August 18, 1856); (3) his revision of *Rip Van Winkle*; (4) his Southern play, *The Octoroon*; (5) his Irish plays; and (6) his numerous "sensational dramas" or melodramas. Although a man of the theater, he tended to emphasize the play and the characterizations within the play rather than the personalities of the actors. He also initiated the traveling company which performed a single play, devised new advertising methods, and invented a solution which made scenery fireproof. His ideas concerning acting brought him distinction, while his essay on "The Art of Dramatic Composition" showed his concern for Aristotle and the classical Greek and French dramatists. In the theater as well as the drama, he was a figure of some significance in America.

Although he bowed to the demands of his audience and resorted overmuch to the burning of ships and houses, Boucicault tried to make the sensationalism of his melodramas realistic and to bring social significance to his plays. *The Octoroon* was concerned with the evils of slavery; his Irish plays brought sympathy for Ireland's struggle for freedom. *The Poor of New York,* adapted from *Les Pauvres de Paris* by Edouard Brisebarre and Eugène Nus, shows Boucicault at his melodramatic best—spectacular realism, sensationalism, and social interest. Odell (*Annals*, VII, 22) said that it was "among the first of those local melodramas of crime, poverty, and riches."

(*Plot*) Frightened at the financial panic of 1837, Paul Fairweather deposits $100,000 in Gideon Bloodgood's bank which is about to fail. Discovering the condition of the bank, Fairweather is refused permission to withdraw his money, becomes excited, and dies of apoplexy, dropping his deposit receipt on the floor. Next morning his body is found in the street; Bloodgood keeps the money, and the only witness to the event, a clerk named Tom Badger, keeps the receipt. Twenty years pass and people are in the depths of the panic of 1857. Fairweather's widow and children, Lucy and Paul, are poverty-stricken; Bloodgood is well off but is still trying to get the receipt from Badger, whom he has had arrested, hoping to find the receipt on his person. Desperate, Bloodgood sets fire to the house in a final attempt to destroy the receipt. The scene is spectacular; police arrive and the villain is arrested, while the lives of Badger and the Fairweathers will be filled with the serenity that only melodrama can provide.

D. Shortcuts to Popularity: Adaptations, Translations, Burlesques

From the very beginning, American dramatists looked to Europe—especially England—for the material of their plays—characters, settings, themes, plots. William Dunlap was a prodigious borrower, adapter, and translater—from English, French, and German drama—in spite of his enthusiasm for native American drama. John Howard Payne, Nathaniel Parker Willis, James Nelson Barker, Richard Penn Smith—many of the best American dramatists at one time or another borrowed material from Europe, either (1) a complete play adapted to American circumstances or translated for an American audience, or (2) particular characters or plot themes from successful plays, or (3) the language of the foreign dramatists.

As the century progressed, John Brougham and Dion Boucicault became the major adapters of foreign literature. And the reasons for adaptations and translations are not hard to find. American managers and actors had always been suspicious of native authors, feeling that Europeans were better in the arts than Americans. Generally, the theater manager thought it was safer to produce a successful French play adapted to an American audience or to adapt a successful novel to the stage than to speculate on an untried play. Translations and adaptations, then, were faster and easier for the average dramatists, safer for the theater manager, and usually popular with the audience.

The three most successful adaptations of mid-nineteenth-century America are *Ten Nights in a Bar Room*, from the novel by T. S. Arthur; *Uncle Tom's Cabin,* from H. B. Stowe's novel; and *Rip Van Winkle*, from Washington Irving's story. A great number of the historical adventure novels, however, were put into play form, although almost always by some person other than the novelist. Quite popular were the dramatized novels of Cooper, Robert Montgomery Bird, William Gilmore Simms, and John Pendleton Kennedy. Hawthorne's *The Scarlet Letter* saw the stage at least twice, in 1857 and 1858; Poe's *The Gold Bug* was dramatized in 1843. Even the domestic sentimental novels of Mrs. E. D. E. N. Southworth were adapted to the stage. And the list goes on!

Burlesques of plays—a ridiculous mocking of the original work—were not as frequent as adaptations or translations, but the reasons for writing them were somewhat the same. If a play had been a hit, it was assumed that a burlesque of that play would also be a hit. John Brougham was one of the most able and successful writers of burlesque with his attacks on *Metamora* (1847) and *Pocahontas* (1855). Apparently, however, the type was well appreciated by audiences. *The Lady of Irons* (1842), an anonymous burlesque of Bulwer-Lytton's *The Lady of Lyons*, and *Hiawatha; or, Ardent Spirits and Laughing Water* (1856) by Charles M. Walcot suggest other objects of dramatic ridicule.

E. Poets and Novelists as Playwrights

The drama seems always to have had an almost irresistible appeal for writers. Something about the immediacy of the audience's response and the fascination of seeing one's characters brought to life on the stage impels both those with and those without the dramatic touch to put their thoughts into dialogue and action. The results, however, have not always been happy. In no instance, for example, has a first-rate American novelist or poet become a successful dramatist. Of America's major writers, Washington Irving collaborated—anonymously—with John Howard Payne in the successful play *Charles the Second* (1824); Poe wrote a fragment of a poetic drama which he called *Politian* (1835); and Longfellow wrote some poetic dramas—*The Spanish Student* (1842), *The Golden Legend* (1851), and a few others—which did not answer the needs of the theater.

Several second- and third-rate figures achieved some success, both in literature and in the drama. Robert Montgomery Bird became a successful novelist after he stopped writing plays. Nathaniel Parker Willis wrote minor essays and

poems, while George Henry Boker was a poet of some reputation. The author of the popular novel, *The Dutchman's Fire-
side* (1831), James Kirke Paulding, wrote *The Lion of the
West* (1831) and *The Bucktails; or, Americans in England*
(1847). John Neal, a Gothic novelist (*Logan*, 1822) and a
critic, wrote *Otho* (1819), the tragedy of the Byronic hero,
Otho the Bastard, who battles with Prince Irman for the love
of Princess Ala and is killed by Irman's father, who discovers that Otho was his son. Another novelist, William Gilmore Simms, wrote *Michael Bonham; or, The Fall of Bexar*
(1852), a melodrama concerned with the fighting in Texas
before the Mexican War; and a tragedy in blank verse, *Norman Maurice; or, The Man of the People* (1851), dealing
with the attempts of a candidate for senator from Missouri
to combat a smear campaign. With the exception of *Michael
Bonham*, the plays of Neal and Simms were not produced.

Of the numerous other playwrights mentioned in this
book, several wrote fiction, poetry, or essays. Samuel Woodworth (*The Forest Rose*, 1825) is probably most familiar to
the average reader as the author of "The Old Oaken
Bucket." T. D. English (*The Mormons*, 1858) was a doctor
by profession but has some reputation as the writer of "Ben
Bolt." Many were editors or journalists; Isaac Harby (*The
Gordian Knot*) and Epes Sargent (*Velasco*) are excellent examples. A. C. M. Ritchie (*Fashion*) also wrote a novel. A
good number of the playwrights, however, were in some way
connected with the theater which may have enabled them to
become generally more successful than the doctors, lawyers,
teachers, and poets or novelists who tried their hands at
pleasing theater managers and audiences during this most difficult time for playwrights.

F. Transatlantic Evaluation: American Drama
in England before the Civil War

It is not generally realized that, long before the Civil
War, American plays were produced in London theaters
with a certain regularity and some success. Although some
plays had been produced earlier in London, the production
of J. H. Payne's first play at Covent Garden in 1815 established a foothold for American drama in the London theater

which it has never relinquished. Most enthusiastically received were the plays which exhibited the peculiar traits of Americans. Yankee plays, Negro minstrels and skits, and pioneer adventure plays enjoyed long runs in London. American social caricatures were also appreciated in London, along with popular plays such as *Uncle Tom's Cabin* and *Rip Van Winkle*. For the appreciative attitude which many English people had toward American plays before the Civil War, much credit is due such people as Edwin Forrest, Charlotte Cushman, Anna C. M. Ritchie, Dion Boucicault, and the various Yankee and Irish character actors.

1. JOHN HOWARD PAYNE

Payne's success in the English theater can be traced (as with other American playwrights) through the records of the Enthoven Collection of the Victoria and Albert Museum in South Kensington, London. After the production at Covent Garden in 1815 of his first translation, *Trial Without Jury,* Payne became a well-known, if not a popular, playwright in London for the next fifteen years. Mainly, the critics approved. *Brutus* was received with "the utmost height of popularity and universal approbation" and continued its success for many years. During the 1822 season, Payne had seven new plays produced in London theaters—a considerable achievement for an American dramatist. His most successful plays were *Charles the Second; or, The Merry Monarch*, opening on May 27, 1824; and *Clari; or, The Maid of Milan,* first played under this title on May 8, 1823—both at Covent Garden. His most controversial play, *The French Libertine* (*Richelieu*), opened at Covent Garden on February 11, 1826, and inspired exciting critical debates from political as well as dramaturgical views.

There can be little doubt that Payne's work paved the way for a more appreciative view of American drama. After William Dunlap's *Tell Truth and Shame the Devil* was performed at Covent Garden on May 18, 1799, American plays only occasionally found their way across the Atlantic. As the new century progressed, however, the number of American plays produced in England increased. When M. M. Noah's *Wandering Boys; or, The Castle of Olival* was presented at

Covent Garden on February 24, 1814, it was anticipated by this rather negative and significantly skeptical comment: "It will no doubt resemble melodrama in general, in being full of sound and show, and good for nothing—too dull . . . and too absurd to entertain the maturer frequenters of a theatre." Then Payne came to London, and ten years passed. On September 13, 1824, at Sadler's Wells, Samuel Judah's *The Mountain Torrent* was well received by the reviewer of the *Theatrical Observer*: "In our opinion, it is decidedly the best piece of the kind ever witnessed here: the plot is completely original, the incidents peculiar and pleasing . . . the characters . . . finely delineated." Both Noah and Judah have been reduced by time to very minor figures in a history of American drama, but the individual receptions accorded their plays in England suggest a turning point in the attitude of English reviewers toward American plays.

2. POETIC DRAMA ON THE ENGLISH STAGE

American poetic tragedy had a mixed reception in England. Edwin Forrest, the actor, took J. A. Stone's *Metamora* and R. M. Bird's *The Gladiator* to London in 1836. While *Metamora* was condemned by the English critics—"utter rubbish" they called it—*The Gladiator* met with a mixed response. Representative is the critic who saw "great crudity in this work, taken altogether"—but went on to call Bird's work "an ornament to the literature of any country." When Charlotte Barnes Conner's tragedy *Octavia Bragaldi* played at the Surrey Theatre in 1844, advertising capitalized on the American authorship of a play that had been very successful in America. On May 10, 1849, G. H. Boker's tragedy *Calaynos* was produced with "merited success." Generally, however, poetic dramas were not among America's successful dramatic exports.

3. YANKEE PLAYS

Certainly, the most popular plays of this period exported to England were the Yankee plays; next in popularity were the Irish plays, the backwoodsman plays, and minstrel sketches. The American Yankee actor took the American-

made Yankee successfully to England in such plays as
Yankee Land, The Yankee Pedler, The Forest Rose, and
The People's Lawyer. And the Yankee's popularity grew. In
1852, for example, at the Adelphi Theatre, Josh Silsbee
played Hiram Dodge in *The Yankee Pedler* for 125 nights,
having previously completed 99 performances of Jonathan
Ploughboy in *The Forest Rose.* In general, English audiences
found the Yankee great fun and kept him in the theaters
for nearly thirty years, even enticing English playwrights to
try their hands at writing Yankee plays.

4. IRISH PLAYS

The Irish character acting of Barney Williams helped
promote the success of American Irish plays in London.
Irish Assurance and Yankee Modesty was standard in Mr.
and Mrs. Williams' repertory. Another American acting cou-
ple long associated with Irish farces, Mr. and Mrs. W. T.
Florence, were successful in London, particularly in T. D.
English's Irish play, *Handy Andy.* In a later production of
Handy Andy at the Haymarket, December 1, 1860, the
American actor John Drew was extremely popular.

5. BACKWOODSMAN PLAYS AND THE WESTWARD MOVEMENT

Of the backwoodsman plays, *The Kentuckian; or, A
Trip to New York,* adapted by William Bayle Bernard from
James Kirke Paulding's *The Lion of the West,* was one of the
more popular. After its Covent Garden production beginning
March 9, 1833, one critic wrote: "At Covent Garden the
novelty has been a farce called *The Kentuckian,* in which a
good satire is conveyed against old Mother Trollope, the lady
who has obtained so much reputation by exhibiting a due
disgust for American vulgarity." A smiliar attitude regarding
"rough material" was expressed toward another backwoodsman play, L. Reade's *The Game Cock of the Wilderness,*
which appeared at the Olympic Theatre in 1845. Adaptations of James Fenimore Cooper's novels, on the other hand,
were perhaps more successful in England than in America.
A version of *The Pilot* by Edward Fitzball played for 200

nights at the Adelphi Theatre in 1825–26. The movement to California was represented on the English stage in part by the light farces of J. S. Coyne—*Cockneys in California,* at the Adelphi in 1849; *Wanted, 1000 Spirited Young Milliners for the Gold Diggings,* at the Olympic in 1852. In contrast to Coyne's American reception, one critic wrote: "There is not a more successful contributor to the light literature of the stage than Mr. Stirling Coyne."

6. *UNCLE TOM'S CABIN* AND THE SOUTH

Mrs. Harriet Beecher Stowe published her novel *Uncle Tom's Cabin* in March, 1852, and almost immediately, in a number of adaptations for the stage, it became a hit in England. Allardyce Nicoll records eight versions of the play in London during 1852, all anonymous. Appearing at the Olympic Theatre September 20, 1852 (only a month after C. W. Taylor's version had been presented in New York and before the successful Aiken version was produced), the play was subtitled "Negro Life in America" rather than "Life Among the Lowly" and had a happy ending with freedom for the slaves. Concerning another version of the play called *Slave Life,* produced in March of 1853, reviewers hoped that it would "make America ashamed of herself for suffering such an anomaly in her institutions."

Other American plays treating Southern problems include *Ida May; or, The Secrets of the Slave Trade,* at the Victoria Theatre in May of 1855; *Dred, A Tale of the Great Dismal Swamp,* adapted by a Mr. H. Young, and a tremendous success at the Victoria Theatre during the fall of 1856; and Dion Boucicault's *The Octoroon,* which was enthusiastically received by the audiences at the Adelphi Theatre during 1861. Just as the Civil War seems to interest modern English historians more than any other aspect of American history, the problems leading up to the Civil War had their fascination for contemporary English audiences.

7. *RIP VAN WINKLE*

Commissioned by Joseph Jefferson, Dion Boucicault adapted *Rip Van Winkle* for the stage, and on September 4,

1865, his version was presented at the Adelphi Theatre, where it ran 170 nights. Hailed as "triumphantly successful," *Rip Van Winkle* was played at several London theaters during the nineteenth century.

8. OTHER PLAYS AND CRITICAL REACTION

Numerous other American plays were produced in England before the Civil War—Mrs. A. C. M. Ritchie's *Fashion;* many of Boucicault's plays; *Nick of the Woods,* a version of Bird's adventure novel; *Pocahontas;* and others. In both scope and quality, the English got a reasonable idea of American drama before the Civil War. Although the critical reaction was occasionally stuffy, the critics themselves were interested and not a little amazed. Moreover, it remains historically significant that English audiences at so early a date found entertainment in American plays, and that criticism was sufficiently favorable for English theater managers to find it to their advantage to produce American plays as a regular feature of their seasons.

V. YANKEE ORIGINALITY: AMERICA'S CONTRIBUTION TO WORLD THEATER
The Minstrel Show, The Showboat Theater, The Tom Show

It is generally agreed that the minstrel show is America's original contribution to world theater; certainly, it could have started nowhere else. Although the Tom shows and the showboat were not original theater in the same way that the minstrels were, they were distinctive theatrical innovations. And in a sense, all three—the minstrel, the showboat, and the Tom show—were bound together by a common philosophy and technique. They created excitement; they reached out to the average man and made him laugh and cry. As soon as possible after the showboat docked, or the minstrel car pulled onto its siding, or the wagons of the Tommers appeared in town, the man on the street was made aware of the arrival by a parade as colorful as the company's resources could make it. Come one! Come all! Here is the kind of entertainment and excitement that you want, born in America!

A. Introducing Sambo and Bones!

One night in 1828, an itinerant actor named Thomas Dartmouth Rice was walking behind a hotel in Louisville, Kentucky, and happened to see a Negro currying a horse. He was an unhappy-looking Negro with a deformed right shoulder and rheumatism in his left leg and his knees, but he sang as he worked; and at the end of each verse of his song, he gave a little jump and set his "heel a ricken' " as he landed. Rice was fascinated. Watching closely, he soon learned the song and mastered the little jump:

> Turn about and wheel about,
>   An do jis so;
> And ebery time I wheel about,
>   I jump Jim Crow.

Then with clothes borrowed from the old Negro, Rice began performing the song and dance between the acts of the play in which he had a part. Surprisingly enough, his success was astounding both in America and England, and his Jim Crow routine earned him the title of the Father of American Minstrelsy.

The first public presentation of a minstrel show was that of the Virginia Minstrels at the Bowery Amphitheatre in New York, February 6, 1843. Actors had impersonated Negroes on stage since the late eighteenth century, but Rice had performed a single blackface act. The quartette of Virginia Minstrels added instrumental music—fiddle, tambourine, banjo, and bones—and jokes. By the last quarter of the nineteenth century, minstrel companies sometimes included a hundred people, and the minstrel show with its definite pattern was an evening's entertainment in itself. There were six or eight blackfaced end men, having either bones or tambourines, who were introduced in pairs by the whitefaced interlocutor before being seated in a shallow half circle on either side of him. Behind them was the chorus. E. P. Christy is usually credited with the division of the night's entertainment into two parts. Part I consisted of songs and jokes; Part II was an "olio" of variety acts and a sketch, or afterpiece.

After the success of E. P. Christy's Minstrels in New York in 1846, scores of minstrel companies were started. Some flourished. Bryant's Minstrels had a run of eighteen years in New York (1857–1875). Other companies left their names and memories and usually great debts—Spencer's Minstrels, Gorman Brothers Minstrels, Beach and Bowers Minstrels. By 1908, when one of the greatest minstrel companies, the Cohan and Harris Minstrels, toured the country starring "Honey Boy" George Evans with "One Hundred Honey Boys," the character of the minstrel had changed to become a spectacle show; songs were still important but little of Negro life remained in it. The afterpiece, however, could not compete with the better-quality farces written by such dramatists as Charles Hoyt, and the variety acts were rivaled by vaudeville entertainment. By the second quarter of the twentieth century, America's only "original contribution to world theater" had been left to the movies and the amateur stage for whatever means of survival it could manage.

B. Here Comes the Showboat!

Perhaps all theater should answer a felt need, but there are few better examples of a theatrical institution designed for a particular purpose than America's showboat theater. Although Noah M. Ludlow had probably used a Mississippi flatboat as a theater in 1817, it was not until July of 1831, when William Chapman's "drama barge" floated down the Ohio and Mississippi Rivers giving one-night shows, that the era of the showboat started.

With the success of Chapman's "Floating Palace," imitations of all kinds appeared by the dozens. Chapman had produced legitimate plays. Soon the entire gamut of theater fare—Shakespeare, minstrels, melodramas, the latest New York plays—could be seen on showboats run by some of the most colorful theater people. Captain French—banjo player, magician, and general showman, married to a wire walker—started on the rivers in the late 1870's with a small barge called the *New Sensation*, seating only eighty-nine people. Soon he added the luxury of a pusher boat; and by 1887, his newest *Sensation* boasted a steam calliope that could be heard for several miles on the river, a ten-piece band for parades, and an advance man who plastered his advertising on available fences and trees. In 1909, W. R. Markle's *Golden-rod* was an extravagant boat—two hundred feet long and forty-five feet wide with lots of gilt, 2500 lights, draperies, carpets, full-length mirrors, and a seating capacity of 1400.

The problems of the showboat actor were many and varied, but they are not the reason that the showboats nearly stopped running. By the late nineteenth century, the need which stimulated the showboat theater business was lessened by stock and touring theater companies. Revived as a curiosity in the early twentieth century, the showboat was sunk by the Depression of the Thirties. Now once again, mainly through universities, plays are being produced on the showboat!

C. "The World's Greatest Hit"

"Poor old Uncle Tom," moaned George Shelby, "he's gone!" And perhaps this is true. After more than ninety years on the stage, *Uncle Tom's Cabin* has joined the minstrel show and the showboat as a curiosity in the history of American drama and theater. Based on Harriet Beecher Stowe's great novel, this play—which the New York *Herald*, in 1852, warned would "poison the minds of our youth with the pestilent principles of abolitionism"—owed its early success to its attack on slavery and then continued to be produced as a melodrama and spectacle play. It truly deserves the title, "The World's Greatest Hit."

Although Mrs. Stowe never gave permission for the dramatization of her novel because, as she wrote to one actor, "the world is not good enough yet for it to succeed," in August following the March, 1852, publication of the novel, C. W. Taylor's dramatization appeared on the New York stage. The best dramatization of the novel, however, seems to have been George L. Aiken's, which was produced first in the Troy (New York) Museum on September 27, 1852, with Cordelia Howard, who was eventually to become a famous Little Eva. One characteristic of *Uncle Tom's Cabin* is the variety in the stage versions; the play seemed to grow. By 1879, Great Danes masquerading as bloodhounds were pursuing Eliza across the river. Simon Legree got meaner and meaner and more adept with his whip. But it must have been an extravagant enthusiasm for novelty that caused one company to double the number of its parts: two Simon Legrees and two Uncle Toms.

As time went on, members of the theater companies that played *Uncle Tom's Cabin* became known as Tommers, and their shows were called "Tom Shows." Interested in only the one play, these players were quite like a family of troubadours living the various characters in the melodrama. A girl who started as Little Eva might eventually become Eliza. The boys and the men had to have several talents—tending Mark's mule, playing in the band, and perhaps acting two or three minor characters in a single performance. But the Tommers were a dauntless clan, and however varied the scenes, the aim of the play was always the same: virtue must be rewarded and sin punished!

The complexity of Mrs. Stowe's novel was mainly responsible for the great number and diversity of play versions. Some scripts followed a simple theme and were almost sketches; other versions lasted as long as five hours and included some fifty scenes. One of the better-known dramatizations is that of A. E. Thomas, who, modeling his version on the earlier one by Aiken, wrote a play of three acts and twenty-three scenes.

(*Plot*) George Harris, a mulatto slave owned by Haley, a villainous slave trader, appears at the Shelby Plantation to tell his wife and son, Eliza and Harry (who are Shelby slaves), that he is running away to Canada. Eliza, learning that Shelby is in debt and must sell Harry and Uncle Tom, warns Tom, who will not leave, and flees with Harry, only to be stopped by the ice-filled Ohio River. Faced with capture by Haley and Lawyer Marks, she jumps through a window of the tavern where she has been hiding and is next seen floating down the river on a piece of ice.

At the St. Clair household, Mr. St. Clair has just bought two new slaves: Topsy for Ophelia, the would-be social reformer from Vermont, and old Uncle Tom for his daughter, Little Eva, a sickly but overwhelmingly sweet and virtuous little girl. Meanwhile, George, Eliza, and Harry are united with the help of Phineas Fletcher, although they are continually hunted by Haley and Marks. Back at St. Clair's, Little Eva dies with a final wish that Uncle Tom be given his freedom, but before the papers can be signed, St. Clair is killed in a fight. With the St. Clair Plantation in debt, the slaves are sold: Topsy to Ophelia; Uncle Tom and Emmeline, a good woman, to Simon Legree, the most heartless slave owner in the entire country. At Legree's plantation, Uncle Tom is ordered to flog Emmeline, who has just refused to go with Legree into his house, and is whipped when he disobeys and left to suffer with another slave, Cassy. In the meantime, young Shelby, who has come to buy back Uncle Tom, and Marks have found a man who swears that Legree stabbed St. Clair. At Legree's house, they accuse him of murder and are dramatically saved from his anger by the slave, Cassy, who stabs Legree fatally. Then the end comes rapidly as Uncle Tom dies in Shelby's arms. "Poor old Uncle Tom—he's gone!"

VI. THEATER BEFORE THE CIVIL WAR
"The life that is moving and calling us"

From 1800 to the period of the Civil War, the American theater developed from a largely imitative form of entertainment to a point where it could contribute to world theater. It had produced some very capable actors and actresses and some startling innovations in production methods; and it now reached—although with some gaps—from coast to coast. No serious critic of the drama or theater had appeared, but this only meant that anyone had an opportunity to fling brickbats or bouquets. Meanwhile, the actors—deserving or undeserving; tyros or artists—carried on their tradition. As they grew with the country, this toast of later years might have been theirs: "To the life that is moving and calling us!"

A. Criticism of the Theater

In a column entitled "The Stage" from *The Philadelphia Repository and Weekly Register* (I [April 11, 1801], p. 171)

the comment was made that "such a thing as a well con-
ducted theatre has never existed nor can it, because a sufficient number of good plays cannot be collected to support a
public theatre." Other critics saw the problem in the institution: "The stage is the direct School of Vice." Still others
could find fault with the physical theater, with the poor lighting and the odor and smoke of the oil-pots on the stoves.
And there was violence in the gallery, assorted improper
activities in the boxes, and rats and vermin in the pit.

One might easily sympathize with the recommendations
of Jonathan Oldstyle (Washington Irving):

> To the actors—less etiquette, less fustian, less buckram.
> To the orchestra—new music, and more of it.
> To the pit—patience, clean benches, and umbrellas.
> To the boxes—less affectation, less noise, less coxcombs.
> To the gallery—less grog and better constables; and
> To the whole house, inside and out—a total reformation,
> And so much for the theater.

The theater remained a rowdy place for many people. It is
perhaps little wonder that Mrs. Frances Trollope in her report
on American manners during the 1830's found irritations in
the theater: men spitting and drinking, "a lady performing
the most maternal office possible," and "a general air of contempt for the decencies of life." Nor did such activities in the
theater cease before the Civil War. As the "Wild West" was
opened, the theater, perhaps an index of civilization, was
only slightly aware of the "decencies of life."

To help the reformation which Washington Irving suggested, there were the critics; at least, there were people who
undertook to comment on plays, point out flaws, and suggest
opportunities for improvement. Newspapers and weekly magazines had theater columns; some magazines were devoted
entirely to theater criticism, such as *The Theatrical Censor*
or *The Thespian Monitor*. Irving's witty and intelligent observations on the theater in the *Salmagundi* papers were outstanding. In defining the objectives of dramatic criticism, a
writer in *The Theatrical Censor*, I (December 9, 1805)
noted that the critic was not the enemy of the drama nor
of the public, but the "voice of an enlightened audience."

Unfortunately, few who wrote about the theater seemed to meet these qualifications. Of the numerous critics, John Neal commented bitingly on the drama but with some insight; Poe was erratic in his observations, but generally the most astute observer of the period. Theater criticisms in general became little more than theater advertising as the century progressed. One becomes more aware of this as he understands the power of the acting stars. Walt Whitman, writing for the Brooklyn *Eagle* in 1847, said that he found no independent drama critics, only "slaves of the paid puff system." The condition of theater and drama criticism was not a happy one.

B.   Westward Ho! and Southward Y'all!

Before the Revolution, the theater had been active in Southern cities such as Charleston and Williamsburg; Philadelphia and New York had also been responsive to theatrical entertainment. Although Boston had no theater until the 1790's, by the turn of the century most of the cities on the eastern coast had theaters. Gradually, however, a center for theatrical activities became recognized, and by 1825, New York was the place. At the same time the theater was spreading westward, and by 1860, there were American theater companies in California and many cities in between.

The push westward and southward started soon after the new century began. From 1815 through 1830, an intrepid actor named Samuel Drake brought plays to Kentucky and Ohio and the Ohio River Valley. In 1817, a member of Drake's company, Noah Ludlow, decided to have his own theatrical company and was soon producing plays in Tennessee (1817), New Orleans (1818), and St. Louis (1819). A little later, an ambitious actor named James H. Caldwell began to establish a chain of theaters along the lower Mississippi. Theater along the upper Mississippi was then not long in coming.

Theater in California existed before the Gold Rush days, but the '49ers provided a tremendous stimulus for theatrical activity. Professional theater came to Sacramento in 1849; within a year, San Francisco had a theater, and by 1851, it enjoyed three theaters and a circus.

C. To Build a Theater

To build a theater was no easy task in a new nation where society was only slowly being established and independence of character was considered a prime virtue. Some audiences would enjoy English drama; other strongly nationalistic people would reject it. Some liked poetic drama; others enjoyed only farce. Theater managers, struggling to please as many people as possible, adopted a number of devices to stimulate success. Of these, the so-called Star System was most significant before the Civil War. Supplementing it were such novelties as the English actor and the specialist. On the other hand, struggling to combat the overwhelming power of the Star System, there were strong resident companies formed in the large cities.

1. ENGLISH ACTORS AND ACTRESSES

One of the earliest attempts to infuse some excitement into the theater was the importation of English actors, a finesse still employed. Two English actors who made reputations in America early in the nineteenth century were the talented Thomas Abthorpe Cooper and the erratic and alcoholic George Frederick Cooke. Charles Mathews' visit to America in 1822–23 provided him with a character idea—the Yankee—which made his fortune. As the century progressed, nearly every celebrated English thespian made his trip to America: Edmund Kean, romantic and successful but so arrogant as to antagonize Boston audiences forever; Charles Kemble and his lovely daughter, Fanny; and William Charles Macready, whose personal and professional antagonism toward Edwin Forrest helped start the greatest theater disaster of the nineteenth century—the Astor Place riot.

2. AMERICAN ACTORS AND ACTRESSES

Although the English performers added a touch of Old World culture to New World society, the American theater was also producing notable performers. John Howard Payne and John Brougham had been successful actors. Junius Brutus

Booth provided some competition for Edmund Kean's romantic acting. Charlotte Cushman received ovations as an actress of tragedy on both sides of the Atlantic at mid-century and enjoyed her reputation for the next twenty years. Joseph Jefferson III, of Rip Van Winkle fame, was just starting his outstanding career during the period before the Civil War.

Dwarfing all of these people in style of acting, pecuniary success, and violence of temperament was Edwin Forrest, a man who prided himself on his physical and personal power. The popular acting style of that day was declamatory, and Forrest has been compared to Daniel Webster, their elocutionary styles being not significantly different. There was no question of Forrest's leadership in American theater, and his interest in native plays (that is, those tailored to his specific acting requirements) adds to his position in the American theater. His various successes in England were marred only by his Edinburgh hiss of William Charles Macready's Hamlet. With this incident, the personal antagonism between these two actors developed until it reached a climax in the infamous Astor Place riot. There on May 10, 1849, when Macready played Macbeth in the Astor Place Opera House of New York, supporters of Forrest precipitated a riot which ended when the militia fired into the mob, killing thirty-one persons and wounding at least 150. But for Forrest, this was only the climax of one act of an exciting life: a scandalous divorce suit provided another. The success of his acting career is matched only by the sensationalism of his life.

3. THE SPECIALIST

One way to become outstanding in a career is to become extremely proficient in a certain speciality. In the theater, as in other professions, there arose the specialist, the most numerous and popular being the Yankee actors—James H. Hackett, George Handel "Yankee" Hill, Dan Marble, John Owens, among others. Thomas Dartmouth Rice made his name with Jim Crow skits and Negro parts. Francis S. Chanfrau was a tremendously popular actor as Mose, the New York Fire B'hoy; and Joseph Jefferson III practically made a career out of his portrayal of Rip Van Winkle.

4. THE STAR SYSTEM: ALL CHIEFS AND NO INDIANS

All that has been discussed, of course, was simply the Star System in action, a technique of the theater people to add interest to a production by "puffing" the talents of a single actor or actress to extravagant proportions. It did add interest, fortune, and glamour; but it also had its bad effects, and opposition to it grew throughout this period. In his *Personal Recollections of the Stage*, William B. Wood cited some of its evils. In its excessive concern for a single star, the theater suffered from a lack of good supporting actors—and a surfeit of poorly prepared actors who were wrongly billed as stars. Such "puffing and lying" did not contribute to a healthy theater. In addition, the Star System rarely allowed time for adequate rehearsals, good casting, or the making of effective scenery. There was also the evil of the benefit nights for which an actor might do a superb job of acting while slacking off on the nights when the management would get the receipts. For these and other reasons, some believed that the Star System tended to harm the theater.

5. NOVELTY IN THEATER PRODUCTIONS

There were other ways, too, of adding excitement to the theater. Charlotte Cushman impressed numerous critics with her portrayal of Romeo; Adah Isaacs Menken achieved notoriety by playing the hero in *Mazeppa* and allowing herself to be strapped naked (in tights) to the back of a horse; and other actresses specialized in "breeches parts," as they were called. *Mazeppa* also introduced the fashion of equestrian drama. Later, P. T. Barnum opened "lecture rooms" in which he presented moral plays like *The Drunkard*. One theory of the theater at this time seemed to be that showmanship was nearly as important as talent for an actor or a manager, and many of the specialists were simply excellent showmen.

6. THE GROWING POWER OF THE RESIDENT COMPANY

The forming of permanent acting companies composed of strong and experienced actors and actresses who could perform with or without the support of a visiting star was considered the best way to improve the theater. By 1860, there were strong resident stock companies in major American cities, companies which had taken considerable time and energy to build. One of the early managers to build a resident company was William Mitchell in New York, 1839; in 1843, W. H. Smith started a resident company for the Boston Museum. Later, William E. Burton, in 1848, and James W. Wallach, in 1855, opened permanent acting companies in their New York theaters. Idealistically, these companies could support a guest star or perform a good repertory by themselves. After reaching a certain point of success before the Civil War, however, such companies were increasingly weakened by the touring of the complete casts of single plays until, by the turn of the century, they had virtually disappeared. Ever since that early time, theater people have dreamed of there being a resident company in every important American city.

VII. SUMMARY

From the beginning of the nineteenth century to the Civil War, American drama was clearly that of a new nation imitating what it considered the fashionable and cultural best of Europe and England, while experimenting with the various possibilities for a native drama. At the same time, the drama mirrored the social, political, and historical movements of this period very closely. Concerned with an immediate appeal to popular tastes in a nation that was strongly nationalistic, playwrights dramatized current events, while romanticizing and making heroic national characteristics and social movements. That the plays of this period were not better may be explained partially by the narrow commercialism of theater managers and certain actors, the unsophisticated tastes of the theater public, and the lack of copyright protection for playwrights. It is also true that there were only a handful of playwrights with sufficient imagination and skill to write a play having both literary quality and theater appeal. In general, this was a weak and stumbling period in the history of American drama, a period of interest in plays for their social, historical, and theatrical significance and for a few plays with qualities of excellence.

It is perhaps ironic that a new and strongly nationalistic country should have produced its best drama in romantic tragedies and melodramas imitative of Europe in style, plot, and theme. In many ways, however, the heroic plot and theme suggested to Americans their own struggle for freedom, while the romantic style reminded them of their own adventures in the New World. Barker's *Superstition* claims its distinction among this group by having a native theme in contrast to two other praiseworthy poetic dramas—Bird's *The Gladiator* and Boker's *Francesca da Rimini*. Other plays which deserve to be included among the best of the period are Anna C. M. Ritchie's *Fashion*, for its clever farce-comedy and caricature of American manners, and Payne and Irving's *Charles the Second*, another witty farce-comedy with literary pretensions.

This period in American drama is also noteworthy for the creation of certain type characters and original contributions to American and world theater. The characters were Jonathan, Sambo, and Metamora, with Jonathan the most popular because he was a national symbol as well as a comic figure. The theater innovations were the minstrel show, arising from a social phenomenon in America; the showboat, a product of American geography; and the Tom Shows, which resulted from the overwhelming success of a sentimental melodrama based on a serious social problem.

As a part of the history of American drama, this period has significance, but compared with American literature of that time, of course, the plays are of minor importance. During the years covered in this chapter, Irving produced his stories and essays; Emerson his celebrated essays on "Nature," "Self-Reliance," and "The American Scholar"; Thoreau his *Walden*; Bryant, Longfellow, Lowell, Holmes, and Whittier some of their best and most popular poems; Hawthorne and Melville their great novels; Poe his stories and poems; and Whitman his *Leaves of Grass*. Obviously, the drama of the period is a country cousin to such literary accomplishments. Yet it was a living and developing drama. As a critic, Poe thought Mrs. Ritchie's *Fashion* worthy of serious consideration. Writing in the Brooklyn *Eagle* in 1847, Walt Whitman pleaded for "American plays" featuring American opinions and institutions and employing American talent—as Emerson and others had asked for an American literature. The need for an American drama to match American fiction and poetry was being felt, but such drama was to come slowly.

SELECTED BIBLIOGRAPHY

America's Lost Plays Series. Princeton: Princeton University Press, 1940–41.

American Periodical Series

Bailey, Thomas A., *The American Pageant.* Boston: D. C. Heath & Company, 1961.

Birdoff, Harry, *The World's Greatest Hit—Uncle Tom's Cabin.* New York: S. F. Vanni, 1947.

Bradley, Edward S., *George Henry Boker, Poet and Patriot.* Philadelphia: University of Pennsylvania Press, 1927.

Clapp, W. W., Jr., *A Record of the Boston Stage.* Boston: J. Munroe & Company, 1853.

Dunlap Society Publications, New York.

Foust, Clement, *The Life and Dramatic Works of Robert Montgomery Bird.* New York: The Knickerbocker Press, 1919.

Graham, Philip, *Showboats: The History of an American Institution.* Austin: University of Texas Press, 1951.

Harrison, Gabriel, *John Howard Payne, Dramatist, Poet, Actor and Author.* Philadelphia: J. B. Lippincott & Co., 1885.

Hewitt, Barnard, *Theatre U.S.A., 1665–1957.* New York: McGraw-Hill Book Company, Inc., 1959.

Hodge, Francis Richard, *Yankee Theatre: The Image of America on the Stage, 1825–1850.* Austin: University of Texas Press, 1965.

Hoyt, Harlowe R., *Town Hall Tonight.* Englewood Cliffs, N.J.: Prentice-Hall, 1955.

Hughes, Glenn, *A History of the American Theatre, 1700–1950.* New York: Samuel French, 1951.

Hutton, Laurence, *Curiosities of the American Stage.* New York: Harper & Brothers, 1891.

Jefferson, Joseph, *The Autobiography of Joseph Jefferson.* New York: The Century Company, 1890.

Moody, Richard, *America Takes the Stage.* Bloomington, Indiana: Indiana University Press, 1955.

————, *Edwin Forrest, First Star of the American Stage.* New York: Knopf, 1960.

Mowatt, Anna Cora, *Autobiography of an Actress.* Boston: Ticknor, Reed, & Fields, 1854.

Musser, Paul H., *James Nelson Barker*. Philadelphia: University of Pennsylvania Press, 1929.

Reardon, John, *Verse Drama in America from 1765 to the Civil War*. University of Kansas, unpublished Ph.D. dissertation, 1957.

Rossman, K. R., "The Irish in American Drama in the Mid-Nineteenth Century," *New York State Historical Association*, XXXVIII, (January, 1940), 39–53.

Stebbins, Emma, ed., *Charlotte Cushman: Her Letters and Memories of Her Life*. Boston: Houghton, Osgood & Company, 1878.

Wemyss, F. C., *Twenty-six Years of the Life of an Actor and Manager*. New York: Burgess, Stringer & Company, 1847.

Wittke, Carl, *Tambo and Bones*. Durham, N.C.: Duke University Press, 1930.

Wood, William B., *Personal Recollections of the Stage*. Philadelphia: H. C. Baird, 1855.

CHAPTER III

From Profession to Art

American Drama from the Civil War to World War I

Dramatic changes in literary movements or theater trends come slowly, with suggestions of change first intruding upon the scene for a number of years. Essentially, the Civil War is only a convenient date for the ending of one historical chapter and the beginning of another; it has little to do with the development of American drama. On the other hand, there are aspects of the drama written during the last third of the nineteenth century which show significant changes from the past, changes which were intensified during the first decade of the twentieth century. The date on which this chapter closes is more logical in a history of American drama. World War I coincides roughly with the organization of the Provincetown Players which, with the plays of Eugene O'Neill, stimulated those changes which are frequently considered the beginnings of modern American drama. During the fifty years from the Civil War to World War I, American drama changed from a profession in which a playwright could eke out a living by combining hack work with imagination to an art in which the dramatist achieved some stature and the play was considered a literary form, subjected to the standards of a developing dramatic criticism.

Although the kinds of plays written during the first half of the nineteenth century persisted in later decades, there were some distinctive changes in form and purpose. Melodrama continued in a sweet and sentimental strain with a rather vivid and violent vein of action; but in the years immediately before World War I, it assumed obligations which caused critics to talk in terms of social melodrama. Farce had always been popular, and it remained so, although it, too, undertook an interest in social commentary. In the last half of the nineteenth century, poetic drama very nearly disappeared, only to reappear with some force in the first decade of the twentieth century in the plays of several poet-dramatists. Spectacle drama continued and developed, both in the amount of plays or entertainment produced—minstrel, burlesque, circus, and musical—and in the method of production.

A major change during the period was a more serious emphasis on realism. Following, although at some distance, the trend of literary realism which distinguishes such major literary figures as Mark Twain, William Dean Howells, and Henry James, the drama of the last third of the nineteenth century reluctantly released its firm hold on romantic melodrama and occasionally shocked its audiences with realistic portrayals of life. In doing this, it emphasized more consistently than before the problems of society. The success of this type of social play plus the growing demands for a literary drama stimulated an interest in social comedy. As the nineteenth century came to a close, these demands upon the dramatist came from a new phenomenon in dramatic circles—the serious dramatic critic. A final new trend in the drama of this period—called "A New Seriousness" in this history—discusses those more thoughtful dramatists of the early twentieth century who not only concerned themselves with social and moral issues of a more enduring thesis than their predecessors, but brought greater artistic imagination and philosophic insight to their themes.

Present criticism of American drama before World War I tends to be severe, but the best plays of that period pointed toward America's debut into world drama. Ibsen had influenced American dramatists, and the plays of other foreign countries had made an impression. At the same time, American plays were being well received in England and had been produced with some success in European countries. By World War I, American drama needed the stimulus of dedicated theater artists and an outstanding dramatist.

I. THE RISE OF REALISM IN AMERICAN DRAMA

The Rise of Realism in American literature is a major literary trend during the last half of the nineteenth century. Starting with local color writers and articulate humorists like Artemus Ward, realism followed a European trend which was stimulated by Balzac's *Père Goriot* in 1834–5. According to William Dean Howells, an American novelist, critic, and playwright who is frequently referred to as the Father of American Realism, realism is nothing more than a truthful representation of life. Definitions, of course, vary. A decided reaction against the sentimental writing of the past, however, realism was a focusing of the universe according to the writer's concept of truth, although his ideas of good taste were also involved.

In addition to a revolt from the past, an explanation of realism involves a listing of the consequences of the twin forces of Science and Democracy which affected all aspects of life in late nineteenth century America: Darwin's *Origin of Species* (1859); Sir Charles Lyell's discoveries concerning the Glacial Age; Friedrich Engels and Karl Marx's *Communist Manifesto* (1848); Auguste Comte's writings in sociology and Herbert Spencer's attempt to apply Comte's theories to biology; the Civil War; the Homestead Act of 1862; reconstruction in the South and politics in Washington; the so-called Robber Barons; Thorstein Veblen's age of "conspicuous waste"; Samuel Gompers and the A.F.L. in 1866. In a large sense, realism in literature came because man was being forced to look at life more realistically, and a more thoughtful and socially conscious literature mirrored this view. This was the trend that the drama followed.

Certain extremes in the Rise of Realism in the drama can be clearly described, but among these extremes realism exists in a variety of forms which must be suggested mainly by reference to particular playwrights. Touches of realism appear before the Civil War in plays that depicted certain sections of America through their peculiar characteristics. Later, this local color drama became mainly pictorial of New England and the West. The climax of realistic drama in the nineteenth century, however, was James A. Herne's *Margaret Fleming* (1890). Before this play, one finds an underlying force for realism in the plays of William Dean Howells, William Gillette, and Steele MacKaye. Realism in the production of a play, of course, was quite another things, and even the wildest melodramas of David Belasco and Augustin Daly can boast some quite realistic stage scenery.

A. Local Color Drama and the Awakening of a Native Tradition

In literature, the term "local color" describes those stories and poems which suggest clearly some particular locale distinct from other places. The distinction was usually made through characters, dialect (using cacography), customs, and scene; and the most frequently mentioned local color writers may be found in New England (Sarah Orne Jewett), the South (George Washington Cable), the Midwest (Edward Eggleston), and the Far West (Bret Harte).

As in fiction and poetry, there are numerous plays which have as one objective the presentation of life in some particular section of America. Also, like the stories and poems, these plays seem to allow cataloging in similar areas—New England, the Midwest, and the Far West, with some interest in the South and in life in New York City. Frequently neither characters nor ideas in these plays are new, but there is a careful concern for realism in custom, character, or dialect. In a sense, earlier character creations now assumed somewhat legendary characteristics, and the local color plays following the Civil War suggested the awakening of a native tradition in American drama.

1. THE YANKEE BACK HOME: NEW ENGLAND LOCAL COLOR

During the 1860's, the Yankee continued to be popular on the New York and London stages, but this Yankee was a caricature, a symbol of America. Following the traditions of Seba Smith's Major Jack Downing and James Russell Lowell's Hosea Biglow, the local color dramatist tried to make the Yankee a believable New Englander, poised against the customs and scenes of his native land. Of all New England local color drama, none was more popular than Denman Thompson's *The Old Homestead*.

(a) Denman Thompson: *The Old Homestead,* 1886

Born in 1833, Thompson graduated from chore boy in a
circus to actor and finally found success acting the main character in a two-scene sketch he wrote about a Yankee farmer.
This was in 1875. It was a lengthened version of this sketch,
then called *The Old Homestead,* which opened at the Boston
Museum to "instantaneous success" on April 5, 1886. Happily
for Thompson, who performed in the play until his death in
1911, the success of the play was as long lasting as it was instantaneous, supposedly earning $3,000,000 over the years. W.
D. Howells ["Editor's Study," *Harper's Monthly,* LXXIX (July,
1889), 317] considered Thompson the originator of a typically
American drama and *The Old Homestead* one of the "sweetest
and simplest" of American plays: "On a wider plane than anyone else has yet attempted, Mr. Thompson gives us in this piece
a representation of American life." The play has been produced
many times in the twentieth century, particularly in Keene, New
Hampshire, the scene of its action.

Essentially a sentimental melodrama with a strong moral
and lots of farce humor, the play includes traditional themes of
temperance and the relative value of city and country life. Realistic touches, however, are exploited: New England customs
(country dances, a sleigh ride, and milking problems), country
scenes, references to the Panic of '73, and the actions and speech
of the main character, Josh, who is sentimentalized in somewhat
the same way as the characters in local color stories and poems.

(*Plot*) At the Whitcomb farmhouse in New England,
Joshua and his sister, Matilda, entertain Frank and Ann Hopkins, the city-bred son and daughter of Joshua's old school
chum, Henry. Joshua, worried about his son, Reuben, who ran
away after being falsely accused of stealing, agrees to visit the
Hopkins family in New York and there look for Reuben. Then,
as a quartet approaches from behind the barn to sing a few sentimental songs, Happy Jack appears, a victim of drink but a
clever talker; and soon Joshua gives him ten dollars if he will
promise to stop drinking.

At the Hopkins mansion in New York, Joshua, as "the very
embodiment of honesty and rural simplicity," both shocks and
charms. The next day he hunts for Reuben and becomes involved in the usual greenhorn problems. Meanwhile Happy Jack,
prosperous looking, enters, sees a young man in the hands of the

law, bribes the policeman, and gives the young man a dollar to get something to eat. Then he sees Joshua and repays him the ten dollars, as the young man staggers into view again and into the arms of Josh, who sobs, "My boy Reub!"

Later, back at the Old Homestead on New Year's Eve, fiddle music announces a dance and Reuben's homecoming. With some homespun New England advice for the young'uns, Joshua says a word to the audience—"Now, you fathers that have got wild boys, I want you to be kind o' easy with them. . . . And, mothers, . . . your hearts are always biling over with love and kindness for the wayward child!"—before the music starts and all take their places for the Virginia Reel.

(b) James A. Herne's Downeasters: *Drifting Apart*, 1888; *Shore Acres*, 1892

Herne's primary contribution to American drama is his interest in realism, particularly in his characters, which include some very effective examples of the New England Yankee. Four plays that should be mentioned are *Hearts of Oak,* written with David Belasco (1879); *Drifting Apart* (other title is *Mary, the Fishermen's Child*) (1888); *Shore Acres* (1892); and *Sag Harbor,* (1899).

Drifting Apart is built around New England sea-going Yankees, although its major emphasis is its temperance theme. A sentimental melodrama using a dream technique, it shows local color in its fishing village scene and secondary characters.

Herne's best New England character is Uncle Nat Berry of *Shore Acres.* A kindhearted, tolerant man who has found his happiness in helping others, Uncle Nat seems to personify the basic spirit of sentimental goodness in all melodrama, but his language and actions bind him to New England.

(c) More Local Color from New England

Throughout the nineteenth century, plays based in New England were produced quite regularly. A good example of the Downeast play is *The County Fair* by Charles Barnard and Neil Burgess (1889). The main character is Miss Abby Prue, a New England old maid who combines a liberal amount of shrewdness with an equal amount of sentiment. The plot tells of a farm, a mortgage, a villainous mortgage holder, and a horse that wins enough money at the county fair to pay off the mortgage. Another equally popular play about mortgages, horses, and New England is *David Harum* (1900), a dramatization of E. N. Westcott's very popular novel.

2. THE WILD WEST IN THE EASTERN THEATER

The vogue for western drama goes back to James Kirke Paulding's *The Lion of the West* (1831), when Kentucky was the west. (Other plays showing similar emphasis were mentioned in Chapter II, section III, C 6.) Then in 1868, the sensational appearance of Bret Harte's "The Luck of Roaring Camp" in *The Overland Monthly* suggested characters and actions ready-made for the theater. The romantic adventures touched eastern audiences, and playwrights followed the lead of Harte and Joaquin Miller. The dramatists' major objective, however, was sensational melodrama: violent actions, exciting escapades, and exaggerated characters. Local color was secondary, but it was part of the appeal of these plays.

(a) *Horizon*, by Augustin Daly, 1871

(*Plot*) Going west to occupy lands given to him by a Congressional grant, Sundown Rowse takes with him Captain Van Dorp, an adopted son whose foster father left his haughty wife and ran away with his daughter to the West years before. At the land grant, Rogue's Rest, young Van Dorp is attracted to Med, the daughter of Whiskey Wolf (actually the elder Van Dorp). The rest of the play shows how the sentimental gambler, Loder, protects Med against the Indian, Wannemucka, and prepares the way for young Van Dorp to marry her.

(*Discussion*) Augustin Daly is one of the major figures in late nineteenth century American theater and drama. As theater manager and owner, he contributed to the development of American theater and to its reputation abroad. As original playwright and frequent adapter, he created important plays in the two major trends of late nineteenth-century American drama— the Rise of Realism in the drama and the development of social comedy. Alert to potential audience appeal of popular fiction, Daly dramatized a Bret Harte story in *Horizon*, copywriting it as "a play of contemporaneous events upon the borders of civilization." Suggestive of his interest in realism and social events is this comment, [A. Daly, "The American Dramatist," *North American Review*, CXLII (May, 1886), 485–492]: "Possibly our national drama, from a literary point of view, will reach its best period when native writers vie with each other in illustrating native character and contemporaneous fashion and follies."

Although the main figure in *Horizon* is Sundown Rowse, a caricature of a crooked politician and Washington lobbyist, other characters suggest the West and Bret Harte's creations: the noble gambler, the drunkard who wants to take care of his daughter before he dies, the bad Indian, and the various citizens of Rogue's Rest. Most of the play is laid in the West, but the atmosphere is very moral and romantic. The scene and the characters present local color; the plot involves the melodrama of murders, Vigilante Committees, Indian raids, mysterious letters, and rescue by American soldiers.

(b) *Davy Crockett*, by Frank Murdock, 1872

(*Plot*) Raised in the backwoods with Davy Crockett but now part of city society, Eleanor passes through Davy's settlement with her fiancé, Neil, and a group going west. Worried about a mysterious plot in which Neil is involved, she appeals to Davy, who agrees to help. Later, separated from their group by a blizzard, Eleanor and Neil arrive at Davy's hunting cabin, and while Neil sleeps, Eleanor inspires Davy to declare his love by reading the story of young Lochinvar. Having burned all the cabin furniture, even the bar to the door, to keep warm, they find only one way to keep the door closed against marauding wolves—"The strong arm of a backwoodsman." The next day, swollen arm and all, Davy hikes ten miles to save Neil, who is dangerously ill. When Eleanor later learns that Neil's uncle has power over her guardian and demands the marriage so that he may control her fortune, she tells Davy that she is his if he rescues her, which he does, quoting young Lochinvar as they ride away. At last she is happy in the "heart and home of Davy Crockett."

(*Discussion*) With Frank Mayo in the title role, *Davy Crockett* was a box-office success in England and America until Mayo's death in 1896. Owing some debts to the life of Davy Crockett and other debts to Scottish history and Sir Walter Scott's *Marmion*, this play uses the background of the Tennessee trapper and the contrasting falseness of city and foreign society to build up the idealized picture of the American backwoodsman. Davy was a "naturel gentleman" who followed his father's motto: "Be sure you're right, then go ahead." In local color terms, the play emphasizes something of the language of the backwoodsman and the peculiarities of his life.

(c) Adaptations of Frontier Life: Bret Harte and Joaquin Miller

Many stories by Harte and Miller were adapted to the stage, but these writers also adapted their works or wrote original plays. Miller, known popularly as the "poet of the Sierras," wrote four plays—*The Danites of the Sierras* (1877), based on two of his short stories; *Forty-nine* (1881); *Tally Ho* and *An Oregon Idyll*, both published with his poems in 1910 but presumably never performed. *The Danites* was quite successful on the stage and portrayed a rough but goodhearted group of miners whose lives are changed by the arrival of a widow. Bret Harte, even more anxious than Miller to be a successful playwright, wrote several very weak plays. Five of them never saw the stage. *The Two Men of Sandy Bar* (1876) was not successful; and *Ah Sin* (1877), in which he collaborated with Mark Twain, was scarcely better. The best dramatizations of Harte's stories were done by other people, and of these playwrights Bartley Campbell was the most successful with *My Partner* (1879). Generally, literary figures who were part of the local color movement were not successful in the theater.

(d) Later Drama of the Frontier: Augustus Thomas and David Belasco

One can only suggest the number of plays about the West. T. W. Henshaw's *The Forty-Niners*, called a "great national drama of pioneer life, faithful to the civilization and incidents it portrays," is typical of many that place the scene in the West but show little knowledge of it. Laid in the Sierras, it has an extremely artificial and melodramatic plot which is not related to the Sierras. *Nevada; or, The Lost Mine*, by George M. Baker (1882), is another of the numerous frontier plays in which Bret Harte's characters find themselves in amazingly melodramatic situations.

(i) Although Augustus Thomas is best known as the author of well-made melodramas of a more subtle nature than the frontier drama could boast, he also contributed to the local color drama of the West, the Midwest, and the South. *Colorado* (1901) was a failure. Another western play, *Arizona* (1899), with the usual melodramatic plot but better-than-average characters, is set in a part of Arizona that Thomas had observed closely in 1897 and which he used successfully to provide scene and atmosphere. Western local color plays generally considered, Thomas's work is distinguished by his serious concern for portraying aspects of life realistically.

(ii) David Belasco is a considerable figure as an advocate of realism in the American theater and as a writer of successful melodramas, mainly in collaboration with others. During one period of his complicated career, he wrote plays about the West which show not only his great skill in writing melodrama but also his knowledge of the West and his ability to put realistic detail into dramatic productions. *The Girl of the Golden West* played for three years after it opened in 1905 and was later made into a grand opera by Puccini. As an example of local color, it became popular through its language, characterization, background scenery, and western traditions. Briefly, the play dramatizes the story of Minnie Falconer, known as The Girl, and her first love, Johnson (or Rammerez) the highwayman. She gives him her first kiss, hides him when he is wounded, gambles with the Sheriff for his life and cheats to assure victory, wins over the jury of miners with her pleas for Johnson's life, and finally leaves for a new life with her hero.

3. LOCAL COLOR DRAMA FROM THE MIDWEST

This may perhaps make a too arbitrary division, for it is rather difficult to separate West and Midwest in the drama of late nineteenth century. The following plays, however, do suggest a different locale from the Bret Harte western.

Joseph Arthur's *Blue Jeans* (1891) has an Indiana setting, and in its comedy scenes suggests rural local color. It is, however, a rather conventional melodrama, distinguished mainly by the buzz-saw device employed to intimidate the heroine. *In Mizzoura* (1893) is another Augustus Thomas play of rural setting where realism of customs and character is emphasized, although a melodramatic plot tells how a girl, returning from college to a home of poverty, finds excitement and love.

4. LOCAL COLOR IN THE SOUTH

Plays about the South vary from the popular war plays to plays variously dealing with Southern problems, to numerous

melodramas of the romantic South. Of the latter type, one melodrama seems to have been much like any other, as the following review of Charles Calahan's *Coon Hollow* (1894) makes
clear (New York *Herald*, August 28, 1894): "You know the
recipe for making a play of this sort. The scene can be laid in
Tennessee, because you can thus get a background of the Mississippi by moonlight. The principal ingredients are invariably
an extremely chivalrous 'Southern gentleman,' a mountaineer,
'rough on the outside, but true at the core'—at fitful moments; a
callow youth, who generally wears riding boots and acts fool-
ishly, and a maiden of preternaturally smart naivete. You season
it with a villain of inordinate wickedness and of perfectly in-
credible shortsightedness. Add a dash of steamboat races, Negro quartets and cotton compresses. Garnish with wild moun-
tainous scenery."

5. LOCAL COLOR IN NEW YORK:
EDWARD HARRIGAN

In the "Editor's Study" of *Harper's Monthly* (July, 1886),
William Dean Howells praised Harrigan's various immigrant
characters, whose touches of realism suggested to him "the
spring of a true American Comedy." He called him the American Goldoni, after the Venetian dramatist who presented the
working people of Venice in such interesting detail. Harrigan,
unfortunately, never fulfilled the prophecy, but he did contribute
good farces to American drama and paid shrewd attention to
realistic detail in his creation of the street life of New York. His
views on dramaturgy are stated in *Harper's Weeekly*, XXXII
(February 2, 1889), 97–99. Each of his little plays, he wrote,
was intended as a "series of photographs of life today in the
Empire City." To provide these he used authentic places and
character types, made realistic by close attention to speech,
dress, gestures, and so on. Although he felt that human nature
was "most virile and aggressive among those who know only
poverty and ignorance," Harrigan believed in portraying "the
fact that right-doing, kindness, and good nature are in the majority."

Harrigan (1845–1911) joined an acting company about
1867 and formed a very popular acting team for his farces, playing the male roles himself while Tony Hart impersonated

women. Starting with sketches, he wrote at least ten plays in the 1870's and 1880's concerning the Mulligans. The scene of these plays was Mulligan's alley in New York's Sixth Ward, emphasizing Dan Mulligan's house, of course, the Wee Drop Saloon run by Walfingham McSweeny, an Italian junk shop, a Chinese laundry-lodging combination, and a Negro social club called the Full Moon Union. The Boston *Herald* once aptly referred to Harrigan's plays as the scene of the "war of the races in cosmopolitan New York." Sometimes called the Dickens of America, Harrigan was interested in the conflicts and problems —emotional, social, economic, and political—of various national characters in New York. *Reilly and the Four Hundred* (1890) contrasts social levels; *The Mulligan Guard Nominee* (1880) is a broad satire on politics; *The Mulligan Guard* (1873) is a burlesque of the target-shooting expeditions of military organizations. The plots of the plays provided the excitement; the temperaments of the characters added the necessary violence; and the touches of realism in the people and the incidents gave the plays an immediate appeal with the audiences.

(a) *The Mulligan Guard Ball*, 1879

With more chaos than logic, the play evolves around the planned elopement of Dan Mulligan's son, Tommy, and Katy, the daughter of Lochmuller, the Butcher. Although both sets of parents are violently opposed to the marriage, the couple elope during the intermission of the Grand Ball, which explodes into a great fight when the ceiling collapses and the ball of the Skidmore Guards, a Negro group, being held in the Red Man's Hall above the Harp and Shamrock Ballroom, joins the Mulligans in a "Grand Crash." Finally, the Lochmullers and the Mulligans are reconciled to the new connection when Gus Lochmuller and six of his butchers armed with meat cleavers help Dan Mulligan get rid of the bill collectors for the Ball.

B. Suggestions of Realism
Augustin Daly, Steele MacKaye, William Gillette

The beginnings of realism in the drama can be described only in vague terms. If one accepts Howells' definition of realism as the "truthful representation" of life, one can find truthfulness in many aspects of a pre-Civil War play—the characters, the scene, the incidents, the background customs, or the ideas.

A new emphasis on realism, however, did come after the War bringing with it certain problems, particularly for the dramatist whose success depended upon an immediate appeal to a large, unsophisticated audience. Realists became suspect, however, for people felt that in their effort to be truthful about life, they had forsaken the bounds of good taste and were sometimes even immoral. A few years before World War I, one playwright moaned that "the conflict between romanticism and realism leaves the American playwright in a quandary almost cruel," ["Cruel Dilemma of the American Playwright," *Current Literature*, LI (September, 1911)].

Consequently, few dramatists writing in this period (1865–1914) tried to present truthful incidents of life or to avoid idealized and exaggerated characters. Suggestions of realism, however, may be found in many plays, and the following dramatists are singled out because realism can be considered a distinguishing characteristic of their plays.

1. AUGUSTIN DALY: *UNDER THE GASLIGHT*, 1867

The reputation of Augustin Daly (1838–1899) is divided between playwriting and the theater. His tremendous energies brought him success as a drama critic, theater manager, original playwright, adapter of foreign plays, producer and adapter of Shakespeare, and manager of a company of actors that successfully carried Shakespeare and other drama to Europe. As a drama critic and theater manager, he encouraged American playwrights, but he was not an innovator. He did rather little to promote realism, nor did he try to improve the audience's tastes or to encourage literary drama. His constant advice to dramatists was that they write according to the requirements of the theater managers. He himself wrote sensational melodramas, farces, and a few social comedies, most of which were adaptations. In several early plays—*Horizon, Under the Gaslight, A Legend of Norwood, Divorce, Pique*—he contributed in a meaningful manner to the two most important trends in late nineteenth-century American drama—the Rise of Realism, and the development of social comedy. But, overwhelmed by the demands of the commercial theater, he did not continue in the development of American drama, and both in his theory and practice became a negative influence.

(a) *Under the Gaslight,* 1867

(*Plot*) The play tells the story of Laura Courtland, the extremely virtuous heroine, whose engagement to the wealthy Ray Traffort is broken when the dastardly villain, Byke, claims her as his daughter. Socially snubbed, she leaves New York, protected by Snorkey and Peachblossom, a girl of the streets, but is constantly pursued by Byke and old Judas. For a while she lives with her cousin Pearl, who now plans to marry Ray; but the villains appear once more, and Laura, planning to leave on the morning train so as not to mar the happiness of Pearl and Ray, has herself locked in the baggage shed of the railroad station for the night. Faithful Snorkey follows to protect her, but is overcome by Byke and tied to the railroad tracks before the eyes of Laura, who grabs an axe from a handy bundle in the shed, breaks down the door, and rescues him in just the nick of time. For melodrama, the scene was hard to beat. In the last act, all ends happily for the good and the virtuous: Ray and Laura are to be married; Snorkey and Peachblossom seem to have matrimony in mind; and the goodness of Laura makes it possible for Byke to "emigrate."

(*Discussion*) Although the plot of this play is as fantastic as any of the nineteenth-century melodramas, there are suggestions of realism in the railroad scene; in the one-armed Civil War victim, Snorkey, whose condition is a social comment; in the satirical picture of the snobbish high society; and in the general authenticity of the theater sets.

2. STEELE MACKAYE: *HAZEL KIRKE,* 1880

A significant number of late nineteenth-century playwrights were men of the theater: actors, managers, or producers, as well as playwrights—men like Daly, Boucicault, Belasco, Herne, and William Gillette. Steele MacKaye (1842–1894) was an actor and a teacher of actors, a theater manager and an inventor—best known for his improvements in stage design and equipment, such as the elevator stage, and for his work as organizer and director of the Spectatorium, a part of the Chicago World's Fair of 1893 before it was cancelled. A dreamer of some genius to whom theater was a temple of art and culture, he was interested in increasing personal comfort and in cultivating the most favorable aesthetic conditions for both actors and audiences.

Writing plays was clearly a secondary part of MacKaye's career, but his plays have some significance in the development of American realism. Although most of his work was romantic melodrama, three of MacKaye's plays boast a distinctive realism in characterization. *Won at Last* (1877) is a tender and romantic farce-comedy with a believable hero and a well-drawn heroine, Grace Fleming, who discovers on her wedding day that her husband is completely cynical about love and has married her simply because she is "well bred, cultivated, and good; she will make me at least a tolerable companion and save me the ridicule and disgrace of a fashionable wife's flirtations." Although this comedic situation degenerates into melodrama in the last act, the play was a firm step toward both realism of character and social comedy. Another play suggestive of realism is *Paul Kauver*, first performed as *Anarchy* in 1887, in which MacKaye showed his indignation over what he considered the very unfair trial of the so-called anarchists in connection with the Chicago Haymarket Riot of 1886. The immediacy of the theme and the obvious sincerity of the author produced a realistic tone.

(a) *Hazel Kirke*, (1880)

(*Plot*) When, many years back, Aaron Rodney loaned him money that saved his mill, Dunstan Kirke promised him his daughter, Hazel, for his wife. Now Dunstan discovers that Hazel has fallen in love with Arthur Carringford (Lord Travers), and he turns her out of his home with a curse: "May my eyes never more behold thee." Supposedly married, but tricked by Arthur's valet with a Scottish ceremony on the English side of the border, Arthur and Hazel meet further difficulty when Arthur's proud mother insists that he is to marry another girl. Shocked and contrite, Hazel returns home and promises to be Rodney's wife if he will ask Dunstan to accept and forgive her, but Dunstan refuses. Seconds later, a blind and agonizing Dunstan hears that Hazel is drowning in the millrace. She is, of course, saved by Arthur, who promises her marriage, and is forgiven by Dunstan: "Hazel, Hazel, coom to my heart!"

(*Discussion*) The success of MacKaye's best-known play, *Hazel Kirk,* at the Madison Square Theatre in New York was so great that during the 1882–1883 season there were fourteen companies touring the play. Basically, it is a sentimental melodrama; speeches are sometimes exaggerated and emotions are frequently made melodramatically vivid. But casting a refreshing light over all of this, is a quality of humor and a tendency toward naturalness in the characters and incidents of the play. Dunstan is a stubborn man, willfully wrong in his first actions, but his honor and his passion, are, in Hazel's character, the very qualities which determine her ways and precipitate the conflict.

3. WILLIAM GILLETTE: *SECRET SERVICE*, 1895

Whereas MacKaye was a playwright whose main concern was with stage settings, William Gillette (1855–1937) was a playwright whose chief interest was in realistic acting: "the artistic representation of reality." As an actor, William Gillette's most effective role was that of the calm, clear-headed person who works quietly, quickly, and effectively in very trying circumstances; and almost all of the plays that he wrote, whether farce or melodrama, contained such a character. Of his twenty full-length plays Gillette acted in nine, and was particularly successful as Thomas Beene in *Held by the Enemy* (1886); Captain Thorne in *Secret Service*; and Sherlock Holmes in Gillette's successful dramatization of that fictional character's exploits. He acted until shortly before his death, but his best work was done around the turn of the century. As an actor, he was the major force for realism in his plays, which are now remembered more for his acting than for particular merit.

(a) *Secret Service*, 1895

(*Plot*) Edith Varney, daughter of General Varney of the Confederate Army, loves Captain Thorne and tries to keep him in Richmond by persuading President Jefferson Davis to appoint him to duty in the Telegraph office. Meanwhile, Captain Arrelsford of the Confederate Secret Service, suspecting Thorne of being a Northern spy, one of two brothers operating in Richmond, brings the brother they have in prison to the Varney house. In an exciting scene, the brothers meet; the prisoner whispers a message, grabs Thorne's gun, and shoots himself as Thorne turns him over to Arrelsford. Later Thorne appears at the telegraph office and starts to send the message. Amidst a great deal of action and frustration, Edith shows Thorne's commission from President Davis which she says is only to save Thorne's life—not for "anything else." Sentimental love wins when Thorne revokes his message and is arrested. Because he did not send the message, however, Thorne's death warrant is set aside, and with Edith's love he is marched away to prison.

(*Discussion*) Encouraged by the success of *Held by the Enemy* (1886), a Civil War play plotted around the love of two men for the same woman and the heroism of a Southern spy, Gillette wrote another play on the Civil War, *Secret Service*. It is noteworthy that the play was not a popular success until Gillette started acting the part of Lewis Dumont (Captain Thorne) in 1896. There is realism in the economy of language in the play, and, as usual with Gillette's work, in its action. Interestingly enough, the four acts take place at eight, nine, ten, and eleven o'clock on a particular evening. None of the characters, however, is particularly realistic.

C. William Dean Howells: The Reticent Rebel

Called the Father of American Realism, W. D. Howells (1837–1920) is usually considered a critic and a writer of fiction illustrative of the "commonplace" realism which he championed. He was also, however, a serious dramatist who wrote thirty-six plays, proposed a theory of a realistic drama, and contributed significantly to both the Rise of Realism in the drama and the development of social comedy. Opposed to sentimentality in both fiction and drama, he was a definite rebel among his literary and theatrical contemporaries. His reticence is suggested by his strong concern for taste and morals in his own writing. Although he could approve the more realistic plays of Ibsen and Herne, he could not write as these dramatists did. He was, however, a realist, reticent or not, and his plays are an excellent illustration of the Rise of Realism in the drama.

1. THEORY OF REALISTIC DRAMA

Howells' theory of drama was simply a logical extention of his theory of fiction (see *Criticism and Fiction*, 1891) with the added qualifications made necessary by the limitations of the drama. He saw the drama as "distinctly a literary form" whose purpose was to illustrate life in terms of morality and truthfulness. The dramatist should avoid verse drama, soliloquies, asides, and the *deus ex machina* which were not a part of life. By the turn of the century, his comments on truthfulness in drama matured from truthfulness of characters and action to a fundamental truthfulness of idea. From these criteria he criticized American drama.

2. REALISM IN SCENES, CHARACTERS, AND INCIDENTS

Realistic detail was basic to Howells, and his plays are filled with references to contemporary events and real persons—the invention of the phonograph, the cholera epidemic in New York in 1893, comments on Bill Nye and Josh Billings. Actors' speeches were loaded with commonplace phrases and the overused expressions of average conversation. Plays were built upon his own experiences and those of his friends. (Twelve of Howells' plays employ the same major characters: Mr. and Mrs. Willis Campbell are modelled on Mr. and Mrs. Samuel L. Clemens; Mr. and Mrs. Edward Roberts are Mr. and Mrs. W. D. Howells.) Equally realistic and more significant are the social events or situations around which Howells' plays are built. There were formal dinners or afternoon teas—events where the social background had an important effect on the action and meaning of the play. The activity was of real and ordinary life, where people stayed in hotels, bought flowers, wrote letters of introduction, or bemoaned the Christmas rush.

3. REALISM IN IDEA

Accompanying Howells' concern for the more or less superficial characteristics of realism was his demand for truthfulness and moral value in the drama. In his plays he tried to present problems of real life in which truthfulness was a central issue. *A True Hero: Melodrama,* for example, suggests a way in which man may equate truth and reality in life. *The Unexpected Guests* describes the failure of the socially convenient lie and the triumph of truth. Writing mainly farces, Howells faced difficulties in his objectives, but he was able to involve his characters in his one-act plays in the more meaningful of life's situations by using the same characters in twelve plays and thereby developing them with some completeness. In a few of his longer plays, he maintained his realism of ideas by dramatizing his own novels—*A Foregone Conclusion* and *The Rise of Silas Lapham*.

4. THE REALISTIC FARCE: *THE GARROTERS*

(*Plot*) The scene is the Roberts' living room, a few moments before a dinner party on a cold, stormy night. Having been sent out on an errand, Mr. Edward Roberts enters, exhausted, disheveled, and frightened. A thief had snatched his watch as he crossed Boston Common, and he was obliged to pull him to the ground and recover his property. Mrs. Roberts is at first astounded, but as the guests arrive, she brags about her husband's exploits. Then in the doorway appears poor old Mr. Bemis, Senior—exhausted, disheveled, a woeful creature, and not a little angry. He, too, has been garroted on the Boston Common, and his watch has been stolen. The situation is now clear to Roberts—who has gone to his room and found his own watch on the dresser—and to Willis Campbell, who tries to get him to make a joke of the experience. As Roberts faces Bemis, however, his weak humor deserts him, and he flounders helplessly until Dr. Lawton, another guest, recognizes Campbell's trick, having already disclosed to the other guests that Roberts is the garroter—a badly mistaken and frightened one, at that. And even old Bemis agrees to forgive. Given an intelligent and sophisticated society, the situation is not complicated. Roberts quickly promises to mend the watch chain that he broke, and—dinner is served!

(*Discussion*) When Howells started writing plays, theater managers wanted full-length plays with exciting, violent, and passionate action. Howells, on the other hand, was interested in dramatizing the common, everyday actions of the average man. It was an extremely difficult task, and Howells was not completely successful. His attempt, however, was significant, and his plays, filled with the realism of everyday life, combined some quiet drama with a literary quality that could not be matched by his contemporaries.

The Garroters was one of Howells' more successful one-act plays. As a farce, it has the clever intriguer, the good man who is fooled, the victim, and the hysterical and not-so-hysterical observers. One of his Roberts-Campbell plays, it has the characters familiar to his audiences; and, typical of Howells' realistic farce, the plot was based on an actual event of which Howells had become aware.

D. James A. Herne: An Epoch Marking Realism

Standing quite alone in the history of late nineteenth-century American drama is James A. Herne (1839–1901). An actor-manager-playwright, he had the intelligence and the imagination to rise above the limitations which seemed to control managers and to blind actors. Unlike most of his playwriting contemporaries who were influenced mainly by the people of the theater, he felt the twin forces which challenged all sensitive life of the late nineteenth century—science and democracy. The trend toward realism in literature interested him; the major realistic writers of the period influenced him; and he attempted to combine and focus a sensitivity for good literary drama and a sound knowledge of the theater. Although his success was only relative, his significance lies mainly in (1) his development of realistic themes and characters in his plays, particularly *Margaret Fleming*, (2) his interest in a literary drama, and (3) his creation of a realistic creed for the drama, "Art for Truth's Sake in the Drama."

1. A THEORY OF REALISTIC DRAMA

Unlike other theater realists who emphasized authenticity in scene construction or acting, Herne attempted to create a drama of ideas in the same realistic vein that had altered the development of fiction in America. Although the observation is relative, no contemporary dramatist in America came nearer to Ibsen's playwriting than Herne. When, in February, 1897, the *Arena* carried James A. Herne's "Art for Truth's Sake in the Drama" (XVII, 361–370), Herne was merely trying to do for the drama what had already been done for fiction.

"Art for Truth's Sake," wrote Herne, "emphasizes humanity." As a serious mode of expression, according to him, it was to perpetuate everyday life, develop the commonplace aspects of life, dignify labor, and abhore injustice. The drama, first of all, must "express some *large* truth" which "is not always beautiful, but in art for truth's sake it is indispensable." Like Howells Herne also believed that the drama has a "higher purpose" than to amuse: "Its mission is to interest and to instruct." Although these ideas sound harmless enough, and Herne seems a weak imitation of Ibsen, his most realistic play, *Margaret Fleming*, was as unacceptable to audiences as Ibsen's *Ghosts*. With this play and his essay on truth, however, Herne suggests the real beginning of modern American drama.

2. EARLY PLAYS OF JAMES A. HERNE

Herne's early plays are relevant to a discussion of his realism only in the contrast that they make with his later works. Herne started his acting career in 1854, toured with Helen Western's company, and became a stage manager in San Francisco, where he wrote plays with David Belasco—a dramatization of a story by Gaboriau in *Within an Inch of His Life* (1879), a sentimental and spectacular melodrama about a man who wishes to end an affair with a countess preparatory to his marriage; and *Hearts of Oak* (1879), among others. Herne's first original play, *The Minute Men of 1774–75* (1886), had a conventional melodramatic plot with an historical background, but it was not successful on the stage, although it had some New England local color and a rather forceful heroine.

3. *MARGARET FLEMING*, 1890

The play opens in the private office of Philip Fleming, an easygoing fellow whose motto is "Live and let live." Then Dr. Larkin appears. Angrily stating that he has just delivered a child to Lena Schmidt and that Philip is the father, he demands that Philip visit Lena. Unwillingly, Philip agrees and calls home to explain his absence to his wife, who is having trouble with their child's nursemaid, Maria, whose unmarried sister has just had a baby and is now near death. The next day, after Dr. Larkin has explained that Margaret has glaucoma and must not become excited, Margaret complies with Maria's plea to visit her sister; but when she arrives, the girl, Lena, is dead and Maria bitterly tells Margaret that Philip is the father of Lena's child. In a strong scene, Margaret sends a note to Philip: "I am waiting for you here. That *girl* is *dead*." Then she takes the baby, and "scarcely conscious of what she is doing, suddenly with an impatient, swift movement she unbuttons her dress to give nourishment to the child." A week later at the Fleming home, Margaret, now blind, but with Lena's child as well as her own, awaits news of Philip, who has run away. When he appears, ashamed and contrite, Margaret forgives him, although "the wife-heart has gone out of me." Pleased, Philip tells of his hope to win her back again; and Margaret replies: "I don't know. That would be a wonderful thing. . . . And we must get to work." Inspired, Philip goes to see his children, and a "serene joy illuminates her [Margaret's] face" as the curtain falls.

4. THE RECEPTION OF *MARGARET FLEMING*

After a brief tryout in Lynn, Massachussetts, in 1890, and the subsequent refusal of theater managers to produce his play, Herne was forced to rent Chickering Hall in Boston, where, before Howells, Hamlin Garland, and other realists, the play was presented on May 4, 1891, and ran for three weeks. In December, it was taken to New York but without success; after that, it was seldom produced. Its reception clearly suggests the romantic immaturity of the average theater audiences of that time and supports the consensus of opinion that the theater simply was not ready for a play of that kind.

Some people, however, those interested in more realistic drama, were enthusiastic in their approval. Hamlin Garland's review of the Boston performance ["Mr. and Mrs. Herne," *Arena* (IV, October, 1891), 543–560] applauded the "utter simplicity and absolute truth to life" that made this play superior to others on the American stage "in purpose, in execution, in power." The New York critics, however, were less understanding. The reviewer for the *Dramatic Mirror,* December 12, 1891, found no pleasure in *Margaret Fleming*, only "the details of unpleasant and unhealthy forms of unruly life." Edward A. Dithmar in the New York *Times*, December 10, 1891, noted the realism in the play, which he compared with the news in the morning paper, but he did not see the artistic creation. His view has some validity in ways he did not comprehend, but his general approach relegated the play to the obscurity which other critics suggested.

5. REALISM IN *MARGARET FLEMING*

Reminiscent of Howells' work, Herne's play calls attention to the small details which show realism in character and incident: the speech, instructions to the cook, and—though shocking to the audience—Margaret's gesture of nursing the baby. From the beginning, Philip is an easygoing fellow, insensitive and materialistic. Herne compares him cleverly with Joe Fletcher, a secondary character who turns out to be Maria's husband and provides some comic relief. Joe is the bad example of what liquor and immorality can bring a man to—they are very much alike, but Philip has been luckier. Margaret is a sensitive and emotional, yet protected, person; but when she does face the ugly world, she has all of the strength and power that her faith in the goodness of man has made possible. Sensitive to rights and wrongs, her moral fiber and her forceful will give her a control over her destiny that Philip lacks. At the end of the play, she has contentment in the knowledge that she has done what was right, and this feeling can sustain her.

The theme of the play shows Herne's interest in social philosophy, particularly social determinism. Philip's social standing saves him from suffering the consequences of being the kind of man he is. It is different with Lena, as Dr. Larkin explains: "The *girl's* not to blame. . . . Under present social conditions, she'd probably have gone wrong anyhow." The use of a rose as a symbol of social growth is well integrated into this theme. Margaret's lullaby tells of blossoms that must go out into the world and weep. She had wanted a particular rose to bloom on her baby's birthday, but it did not and Philip later plucked it. She loves flowers and in Act IV appears with an armful of roses. The doctor, however, confesses that his roses are full of bugs, and she advises him to spray them: "Don't you know that the time to prevent trouble is to look ahead? From potatoes to roses, spray before anything happens—*then* nothing *will* happen." But who can do the spraying? Only those who rise above their fates!

6. REALISM AND *THE REVEREND GRIFFITH DAVENPORT*, 1899

Based on a novel by Helen H. Gardener, entitled *An Unofficial Patriot*, the play tells the story of a man who is morally opposed to slavery, although he has slaves of his own. When the Civil War begins, one of his sons fights for the North, the other for the South. He himself is misunderstood by the slaves he has freed, and his anti-slavery theories arouse bitterness among his neighbors. Forced to leave his home, he goes to Washington and, at Lincoln's request, prepares a map of Virginia and leads Union troops to his home, where he is captured by his own son. As the play ends, he is taken away to prison. In his review of the play, John Corbin ["Drama," *Harper's Weekly,* XLIII (February 11, 1899), 139] called it an essay in stage realism— "quiet, humorous, sincere, deeply intelligent, and artistic."

II. THE BEGINNINGS OF THE SOCIAL DRAMA: COMMENT, COMEDY, AND MELODRAMA

Hand in hand with the Rise of Realism in American drama was the continued development of a drama built around various aspects of society. American plays had mirrored society— albeit with some distortion—since Revolutionary times; but by the turn of the century, there were melodramas dealing with serious subjects as well as strong beginnings for a social comedy. The American drama critic, John Corbin, noted these beginnings in "The Dawn of American Drama," [*Atlantic Monthly,* XCIX (May, 1907), 632–44]. Difficulties existed, of course. In the first place, Americans hardly had a sufficiently established society to make a social drama possible. Corbin pointed out the refusal of theater managers to produce a play by Shaw as an illustration of their lack of artistic judgments. Public taste continued to demand farce and melodrama.

It is also questionable whether any of the playwrights during this period were capable of writing true social comedies. Howells could write the witty dialogue and describe the society, but he lacked the dramatic instinct. Daly was interested in supplying a commodity; Gillette wanted to act; Steele MacKaye was concerned with the development of the theater; Belasco and Boucicault enjoyed spectacles; Bronson Howard had some good plots but lacked literary skill and could not seem to avoid melodrama; Clyde Fitch came closest. Social comedy, on the other hand, required an interested theater management, a sophisticated audience atmosphere, and an imaginative playwright's talents. Hence, America enjoyed mainly melodrama with comment and comedy.

In an essay entitled "The Development of American Drama" [*Harper's*, XLII (December, 1920), 75–86], William Archer, the English critic, wrote: "A favorite generalization with regard to the American stage is that it excells in 'shirtsleeve drama' and is weak in the drama of society." It is a combination of the "shirtsleeve" or realistic drama with an awareness of society and its problems which distinguishes the drama of this period. Mainly in melodrama and more or less seriously, the playwright began to treat the social, economic, political, and religious issues of the day. It was an active period—from the Civil War to World War I—and a period of growing social problems that frequently appeared in one form or another on the American stage.

A. Toward a Social Comedy

Social comedy is a witty portrayal of fahionable life, where the complex manners or moral actions of the characters become a major concern of the dramatists, who must create motivated actions and believable characters with a facile pen and a detached attitude. The plays written during the period under consideration unfortunately do not fulfill completely these requirements, but the faults and foibles of society were beginning to attract dramatists. John Geoffrey Hartman, in *The Development of American Social Comedy from 1787–1936* (1939), called the years between the Civil War and 1900 the Transition Period, placing it between the Period of Caricature, 1787–1860, and the later Establishment of Social Comedy by Clyde Fitch. With due consideration for Fitch's frequent melodramatic tendencies, however, one would accept his plays and those of Langdon Mitchell only as the ones most nearly approaching social comedy in America before the social problems plays of Rachel Crothers and Charles Rann Kennedy. Showing some interest in social comedy themes or techniques before Clyde Fitch were Augustin Daly, Bronson Howard, and W. D. Howells.

1. AUGUSTIN DALY AND SOCIAL COMEDY

Two plays by Daly which indicate his concern for social comedy are *Divorce* (1871) and *Pique* (1875). Both were popular successes, and both were adapted, at least in part, from English novels. The basic situations in both plays suggest social comedy—marriage problems, divorce—but in each instance, Daly failed to be detached and manipulated his characters and action into melodrama. In *Divorce*, his satire on the hypocrisy of divorce lawyers provides an interesting side issue.

(a) *Divorce*, 1871

Encouraged by her ambitious mother, Louise Ten Eyck marries the old but wealthy Dewitt, while her sister Fanny accepts Alfred Adrianse, a childhood beau who has just inherited his father's fortune. Grace, a cousin of the Ten Eyck sisters, is in love with Harry, a young minister; but being poor, they must postpone marriage. Three years later, Louise and Dewitt are about to separate, and Alfred is jealous of Fanny's attentions to a Captain Lynde. The plot becomes farcical as the lawyers try to create good cases for divorce and fail when the two couples forget and forgive. Even Grace and Harry will become part of that sentimental group of poor but happily married people.

(b) *Pique*, 1875

Lovely Mabel Renfrew, part of a very fashionable society and much sought after by men, is refused by the man she loves, Raymond, because she has no money. To make the insult more stinging, the cad then addresses his attentions to Mabel's rather young and widowed stepmother. But this comedy situation is not fulfilled. Mabel reacts impulsively and with pique: she hastily accepts the marriage offer of Arthur Standish, an honorable and likable fellow whom she had once refused. Unable to adjust to life with Arthur, however, she angrily tells him that she married him only from hurt pride and that she still loves Raymond. Then the play becomes melodramatic. Arthur leaves; their child is kidnapped; with the help of her father-in-law Mabel foils the villains; she and Arthur are reunited; and Raymond marries her stepmother.

2. BRONSON HOWARD: "THE DEAN OF AMERICAN DRAMA"

A serious dramatist, who evolved his own principles of dramaturgy ("The Laws of Dramatic Construction") and was one of the most successful of American playwrights during this period, Bronson Howard (1842–1908) earned the title of "Dean of American Drama" by making a professional career out of playwriting. Although he was not interested in drama as literature, he was concerned with the playwriting profession. He founded the American Dramatists Club in 1891 and worked to extend legal protection to the dramatist's art. His established success in both England and America was along the lines frequently suggested by Augustin Daly: he was a fine craftsman, who collaborated with the theater people and used well his expert knowledge of the stage and the actor's art. Although he was a member of the "Syndicate School"—dramatists for the Theater Syndicate that controlled most theaters of this time—he had greater vision than his commercial-minded contemporaries. He saw, for example, that the direction of the drama was toward social comedy and that in America the business man was becoming increasingly important. He also emphasized the international aspect of life and by so doing attempted to dramatize themes with which W. D. Howells and Henry James had had great success in fiction. Original in much of his work and interested in a theory of drama, Howard was limited by many conventions and requirements of the theater, but he did point the way for others who, with greater talent and more interest in literary drama, were to follow him.

Both Brander Matthews and A. H. Quinn emphasize the point that Howard worked in a transition period. Before him, a staple of the American stage had been foreign plays; yet during his lifetime, Howard was able to give the American dramatist greater importance in the theater. Although he adapted a few of his plays and retained in his work many of the conventions and devices that had made foreign drama popular to America, he forced managers to see the value of American playwrights, and he paved a more secure way for the younger dramatists who would follow him. He accomplished much of this through personal force and written precept. His creative work, on the other hand, may be divided into three general categories: the plays that deal with some aspect of society, those that emphasize American business, and his single war play, *Shenandoah.*

(a) A Theory of Drama

Bronson Howard's "Laws of Dramatic Construction" as he described them in *The Autobiography of a Play* present his more important ideas on the drama. Mainly, he demanded a well-constructed or "satisfactory" play—which meant that the play must be "satisfactory" to the audience. For example, audiences in England and America would not accept, Howard felt, the death of a heroine in a play; they demanded the happy ending. Recognizing this, Howard changed the ending of *The Banker's Daughter* (1878). Obeying his laws of dramatic construction, Howard stated, was "merely the art of using your common sense in the study of your own and other people's emotions." The playwright, he noted, should deal "so far as possible, with subjects of universal interest." He should put upon the stage the best work he can do, acknowledging the advice and assistance of others; and he should always keep in mind the sympathies of his audience, as well as the motives and actions of his characters in a play.

(b) The Social Plays of Bronson Howard

Howard's early farces were distinctive only for their better-than-average dialogue and some ingenuity in plot, but they suggest his interest in contemporary society. *Saratoga* (1870) is a good example. Using a favorite American resort as its scene, it presents the farcical involvement of Bob Sackett with four women, while fashionable society provided a good background for the situations. The fact that *Saratoga* was adapted by Frank Marshall for the English stage under the title *Brighton* (1874) suggests a current popularity more than a universal appeal, however. *Diamonds* (1872), called a "comedy of contemporaneous manners" by Brander Matthews, American writer and critic, follows society down state to New York City and Staten Island. *Hurricanes* (1878) is the same type of play.

As American fortunes began to increase, an awareness of European culture became fashionable. Consequently, the international comedy of manners became a strong social theme for writers, and Howard plumbed its possibilities in several plays. *Met by Chance* (1887) uses an international contrast as a basis for its plot. Howard's last play, *Kate* (1906), dramatizes the story of a rich American girl who becomes engaged to an English earl. *One of Our Girls* (1885) contrasts Julie—living in France and engaged to a French count to satisfy her interest in a title and his concern for her dowry—with her rich cousin from America, Kate. The plot is melodramatic, but an effective contrast is made between the freedom in choosing a mate which Kate enjoys and the traditional restrictions which bind Julie.

(c) The Business Plays of Bronson Howard

Bronson Howard emphasized the American businessman in drama at a time when the businessman in America was making giant strides. His conscious use of a social-economic movement and his employment of fashionable society as a background are significant contributions to American drama of this period.

(i) Young Mrs. Winthrop, 1882

Young Mrs. Winthrop is praised by Odell (quoting "some critics," *Annals of the New York Stage,* XII, 19) as "the great American drama so long and so ardently awaited." "This beautiful piece," Odell wrote (p. 18), "was in accomplishment and solid effect one of the finest things yet written for the American stage." In this play, Howard dramatized that increasing complexity of the business and social worlds which can prevent a man and a woman from finding happiness together in their home. Left alone by a husband immersed in business, Mrs. Winthrop finds some relief in the social whirl. After a brief separation, husband and wife are reunited through Howard's preachments.

(ii) The Henrietta, 1887

A very successful play satirizing life on the Stock Exchange, *The Henrietta* was concerned with the financial rivalry of Nicholas Vanalstyne, Sr., known as "the Napoleon of Wall Street" and his son Nicholas, Jr. Both are unscrupulous men to whom business is "health, religion, friendship, love—everything." Taking its name from the Henrietta Railroad, which was an issue of control, the play was hailed by John Corbin as the earliest of a new kind of play—the business play.

(iii) Aristocracy, 1892

Aristocracy presents the American businessman in the international situation. Jefferson Stockton is a California capitalist, a millionaire who knows that new millionaires are not good society. When his daughter, Virginia, is refused by Stuyvesant Laurence, the son of an old and proud New York family, he realizes immediately that the quickest way to enter New York society is via London society. The rest of the play caricatures society in London before the Stocktons return to New York and, presumably, happiness.

(d) War Play: *Shenandoah*, 1888

(*Plot*) After a ball in a Charleston home, some of the guests wait to see if Fort Sumter will be shelled. Among those waiting are Kerchival West and Robert Ellingham, lieutenants in the U.S. Army, who discover that they are in love with each other's sisters—Madeline West and Gertrude Ellingham. But Kerchival and Madeline are from the North, and the Ellinghams are from the South. As the shells burst over the Fort, they have to part to fight on opposing sides, but their love becomes the major plot complication.

(*Discussion*) Whatever Howard's reason for writing *Shenandoah*—perception of the tastes of the time or the imitation of Gillette's successful *Held by the Enemy*—the play is a thoroughly romantic tale in which the author attempts some realism in his characters and in his picture of society. Against the background of war and employing the circumstances of war to advance his plot, Howard constructed an entertaining and sentimental farce-melodrama.

3. W. D. HOWELLS AND THE COMEDY OF PROPER SOCIETY

Howells called most of his one-act plays farces, but one cannot apply this term generally without serious reservations: several of these plays revealed characteristics of social comedy. In addition to his one-act plays, Howells quite early wrote two long comedies: *Out of the Question* (1877), concerned with a problem of propriety—What constitutes a gentlemen?; and *A Counterfeit Presentment* (1877), one of Howells' more successful stage plays. Presenting some charming and witty comments on society, the latter play tells of a delicate heroine, who is brought to a New England resort hotel by her parents to recover from an abortive romance, only to meet a man whose appearance is identical to the man who she thinks jilted her.

It is mainly in his one-act plays, however, that Howells

presents the society that he knows best—Boston's Back Bay aristocracy. His comments clearly reveal his acute powers of observation, as well as the high degree of critical insight required of the social-comedy dramatist. The formal dinner was Howells' favorite scene, and his favorite people, the Robertses and the Campbells whom he featured in a dozen plays which explore various social emergencies.

(a) The Roberts-Campbell Plays of W. D. Howells

The first of the Roberts-Campbell plays appeared in 1883, and during the next ten years, Howells wrote ten more plays with these characters, returning to them only once after that period in a most inadequate play called *The Smoking Car* (1900). Although there is a disparity in the dramatic value of these plays, a good number of the characters are believable and human. Amy Campbell is usually a shrewd little woman, while Mrs. Roberts is as scatterbrained as she is kind and lovable. Dr. Lawton is a delightful talker, and Willis Campbell can be a charmer as well as a schemer. Enacted within an atmosphere of propriety, the Roberts-Campbell plays generally show a mature, somewhat sophisticated, convention-bound society, where tradition has replaced thought, and action and words have become nearly equal in importance.

What may be called a twelve-act play starts when Mrs. Roberts returns to her home in Boston in *The Sleeping Car* (1883) with her baby and her Aunt Mary, whom she has just visited in Albany. It is Christmas time and doubly meaningful this year because Mrs. Roberts' brother, Willis Campbell, is returning to Boston from California, where he has lived for a number of years. Two Christmases later, in spite of an elevator mishap (*The Elevator*), the Robertses give a formal dinner, and the audience meets their friends—the Millers, the Curwins, old Mr. Bemis, his son Alfred, and Dr. Lawton's daughter, Lou. Alfred and Lou will be married before the next Christmas dinner at which poor old Mr. Bemis will be mistakenly garroted by Mr. Roberts in *The Garroters*. The next three plays follow the activities of Willis: first, as he becomes engaged to the young widow, Amy Somers, who has by *Five O'Clock Tea* waited the proper period of time since the death of her husband; then, as he flirts with Amy's ire and adoration in *The Mousetrap*; and finally, as he becomes involved in the problems of being a husband in *A Likely Story*. Other plays show Willis as a farce intriguer, taunting Mr. Roberts, who must meet a new cook whom Mrs. Roberts had hired in *The Albany Depot*, and helping Roberts find his dress suit in *Evening Dress*. Much better plays for social comedy are *A Letter of Introduction* in which Roberts' absentmindedness is exploited, and *The Unexpected Guests* in which Amy Campbell faces that social emergency. *The Smoking Car* is a weak farce; but *A Masterpiece of Diplomacy*, in which the Robertses face the problem of having called two doctors of different medical persuasions for a very simple illness, shows more of the Howells' wit and charm.

(b) Social Comedy Themes and Satire in Howells' Plays

One comedy theme which seems to have fascinated Howells was the ever-present struggle between man and woman—a frequent theme in his Roberts-Campbell plays. Numerous times, however, Howells treats this conflict in a plot involving an engagement, which is either being made for the first time or being patched up after some confusion. No fewer than seven plays— *The Register, An Indian Giver, A Previous Engagement, Her Opinion of His Story, The Parlor Car, Parting Friends, Self-Sacrifice*—have similar plots on this theme.

One of Howells' major strengths in the drama was his ability to depict brilliant conversation—far more witty and clever than anything being written in American drama of this time. Enhancing his wit was his satire. With a certain mischievousness, he pointed out the ridiculous attitudes and foibles of society and the socially acceptable person. A good illustration of this characteristic is *A Letter of Introduction* in which he ridicules Englishmen, New Yorkers, critics, Boston snobbery, the cultivated family of Boston, American artists, American language, and American culture. In his later plays—*The Night Before Christmas* and *The Impossible*—Howells was more serious, less flippant, and more pessimistic in his satire.

4. CLYDE FITCH AND THE SOCIAL WORLD

The traditional criticism of Clyde Fitch (1865–1909) describes him as a skillful man of the theater and a master of stage effects, who brought with him the practiced eye of the observer of society and a singular talent for writing realistic dialogue. Although he lacked genius, he was immensely clever at capturing the idiosyncrasies of people and society—particularly that of New York. To satisfy the actors and theater managers for whom he wrote, he used some of the devices of melodrama that had proved successful, but he otherwise became absorbed in detailed observations of social life which, in his most successful plays, magnified a particular social or personal foible into a social comedy with effective scenes. When he carried his enthusiasms for this truthful detail to excess, however, the result was either a caricature or an over-abundance of what was termed "Fitchian detail."

(a) Popular, Prolific, and Prosperous

A colorful figure who sported a twirlable black mustache, Fitch was a conscientious and hard-working playwright. Asked to write a play for Richard Mansfield, the actor, he produced *Beau Brummell* (1890) and during the next nineteen years, wrote thirty-three original plays and made twenty-two dramatizations of novels or adaptations of foreign works. Writing easily and without haste, he was able to work on as many as five plays at the same time. His popularity is indicated by the 1901 theater season in which four of his plays were produced in different New York theaters at the same time. In his history of the American theater, Glenn Hughes suggests that Fitch was the first dramatist to make a million dollars. John Corbin, "The Dawn of American Drama," considered him the only member of the "Syndicate School" whose power was still on the ascendant in 1907. In England, several of Fitch's plays met considerable success, particularly *The Truth* which—acted in several European countries—gave him an international reputation.

(b) Fitch's Theory of the Drama

In *The Clyde Fitch I Knew* (1909), Archie Bell quotes the information which Fitch usually gave to aspiring playwrights: "Write the play as it seems to you. Brevity is important. Things must move fast. Study the works of others, but don't imitate. Don't follow rules, but there are guiding principles. Revise your work thoroughly. Study doubtful situations. Prune out superfluous words. Try to be truthful." Fitch wanted to reflect "absolutely and truthfully the life and environment about us; every class, every land, every emotion, every motive, every occupation, every business, every idleness!" But his concern for truth was without the larger perspective of life, and his lack of meaningful ideas is noticeable. His plays are melodramatic, but written with a sensitivity for life which made critics describe Fitch as a man of whom better work could be expected.

(c) Social Plays: On Married Life

Of Fitch's fifty-five plays, only six or seven are worth serious discussion as social drama, treating the problems of married life, individual faults and foibles, and social climbers. Fitch's first full-length study of society, *A Modern Match* (1892), tells the story of a flippant and selfish wife, who refuses to assume the responsibility of marriage, and therefore must suffer the consequences of the unfaithful wife. There is, however, little of Fitch's later talent here among his exaggerated characters, artificial stage directions, and melodramatic plot.

Her Great Match (1905), which shows Fitch's understanding of European as well as American manners, involves an international contrast between an American girl and the Crown Prince Adolph of Eastphalia. *A Happy Marriage* (1909), although better than the previously mentioned plays, indicated that Fitch was never quite capable of writing a good comedy on the theme of marriage. The dinner scene at the beginning is excellent Fitch, but the play dissolves into an uninspired discussion of marriage.

(d) Social Plays: Social Climbers

In *The Social Swim* (1893), an adaptation of Sardou's *La Maison Neuve*, Fitch describes two people who embark on an extravagant social life and become frivolous, immoral, and bankrupt. Beneath a melodramatic plot, *The Climbers* (1901) satirizes aspects of the New York social life and, in particular, the "climber." Although considered shocking by some New York managers, the opening scene of the play is one of its best from the point of view of social drama as it ridicules the hypocrisy and unfeeling materialism of the members of the Hunter family after the funeral of Mr. Hunter. This scene also prepared the way for the play's theme: "Oh, my dear, that's just it! The watchword of our age is self! We are all for ourselves; the twentieth century is to a glorification of selfishness, the Era of Egotism."

(e) Social Vices: Individual and Collective

Fitch never became a social dramatist of the first order because he remained "a man of the commercial theater." In his best plays, however—*The Girl with the Green Eyes, The Truth,* and *The City*—he emphasized social vices and concerned himself with character development, the realistic details of conventional society, and a more socially significant conflict and struggle.

(i) The Girl with the Green Eyes, 1902

Jinny Tillman is a jealous, nervous person who shows her weakness from the day she marries Jack Austin. The plot is complicated by the fact that Jinny's brother, Geoffrey, had secretly married a social inferior, Maggie, when he was in college but is now in love with Ruth Chester. Jack's attempt to help Geof inflames Jinny with the fire of jealousy; and circumstantial evidence further clouds the truth, as a dense and rather unfeeling Jack causes Jinny to attempt suicide. She is saved by the dramatist's manipulation of time and Jack's inconsistent character, and all ends happily.

The exposition for this play employs the traditional servant scene, and the jealousy is clearly foreshadowed. Minor characters provide humor in a Dickensian fashion. Although Jinny is clearly motivated, Jack's unbelievable character only forces the melodrama. There is, however, some good wit and irony and excellent satire, not only on New York society but also on American tourists and European guides. The happy ending was, of course, a requirement of the "Syndicate School" to which Fitch belonged.

(ii) The Truth, 1906

The heroine of *The Truth* is Becky Warden who, like Jinny Austin, has inherited a particular vice: she is a pathological liar whose husband is as honest as Jack Austin is blindly unsuspecting. Called "the greatest play ever written by an American author" when it was tried out in Boston, *The Truth,* nevertheless, failed on the stage in New York in 1907. Soon afterwards, however, it was produced in several European countries and played in London for over a year. Barrett Clark called it "one of the few genuine American comedies of manners."

(iii) The City, 1909

In Middlebury, New York, the Rand family is preparing to move to New York City until George Rand, Sr. tells his son,

George, that he is being blackmailed by his illegitimate son,
Hancock, and then dies of shock. Years pass; the family has
moved to New York; and George is about to become a candidate for governor. As he prepares to show that his record is
clean, Cecily, his sister, arrives to tell him that she and Hancock were married that morning. When he tells the pair that
they had the same father, a mentally deranged Hancock kills
Cecily, and tries to commit suicide. George is forced to explain
everything to the police, and the scandal ruins his political career, while he and his wife, now facing the truth, turn their
backs on "the city" and see hope for the future.

In this play, Fitch suggested a change in theme from individual vices to the evils that characterized society: for people
bred in a small town the city has an evil influence. This thesis,
however, is not well dramatized in the play. The unhappiness
of Fitch's people comes, at least in part, as a consequence of
the plotting of a degenerate offspring born of moral hypocrisy
in that small town. The evil was in the person, not in the city.
The language, like some of the ideas in the play, was stronger
than Fitch's usual fare and suggested a more naturalistic tendency in Fitch's work, but the tone is still melodrama.

(f) Achievements of Clyde Fitch in Social Drama

Fitch contributed to the reputation of American drama
abroad by being the first American playwright with a significant
international reputation. As an influence in the development of
American drama, he has a place, although, typical of the time,
he was less a literary figure than a man of the commercial theater. Walter Pritchard Eaton in the "Dramatist as Man of Letters," [*Scribner's Magazine*, XLVIII (August, 1910), 490–
497], thought of him as a theater craftsman who combined
acute powers of observation with skill in characterization and a
concern for careful productions. The result was, occasionally, a
faithful and colorful documentation of American life around
the turn of the century.

Rather than establish a social comedy in America, Fitch
defined more clearly than his predecessors a base from which
social comedy could be written for American theaters. Just as
Howells regularly presented his truthful observations about society in farce, Fitch developed some believable characters and
painted his social observations on the backdrop of melodrama.

5. LANGDON MITCHELL: ONE "STERLING COMEDY"

Langdon Mitchell (1862–1935) was a dramatist and poet whose reputation rests mainly on one play: *The New York Idea* (1906), which Quinn called a "sterling comedy." Since its first production with the celebrated American actress, Mrs. Fiske, in the leading role, *The New York Idea* has been successfully revived and translated into several foreign languages. Other plays by Mitchell include a poetic tragedy, *Sylvian* (1885), and a successful adaptation of Thackeray's *Vanity Fair* called *Becky Sharp* (1899).

(a) *The New York Idea*, 1906

(*Plot*) In the Phillimore living room, the mother, sister, and aunt of Philip Phillimore, a pompous Supreme Court judge, just divorced from Vida Phillimore, coolly greet Philip's fiancée, Cynthia, the ex-Mrs. John Karslake. When Vida Phillimore and Cynthia's ex-husband, John Karslake, drop by for various reasons, a farcical chaos results. Disturbed by the Phillimore family, Cynthia, a race horse enthusiast, delays the wedding for a trip to Belmont Park. She is also tormented by indecision and jealous of Vida's attentions to John. Finally, when the wedding starts and the bored choir boys burst into song, Cynthia realizes her mistake and runs off to prevent John from marrying Vida. She is successful, of course, and once she and John talk, the play turns into melodrama, and love finds its way.

(*Discussion*) The play is filled with quotable lines about marriage, divorce, society, and family. "Marriage is three parts love and seven parts forgiveness of sin." The wit and literary quality of parts of the dialogue contrast with the farce action and elevate the theme, which is dramatized with more seriousness and also more melodramatic sentiment in the last act of the play. Generally, *The New York Idea* strikes the modern reader as an effective farce-comedy.

B. Issues and Attitudes

Writing of "The Tendencies of the American State" [*Cosmopolitan*, XXXCIII (November, 1904), 15–22], Daniel Frohman, the American theater impresario, noted that the theater had made inroads into many aspects of everyday life. He was optimistic that there was "much that should furnish good, sound, convincing and interesting material for a successful American play." And he was right. Beginning in the late nineteenth century and becoming stronger in the twentieth century, there was a definite interest among playwrights in various issues and attitudes. Using farce, comedy, or melodrama, playwrights now joined other writers who were trying to say something meaningful about the many forces and institutions that were America.

1. SOCIAL ISSUES AND ATTITUDES

The social concerns of the dramatist increased as society became more complex, although old themes remained popular. Temperance was always a thesis dear to the stage. Several of James Herne's plays show the evil of drink. Charles H. Hoyt's *A Temperance Town* (1892) attacks the problem by pointing out that although forced prohibition is not a good thing, temperance is. Alice Brown's *Children of Earth* (1915) dramatizes the problems of the drinking wife.

Plays also continued to emphasize aspects of small town living—Charles Barnard and Neil Burgess' *The County Fair* (1889), and James Forbes' *The Travelling Salesman* (1908) and *The Commuters* (1910). Winchell Smith's *The Fortune Hunter* (1909) shows the reaction of a small town to the farce hero whose plan is to go to a small town, get a job, and marry the daughter of the local millionaire. George Ade's *The County Chairman* (1903) shows the politician in a small town. Two other plays by Ade, a successful writer of farce, suggest attitudes toward education: *The College Widow* (1904) and *Just Out of College* (1905). Audiences, however, were capable of enjoying a greater sophistication; and American life, as Daniel Frohman suggested, could provide the material for the playwright.

(a) Race Differences

Illustrating one of those inconsistencies in a land where all men are created equal, Americans were interested in racial and national differences. In the early American plays, dramatists had exploited the distinctive characteristics of Negroes and Indians as well as Yankees, who were almost a race in themselves. Soon the Irishman and the German became characters in the drama. After the Civil War, Edward Harrigan emphasized the international flavor of New York, and the Yankee became a New Englander. Meanwhile, the Indian nearly disappeared from the stage; the Negro continued as a minstrel and as a sentimental retainer, occasionally becoming the subject of serious drama; and the Jew appeared.

(i) The Jew

The Jew was primarily seen as a businessman. George H. Jessop's *Sam'l of Posen* (1881) showed Sam as a Jewish immigrant store clerk who vowed to own the business in a year. Odell (*Annals of the New York Stage* XI, 257) wrote that "*Sam'l of Posen* was the Jewish commercial traveler, with most of the brass required by his profession." *Caught in a Corner* (1886) by W. J. Shaw portrayed Isaac Greenwald, the Chicago Board of Trade, and an attempt to corner the wheat market by a woman speculator. A more serious but still melodramatic picture of the Jew is Augustus Thomas' Dr. Seelig, who acts as the *raisonneur* in *As A Man Thinks* (1911). Edward Harrigan also pictured the Jew in the New York scene, and the Jew's melodramatic stage character became solidified during the late nineteenth century.

(ii) The Indian

The Indian lost his popularity in the drama when John Brougham burlesqued Pocahontas but continued his theater career in the late nineteenth century mainly as friend or foe in the Western melodramas. Then slowly a change came, and the Indian became a part of the social climate. *Squaw Man* (1905) by Edwin Milton Royle dramatized the struggle within an English solider who must choose between the Indian squaw whom he loves and has married and the girl and the earldom which wait for him in England. That same year, 1905, William C. DeMille's *Strong Heart* presented a love story of an American Indian boy and a white girl. Racial discrimination was involved as the heroine first decides to marry the boy and then changes her mind when he has to return to his tribe as chief, knowing she could not endure the primitive living. By far the best portrayal of the Indian was Mary Austin's *The Arrow Maker* (1911)—the story of a medicine woman's love for a young Indian—but there was no racial discussion here.

(iii) The Negro

A familiar sight in minstrel shows and as the sentimental or humorous servant in plays, the Negro was occasionally dramatized as an object of racial discrimination, as in Herne's *The Reverend Griffith Davenport* (1899). One of the few plays to show the Southern view of the Negro was *The New South* (1893) by Clay Greene and Joseph Grismer, which emphasized that the Negro should be kept in his place because he was an undesirable character. A different treatment of the race problem is Edward Sheldon's *The Nigger* (1909) which tells of a Negro-hating governor who discovers that he has Negro blood. As a melodrama, it has its artificialities and improbabilities, but it shows a rather forceful character in Governor Morrow who, at the end of the play, leaves the Southern girl to whom he is engaged and prepares to tell the people of his past. A current reviewer, Clayton Hamilton ["New Theatre and Contemporary Plays," *Bookman*, XXX (January, 1910)], found it impossible to consider the play seriously, but as a serious theme it would be used many times.

(b) Marriage and Divorce

The plays to be discussed in this and the next two sections —*A Woman's Place* and *Problems of Immorality*—are closely related as well as being rather staple themes for social comedy. (See section on Social Comedy.) Henry C. DeMille and David Belasco, for example, wrote *The Wife* (1887), which tells of the hurried marriage of a jilted girl to a man who, upon discovering his wife's earlier love, decides to try to win her fairly—a twist on Bronson Howard's *The Banker's Daughter*. And the number of such plays grew steadily! By 1900, Edward A. Dithmar in *The New York Times* of April 8, writes of *A Man and His Wife* by "George Fleming," pseudonym of Julia C. Fletcher, that it has the "old, old subject of marital infidelity, the subject of so large a portion of all the comedies."

The marriage scene—struggle, separation, and reunion—was a more than frequent theme. Consider the plays of Fitch, Mitchell, and Crothers. Two of A. E. Thomas' pre-World War I plays deal with husband and wife relationships—*Her Husband's Wife* (1910) and *The Rainbow* (1912). Thinking that she is dying, a woman decides to choose *Her Husband's Wife*, but she is too successful and must discourage her "choice" while her husband mentions divorce to shock her into contentment. *The Rainbow* shows how the daughter of separated parents brings about their happy reunion.

(c) A Woman's Place

Henry Adams, historian and author of America's most distinguished autobiography, *The Education of Henry Adams,* once wrote that "the proper study of mankind is woman." Playwrights have evidently always known this fact. From such a play as Dion Boucicault's *Formosa: The Most Beautiful; or, The Railroad to Ruin* (1869), which dramatized the fallen woman, to Rachel Crothers' plays featuring the self-sufficient woman was a tremendous step. Here that development can only be suggested—relating it to the social, political, and economic independence which women fought for during this period.

(i) The Late Nineteenth-Century Woman

Picture the famous scene in Daly's *Under the Gaslight* (1867)! Snorkey is tied to the railroad tracks. Inside the baggage shed Laura is slashing at the door with an axe. Finally she bursts out. "Victory! Saved! Hooray!" he shouts. She pushes the railroad switch. "And these are the women who ain't to have a vote!" says Snorkey, in one version of the play. A new force of woman was beginning to be apparent. As the century came to a close, more realistic struggles of women were dramatized. W. D. Howell's plays—*The Mousetrap,* for example—frequently emphasized the moral superiority of woman. James A. Herne's *Margaret Fleming* showed a woman of great moral strength and courage. By the end of the nineteenth century, women on the stage had to contend not only with the social world but with the "cruel world."

(ii) Woman and the Early Twentieth Century

During the decade before World War I, the consequences of woman's struggle for rights appeared in the theaters. *Margaret Fleming* had suggested that there was a double standard; Rachel Crothers attacked the double standard in *A Man's World* (1909). When an independent and self-supporting woman writer named "Frank" Weir, living with an adopted child, discovers that the man she loves is the father of that child and the destroyer of the child's mother, she expects him to accept some of the blame for his actions. But he demurs: "What do you expect? We don't live under the same laws. It was never meant to be. Nature made men different." Other Crothers plays emphasize a similar related theme: *He and She* (1911), *Ourselves* (1913). Augustus Thomas' *As a Man Thinks* (1911) presents another view. Dr. Seelig, the voice of truth, declares: "There is a double standard of morality because upon the golden basis of woman's virtue rests the welfare of the world."

Differing views appeared and disappeared, but the feminist question remained popular in the theater. Edward Sheldon's *The High Road* (1912) traces the spiritual growth of a modern woman who is self-supporting and therefore responsible for her own decisions in life. George Middleton's *Nowadays* (1914) dramatizes the equality of woman; his heroine proposes to a man and also satisfies her right to a career. The emphasis on woman in the drama reached such proportions that Florence Kepper in "Some American Plays" [*Forum*, LI (June, 1914), 921–31] wrote: "Every play produced on the American stage, with perhaps a few negligible exceptions, has its say on the feminist question." As plays dramatized the woman's growing strength in the world at large, however, the inevitable burlesques appeared. One was William C. DeMille's one-act farce, *In 1999, A Problem Play of the Future* (1914). In this play the man cares for the child, and the woman has become the breadwinner and the family protector. The double standard still prevails, however, and while she flits around from sin to sin, he fears the false step which will damn him forever. Boucicault's *Formosa* had returned!

(d) Problems of Immorality

Another issue that some dramatists treated was that of immorality, which they, of course, opposed in proper fashion. Adultery was often suggested but always indirectly, and the woman involved was never allowed to escape uncondemned. Bronson Howard had made such a denouncement mandatory in his discussion of *The Banker's Daughter*: "The wife who has once taken the step from purity to impurity can never reinstate herself in the world of art on this side of the grave." Seduction was similarly treated in such plays as *The Charity Ball* (1888) by Henry C. DeMille and David Belasco, where the seducer is made to marry the girl; or in the Western plays, where a villain made an honest woman of the girl before he was hanged. W. D. Howells had stated that every dramatist was also a moralist, and dramatists of the late nineteenth century generally took it upon themselves to be judges.

(i) A Realist's Approach: Eugene Walter's *The Easiest Way*, 1908

Eugene Walter (1874–1941) was a newspaper man who became a writer of well-developed and skillfully-constructed melodramas. *Paid in Full* (1908) contrasts the strong woman and the weak man with some realism, but *The Easiest Way* (1908) as a study of a weak woman is one of the most effective melodramas of the period, showing definite changes in theater taste and a concern for disagreeable truths. Laura Murdock is the money-loving, easygoing heroine. When she meets and falls in love with John Madison, she has lived with many men, most recently with Willard Brockton. An agreement is made: if she will stop living with Brockton, John will marry her when he has made enough money. Back in New York, Laura pawns everything as things go from bad to worse; finally, she goes back to Brockton but tries to deceive and marry John when he arrives in New York, his fortune made. But Brockton forces her to tell. John then gives her up; and Laura, after a weak attempt at suicide, heads for the theater and "to hell with the rest." Brockton is a worldly person; he knew what Laura would do. The study of Laura, however, as a woman defeated by her basic desires, provides a strong drama with some psychological insight.

(ii) Immorality on the Stage

When a house of prostitution was portrayed on the stage by Bayard Veiller in a play called *The Fight* (1913), the critics voiced bitter indignation at "all its tawdry horrors." Veiller, however, defended his plot in *The New York Times* (September 21, 1913), stating that it "was taken incident for incident from a warning sent out last year by the Traveler's Aid Society to girls in all parts of the country." That same year, 1913, Charles Rann Kennedy's one-act play on prostitution, *The Necessary Evil*, was also produced. Witter Bynner's short play *Tiger* (1913) showed how a girl was lured into a house of prostitution thinking that she would marry the man who took her there. In a sensational climax, she is saved by her first customer, who turns out to be her father. The theater was becoming increasingly realistic in presenting the more sordid aspects of life, but it was not without its critics.

2. ECONOMIC ISSUES AND ATTITUDES

American drama made spectacular and melodramatic use of economic and industrial advances and problems. When Augustin Daly made use of his sensational railroad scene in *Under the Gaslight,* he introduced a suggestion of economic progress which appealed to his audience. Soon Daly's success prompted other playwrights to look closely at industrial America—with a noticeable result. The heroine of Joseph Arthur's *Blue Jeans* (1891) nearly had her head sawed neatly in half by a buzz saw, while the heroine of William Haworth's *A Nutmeg Match* (1892) prevented the villain from releasing a steam pile driver which would crush her husband's skull. In the South—Charles Calahan's *Coon Hollow* (1894)—the cotton press replaced the buzz saw or the railroad tracks as a means of intimidating the heroine.

Many plays did, however, either comment on economic issues or use an issue to some purpose in their plots. In this way, the struggles of capital and labor, the problems of speculators and financiers, and the troubles wrought by money became a part of American drama. Reform was occasionally an issue, and plays like William Hurlburt's *The Writing on the Wall* (1909) suggested the varied places where reform was urged. In this melodrama, for example, the objective was reform in city building laws and fire safety in tenant dwellings.

(a) The Struggles of Capital and Labor

In "The Future American Drama" [*Arena,* II (November, 1890), 625] Dion Boucicault had urged a new drama concerned with social and scientific problems, such as "the great struggle between labor and capital." He was, of course, asking for serious drama in contrast to the sentimental melodrama which for the previous twenty years had used poor working girls as heroines and dramatized the consequences of criminal labor conditions. Charles Foster's *Bertha, The Sewing Machine Girl* (1871) chronicled Bertha's life from her fourteen-hour work day for $6 to $8 a week, to prison for a theft she did not commit, and almost to "a fate worse than death" before she is rescued by the hero. *The Waifs of New York* (1871) by Thaddeus W. Meighan, recounts the trials of an orphaned pair, a bootblack and a sewing girl, among the villains of New York. The heroine of Leonard Grover's *Lost in New York* (1887) says: "I work sometimes eighteen hours a day for a bare living. They say slavery is abolished, but there is more slavery among women who sew in New York than was ever known among the Negroes."

Few plays presented a definite protest against labor and economic conditions until well after the turn of the century. The workingman is treated very slightly in Bronson Howard's *Baron Rudolph* (1881); and James A. Herne gave only a brief picture of the common workers in *Margaret Fleming*. Hamlin Garland's *Under the Wheel* [*Arena,* II (July, 1890), 182–228] is much more realistic in its presentation of labor conditions. There were occasional plays about strikes—*The Strike* (1877), *The Workingmen's Strike* (1881)—and in 1891, Henry C. DeMille in *The Lost Paradise,* an adaptation of a foreign work, used a social philosopher to win both a factory strike and the factory owner's daughter. Another play, Augustus Thomas' *New Blood* (1894), was sympathetic to labor as it dramatized conditions in a manufacturing company. During the early years of the twentieth century, the outstanding labor play was Edward Sheldon's *The Boss* (1911), which used labor-management struggles as a background to portray the breakdown and humanizing of a political and economic boss. Other plays which stress labor's problems include Charles Kenyon's *Kindling* (1911), which dramatizes the poverty and desperation that a labor strike can precipitate, and Charles Klein's *Daughters of Men* (1906), which also deals with a strike situation.

(b) Speculators and Financiers

In the public's mind the successful businessman merged with the financier and the speculator who could be easily caricatured. *The Gilded Age,* a novel by Mark Twain and Charles D. Warner which gave its name to a period of speculation and created a character who will always be remembered as a speculator, Colonel Mulberry Sellers, was dramatized by G. S. Densmore in 1874, and with John T. Raymond as Sellers became a great success. Bartley Campbell's *Bulls and Bears* (1875) was an adaptation of the same foreign play that Augustin Daly made into *The Big Bonanza* (1875), in which a professor pits his intellect against the skill of a Wall Street broker. Benjamin E.

Woolf's *The Mighty Dollar* (1875) concerns a political speculator who, like Colonel Sellers, is involved in a railroad land
grant. In the 1880's, Henry C. DeMille's *John Delmer's Daughters* (1883), Bronson Howard's *The Henrietta* (1887), and
Brander Matthews and George H. Jessop's *A Gold Mine* (1887)
suggest the financier's popularity in the theater. After a critic for
the New York *Dramatic Mirror* (May 9, 1891) mentioned "the
average Wall Street play, of which we have had so many," one
imagines that George Broadhurst's 1896 failure, *The Speculators,*
was just another play on the financial situation.

(c) Man and Money

By the twentieth century, playwrights were beginning to find
out just what money could do. Smith and Ongley's *Brewster's
Millions* (1906) was one of the more successful plays in this new
exploration. How does one get rid of a million dollars? Charles
Klein's *The Lion and the Mouse* (1905) depicts financial interests that circumvent the law. In *Get-Rich-Quick Wallingford*
(1910), George M. Cohan provides a hero who does just that;
while *Fine Feathers* (1913), by Eugene Walter, shows the
power of money to corrupt man and create a greed that will
drag him to ruin. *It Pays to Advertise* (1914) is an amusing
farce by R. C. Megrue and Walter Hackett built around a rich
man's bet that his son can make more money than another
man's son. In all of these plays and many more, it is money that
makes the plot go.

3. POLITICAL ISSUES AND ATTITUDES

Political themes are as old as American drama—(*Andro-
boros,* 1714)—but not until the last part of the nineteenth century does one find politics or politicians becoming the central
issue of a full-length play. There were, however, many references
in nineteenth-century melodrama to political maneuvers, campaigns, elections, and graft: the dramatization of Mark Twain's
The Gilded Age (1874) satirized politicians; Edward Harrigan's
The Mulligan Guard Nominee (1880) ridiculed all politics; and
David Lloyd's *For Congress* (1884) satirized Congressional
practices. One of the first plays to have its plot woven around
the maneuverings of a politician was *The Senator* (1889) by
David Lloyd and Sydney Rosenfeld. A mixture of romance and

politics with humorous but loosely plotted incidents, the play burlesqued life in Washington through the love life and political activity of Senator Hannibal Rivers, an honest gentleman who stirred the sensitive heart.

(a) The 1890's

Numerous plays on political issues and politicians came to the theater in the 1890's. Henry G. Carleton's *Ambition* (1895) pictured the self-made man of integrity, Senator Obadiah Wreck. Augustus Thomas' *The Capitol* (1895) suggests the financial and religious influences that are exerted in Washington. That same year, Charles Klein's *The District Attorney* attacked political corruption and Tammany graft. Washington was always an object for satire, but the major political issue on the stage during this decade was that of imperialism in Cuba. Such titles as *Cuba's Vow, The Maine Avenged,* and *Devil's Island* indicate the popularity of such themes.

(b) Influence, Corruption, and the Political Whirl

With the new century, playwrights began to probe the world of the politician, and soon the wide political scene came to the stage—from the importance of the First Lady to the trickery of the county chairman. Casper Nannes (*Politics in the American Drama,* 1960) calls George Ade's *The County Chairman* (1903) the "finest play on the subject yet to come out of American drama." It shows the small-town politician to perfection—a shrewd but cynical trickster whose only interest is winning. That same year, George M. Cohan wove a love story into a mayoralty campaign in *Running for Office.* In Charles Klein's very successful political melodrama, *The Lion and the Mouse* (1905), the influence of big business in Washington politics becomes an almost overwhelming force. Two other political plays —George Broadhurst's *The Man of the Hour* (1906) and *The Undertow* (1907) by Eugene Walter—successfully revealed the political machinery in a large city, New York.

4. RELIGIOUS ISSUES AND ATTITUDES

Although American dramatists were generally concerned with strong moral quality, they stayed away from the strictly religious plays. By the late nineteenth century, however, there was clearly a growing interest in religious figures and ideas —an interest which was to develop before World War I.

(a) Stereotyped Religious Figure Changes

During the two or three decades before the new century, religion was sometimes mentioned in plays but never discussed, and the representative of a religion was a safe figure working for the good. If a Biblical thesis were put into a play, it was customary to make it a poetic drama: G. H. Hollister's tragedy, *Thomas Á Becket* (1866). In other plays at this time, ministers or priests appeared seldom and briefly. Charles Hoyt in *A Temperance Town* (1892) created the Reverend Ernest Hardman, a limited but good man who worked doggedly for what he believed was right. A more sophisticated presentation of religion appeared in Augustus Thomas' *The Capitol* (1895), which discussed the lobbying practices of the Catholic Church in Washington. It was a difficult theme, and Augustus Thomas took care that it would offend no one. James A. Herne's *The Reverend Griffith Davenport* (1899) focuses on a humanitarian minister, but his basic religion is not dramatized—only his interpretation of human rights.

(b) Religious Historical Drama

Historical melodramas of the spectacular type occasionally portrayed the Christian theme. In 1901, there were two dramatizations of Henryk Sienkiewiczs' *Quo Vadis*—the Whitney version and an adaptation by Jeanette Gilder. Thomas Ewing, Jr.'s poetic tragedy, *Jonathan*, appeared in 1902. Morst memorable of this period, however, is William Young's ambitious and spectacular melodrama, *Ben Hur* (1899), a dramatization of Lew Wallace's now famous novel.

(c) More Serious Concern with Religious Themes in the Twentieth Century

Consistent with nineteenth-century practice, the poetic drama was used for religious themes more frequently than prose plays. The outstanding example is William Vaughn Moody's poetic trilogy: *The Masque of Judgment* (1900), *The Fire Bringer* (1904), and *The Death of Eve* (unfinished). A superior poetic drama which presents the Christ figure as "the Lonely

Man" is Josephine Preston Peabody Marks' *The Piper* (1910), a dramatization of the Pied Piper of Hamlin story.

Moody, the Anglo-American Charles Rann Kennedy, and Edward Sheldon used clergymen and religion to help dramatize the ideals in their plays. Sheldon's Archbishop in *The Boss* is a strong and powerful figure who thoroughly cows the belligerent Regan. Kennedy, one of the few dramatists of the period who combined a searching and intelligent mind with fair dramatic technique, created an effective Christ figure in *The Servant in the House* (1907) and an interesting Crucifixion theme in *The Terrible Meek* (1912). *The Faith Healer* (1909) by Moody gives a penetrating and realistic study of a practitioner of the occult who found love and the fulfillment of his mission at the same time. Another play which undertook a difficult problem was Joseph M. Patterson's *Rebellion* (1911), which dramatized the inner struggle of a Catholic woman who has to decide whether to divorce her drunken husband and marry again or remain true to her beliefs in a Catholic marriage.

5. ATTITUDES TOWARD SCIENCE

Science and democracy—truth and equality—are consider the twin forces most responsible for the movement toward realism in late nineteenth-century American literature. Few playwrights were concerned with the effect of science upon society. Dion Boucicault's early use of the camera in *The Octoroon* is a good illustration, and Howells frequently used new inventions like the telephone (*The Unexpected Guests*) and the elevator (*The Elevator*). Otherwise, it was a long time before the playwright used anything or anybody but the family doctor to indicate an attitude toward science.

(a) Scientist as Doctor

In spite of the inadequate training of the medical doctor of the late nineteenth century as compared with modern medical school requirements, most playwrights saw the doctor with his interest in chemistry, anatomy, biology, and psychology as a representative of science, and used him to suggest scientific truthfulness. In James A. Herne's *Margaret Fleming*, the doctor is the very moral voice of truth. Dr. Littlefield in *The Faith Healer* represents the dogmatic skepticism that science has toward the occult. In Steele MacKaye's early comedy, *Won at Last* (1877), there is both Professor Tracy, "a man of science," and Dr. Sterling, "a man of fact." The distinction is interesting, although as characters in the play their particular descriptions are not dramatized. Before World War I, however, the scientist was becoming more popular and more human. In *Fine Feathers* (1912) Eugene Walter has Bob Reynolds, a chemist-scientist, take a bribe and suffer the consequences of the damned.

(b) Science in the Drama

Among the significant American dramatists of the period, James A. Herne and W. D. Howells seem to have had the most inquiring minds about science. Most of Howells' concern was combined with an interest in psychical research and was developed in novels rather than in plays, although Howells' *The Mother and the Father* (1909) and *The Impossible* (1910) show his interest. Relating science and realism, Herne believed in evolution, made references to the beliefs of Darwin and Herbert Spencer in his plays—scientific agnosticism in *Shore Acres*; determinism in *Margaret Fleming*—and said that he had an "unbounded respect for scientists and the scientific method." A very interesting play in the scientific vein, written by Percy MacKaye, son of Steele MacKaye and a poetic dramatist of some stature, is *Tomorrow* (1913), a study of positive eugenics, concerned with "the improvement of the human breed through selection."

III. THE AGE OF MELODRAMA

Taking his title from the best-remembered line of Owen Davis' popular melodrama, *Nellie, the Beautiful Cloak Model,* " 'Why do you fear me, Nellie?' The Melodrama of Forty Years Ago," [*Harper's,* CLXXXIII (July, 1941), 164–170], Walter Prichard Eaton mourned the passing of the old-fashioned melodrama of intense excitement and unsophisticated emotion. Before the movies usurped this type of entertainment for their stock in trade, theaters did a rushing business in sensational melodrama. Vivid and violent, sweet and sentimental, these melodramas combined simple emotions and complicated plots, undeveloped characters, and involved stage machinery. The object of the play was to thrill, and the playgoer had only to weep, scream, hiss, or shout for joy as his emotions dictated. It was "satisfactory" entertainment.

Melodrama is more complicated than Eaton suggested, although the type that he mentioned was dominant in American drama from the Civil War to shortly after World War I. The term melodrama was invented by Jean Jacques Rousseau for his play *Pygmalion* (1766), which was quite different from the plays now called melodrama. In Paris, toward the close of the eighteenth century, the Boulevard du Temple became a laboratory for this type of play which exhibited physical and emotional thrills with a villain-hero conflict, a musical accompaniment, and a happy ending. Pixerécourt originated the stock characters—the pure heroine, the dark villain, the intrepid hero, and the comic. From Paris, the melodrama soon crossed the English channel. Thomas Holcroft's *A Tale of Mystery* (1802) is technically the first English melodrama. America's master of the melodrama was David Belasco, but he shared his popularity with many others during the twenty years before 1900 and the ten years or so that followed. This was the Age of Melodrama in America.

Best defined through what it is supposed to do, melodrama must thrill rather than comment on life. Limited by one-dimensional development, characters must provide excitement or comedy. "For every smile a tear, for every tear a smile," announced the posters. Because the objective was vivid sensation and violent or sentimental emotions, there was no logic and little plot in a melodrama but an abundance of situations— usually well-tried situations made novel by the skill of the actor or the stage carpenter. One of the key words in a melodrama of this period was "Saved!" And any rescue—though sure to come—was always delayed until the last second.

Because the periods of the Rise of Realism in the drama and the beginnings of social drama are also the Age of Melodrama, a large number of the plays already discussed are obviously melodrama. Here, in chronological order with special attention to the works of Dion Boucicault, Augustin Daly, David Belasco, and Owen Davis, the more popular types of melodrama will be discussed; then a consideration of historical and romantic melodrama, melodrama of crime and detection, and social melodrama will follow. In all such plays, the major characteristics of melodrama remain; the objective is to stimulate feeling rather than thinking, and the scenes are put together with a view to sensational entertainment.

A. Melodrama: Vivid and Violent, Sweet and Sentimental

When one thinks of melodrama, he usually pictures in his mind the stock situations that have excited so many for so long. [See H. J. Smith, "Melodrama," *Atlantic Monthly,* XCIX (March, 1907)] There is the heroine looking demure and helpless as she tremulously cries, "I swear to you that I am in-nocent," while the audience breaks into cheers; later, bound and gagged and left on a railroad track, she is rescued at the last minute by her two Landseer dogs, "possessed of an intelligence almost human." Meanwhile, the not-too-bright hero nearly succumbs to the wiles of the scheming "Zidella of the purple gown and reptilian eyes." Across the stage slithers the arch-villain with a horrible leer upon his mustachioed face, and—well, the story goes on until all are saved. It was that simple, but it was awfully exciting. This is melodrama, and nineteenth-century America had no peers in its creation.

1. DION BOUCICAULT

When William Winter wrote down his thoughts about Dion Boucicault for his book, *Other Days, Being Chronicles and Memories of the Stage* (1908), he listed Boucicault's "supreme achievements" in drama as "the ticking of the telegraph, in 'The Long Strike'; the midnight farewell of the schoolmaster in 'The Parish Clerk'; the incident of Jessie's concealment of the broken floor, in 'Jessie Brown'; the heroic self-sacrifice of Shawn, in 'Arrah-na-Pogue'; the sentinels in the opening scene of 'Belle Lamar'; and the pathetic situation wherein the poor old father learns that his son's honor has been vindicated, in 'Daddy O'Dowd.' " Few modern students of the drama would find themselves in agreement with many of Winter's other statements, but he obviously showed some critical perspicacity in choosing the creation of melodramatic incidents as Boucicault's forte. In American drama, Boucicault's achievement was in melodrama.

Boucicault's type of melodrama, however, declined soon after his death in 1890, and within a few years critics were beginning to apologize for his work and wonder how they ever enjoyed his plays. Once considered "the apostle of realism on the stage," with his fire-and-water spectaculars and his opportunities for self-indulgent acting, his plays became a casualty to changing techniques in acting and writing melodrama.

(a) Boucicault Melodramas

Boucicault's first play to be produced after the Civil War was *The O'Dowd* (1873), an adaptation of a French play, whose scene and circumstance he transported to Ireland. Emphasizing the prodigal son theme, the play dramatizes both the sacrifice that the father must make to save his son from ruin and the heroic actions of the son to redeem his name and fortune. More traditional in melodrama and very successful on the stage was Boucicault's *Led Astray*. Produced the same year as *The O'Dowd* and also adapted from a French melodrama, *Led Astray* managed to change a French love triangle into an Irish triangle and even heighten the effect. *Belle Lamar* (1874) is a melodrama of the Civil War. Boucicault's last popular melodrama was another in the Irish vein, *The Shaughraun* (1874), loosely defined as "the Wanderer." Based on an incident in the Fenian insurrection in 1866, it tells of the adventures and escapes of an Irish gentleman under sentence of death as a Fenian.

After this success, Boucicault wrote and adapted several plays, but his fortunes slowly melted away. Finally, he was reduced to teaching in a school for actors, a melancholy end for one whose contributions assure him a niche in the history of American drama and theater.

2. AUGUSTIN DALY

In *The Theater of Augustin Daly*, Marvin Felheim entitles his chapter on Daly's major melodramas, "Blood and Thunder Dramatist." These plays included *Under the Gaslight* (1867), *A Flash of Lightning* (1868), *The Red Scarf* (1868), *Horizon* (1871), and *Undercurrent* (1888). Of these plays, *Under the Gaslight* is the most famous and the most successful, the railroad scene becoming a hallmark of melodrama.

(a) *A Flash of Lightning*, 1868

(*Plot*) Having two daughters, Garry Fallon shows his partiality for Rose by giving her a necklace, and his dislike for

Bessie by accusing her of theft when the necklace is missing and by turning her over to the police in the person of Skiffley. By accepting her fate, Bessie tries to shield the man she loves, Jack. The rest of the play shows the attempt of Skiffley, the villain, to gain control of Bessie, while Jack tries to save her and prove to her that he is innocent of the theft. Somehow they get aboard a Hudson River steamer which blows up and catches on fire— providing equally heroic opportunities for Jack and the stage carpenter. Both are successful; and in the final act, Jack proves that lightning destroyed the necklace, but not before Bessie almost does away with herself in anticipation of a jail sentence.

(*Discussion*) The water and fire spectacles in *A Flash of Lightning* added nothing new for New York audiences who had seen burning buildings in *The Poor of New York*, burning ships in *The Octoroon*, and a water spectacle in *The Colleen Bawn*— all by Boucicault. The play was successful, however, and Daly soon wrote *The Red Scarf; or, Scenes in Aroostook*. In this play, he tied his hero to a log which was about to be sawed in two in a sawmill before he burned down the mill. But Daly's heroines were inevitably brave and quick on their feet, and all characters were able to appear for their bows. This type of action was typical of the Daly melodrama.

3. DAVID BELASCO

In his bitter and cynically clever work, *The Devil's Dictionary*, Ambrose Bierce defined a dramatist as "one who adapts from the French." The phrase is an apt description of a number of American dramatists of the nineteenth century, including David Belasco (1853–1931), master of sentimental and romantic melodrama. As actor-manager-playwright and innovator in the theater, his attention to minute detail became a mark of the Belasco production. His interest in the use of electricity caused Montrose Moses (*The American Dramatist,* 1918) to relate his discussions of Belasco to the "Switchboard Theater." His plays are mainly collaborations with a number of playwrights, including James A. Herne (*Hearts of Oak*), Henry C. DeMille (*The Charity Ball*), Franklyn Fyles (*The Girl I Left Behind Me*), and John Luther Long (*Madame Butterfly*). Belasco had that skill of being able to add the particular touch which made a play successful on the stage. With DeMille, he wrote social melodrama; with Long, he wrote romantic melodrama; but his forte was the robust melodrama of violence and sentiment. Of the sixty Belasco plays that Quinn lists as having been written after 1872, twenty-three were adaptations or dramatizations of material not his own; in nineteen of the sixty, he collaborated with a total of twelve people.

(a) *The Girl I Left Behind Me*, 1893

In an intense and violent melodrama of life on an army post in Sioux country, the General's daughter, who is engaged to a scoundrel, discovers that she loves another. Outside the fort, the Indians attack, led by Scarbrow, the Sioux chieftain. Complications arise when it is clear that Scarbrow's daughter and the General's daughter love the same man. The Indian girl's death facilitates a happy ending, although for a while it seemed that the General might have to kill his daughter to prevent her from being captured by the Indians and thus leave the melo-drama without a heroine. But "Saved!" is the byword, and the rescue comes as the Indians retreat before the U.S. Cavalry.

(b) Belasco and His Stars: Mrs. Leslie Carter

As a theater manager, Belasco was interested in creating stars. Mrs. Leslie Carter, one of his greatest stars after her sensational divorce from a socialite family, tells in her memoirs how intense his training was—in gesture, in voice projection, and in physical feats. Her physical actions and her stamina never failed to bring comments from the critics. Belasco wrote several plays for Mrs. Carter before they parted ways, the first one being *The Heart of Maryland* (1895) in which Mrs. Carter played the part of Maryland Calvert who risks life and limb for her lover. For three years she brought a warm joy to the hearts of the audience by refusing to let the curfew sound which would bring doom to her lover. Her method was simple but startling— she clung to the clapper of the bell, swinging with it.

Three years later, 1898, Belasco adapted *Zaza* from the French, especially for Mrs. Carter. As Zaza, "the wicked and of course irresistible music-hall singer," Mrs. Carter had ample opportunity to exploit her beauty, the violent ebb and flow of her emotions, and her limitless energy. Because the scene was a theater, Belasco exercised his tremendous talent in stage management with exhibitions of theater machinery. *Zaza* well exemplifies Belasco's melodramatic art: a play adapted from the

French, a plot filled with sensationalism, a single star with an emotional appeal, an exhibit of the stage manager's skill—in essence, a spectacle in character, action, and scene.

4. MELODRAMA BY OWEN DAVIS

Al Woods and Owen Davis as theater manager and playwright, respectively, may well have produced more "thrillers" than any other team in the American theater. Starting in 1899 with *Through the Breakers*, Davis found the market pressing and the results so lucrative that for nearly fifteen years he wrote a melodrama every month or six weeks—129 melodramas before he wrote *The Family Cupboard* in 1913, which marked his switch to comedy and a more serious interest in drama. The titles of some of his melodramas are *Convict 999*; *Confessions of a Wife*; *Nellie, the Beautiful Cloak Model*; and *Gambler of the West*, which he considered the best of his sensational melodramas. Eventually, however, he tired of writing sensational melodrama, began to write more realistic drama, and finally won a Pulitzer Prize with *Icebound* in 1923.

During the period in which his melodramas were so enormously successful, his philosophy of writing was very simple. The theater, he felt, should provide not screams or political speeches but "amusement, or some excitement, or something that will bring about a mood of hope, faith, or exaltation." (See Owen Davis, *My First Fifty Years in the Theatre*, 1950.) To do this he devised certain techniques, such as dividing a play into "no less than fifteen scenes, the end of each being a moment of perilous suspense or terrifying danger." Cheap to produce and seventy per cent successful, the Davis melodramas were more a product of knowledge of the theater and theater audiences than of artistic imagination, but they deserve mention in a history of American drama.

5. SOME SENSATIONAL MELODRAMAS

To suggest the variety and scope of the sensational melodrama throughout this period, brief plot outlines are given for a number of the better-known and most popular "thrillers." Plots must remain sketchy, however, because one characteristic of these melodramas was an almost inextricably involved story.

(a) *East Lynne*, 1863

(*Plot*) Archibald Carlyle has just brought his bride, Isabel, to the Old Homestead in East Lynne, but their serenity is soon disturbed by Barbara Hare, who begs Archibald to help her brother who is suspected of a murder. Suspicious and jealous, Isabel is readily deceived by Francis Levison, a scoundrel, and runs away with him. Years later, abandoned and repentant, Isabel, disguised as Madame Vine, returns to East Lynne where, working as a governess for Archibald and Barbara, who have married, she finally reveals herself when one of her children dies in her arms. In the final act, it is necessary only to punish the villain, who has been identified as the murderer in question, and to forgive Isabel who conveniently dies, relieving Archibald of bigamy.

(*Discussion*) To many modern Americans, *East Lynne* means melodrama. Based on a novel by Mrs. Henry Wood, an Englishwoman, and adapted by Clifton W. Tayleure, it opened at the Winter Garden in New York in 1863. William Winter, dramatic critic, (*Albion*, March 28, 1863, quoted in Hewitt) declared that a "flimsy and stupid novel has been resuscitated into a flimsy, unnatural, incongruous and feverishly sentimental play." And yet the play is still in print and still occasionally produced.

(b) *Rosedale*, 1863

(*Plot*) Lady Florence and her son, Arthur, live comfortably on the fortune left by her deceased husband, half of which will go to her uncle, the Colonel, if she marries without his consent. A greedy man, the Colonel has Arthur kidnapped, but is forced to relinquish his rights to the money when his plot is revealed. Lady Florence is then free to marry the man she loves.

(*Discussion*) Written by the popular actor, Lester Wallack (1820–1888), and replete with disguises, discoveries, and much sentiment, *Rosedale; or, The Rifle Ball*, based on a novel, *Lady Lee's Widowhood* by Edward B. Harnley, was a popular hit for many years.

(c) *The White Slave*, 1882

(*Plot*) Lisa, the illegitimate white child of the Judge's daughter, is loved by Clay, the Judge's adopted son; but they are kept apart by the assumption that Lisa has Negro blood.

When the old Judge dies, his debts force the sale of the plantation and the slaves, including Lisa. Lacy, the villain, buys Lisa,
who goes to work in the fields rather than meet Lacy's demands:
"Rags are royal raiment when worn for virtue's sake! Rather a
hoe in my hands than self-contempt in my heart." Finally Clay
rescues Lisa, who is shown to be the Judge's white granddaughter by a baptismal record; Lacy is accused of murdering a
Negro; and Lisa, Clay, and their slaves return to the Judge's
plantation and a wedding.

(*Discussion*) The author of *The White Slave,* Bartley Campbell (1843–1888), was a dramatist of considerable reputation
for the brief period from about 1879 to 1885. Not only was he
the most popular dramatist of that day, but many critics considered him one of the best. Other Campbell melodramas include
My Partner (1879), a dramatization of Bret Harte's story; *The
Galley Slave* (1879), which has a foreign setting; and *Paquita*
(1885), which dramatizes a surgeon's struggle as he performs a
life-saving operation on his wife's lover. Most of the plays were
performed abroad with success. *The White Slave* toured coast
to coast after its initial success in New York.

B. Historical and Romantic Melodrama

Sensationalism was a major aspect of a melodrama's appeal, and the stage manager's art was always evident. In plays
which used an historical incident or character or emphasized a
tense love story, however, characterization and idea assumed
some importance.

1. HISTORICAL MELODRAMA

Historical events and personalities did not generally appeal
to playwrights of the late nineteenth and early twentieth cen-
turies as they did to their counterparts of the earlier nineteenth
century. Bronson Howard and Brander Matthews wrote *Peter
Stuyvesant* (1899), embellishing the life of the early New York
governor. Clyde Fitch wrote *Beau Brummell* (1890), *Nathan
Hale* (1898), and *Major André* (1903). The most popular historical melodramas, however, were either of a religious nature
or had a foreign setting. Two dramatizations of *Quo Vadis,* an
historical novel by Henryk Sienkiewicz depicting the time of

Christ, were presented in 1900. In the religious melodramas, too, spectacle was the object.

(a) *Ben Hur*, 1899

(*Plot*) At the palace of the Hurs, who are Jewish, Ben Hur is insulted by Messala, a Roman and former friend. When Ben accidentally causes the death of a Roman leader, he is arrested by Messala and is sentenced to row on a Roman galley. During the battle in which the galley is destroyed, Ben saves the life of a Roman officer and then lives with him as his adopted son until the man dies, whereupon Ben returns to his home and searches unsuccessfully for his mother and sister. But he learns of the coming King, and with the Arabian horses of Ilderim, he wins a desperate chariot race with Messala. Later, having discovered that his mother and sister have leprosy and hide in a cave, Ben finds them healed by Jesus and is happily reunited with Esther, his very faithful sweetheart of earlier days.

(*Discussion*) Dramatized by William Young, Lew Wallace's spectacular historical novel, *Ben Hur,* held the stage for a number of years. Much of the excitement was due to the art of the stage manager and his carpenters—in particular, the tremendously effective chariot race with eight horses on treadmills prancing in front of the audience.

(b) *DuBarry*, 1901

(*Plot*) Trimming hats in a Paris milliner's shop, Jeanette flirts happily with Cosse; then Jean DuBarry brings her to the attention of Louis XV, who makes her his mistress, gives her a title, and keeps her at Versailles, the most powerful woman in France. During an uprising of the people, however, she is forced to betray Cosse in order to save his life. Later, when the French Revolution is under way, Cosse has to condemn her to the people's court for this betrayal. In a final dramatic scene, she is drawn away in a cart through the streets of Paris—toward the guillotine.

(*Discussion*) An historical melodrama of quite a different nature is David Belasco's *DuBarry*, which he embellished with his usual concern for realism, getting many of his stage properties from Paris. Glamorous in a spectacular sense, it became a popular vehicle for Mrs. Leslie Carter.

2. ROMANTIC MELODRAMA: FROM STRANGE LANDS

Most melodrama has at heart a touch of the romantic, usually more than a touch in its love episodes. The reference here, however, is to the romance of fancy and of distant places with strange-sounding names. Only a few dramatists seem to have been interested in writing it. David Belasco's collaborations with John Luther Long are outstanding: *Madame Butterfly* (1900), *The Darling of the Gods* (1902), and *Adrea* (1904). Richard Tully's *Bird of Paradise* (1912), George C. Hazelton and J. H. Benrimo's *The Yellow Jacket* (1912), and Edward Sheldon's *The Garden of Paradise* (1914), which builds upon Hans Christian Andersen's "The Little Mermaid"—all suggest a kind of romantic fantasy. Most of the plays of Edward Knoblock are romantic melodrama—*The Cottage in the Air* (1909) and *Kismet* (1911), his greatest success.

(a) David Belasco and John Luther Long: *Madame Butterfly*, 1900; *The Darling of the Gods*, 1902

(i) Madame Butterfly is based on a story by John Luther Long. Highlighted with tender and romantic song, the play tells of Cho-Cho-San, Madame Butterfly, who waits with her child, Trouble, for the return of Lieutenant B. F. Pinkerton, an American naval officer to whom she feels herself married. All night long she waits—a night created by lights for a period of fourteen minutes, during which no words are spoken—only to discover that Pinkerton has brought an American wife. Going behind a screen, she wounds herself with her father's sword—"to die with honor, when one can no longer live with honor"—binds her throat with a scarf, and dies embracing her child.

(ii) The Darling of the Gods, a play of Japanese background, carries the exotic quality of the oriental fantasy. Yo-San, the daughter of the Prince of Tosan who wants "only to be perfectly happy all my life," falls in love with Kara, the outlaw leader of the two-sword men, and protects him when he is wounded. But she is later tricked into betraying the hideout of Kara and his men. For her betrayal, Yo-San must wander one thousand years before going to heaven, but as Kara promises to wait, they kill themselves saying, "Sayonara." In the last

scene, the thousand years has elapsed; Kara and Yo-San meet in the first Celestial Heaven and ascend to the next together.

C. Melodrama of Crime and Detection

With Indians to fight, the wilds of nature to contend with, and the most horrible of black-mustachioed villains to foil, melodramatists of the nineteenth century did not bother much with criminals. Generally, the heroes or the heroines solved their own mysteries and handed the villains over to some nebulous person called the law. All of the good people, of course, respected the law, and the bad people showed their disdain for it in many ways. But the thrills of cops and robbers evidently had to wait until some progress was made among cowboys who killed Indians and the heroes who must subdue numerous tall-hatted villains.

For some reason E. A. Poe's (1809–1849) great detective, Monsieur Dupin of "The Purloined Letter" and "Murders in the Rue Morgue," did not attract playwrights, although William Gillette's *Sherlock Holmes* (1898) owes something to Poe's creation as well as to Conan Doyle's. One of the few popular American detectives of the period, Dick Brummage of *The Great Diamond Robbery*, knew many disguises and tricks, and was incorruptible as well as persistent; but though he shared their self-confidence, he clearly lacked the wit, finesse, and intelligence of the two detectives of short-story form. The play by Edward M. Alfriend (b. 1843) and A. C. Wheeler (1835–1903) illustrates the type of melodrama popular in the Ten-Twenty-Thirty (10¢-20¢-30¢) theater—simple, clean-cut characters, complicated situations, and fast-moving action, all requiring an emotional rather than a thoughtful reaction.

1. POPULAR CRIME MELODRAMA

About the beginning of the second decade of the twentieth century, crime melodrama achieved a popularity that is worth noting, although as early as 1895 Charles Klein had written *The District Attorney* with Harrison G. Fiske.

(a) A Fad of Crime Melodramas

In the spring of 1912, Bayard Veiller produced *Within the Law*. Combining action and sentiment, it tells of a girl, unjustly convicted of stealing from a shop where she worked, who seeks revenge by marrying her former employer's son and leading a gang that worked just within the law. Extremely successful, it suggested a fad in crime-detection plays—a "flood of melodrama featuring criminals hunted by detectives and police" [*Bookman*, XXXVI (February, 1913), 638–49]. *The Conspiracy* (1912) by John Emerson and Robert Baker tells of a girl who helped round up criminals by working for an amateur criminologist. *Under Cover* (1914) by Roi Cooper Megrue is concerned with some jewel smugglers and a girl whose misplaced love tempts her to help them. Elmer L. Reizenstein's (Rice) *On Trial* (1914) is the dramatization of the prosecution and defense of a man charged with murder in the first degree.

(b) *Seven Keys to Baldpate,* 1913

A mixture of melodrama and farce, George M. Cohan's *Seven Keys to Baldpate* is one of the best examples of the early crime melodrama. Having bet the owner of the Baldpate Inn that he can write a novel there within twenty-four hours, Mr. Magee discovers in the Inn some crooks and a newspaper girl who is trying to expose their crime. One by one, however, Magee and the girl catch the crooks. Then the farce starts: the crooks seize control, kill the girl, blame Magee, and fool the police until the owner of the Inn appears and calmly kills the two policemen before he explains that the people are all actors in his employ. Presumably Magee has lost his bet, but in the epilogue Magee is typing: everything portrayed has been his story!

D. Social Melodrama

In an article on the "Characteristics of American Drama," Alfred Hennequin [*Arena,* I (May, 1890), 700–709] maintained that the French melodrama had combined with English melodrama to produce a very prevalent type of American play—social melodrama. One may see social melodrama as a compromise on the part of the playwrights, managers, and audiences. It suggested a break toward the modern drama of Ibsen and Shaw at the same time that it kept safely within the bounds that managers and playwrights knew were successful at the box office. Clayton Hamilton, a popular writer-critic of the period, saw the change from early melodrama as a degeneration ["Melodrama, Old and New," *Bookman,* XXXIII (May, 1911, 309–14]. He found "a new species of melodrama that is ashamed of itself"—it takes the form of "a serious study of contemporary social problems." Social melodramas, however, retain the characteristics of melodrama and use or comment on social problems or conditions rather than treat them intelligently and imaginatively.

1. WRITERS OF SOCIAL MELODRAMA

Of the playwrights whose melodramas commented on social problems and conditions, Clyde Fitch's work provides a good starting point with two social melodramas (1901)—*The Way of the World,* concerned with life in New York, and *The Girl and the Judge,* which shows the reaction of the daughter and husband of a kleptomaniac. Charles Klein's plays were mainly melodramas involving social, political, or economic issues. George Broadhurst's *Bought and Paid For* (1911) exploits the problems of a wealthy self-made man who owns his wife among other assets. Life in a newspaper office is exaggerated dramatically in *The Fourth Estate* (1909) by Joseph Medill Patterson and Harriet Ford. In general, the writer of social melodrama was restricted in his choice of material only by what he considered unwise for the box office.

(a) Eugene Walter, *Paid in Full,* 1908; *Fine Feathers,* 1913

The most significant writer of social melodrama was Eugene Walter whose best play, *The Easiest Way*, has already been discussed. *Paid in Full,* a study of human weakness in a husband contrasted with the strength of the wife, captializes on a melodramatic situation in which the husband, accused of embezzlement, begs his wife to visit his employer and bargain for his freedom with her physical charms.

Walter's *Fine Feathers* dramatizes the evils of greed and temptation and the weakness of man, as a young chemist is bribed to use poor materials in a dam which breaks with appalling loss of life. Faced with running or staying, the chemist stays, calls the police, and then ends his life with a bullet.

(b) Elmer L. Reizenstein's (Rice) *On Trial,* 1914

On Trial is a social melodrama of the criminal courts having

a number of stage devices, particularly flashbacks, which added
to its effect on the stage. According to *The New York Times*
reviewer, August 20, 1914, it was a "new thing to have an
entire play written out of the record of a murder trial." Deceived
by a man before her marriage, a young woman is forced by circumstances to visit this man for fear he will ruin her husband.
Finally, he is killed by her husband, who complicates his trial
by trying to shield his wife.

IV. THE POPULAR FARCE

There will always be farces in the theater, and it is likely
that they will always be popular. A good number of the plays
discussed in this chapter have some farce characters, but the
farce in American drama had greater significance during the
years from the Civil War to World War I than simply as an
aspect of comedy and melodrama. Before the Civil War, the
farce was mainly an afterpiece or a means to exploit a character
such as the Yankee. By the turn of the century, it had become an
evening's entertainment. Amidst the social and industrial difficulties of late nineteenth-century America, people wanted mainly
the vicarious excitement of melodrama and the laughter of farce.
And farce then reached its highest point of popularity in the history of American drama.

A. Farce and Its Varieties

If farce is successful, the audience laughs. Dramatizing
either novelty or the common life, the plot in farce has no major
conflict but a series of minor incidents in which external, physical, and trivial situations are exploited. Focusing on an
improbable situation, the playwright creates confusion and embarrassment purely for their own sake. Characterization is
avoided. Generally, with the single exception of the intriguers
who start the confusion, stock characters and unalert people
become the dramatis personae in farce. If people used their intelligence, in fact, there would frequently be no play. Specifically,
characters do not determine or influence events, and the play
progresses, not by what the characters do, but by what happens
to them. Farces, then, are compounds of absurdity, improb-
ability, and contrivance. There must be, however, sufficiently

recognizable human traits in the characters or in the situation that the audience will want to see how it all ends.

1. SITUATION FARCE

The situation farce was the most successful of the period, and one of the popular figures of this time was also a prolific writer and adaptor of farces—Augustin Daly. One of his most successful farces was *A Night Off* (1885), which tells of an absent-minded professor who loves the theater and, while his wife is away, has numerous experiences when a romantic tragedy he wrote in college is produced. William Gillette was another effective writer of farces with *The Private Secretary* (1884) and *Too Much Johnson* (1894). *Why Smith Left Home* (1898), which describes the problems of Smith and his bride who are visited by so many relatives that they can never be alone, is typical of the farces of George Broadhurst. Perhaps two of the best-known farces of this period are Winchell Smith and Byron Ongley's *Brewster's Millions* (1906), which tells of a man who must spend—not give away nor acquire any property—one million dollars; and Margaret Mayo's absurd situation farce, *Baby Mine* (1910). Another very successful farce was Charles Klein's *Potash and Perlmutter* (1913), which exploits the Jewish businessman.

2. SECONDARY PURPOSE: RIDICULE

Objects of ridicule in farce are not limited, and almost all plays that attempted satire did so through farce techniques. Politics, of course, is always an object of ridicule. *The Nominee* (1890), adapted from the French by Leander Richardson and William Yardley, describes an election in which a man ran for Congress as a Jacksonian Democrat and was elected as a Republican Protectionist. *For Revenue Only* (1892), attributed to Milton Nobles, exaggerates aspects of politics and tells of a candidate for Congress whose unscrupulous campaign manager turned out to be his long-lost son. *It Pays to Advertise* (1914) by Roi Megrue and Walter Hackett is an early play ridiculing the advertising business. George M. Cohan's *Broadway Jones* (1912) also makes fun of the business and advertising world. Numerous plays, mainly of doubtful merit, exploited the absurdities of the stock character of the speculator—Benjamin E. Woolf's *The Mighty Dollar* (1875), Daly's *The Big Bonanza* (1875). From Bronson Howard's *Saratoga* to Langdon Mitchell's *The New York Idea*, farce was the popular means for ridiculing society. Such was the popularity of farce.

B. Everyone Writes Farce

Most playwrights of this period wrote farce—some intentionally, some because they lacked the skill to avoid it. Farce as a genre, however, has its admirable qualities and should not be disparaged if it is written properly.

1. CLYDE FITCH

Some critics will contend that Fitch wrote mainly farce; certainly he resorted to contrivance in creating both plot and characterization. In several plays, however, he illustrated his talent for creating the unpretentious but entertaining farce. *The Blue Mouse* (1908), adapted from the German, is a good example. A young man, ambitious to advance in his business and knowing that his boss is susceptible to pretty women, hires a chorus girl to act as his wife. As both boss and young man are married, the misunderstanding between "hired" wife and real wives produces much ludicrous entertainment.

2. AUGUSTUS THOMAS

A craftsman of the theater who achieved some success by dramatizing the interests of a changing society, Thomas (1857–1934) wrote for the commercial theater, generally with a particular actor or actress in mind. He followed a contemporary interest in regionalism (*In Mizzoura*, 1893; *Arizona*, 1899), in labor (*New Blood*, 1894), in politics (*The Capitol*, 1895), and in new fads such as mental healing (*As a Man Thinks,* 1911). In his best-known play, *The Witching Hour* (1907), a conventional melodrama of sentiment and morality which exploits a popular interest, he dramatizes the story of a young man who, under the influence of hypnotism, has killed a man. Generally, Thomas was a master of the well-made play.

Most of his plays, however, were farces. *On the Quiet*

(1901) tells of a college student who, contrary to an earlier promise, secretly marries an heiress, and of the subsequent complications. Wishing to be anonymous while visiting America, an English earl (*The Earl of Pautucket*, 1903) borrows an American's name and of course—his many problems.

3. W. D. HOWELLS

During his playwriting career, Howells wrote twenty-five one-act plays, most of which he called farces. A few of them came closer to comedy than to farce, through his development of the basic situation, the characters, and the dialogue. Many are simple farce—*Evening Dress* (1893), in which Campbell exploits Roberts' wardrobe while trying to find his dress suit; *Room Forty-five* (1900), in which a woman cannot sleep because the man in the hotel room below her snores; *Parting Friends* (1911), in which two young people are so bothered by visitors that they cannot kiss goodbye before she leaves on the steamer for Europe. Few of these farces were produced on the professional stage.

C. Masters of the Farce

Of the many who wrote farce for the commercial theater, two of the most talented and successful were Charles Hoyt and George Ade. Both playwrights relied heavily on satire and situation, but whereas Hoyt wrote straight farce and followed in the footsteps of Edward Harrigan, Ade emphasized effective dialogue and more recognizably human characters.

1. CHARLES H. HOYT

Called the forerunner of George S. Kaufman and Moss Hart, Hoyt (1859/60–1900) exploited farce and satire to become the most popular writer of "hilarious confusion" in the late nineteenth century. Drawing his material from his own experiences—small-town life, politics, temperance and suffrage meetings, law school, and sporting events—his plays developed from an early emphasis on slapstick comedy to an awareness of social problems. In a quite Puritan but not always a careful fashion, he poked genial fun at many aspects of American society. *A Temperance Town* (1892) satirized prohibition; *A Milk White Flag* (1893) burlesqued the hypocrisy of home guard companies; *A Runaway Colt* (1895) told of a gambler's attempt to bribe a baseball player. His objective was to entertain, and his box office success suggests his place in American farce-comedy.

(a) *A Texas Steer; or, Money Makes the Mare Go*, 1890

A satire on Washington politicians and their methods, the play opens in Texas, where Maverick Brander's daughter, Bossy, and a Captain Bright are arranging to have Brander elected to Congress because Bright is being transferred to the Capitol and they would like to be together. The election is chaotic but not too expensive at $5.00 a vote. With the Branders in Washington, there are the usual greenhorn problems with elevators and blackmail, but the Texans are distinctive with their ever-ready guns. Brander, of course, does nothing as a Congressman and is investigated by three gun-toting Texans who shoot up the place, lose Brander friends in Washington, but assure him that he will be re-elected by Texas.

2. GEORGE ADE

Undoubtedly using Hoyt as a model, Ade (1866–1944) wrote numerous farces and farce-melodramas. He used satire yet was not a penetrating satirist, nor was he seriously critical in his plays. Enjoying people and situations more than plot, he became a popular playwright during the first decade of the twentieth century. In *The College Widow* (1904) he created a fine farce situation. In order to persuade a certain boy to come to Atwater College to play football, the coach asks his girl friend to show interest in the boy. She is successful, of course, and the football team wins its big game. The crisis comes when the coach's plot is revealed as well as his girl friend's love—for the football player. *The Sultan of Sulu* (1902) is a musical farce which uses an army base in the Philippines to poke fun at government procedures. *Just Out of College* (1905) satirizes the value of a college education in the business world. *Artie* (1907) describes a clever and flippant young man who jollies his way to material success. George Ade wrote plays for the next twenty years but was lost in a theater dominated by Eugene O'Neill.

V. POETIC DRAMA
Civil War to World War I

Poetic drama from the beginnings of American drama to the Civil War included the most significant of the plays being written. From Thomas Godfrey through William Dunlap, James Nelson Barker, Robert Montgomery Bird, to George Henry Boker, poetic drama grew in America until it could compare well with the best poetic dramas written in the contemporary world. The best actors (such as Edwin Forrest) presented it as a major part of a repertory slanted toward an artistic as well as a commercial success. Essentially, poetic drama seemed to have caught the attitude of a part of early nineteenth-century America. After the Civil War and until the turn of the century, poetic drama did not fit the requirements of the Rise of Realism. Then during the ten years before World War I, there was a revival of interest in poetic drama.

A. Poetic Drama and the Rise of Realism

With the exception of the work of George Henry Boker, the poetic drama of the period from the Civil War to the turn of the century was considerably less inspired than what had come before. Times had changed; the demands of the theater had changed; and the playwrights followed the direction taken by the commercial theater. The people were being forced to look at life more realistically, and the drama mirrored that change in society. Therefore, when W. D. Howells, the spokesman for realism, declared that any play which proposed to be a faithful representation of lives of men and women should not be written in verse form, few people questioned his statement. The Rise of Realism in literature, then, not only did not promote poetic drama; it laid down a dictum under which poetic drama would be considered false. Poetry, in fact, was not a significant part of the Rise of Realism.

1. POETIC PLAYS—1865–1900

From 1865 until 1900, few poetic dramas were written; fewer reached the stage. (The plays of George Henry Boker have been discussed in Chapter II, and the efforts of Longfellow mentioned.) Some of the poets of the period, however, attempted dramatic poetry, such as *Prince Deukalion* (1878) by Bayard Taylor. In 1881, William Young dramatized part of the Arthurian story in *Pendragon*, and Ernest Lacy wrote *Chatterton* (1893), a study of the poet's life, for the actress Julia Marlowe.

2. THE POETIC DRAMA OF W. D. HOWELLS

During the 1870's and early 1880's, there was a slight revival of interest in poetic drama occasioned mainly by the temperament and acting abilities of Lawrence Barrett. One poetic drama which Barrett acted for more than twenty years was written by none other than W. D. Howells, the Father of Realism who occasionally slipped from his throne of realism and cavorted with the romantics. For his first play, Howells chose Ippolito D'Aste's *Samsone*, which he translated and adapted as *Samson* (1874) for the actor Charles Pope. In 1878, he adapted and translated Tamayo Y Baus' *Un Drama Nuevo*, a play he eventually called *Yorick's Love*. Employing a play within a play, it tells the story of an actor, Yorick, who discovers that his young wife loves another when she acts the part of an unfaithful wife with him in a play.

Howells also wrote three other poetic dramas: *Priscilla: A Comedy* (1879–82), a dramatization of Longfellow's "The Courtship of Miles Standish"; *A Sea Change; or, Love's Stowaway* (1888), an operetta with music by Georg Henschel; and *The Mother and the Father* (1909), a series of three plays showing the reactions of mother and father to the birth of a daughter, her later marriage, and her untimely death. But Howells was not an exceptional poet, and these plays were never produced by professionals.

B. A Revival of Interest in Poetic Drama

From about 1900 until World War I, there was a renewed interest in poetic drama in both America and Europe. In England, William Poel had started reviving Elizabethan plays with particular success in productions of *Everyman* and Shakespeare's plays. William Butler Yeats was writing exceptional poetic drama; and on the Continent, Rostand, Maeterlinck, and Hauptmann contributed poetic plays. In America, conditions were still not particularly conducive to poetic drama, even though Percy MacKaye had declared that "the drama of democracy will be a poetic drama." It was a period ruled by pragmatic people, described by the Muckrakers, and interpreted by naturalistic moralists like Theodore Dreiser. Poetic drama presented a great contrast to reality because it did not seem to mirror life, and people did not look to poetry for truth. The poetic dramatist, however, wanted to portray both beauty and truth. Hence he copied from the past, and most of his themes concerned historical plots, romantic legends, or Greek myths. In spite of the contrast, however, several poetic dramatists of the first part of the twentieth century managed some success and attracted some favorable attention.

1. WILLIAM VAUGHN MOODY: RELIGIOUS AND UNIVERSAL THEMES

Of American poet-dramatists before World War I, the one with the best reputation as a poet is William Vaughn Moody (1869–1910), the stern teacher of English at the University of Chicago, best known for his "Ode in Time of Hesitation." As a poet, Moody was a transition figure—ever aware of new ideas and a moving, progressive culture and society, and at the same time one who employed the style and form of the older poets. In the history of American drama, Moody is most noteworthy for two prose plays—*The Faith Healer*, and *The Great Divide* —which indicate his concern for a serious, realistic, and progressive drama. His poetic plays suggest similar themes and contain some effective poetry, but they did not reach the stage.

(a) A Poetic Trilogy
The Masque of Judgment (1900). Based on the Bible and dramatizing the conflict between God and the creatures He had created, the trilogy begins with the Incarnation and continues through the Day of Judgment with the Angel Raphael as the protagonist. This play shows that man's desires, for which God is responsible, make him susceptible to evil. When man rebels and is conquered by the serpent, it is God's mistake.

The Fire Bringer (1904). Another story of rebellion— Prometheus' struggle with the gods and his subsequent punishment—this play pictures an unreconciled god at the end of his tyrannical attempt to destroy man.

The Death of Eve (1912), a fragment. This play is concerned with the reconciliation of God to man through woman, who had first separated them. To Moody, who saw disunity as oblivion, man and God must be united.

2. PERCY MACKAYE: ROMANTIC EXPERIMENTER

Percy MacKaye (1875–1956) is known in drama circles through the work of his father, Steele MacKaye, and through his own work in poetic, pageant, and experimental drama. His contribution, particularly in spectacle and pageant drama is undeniable, although his works were never popular in the theater. His first poetic drama, *The Canterbury Pilgrims* (1903), was a blank-verse comedy of four acts which emphasized the character of the poet Chaucer and his sentimental attitude toward the Prioress, as the Wife of Bath tried to make him her next husband. *Sappho and Phaon* (1907) tells the sad story of the Lesbian poetess in love with the slave Phaon. One of his best poetic plays was *Jeanne d'Arc* (1906), a five-act play in blank verse which presents a romantic and rather sentimentalized Jeanne who is driven toward her destiny by the guardianship of St. Michael and by her love for her people.

3. JOSEPHINE PRESTON PEABODY MARKS: HUMANITARIAN POET-DRAMATIST

Josephine Peabody Marks (1874–1922) is the most significant of the early twentieth century poetic dramatists. An intelligent woman with both talent and imagination for writing poetry, Mrs. Marks owed some of her interest in the drama to William Vaughn Moody, one of her college teachers. After a one-act verse play, she wrote *Marlowe* (1901), an idealized if unsuccessful play. A later drama, *The Wolf of Gubbio* (1913), dramatizes the selfishness versus the love in men's lives against the background of Christmas and the influence of Francis of Assisi, whose love controls even animals.

(a) *The Piper,* 1910

(*Plot*) After the Piper rids the town of Hamelin of rats, he is refused his fee by the selfish people. Only Veronica, who is not Hamelin born, and her crippled little boy, Jan, have sympathy for the Piper; while Barbara, daughter of the Burgomaster, falls in love with Michael, the sword swallower, a member of the Piper's group of strolling players. Into the hills, the Piper takes the children, and there he struggles—his prideful wish to punish the villagers conflicting with his love for the children and his human sympathy. When he discovers that Barbara will be placed in a nunnery as penance for the village and hears of Veronica's faith that he will return the children, he does bring the children back to the villagers. People are still greedy, but there is love in the world, and this knowledge seems to have changed the Piper.

(*Discussion*) This play won the Stratford Prize Competition in 1910. For Mrs. Marks, the Piper became not a fairy, but a human, a "fanatical idealist." The play becomes one of character and forces, in which the poetry provides a decided emotional appeal. There is the conflict between the greed of the villagers and the love of Jan for "the Lonely Man," the Crucifix in the village. The forces of greed, love, Christianity, and the supernatural (the pipes of the Piper) act upon the complex struggle within the Piper, who is torn by strong pride and human sensitivity, a cynical bitterness and a self-denying love. Pitting himself even against God, he is finally overcome by the Christian force.

4. MORE POETIC DRAMA, 1900–1914

Other writers of poetic drama during these years include Mary Johnson, the novelist, *The Goddess of Reason* (1907), a blank-verse play in four acts, concerned with the love of a lord and a peasant girl during the French Revolution; Cale Young Rice, *A Night in Avignon* (1907), one act; T. B. Aldrich, *Judith of Bethulia* (1904), the story of a woman who resists love, and assassinates the ruler of the army which surrounds her town, with the consequence that the town is saved and she is honored; George Cabot Lodge, *Cain* (1904); and plays by Ridgely Torrence and Edwin Arlington Robinson.

VI. A NEW SERIOUSNESS

Obviously, from the beginning of time, those who have been interested in drama have had different objectives for writing plays. In early American drama, the traditions behind the writing of plays in prose and poetry suggested to the playwrights that poetry was more the language of serious drama than prose. With the change of attitudes toward life which permeated society after the Civil War in America, the medium for seriousness in drama changed. The romantic wrote in poetry, and although he attempted serious themes, his attempts were generally lost upon a society which demanded that the serious writer express himself in prose. Thus the serious drama of the last part of the nineteenth century was realistic in keeping with the realism of Howells and James. By the turn of the century, others joined the ranks of those few who not only wanted to make commercial successes on the stage but had something of importance to say; yet the means of presenting a serious theme had changed again. Convention now dictated that serious drama be at once comedy, problem play, and criticism of society. The mode was comedy or melodrama, but themes of these serious plays reflected the dramatists' concern for problems in contemporary society.

Few of the plays of this particular period are memorable, but those few have significance for that quite misunderstood decade and a half before World War I. It was a period of change and movement, but it was also an innocent and naïve period. Most of the dramatists dealt with questions of simple propriety and never penetrated into the deeper concerns of morality and truth. A few tried, with varying success and failure, to be meaningful: William Vaughn Moody, Rachel Crothers, Edward Sheldon, and Charles Rann Kennedy.

A. William Vaughn Moody: Believer in Men

An intellectual rather than a commercial playwright, Moody wrote only on themes which he felt significant in modern life. He was interested in intense emotional conflicts, both within individuals and between ideological and social groups. In *The Great Divide* (1906), he contrasted the independent freedom of the West with the inhibiting traditions of Puritan New England, but the major conflict of the play is the internal struggle of a New England girl whose basic desires war against her heritage. Melodramatic touches mar the hero and the plot development, but the serious intent of the playwright in idea and language is prominent. *The Faith Healer* (1909) dramatizes the conflict between earthly love and a sense of divine mission. In all of Moody's plays, there is the strong thesis of the necessary unity of man and a Spiritual Being. A somber idealist, Moody tried to be both practical and profound—to bring meaning to a commercial theater.

1. *THE GREAT DIVIDE*, 1906

An Easterner visiting the West with her brother and fiancé, Ruth Jordan finds herself in the clutches of three men. Unable to protect herself, she offers herself to the strongest, Stephen Ghent, who buys her with a string of gold nuggets. Later, married to Ghent, Ruth buys back the nuggets and returns to the East, where Ghent's child is born. But life is meaningless for Ruth until Ghent appears, explains his love, and promises to begin life again in order to bring her happiness and to remove the guilt of the past.

2. *THE FAITH HEALER*, 1909

Mary, the wife of a midwestern farmer who believes in Darwin and Spencer, is able to walk for the first time in five years when treated by Michaelis, a faith healer. But Michaelis begins to doubt his divine mission when he feels the strength of his love for Rhoda, Mary's niece. His subjection to the scorn of a medical doctor and an orthodox clergyman causes him to lose his powers, and Mary finds that she cannot walk. Finally, however, through his own inner searching and his love for Rhoda, he regains his power, and the play ends with his triumph.

B. Rachel Crothers: Historian of Manners

Although her name is forgotten, for a period of over twenty-five years Rachel Crothers (1878–1958) contributed a play of some significance to American drama almost every season. It has been suggested that her plays form a study of the manners of woman during the first quarter of this century, and to a degree this is true. She wrote of the double standard in *A Man's World* (1909), showed woman's position in *When Ladies Meet* (1932), and discussed the problems of the younger generation in *New People* (1920). But her observations now seem mainly standard: self-expression doesn't mean freedom (*Expressing Willie,* 1924); saying you believe doesn't make you believe (*Susan and God,* 1937); a woman's place is in the home (*He and She,* 1911); parents can disillusion their children (*Mary the Third,* 1923). Dressed in the craftsmanship which marked her plays, these ideas are more impressive than in a list. But she was not a particularly penetrating critic of society and sometimes mistook proprieties for moral values.

All of her plays, however, are not without significance. She did have some insight into the problems of her contemporary society; and in a serious and sometimes excitingly dramatic fashion, she arrived at some meaningful conclusions. Love and honesty are important in family relations; a woman must be true to herself. In a rather homely and seemingly Victorian fashion, Rachel Crothers' plays before World War I mark a decided step in the development of serious social comedy. Her plays, however, are clearly a part of pre-O'Neill drama and tend to be dated in idea and language.

1. *HE AND SHE,* 1911

Tom and Ann Herford, both sculptors, decide to enter separate designs for a commission. So as not to bother them while they work, their teenage daughter is kept away at school. Meanwhile, Keith, Tom's assistant, decides that he really doesn't love Ruth, a prim career girl, but sees great possibilities in Daisy, Tom's home-loving sister. Tom is broken when Ann gets the commission, but the tables turn quickly as the daughter comes home from school, having decided to marry a fellow who cares for her. Ann immediately gives Tom her designs and decides to spend her time winning back the faith of their daughter.

C. Edward Sheldon: Romantic Realist

The variety of Sheldon's (1886–1946) plays makes him difficult to classify, but his early plays gave him a reputation as a precursor of the realists of the 1920's. Although he wrote mainly melodrama, he is an interesting combination of the realist and the romanticist whose significance comes from his imaginative experimentation and his courage and concern for truthful social themes. Beauty of thought and expression interested him, too, and his use of fantasy, romanticism, and realism suggest the range of his imagination.

Sheldon's plays after World War I—*Bewitched* (1924) with Sidney Howard; *Lulu Belle* (1926) with Charles Mac-Arthur—are not effective. His first professional play, *Salvation Nell* (1908), suggested realism in the variety and activity of its minor characters in the barroom scene, but it is clearly a melodrama of a girl who worked for, waited for, and won to the right cause the man she loved. *The Nigger* (1910) courageously dramatizes the story of a Southern governor who discovers that his grandfather was a Negro slave. After *The Boss* (1911), Sheldon's concern for romanticism became dominant. *Romance* (1913), one of his most successful plays, uses the story of a young American clergyman's grand passion for an Italian opera singer to prepare for the marriage of the clergyman's grandson to an actress. Romanticism determined the action in this play, and also determined that the theme of a search for beauty in *The High Road* (1912) would be treated not as realistic tragedy but as romance. Sheldon's romantic and poetic imagination is seen at its height in *The Garden of Paradise* (1914), a dramatization of Andersen's "The Little Mermaid" in which the characters are humanized. Essentially, Sheldon always tried to present a truthful theme, but his early concern for realism disappeared in later plays.

1. *THE BOSS*, 1911

(*Plot*) When Griswold and Company, Contractors, are forced to near-bankruptcy by Regan, a rival contractor, and the bank which Griswold directs is in danger of losing money which belongs to the poor people of the city, Regan offers to join forces with the stipulation that he be allowed to marry Griswold's daughter, Emily, and thereby gain social position. Emily, a very serious social worker, agrees to the marriage— in name only. Complementing this conflict is young Griswold's union activity in organizing Regan's men, their subsequent strike, and the riot during which Griswold is hit with a brick. Regan is accused of instigating the incident and put in jail, where his belligerent spirit is broken. But with Emily's help, Regan's moral spirit is strengthened and, freed after another confesses throwing the brick, he goes home, a good man, with his wife.

(*Discussion*) *Salvation Nell, The Nigger,* and *The Boss* show Sheldon's concern for a realistic portrayal of American life. Against an interesting background of business, political, and labor conditions, the dramatist created a romantic incident —the forced marriage—and a stageworthy if melodramatic hero. The play is frequently realistic in character, scene, and action, but it is not a realistic study of labor problems or of a labor boss.

D. Charles Rann Kennedy: Christian Idealist

A scholarly Englishman who married an actress, Edith Wynne Matthison, and became an American citizen in 1917, Kennedy (1871–1950) was a serious advocate of Christian principles, which he dramatized with more courage and ardor than theatrical effectiveness. Quinn complains that his work became progressively less dramatic, and one cannot countenance the talky quality of his plays, although their ideas are vital. His sincerity and concern for social problems show his attachment to the Social Gospel Movement, and in all of his plays there are strong religious and sociological implications. Adding a literary distinction to his work is his thoughtful and effective use of symbolism. Although he continued to write plays after World War I, he reached the height of his reputation about the middle of the second decade of this century.

Kennedy's Christian idealism is the dominant aspect of his work. Believing that "God does things as a dramatist would," he set out to dramatize Christianity. In *The Servant in the House* (1907) he presented a Christ-figure who reveals the hypocrisy of organized religion and the idealism of love and truth in life. Another play, *The Winter Feast* (1908), portrayed, he said, "the hate and lies in life that destroy." These were the first two of a proposed but unfinished five-cycle play; the third, *The Idol Breaker* (1914), dramatized the thesis of freedom. A later trilogy consisted of *The Chastening* (1922), on Jesus of Nazareth; *The Admiral* (1923), on Columbus as discoverer, which G. B. Shaw called a "magnificent play"; and *The Salutation* (1925), on Paolo and Francesca.

(a) *The Terrible Meek*, 1912

A daring play, *The Terrible Meek* "portrays a soldier's awakening consciousness." In the darkness, a woman whose son has been killed talks with the Captain and soldier who executed him. Finally, the scene is faintly revealed, with the Crucified Christ in the background. Exploring a thesis that "the real meek are beginning to inherit the earth," Kennedy sent his published play to all kings, emperors, presidents, war ministers, munition-makers, etc. in the world.

(b) *The Idol Breaker*, 1914

Concerned with individual freedom and man's relationship to God and society, this play tells of Adam, the bastard blacksmith bound to the village of Little Boswell, and Naomi, the gypsy girl who represents that quality which unites all men beyond time and space. Adam, married to Ellen, who represents the "smallness" of Little Boswell, has made a clock, "God's clock!" with a living heart and a tongue which tells the truth as well as the time, thus revealing man's hypocrisy and superficiality. But Adam is misunderstood by everyone and condemned as an atheist, an egotist, and an anarchist. In the plot, which is not always clear, a new character appears—Jake, Naomi's husband, who represents the freedom of hate in contrast to Naomi's freedom of beauty and understanding. After a fight over Naomi, Jake dies, and Adam and Naomi leave to bear children before returning to Boswell, where Adam will become the Blacksmith of the World.

VII. BEGINNINGS IN DRAMATIC CRITICISM

Many years had passed since Washington Irving had called critics the "pests of society," but the thought remained in many people's minds. During the first hundred years of American drama, theater developed, plays improved, but dramatic criticism remained an unenlightened pastime—although one must admit that complaining about dramatic criticism will always be a hobby of playwrights. With few exceptions, however, dramatists before the Civil War had not bothered to evolve theories of drama, and criticism of plays generally meant paid "puffing" or biased comment on the way the play had been produced. Toward the end of the nineteenth century, however, attitudes toward criticism began to change. There had always been three emphases in dramatic criticism—moralistic criticism, technical criticism, and literary criticism. These continued, but the last one became relatively more significant by the decade before World War I.

A. Whither American Drama?

By the last quarter of the nineteenth century, many people were beginning to ask this question, and the answers suggested a new period in dramatic criticism. Although Augustin Daly accepted "The American Dramatist" [*North American Review,* CXLII (May, 1886)] only in terms of the dramatist's willingness to collaborate with a theater manager, Brander Matthews viewed "The Dramatic Outlook in America" [*Harper's,* LXXVII (May, 1889)], Alfred Hennequin described the "Characteristics of American Drama" [*Arena,* I (May, 1890)], and Dion Boucicault was optimistic about "The Future of American Drama" [*Arena,* I (November, 1890)].

Although it is difficult for some post-World War II critics to feel the significance of pre-World War I drama, there is much to be said for dating the beginnings of modern American drama in 1890. During this year, America's most serious imitator of Ibsen, whose plays generally designate the beginnings of modern drama, produced his best play, *Margaret Fleming.* And by this time, critics and dramatists wrote in terms of an American drama and were concerned with what it was and where it was going.

B. American Dramatic Theory

"American Playwrights on the American Drama" [*Harper's Weekly,* XXXIII (February 2, 1889)], written by Edward Harrigan, William Gillette, John Grosvenor Wilson, Steele MacKaye, William Winter, Bronson Howard, and Augustin Daly, is an unsuccessful attempt to define or discover agreement on the nature of American drama, but it does show clearly what each dramatist wanted to do on the stage. In contrast to earlier times, it became rather normal for a dramatist to pronounce his theories of the drama in a published essay.

Bronson Howard wrote "The Laws of Dramatic Construction" in which he described a "satisfactory" play. In numerous essays, W. D. Howells propounded his dramatic theory which was later imitated by James A. Herne in "Art for Truth's Sake in the Drama," (*Arena,* February, 1897). By the turn of the century, some dramatists, such as Langdon Mitchell, lectured on their theories of drama. Others were being interviewed more adroitly by newspaper and magazine writers with the consequence that a playwright had more opportunities to discuss his theories.

C. Dramatic Criticism

Historically, criticism of the American drama came from three different views—moralistic, technical, literary. In practice, there were (1) critics who were paid to "puff" a certain play, (2) newspaper and magazine critics who were completely without the necessary intellectual or imaginative equipment to criticize a play, and (3) a few literary critics concerned with works of art rather than theatrical performances. Publication sources also became a meaningful part of the history of dramatic criticism in America.

1. PUBLICATIONS FEATURING DRAMATIC CRITICISM

Once reported as part of the sporting world, theater news achieved sufficient importance to warrant particular journals soon after the Civil War. The first significant theatrical papers were the New York *Dramatic News and Society Journal,* 1874; the New York *Dramatic Mirror,* 1879; and the New York *Dramatic News,* 1881. *Leslie's Monthly Magazine* gave special attention to the theater, mainly on stage sets, about this same time. During the late 1880's, W. D. Howells used *Harper's* "Editor's Study" to comment as he wished on the drama and theater. A most significant step was the appearance in 1900 of *Theater Magazine,* edited by Arthur Hornblow. As varied newspapers and magazines employed more steady reporting of activities in the theater, dramatic criticism increased in both quality and quantity.

2. THE NEW CRITICS

Dramatic criticism from the point of view of morality lessened somewhat from its earlier emphasis but remained prominent in such essays as "Filth on the Stage," and "Indelicacy of Modern Plays." Criticism from a technical point of view was still a major interest of the reviewers—William Ellsworth's observations on *Ben Hur* in *The Critic* (XXVI, March, 1900), and many comments by prominent theater figures such as Steele MacKaye, William Gillette, and Dion Boucicault. The innovation of this period was an interest in drama as literature. W. D. Howells commented on the plays of every major contemporary dramatist during the two decades that surround the turn of the century. He was particularly effective in his criticisms of Edward Harrigan, James A. Herne, Ibsen, and Shaw. Henry James spent considerably less time writing about American drama, but he published several interesting essays on contemporary drama. Among the most active of the other serious critics were Brander Matthews, Laurence Hutton (*Curiosities of the American Stage*, 1891), and Walter Prichard Eaton (*The American Stage of Today*, 1908).

3. JOURNALISTIC CRITICS

It is possible here only to note the great variety of journalistic critics. Howells complained that the same reporter who described a fire in the morning reviewed a theater performance that evening. This was one problem. Another was paid "puffing." The Syndicate Theater, for example, controlled not only theaters and playwrights but newspaper criticism. Certain critics, then, are completely unreliable in their reviews. A few were independent and astute in their observations and deserve some mention. William Winter wrote many criticisms of plays and dramatists (collected in *The Wallet of Time*, 1913), but his close association with some dramatists, such as Daly, limits the value of his work. Alan Dale and James G. Huneker were among the best reviewers. John Corbin deserves attention for his observations, particularly those in "The Dawn of American Drama" [*Atlantic Monthly*, XCIX (May, 1907)]. Clayton Hamilton was a particularly prolific critic of all drama, although inclined to be more conservative than inspired in his work.

VIII. A DEVELOPING THEATER

During the fifty years that separated the Civil War from World War I, the American theater changed dramatically. Following its own inclinations concerning spectacular melodrama and stimulated by the realism movement in literature as well as the products of industry, theater performances became more realistic. The style of acting as well as the entire procedure for producing a play underwent changes in the hands of the new director-producers. With the social and economic development of the spreading country, the need for entertainment grew, and new kinds of theater entertainment also became popular. Growth meant money, and one consequence of potential wealth was the establishment of the monopoly known as the Theatrical Syndicate. If a phrase were needed to describe the theater of the early twentieth century, it would be "Big Business!"

A. Realism in the Theater

Realistic theater did not necessarily mean a truthful theater in terms of ideas presented on the stage. Essentially, it meant that the audience need not "suspend its disbelief" so willingly. The acting, the action, the scenery, and the stage properties became more realistic. Dramas which suggested realism of idea, such as Ibsen's *Ghosts*, did not become acceptable in the American theater until after the twentieth century began.

1. REALISM IN SCENE

Before the Civil War, Boucicault was producing realistic spectacles of a building on fire in New York City or a boat exploding. Later melodramas employed the buzz saw, the pile driver, or the cotton press in an effort to capitalize on the popular appeal of realism. The log cabin and the wolves in *Davy Crockett* as well as the storm suggested the realism made possible by the stage carpenter. Such plays as *Ben Hur* with palaces, horse races, and galley fights were outstanding for stage realism. On the other hand, Edward Harrigan and Howells, as previously mentioned, were interested in more detailed stage realism of a less spectacular nature.

2. BELASCO REALISM

As director and producer, David Belasco insisted on a realism limited only by the abilities of his stage carpenters and property men. The details interested him. If soldiers were supposed to be tramping through North Carolina, he demanded North Carolina mud. For one play that required a certain kind of room, he visited a poverty-stricken neighborhood in New York and bought the contents of a room—wallpaper and all. Many props for *Du Barry* came directly from Paris. He was meticulous, even to the indentation in a pillow which would suggest that a person had just left his bed, or the right kind of biscuit in the cupboard of an actress down on her luck. This was the realism of which Belasco was a master.

3. ONE-CHARACTER ACTORS

A select number of actors achieved reputations for realism through their development of realistic details in their character portrayals. Joseph Jefferson III was such an actor in *Rip Van Winkle*; so were Frank Mayo in *Davy Crockett*, and James O'Neill in *The Count of Monte Cristo*. William Gillette's acting of Sherlock Holmes and Denman Thompson's in *The Old Homestead* also suggested a concern for particular realism.

B. Innovations in Theater Management

The theater manager was usually the person who owned the theater, chose the plays, hired the actors, and collected the money. Actors learned their "lines of business" and as "walking gentlemen" or "leading ladies," for example, performed in plays. This arrangement changed when the producer-director came into existence, although the job of the director as it is now understood did not appear until much later. This new "manager," however, pitted himself against the star system as it had been; *he* created stars. He also created a tyranny which was both good and bad. A very helpful innovation was the establishment of the booking office, but with this service there was a means for controlling performers and plays which was eventually exploited by the Theatrical Syndicate.

1. AUGUSTIN DALY: "THE AUTOCRAT OF THE STAGE"

No one could have become more absorbed in the theater than Daly, and few were as powerful. He "lived" in his theater; chose, wrote, or adapted his plays; selected his cast, not for "lines of business" but as he understood the parts; and controlled and rehearsed his actors in a dictatorial but effective manner. His standards in art and personal morality were high, and his achievements in encouraging a certain kind of American play, in bringing European drama to America, and in carrying Shakespeare to England are significant.

2. STEELE MACKAYE: MAN OF CREATIVE IMAGINATION

Another producer-director, MacKaye was interested in the technical theater. His innovations in theater management include the elevator stage, improved ventilating systems, fireproofing for scenery, and a curtain of light. MacKaye is also remembered for the theater he planned for the 1893 Chicago World's Fair—the Spectatorium. With a stage opening of 150 feet by 70 feet, a seating capacity of 10,000, and numerous devices for a variety of stage spectacles, it was the product of an extravagant imagination. Unfortunately, when the economic Panic of 1893 curtailed expenses for the Fair, the Spectatorium was cancelled.

3. THE THEATER SYNDICATE

The key to theater success in the late nineteenth century came through the booking agency: control bookings and control theaters, actors, and playwrights. With the growth of a nationwide network of theaters, it is little wonder that a monopoly in the form of a Theater Syndicate settled over America. It started in 1895, when six men representing different sections of the country joined forces to control entertainment: Sam Nixon and Fred Zimmerman (Philadelphia to Chicago), Charles Frohman (New York, New England, and the Continent) Al Hayman (the important towns west of the Mississippi and the

Far-West), Marc Klaw and Abe Erlanger (south from New York to New Orelans, north to Chicago). Their objective was power. Syndicate theaters could not hire independent actors; syndicate acting companies could not play in free theaters; and the Syndicate took 5 per cent of the theater gross. It was a tough system, and few tried to buck it—Belasco, Minnie Maddern Fiske, James A. Herne. For ten years, the control was strict, but it weakened finally—from internal discord, excessive greed, questionable contracts with actors and companies, and from such ambitious impressarios as Keith and Albee and the Shubert brothers.

C. Theater Activity: Expansive and Experimental

During the last quarter of the nineteenth century and the first decade of the twentieth, American theater was a varied and frequently extravagant business. The minstrel shows, the Tom Shows, and the showboats have been discussed. Burlesque and variety acts probably started when the first dance-hall girl climbed onto the bar and started to sing or dance, but greater publicity came with Lydia Thompson and her British Blondes in 1869. Legs were no longer hidden. Musical comedy goes back to the eighteenth century, but *The Black Crook* (1866) by Charles M. Barras is usually considered the beginning of modern musical comedy. Other kinds of entertainment include the Wild West Show, the Can Can, the Circus, and the Honky Tonk. The work of George M. Cohan added to American musicals after the turn of the century; and in 1907, the Ziegfeld Follies started their particular kind of revues. American vaudeville started in the variety houses toward the end of the nineteenth century with such acts as Weber and Fields or McIntyre and Heath and reached top popularity during the First World War.

1. ACTORS, IMPORTS, AND EXCITEMENT

Beyond variety, this was the age of some big names in American theater. Actors like Lawrence Barrett and Edwin Booth were matinee idols; Nat Goodwin was one of the fore-

most comedians. Richard Mansfield and Minnie Maddern Fiske
were leaders of the theater when Ethel Barrymore made her
debut in 1894. By the turn of the century, America was im-
porting not only popular melodrama but, with some daring and
some dissension, the plays of Ibsen, Shaw, Synge, Barrie, and
Rostand. Both the plays and players sometimes caused excitement, but the single greatest catastrophe was the Iroquois Theater fire in Chicago on December 30, 1903, which claimed
over 500 lives.

2. NOTABLE EXPERIMENTS: PERCY MACKAYE AND DAVID BELASCO

Among various theater experiments, two plays by dramatists of particular imagination and theatrical skill are outstanding. Percy MacKaye's *The Scarecrow* (1908) takes its theme
from Hawthorne's story, "Feathertop," and tells of a scarecrow
which is created before the audience's eyes, comes to life as
Lord Ravensbane, and achieves a considerable sense of humanity before it succumbs to its own artificial construction. The
fantasy of the play, its challenge to actor and director, and its
literary quality make it outstanding. Belasco's play of the supernatural, *The Return of Peter Grimm* (1911), is another experimental fantasy. Peter returns from the dead to be an unseen
influence on the lives of the living and finally to carry away
with him the little boy who dies. The thesis is love, and there is
sentiment in the play; it was, however, effective theater and not
maudlin experimentation.

IX. SUMMARY

From the Civil War to World War I, drama developed
from a profession that demanded certain acquired skills to an
art which showed seriousness and imagination—from the professionally effective plays of Boucicault and Daly to the artistry
of Herne and Moody. Plots suggested more sophistication;
characterization indicated the dramatists' more probing interest
in life. Early stereotypes—the Indian, the Negro, the Yankee,
the Irishman, and the Jew—became types and finally developed

into the individuals which distinguish characterization in many modern American plays. Before the turn of the century most of the plays were melodrama and farce, but the significant trends were toward realism—as seen in the plays of MacKaye, Howells, and Herne—and the development by Howard, Howells, and Fitch of a social comedy.

The influence of Europe helped the modern, serious dramatist become successful, and with the new century poetic drama experienced an interlude of slight popularity. Social, economic, and political theses were now treated with some seriousness; and social melodrama replaced the vivid spectacle that overwhelmed the stage during the last third of the nineteenth century. Drama, although not yet great or even very good as a body, had certainly become a more meaningful genre in the society of America. Breaking away from the traditions of the past—in theme and technique—the drama and the theater were now ready for the necessary next step: an independent and courageous theater company and an outstanding dramatist.

SELECTED BIBLIOGRAPHY

"American Playwrights on the American Drama," *Harper's Weekly*, XXXIII (February 2, 1889), 97–100.

Bucks, Dorothy Sims, *The American Drama of Ideas from 1890 to 1929*. Unpublished dissertation, Northwestern University, 1944.

Corbin, John, "The Dawn of the American Drama," *Atlantic Monthly*, XCIX (May, 1907), 632–644.

Davis, Owen, *My First Fifty Years in the Theatre*. Boston: W. H. Baker Company, 1950.

Dickinson, Thomas H., *Playwrights of the New American Theater*. New York: The Macmillan Company, 1925.

Felheim, Marvin, *The Theatre of Augustin Daly*. Cambridge, Mass.: Harvard University Press, 1956.

Harper, Robert D., *Economic and Political Attitudes in American Drama 1865–1900*. Unpublished dissertation, University of Chicago, 1949.

Hartman, John Geoffrey, *The Development of American Social Comedy 1787–1936*. Philadelphia: University of Pennsylvania Press, 1939.

Herne, James A., "Art for Truth's Sake in the Drama," *Arena*, XVII (February, 1897), 361–370.

Hughes, Glenn, *A History of the American Theatre, 1700–1950*. New York: Samuel French, 1951.

Hutton, Laurence, *Curiosities of the American Stage*. New York: Harper & Brothers, 1891.

Meserve, Walter J., ed., *The Complete Plays of W. D. Howells*. New York: New York University Press, 1960.

Moses, Montrose J., *The American Dramatist*. Boston: Little, Brown & Company, 1925.

Nardin, James T., *A Study in Popular American Farce*. Unpublished dissertation, University of Chicago, 1949.

Quinn, Arthur H., *A History of the American Drama from the Civil War to the Present Day*. New York: Appleton-Century-Crofts, Inc., 1943.

CHAPTER IV

American Drama Between the World Wars

From the Provincetown to World Renown

With the appearance of the Provincetown Players and Eugene O'Neill, American theater and drama achieved a new significance which by the time of World War II had changed American drama into a recognized force in world drama. The substantial advances made during the twenty-five years preceding 1915, however, should not be forgotten. The Provincetown Players, for example, were only one group of several in a Little Theater Movement rebelling against commercial practices in America. Foreign influences, which were highly significant in the development of modern American drama—from the Moscow Art Theater to the works of Ibsen and Strindberg—were seen long before World War I in the plays of a few serious dramatists. Essentially, the direction had been clearly pointed out by 1915, and dramatic implementation was urgently needed. This was supplied through the creative work of the Provincetown Players and the imaginative genius of Eugene O'Neill—a necessary combination. Then within a few years, American drama was transformed into something much more vital than it had been previously, but the result obtained was the product of forces at work in America since the beginning of the century.

The dramatic impetus having been established and the moment in our social and intellectual history being right, several dramatists of the 1920's began writing plays which were distinguished by imaginative thought and creative characterization. Dramatists, as Thomas H. Dickinson (*Playwrights of the New American Theater*, 1925) pointed out, were no longer concerned only with amusement; they felt the more dynamic responsibility of art toward society and truth—Maxwell Anderson, Paul Green, S. N. Behrman, Philip Barry, Robert Sherwood. Also, the greater freedom which the dramatist now enjoyed was mirrored in the kind of plays he wrote—a new realism, a more poignant social comedy, folk drama, pageant drama, poetic drama.

It is always difficult and a bit artificial to attempt to impose some order on creative work, but the attempt is necessary and the results, in any historical sense, valuable. Underlying a good part of the drama of the 1930's is a social consciousness which may be oriented through the dramatists' intellectual persuasion—left to right, from the most liberal of propaganda plays to the traditional high comedy. On the spectrum between these two points, still going from left to right, are plays of social commentary, problem plays, satirical plays, and plays of domestic and light comedy. In addition to these trends, there were, of course, as in the nineteenth century, always light farces and entertaining melodrama. Outstanding in this period were those few dramatists who aimed at some psychological insight. Although these dramatists did not reach O'Neill's penetration, they were searching for the same meaningful interpretation of life—Philip Barry, Maxwell Anderson, Thornton Wilder, and William Saroyan.

An achievement in American drama of this time was the faint beginning of a substantial dramatic criticism. Before World War I, there were brief sojourns into dramatic criticism by those oriented in literature, but no tradition was established. Only by the end of the Thirties, in fact, does there appear the beginning of a serious literary criticism of the drama. With this necessary adjunct to a more meaningful drama, American plays at the outbreak of World War II assumed a new importance. A perennial but increasingly insistent intruder on the international scene before the war, American drama during the years following 1945 became accepted as a major force in world drama.

I. AN APPROACHING TRANSFORMATION

American drama and theater at the time of World War I enjoyed a potential, though largely unrecognized, that it could not have claimed ten years before. Activity throughout the theater suggested a spirit and vitality which were unknown during the Augustin Daly and Charles Frohman periods of influence. The work of university teachers such as George Pierce Baker, for example, was effecting a healthy influence on playwrights; and art rather than commercialism became a more common objective. Of particular significance in theater history was the Little Theater Movement, which took its impulse from foreign theaters; for the moment, however, foreign influence was less impressive on the work of the dramatist. Largely melodrama, although with an increasing emphasis on social and psychological comment but with infrequent concern for experimentation in form, American drama offered little for someone like O'Neill to imitate. He could, however, follow the direction that the more daring American dramatists suggested—imitate foreign drama—and he could revolt. The seed for a change in American drama and theater had already been planted. The conditions in the theater, the poverty of good plays, and the world situation helped bring about a transformation toward which numerous playwrights, theater people, and critics had been working for a number of years.

A. The Condition of the Theater

Quite simply one might describe the condition of the theater during the second decade of the twentieth century as one of dramatic change. The monopoly of the Theatrical Syndicate had been broken. Of the older director-producers, Belasco was the major figure remaining; and although he was still active during this period, his particular style of production was losing its appeal with audiences. Much more impressive was the influence of André Antoine's Théâtre Libre, the Abbey Theatre, and the Moscow Art Theatre. Within

America, university professors were proving influential both in the writing and production of plays. Certain statistics also indicate a change in the theater. In 1900, there were sixteen first-class theaters in New York; in 1910, there were thirty; in 1925, sixty-one. These theaters produced seventy-two new plays in an average year at the turn of the century; ten years later, they were producing 130 plays; while at the quarter-century mark, they produced 208. Plays on tour during these years, on the other hand, dropped in number from 308 to 198 to 68. As New York asserted its power, there was also a tremendous growth of community and university theaters across the country. These changes inevitably affected the drama.

1. UNIVERSITY THEATERS AND GEORGE PIERCE BAKER

During the late eighteenth century, American universities made a contribution to the drama which they were unable to continue during the nineteenth century. Once again in the early twentieth century, however, they found a niche in the development of American drama. Some of the more effective contributions came from Frederick Koch at the University of North Dakota and later at the University of North Carolina, A. M. Drummund at Cornell, Thomas H. Dickinson at the University of Wisconsin, Thomas Wood Stevens at Carnegie Tech, and E. C. Mabie at the University of Iowa. None, however, was more effective in his work than George Pierce Baker (1866–1935) at Harvard University and later at Yale University. Actor, playwright, director, critic, and teacher, his graduate course in English Composition (English 47), "The Technique of the Drama," known as the "47 Workshop," has become a familiar landmark in theater history. First taught in 1909, the course eventually enrolled, among others, Edward Sheldon, Philip Barry, Eugene O'Neill, Sidney Howard, and Fred Koch. Baker's essay on "Practical American Drama" in 1911 suggests his approach, which was not, unfortunately, looked upon with complete satisfaction by Harvard officials. After pleading for a Harvard School of Drama without success, Baker finally left for New Haven in 1924 to help establish the Yale School of Drama.

2. LITTLE THEATER MOVEMENT AND THE PROVINCETOWN PLAYERS

Eva Le Gallienne, an American actress and director, once wrote that "the true theater of America must be created by the people themselves." In one way her statement effectively describes theater activity during the early twentieth century. It was a protest against the commercial theater that stimulated the founding of the Drama League of America in 1910. Further stimulation for the revolt came from the little theaters abroad—the Théâtre Libre, the Freie Bühne—and the work of Adolphe Appia and Gordon Craig. When the Abbey Players from Dublin toured America in 1911 and Max Reinhardt's spectacular, *Sumurûm,* was produced early in 1912, the necessary impetus had been provided, and several little theater groups started in America: the Chicago Little Theatre, the Toy Theatre in Boston, Stuart Walker's Portmanteau Theatre, and the Washington Square Players. *The Little Theatre Monthly* also appeared, edited by Harold A. Ehrensberger, which soon listed over 1000 community and university theaters in America. A group interest in pageantry which used amateur actors was spurred on at this time by Percy MacKaye. Essentially, the changes in the theater had been brought about by interested amateurs, although professionalism frequently resulted. From among the Washington Square Players, for example, the Theatre Guild was formed in 1918.

(a) The Provincetown Players

The best known of all little theater groups was the Provincetown Players, started by some theater enthusiasts on a wharf in Provincetown, Massachusetts, during the summer of 1915. The next year, 1916, they gave themselves a name, selected George Cram "Jig" Cook as president of the twenty-nine members, and settled at 139 Macdougal Street in Greenwich Village as a subscription theater—"to give American playwrights a chance to work out their· ideas in freedom." Eugene O'Neill joined them during the summer of 1916, and with him and Susan Glaspell as their major playwrights, the group's success mounted. Soon they moved to different quarters; and during the 1920–21 .season, they took *The Emperor Jones* uptown. With success, however, came difficulties. The informality was gone, the spirit that had held them together was dead; and the group split—one part interested in experimental theater; the other concerned with progress and success. After Jig Cook sorrowfully left, the triumvirate took over: O'Neill as playwright, Robert Edmund Jones as designer, and Kenneth Macgowan as director. Again they reached success, and again they disagreed on their objectives— professionalism vs. idealism. In 1925, a third Provincetown group reaffirmed the old ideals but met financial difficulties. Helped by Otto Kahn, they forged ahead into the fall season of 1929, hoping to recoup loses with a production of Thomas H. Dickinson's *Winter Bound*. But it was too late! The Crash ended an era in the theater, too, but not before the Provincetown Players had brought considerable enlightenment to American drama and theater.

B. Suggestions without Excitement: 1915–1919

During these five years, one finds suggestions of interesting potential among dramatists, but little of the excitement of artistic attainment. War conditions prevailed; older playwrights were losing their effectiveness; new playwrights had not yet gained control of their art. The transformation was slow in coming. There were the social melodramas and comedies which commented on society's follies—one received the first Pulitzer Prize in drama—and a few war plays. Worthy of comment, however, were the beginning works— one-act plays, in particular—of playwrights who were to do better things later on. Not until 1919 did the drama seem to suggest in over-all productions the creativity which would characterize the plays of the 1920's.

1. SOCIAL MELODRAMA AND COMEDY: THE OLD AND THE NEW

Among the established dramatists who produced uninspired plays during these years were Eugene Walter, Charles Rann Kennedy, Rachel Crothers, and George Middleton.

Louis Anspacher's *The Unchastened Woman* (1915) enjoyed a measure of popularity, portraying, as it did, a
wealthy but unconscionable society woman's fight for power.
Good Gracious, Annabelle (1916) by Clare Kummer, a
newcomer, is a much more lively play, a situation comedy distinguished by witty dialogue, in which the girl gets her millionaire. Jesse Lynch Williams' *Why Marry?* (1917), the
first Pulitzer Prize winner, seems impossibly dated to have
won such a distinction. Satirizing and defending the institution of marriage, Williams presents a couple who feel that
love is enough, that they do not need marriage. Finally, however, they are tricked into marriage because it is "the best
we [society] have to offer you." Williams' next play, *Why
Not?* (1922) dramatized two mismated couples whom he
brought properly back to an acceptance of social standards
by providing each with a child. The new realism in social
comedy, however, had not yet arrived.

As the 1920's approached, the pace and character of
the drama suggested the explosion of good plays during that
decade. Booth Tarkington's silly but cute farce *Clarence*
(1919) shows how a young soldier-scientist-Ph.D. solves the
problems of the Wheeler family. Zoë Akins' *Déclassée* (1919)
describes a love triangle, the resulting divorce, and the woman's suffering from being déclassée or lowered in social position, and ends with a melodramatic death. *The Famous Mrs.
Fair* (1919) by James Forbes tells of a woman whose war
career overshadows her return to civilized life until she sees
what her place in life must be. Other plays produced in 1919
include Susan Glaspell's first full-length play, *Bernice*;
O'Neill's *The Dreamy Kid*; and Elmer Rice's *For the De-
fence*.

2. MODERN DRAMA IN ONE ACT

The university theater and the Little Theater Movement
changed the nature of one-act drama in America from the
frequently farcical curtain raisers of the past to something of
dramatic significance. Generally, these new plays were the
initial efforts of dramatists who were to do better things.
Lewis Beach's *The Clod* (1914) takes place during the Civil
War in a frontier house and shows how little things reveal

the basic person—even the clod. In Susan Glaspell's *Trifles* (1916) a farm woman has strangled her earthy and unimaginative husband with a rope while he slept. Some women at the farmhouse, gossiping and waiting for their husbands to investigate the crime, discover the woman's favorite canary, which had been her sole company and comfort, with its neck twisted and deduce the motive for killing. *Aria Da Capo* (1919) by Edna St. Vincent Millay is a poetic satire on war. Onto a set arranged for the traditional Columbine and Pierrot come two friendly shepherds who are prodded to greed and finally to murdering each other by Cothurnus, the Masque of Tragedy, before Columbine and Pierrot return to their interrupted dialogue. Particularly outstanding are the one-act plays of Eugene O'Neill—*Bound East for Cardiff, Thirst, In the Zone, Ile, The Rope,* among others—which suggest the characters and themes at his later plays.

II. EUGENE O'NEILL: CREATIVE SEARCHER

Whatever the final criticism of O'Neill's work may be, he arrived on the American dramatic scene at a time when he was most urgently needed; moreover, through his sense of good theater and his desire to make a penetrating comment on life, he has made the most significant single contribution to modern American drama. Writing only plays, he refused to be lionized when his work achieved popular acclaim, and he persisted with a single exception—*Ah, Wilderness!* (1933), a comedy—in his basic desire to write tragedy with American circumstance. His connection with nineteenth-century American theater through his father, James O'Neill, an actor, warred with his own dramatic instincts, which were strongly stimulated by European innovations in experimental theater. At the same time, conflicting agonies arising from personal and family difficulties led him into a concern for contemporary psychology and philosophy, which he was unable to master but which added strength and insight to the human conflicts in his plays. Through a tangled path of dramatized experiment, he searched—haunted and cursed—

for himself. And throughout his career, he found different answers to his questions, none completely satisfying either in form or idea. His lack of detachment is a problem; his stylistic difficulty is another and more serious limitation. All considered, however, his achievements have earned him more critical attention than any other American playwright and an international reputation which ranks him as America's greatest dramatist. Although this reputation may change, O'Neill will always be remembered as a vital, moving force in the establishment of modern American drama.

A. Life and Influences

If a man is the sum of his experiences and the influences that have worked upon him, an interpretive review of such events and ideas will help one understand the emotional and intellectual complexity that was Eugene O'Neill. The story of his life, fascinating and revealing and not a little horrible, must remain a sketch, unfortunately; and the influences upon him may only be suggested.

1. "TRIAL BY EXISTENCE," EUGENE O'NEILL (1888–1953)

Within ten years, the shy young man whom Terry Carline introduced to the Provincetown Players in the summer of 1916 became a major figure in American drama. In another ten years, he had won the Nobel Prize for his contribution to dramatic literature. To accomplish this he had traveled a long way from his birth in a hotel room, the son of the actor, James O'Neill and Ellen Quinlan O'Neill, to life as a sailor on assorted tramp steamers, to six months in a tuberculosis sanatorium, to George Pierce Baker's "47 Workshop" at Harvard, and on to the Provincetown Players and his first theater success. And the way had not been an easy one, as the titles of books about him suggest: *The Haunted Heroes of Eugene O'Neill, Eugene O'Neill and The Tragic Tension, The Curse of the Misbegotten.*

O'Neill's father, James O'Neill, considered himself a tragic person, doomed to act in a single play, *The Count of Monte Cristo.* With self-pity, drink, and a miserly attitude toward money, the elder O'Neill created a family life of misery and horror, which O'Neill partially revealed in his play *Long Day's Journey into Night*. The conditions which led his mother to become a dope addict, his brother an alcoholic, and which made him question his Catholic background haunted O'Neill throughout his life. Married in 1909 to the first of three wives, he immediately left his bride and started on aimless adventures—Honduras, Argentina, the sea—until his time in a sanatarium for tuberculosis gave him an opportunity to read and to think. After attendance at the "47 Workshop" in 1914 and his association with the Provincetown Players, he began his climb to success with his first of three Pulitzer Prize plays, *Beyond the Horizon* (1920). Ever restless and haunted by doubts, he divorced his second wife, Agnes Bolton, in 1929, and married actress Carlotta Monterey. Meanwhile, his plays kept appearing until 1934.

During the late 1930's and the 1940's he worked on a dramatic cycle which, at one time, was to "include eleven individual plays." Parkinson's disease prevented his completing his projected work, but the extant plays have been produced since his death. Haunted by alcoholism, disease, love and hate, and the frustration of his own personal and artistic ambitions, he isolated himself in later years from all but the understanding of his wife. His son by his first wife, Eugene O'Neill, Jr., a brilliant classical scholar, committed suicide in 1950; his two children by Agnes Bolton are Oona, married to Charlie Chaplin, and Shane, who lives haphazardly in the O'Neill shadow.

2. INFLUENCES ON O'NEILL: ACCEPTED AND SUGGESTED

In his book entitled *Twentieth Century Drama*, Bamber Gascoigne questioned the "academic parlour game" of discovering sources and influences. For the immediate enjoyment of a particular work of art, the point is well taken. For the literary historian, however, the placing of an artist's work within a developing social and intellectual frame has its value. Here a few observations will suffice.

Within existing American drama, O'Neill found almost nothing to imitate. He was, however, influenced by it to the extent that melodrama reminiscent of the late nineteenth century is a quality in certain plays. In *Desire Under the Elms,* for example, he burlesques some of the traditional aspects of American melodrama. Admitting the influence of no single dramatist except Strindberg, he was clearly interested in other European dramatists, particularly Ibsen, and European Expressionism. Beyond the theatrical experimentation, he borrowed ideas from Freud, Jung, and Adler (*Strange Interlude* and *Mourning Becomes Electra*). References to the Bible, orthodox religion, and classical myths appear often in his plays. Philosophy fascinated him, particularly that of Nietzsche; and he retreated into a kind of mysticism quite frequently. The Greeks—their practices and doctrines in drama—became central in his experimentation. A restless, searching person who flirted with ideas for their own sake, O'Neill was stimulated, although sometimes only momentarily, by various philosophies, types of literature, and modes of contemporary thought.

B. Experimentation in Form

By inclination and circumstances, O'Neill was forced to experiment in his plays. As he concerned himself with the predicament of man in society, his struggles and inner conflicts, while searching for meaning and order, he became aware of the forces that controlled man. In America, however, with only a few exceptions—Percy MacKaye, for example—he had inherited a theater in which realism was a major objective, brought about mainly by devices and artifices of the stage manager. In dealing with man's inner strengths and his subconsciousness, O'Neill found that realism failed to probe deeply enough. For him, then, Expressionism became a major technique, complementing the earlier naturalism; but he further experimented with monologue, trilogies, symbols, divided characters, and masks.

1. *THE EMPEROR JONES*, 1920: MONOLOGUE, DRUMBEATS, DARWIN

Primarily a monologue, *The Emperor Jones* shows the destruction of man's sense of dignity and pride as he retro-

gresses through a Darwinian chronology to a primitive existence. Elaborate stage sets, strong lighting effects ("the formless
fears"), and the divisions of this play suggest its experimental substance. Concerning the use of sound, O'Neill said
(quoted in *The Curse of the Misbegotten,* p. 131): "One
day I was reading of the religious feasts in the Congo and
the uses to which the drum is put there—how it starts at a
normal pulse and is slowly accelerated until the heartbeat of
everyone present corresponds to the frenzied beat of the
drum. Here was an idea for an experiment. How could this
sort of thing work on an audience in a theater?"

2. *MOURNING BECOMES ELECTRA,* 1931: TRILOGY, GREEK THEME, MASKS, FREUD

Rewriting the Greek myth concerning the House of
Atreus, O'Neill took the Mannon family, placed them in a
Civil War setting, and motivated them in terms of Freud and
Jung. It became for O'Neill "a modern tragic interpretation
of classic fate," "a modern psychological play—fate spring-
ing out of the family." The trilogy is composed of three
plays—"The Homecoming," "The Hunted," and "The
Haunted"—which follow Aeschylus' *Oresteia* in character
and action, although O'Neill with greater severity provides no
escape for any of his characters. The Greek influence is also
seen in the use of the villagers as a choral response and in
the mask-like quality of certain characters as well as the
Mannon house. The emphases on sex, the psychological mo-
tivations, and the Oedipus and Electra complexes point
clearly to Freud and Jung. *Strange Interlude* is another trilogy with Freudian implication.

3. USE OF SYMBOLS AND SPLIT CHARACTERS

Used variously in O'Neill's plays, the symbol is perhaps
most obvious in *Dynamo* (1929). Supposed to be the first
play of a trilogy (which was not continued) investigating the
failure of science to fill the void left by a dead Christianity,
the dynamo, a symbol of science, becomes in this play a
god—a mother-god, because O'Neill had seen the failure of
the father-god in Christianity. Even in physical appearance,

the great dynamo with its dual commutators suggests the female god. In *Days Without End* (1934), O'Neill used two characters to suggest two conflicting qualities within a single person. John Loving is the whole person: Loving is vicious and bitter, "a death mask of a John who has died with a sneer of scornful mockery on his lips." The struggle in the play is between John and Loving, but the other characters in the play see and hear only John.

4. USE OF MASKS

O'Neill made several notes on the use of masks, contending with some seriousness that all characters in plays should wear them, and suggesting particularly the use of masks—or a mask-like quality—in several of his plays. One of his most complicated plays using masks is *Lazarus Laughed* (1928). All members of the Chorus wear masks representing the Seven Ages of Man and seven kinds of people. With such masks as the Simple, Ignorant, Young Manhood type or the Sorrowful, Resigned, Old Age type, there was the possibility of forty-nine masks. His most interesting play of masks, however, is *The Great God Brown* (1926). Young Dion Anthony (Dionysus, "the creative pagan acceptance of life" combined with St. Anthony, "the life-denying spirit of Christianity") must wear the mask of Pan before the world to protect his sensitive and creative spirit. As he grows older, his mask changes into a cynical Mephistopheles. When he dies, Billy Brown steals his mask, thinking that he is stealing his creativity but, in actuality, stealing only the mask in which Dion was forced to face the world. Soon Brown is forced to wear another mask—William A. Brown, successful businessman—before the world. As such, he is unable to become *himself* to anyone. It is a difficult play, and even O'Neill felt obligated to attempt an explanation in an essay.

C. Search for Self

To "justify the ways of God to man" is perhaps the greatest challenge for man's creative imagination and genius. In nineteenth-century America, man's attempt to know God became man's attempt to see himself in relation to his society and to his fellow men. One's concept of nature gained, accordingly, greater import. In this questioning of life, man searched for meaning, for values, for truth. With the advent of Darwin, Comte, and Spencer, man's search became an analysis of the various forces that worked upon him in society. Modern man, however, influenced by the principle of modern psychology, particularly the introversion-extroversion concepts of Jung and Kierkegaard's idea of self, saw his search in life as concentrated in self. Through self-analysis many modern artists attempt to "justify" the ways of God to man, and Eugene O'Neill is such an artist. He takes as his task the expression of the torment and tension within the human mind, and attempts to understand the predicament of man, and therefore his values in life, by dramatizing man's search for the secrets of self. Mainly, O'Neill discovered, man is destroyed in his search; only once did O'Neill see victory for him; and finally, even a life of illusion where one no longer searches proved unsatisfactory.

1. THE PREDICAMENT OF MAN

In his attempt to interpret man and discover basic truths, O'Neill made many observations which he sometimes described as "the sickness of today." This sickness is thought to result from various forces working upon man, and becomes the predicament of sensitive man in modern society. As he searches for his own soul, sensitive man finds a society which destroys mankind in several ways. It may be the force of materialism which hardens and destroys Marco Polo in *Marco Millions*. Or man may be destroyed by his inability to be true to himself and at the same time successful in life, as Dion was destroyed in *The Great God Brown*. If this "sickness of today" permeates the forces of society which make sensitive man miserable and finally destroy him, the desire to "belong" is man's frustrating response—frustrating because man is doomed never to "belong." Yank in *The Hairy Ape* is symbolic of the predicament O'Neill finds for man who tries to understand life; men are those "haunted heroes." Obsessed, driven, suffering, and haunted, man is pictured by O'Neill as searching for truth, trying to discover both himself and his place in the universe.

2. THE SEARCH DEFEATED

With the exception of his comedy, *Ah, Wilderness!*
(1933), and his naturalistic tragedy, *Desire Under the Elms*
(1924), O'Neill's major plays written before he stopped publishing in the mid-1930's show man as defeated in his search
for meaning.

(a) *Beyond the Horizon,* 1920
The setting is a farm where Robert Mayo, poet and
mystic, is planning to leave home on a voyage with his uncle
and see "beyond the horizon." But Ruth Atkins, one of
O'Neill's early dominating women, persuades Robert to stay
and marry her, while Robert's brother Andrew who really
loves the farm goes on the planned trip. All search for
meaning in life, though not consciously, and all fail. Ruth
loses even her will to seek; Andrew sees nothing in the won-
ders of the world he visits; Robert, having been unhappy
with Ruth and having failed to satisfy his dream, dies without having seen beyond the horizon.

(b) *The Hairy Ape,* 1922
A play involving the social problems of the industrial
revolution as a background for a psychological search for
meaning, *The Hairy Ape* was, O'Neill wrote, a "symbol of man,
who has lost his old harmony with nature, the harmony which
he used to have as an animal and has not yet acquired in a
spiritual way. . . . The struggle used to be with the gods, but is
now with himself, his own past, his attempt to belong." Yank, a
stoker on a steamship, attempts to show society who he is,
after being called a "hairy ape" by a member of that society. Physically strong and continually assuming the position
of Rodin's "The Thinker," Yank is completely ineffective in
society. Nobody understands him—the policemen who arrest
him for disturbing the peace, the Industrial Workers of the
·World who consider him a spy—and all he wants is to belong. Finally, he sees a gorilla in a cage as a possible companion, but, once freed, the gorilla crushes him: "Even him
didn't tink I belonged. Christ, where do I get off at? Where
do I fit in?" The answer is, of course, "Nowhere!"

(c) *The Great God Brown*, 1926

As a boy, Dion Anthony must wear the mask of Pan to conceal his sensitive spirit from society. Later, as a man and married, his mask becomes Satan even to Margaret, his wife, and he can remove his mask only before Cybel, the prostitute and mother of all men. But he is a good architect in spite of his drinking, which is his outward response to his inner frustration. Finally, destroyed by his inability to be creative in modern society, he dies, and his mask is stolen by William Brown, his childhood friend, his boss in the contracting firm, and a successful businessman. Brown feels that he is stealing Dion's creativity, but he is, of course, taking only Dion's cynical paganism. Wearing the mask, he assumes his place as Margaret's husband, but soon he must wear another mask—William Brown, Businessman—and patronize Cybel. He can be himself to no one. Frustrated by his fate, he finally abandons the mask of Brown (thus killing him and being accused of his murder) and dies with Dion's mask beside him. Ironically, it is to this mask of Dion that Margaret promises to be true forever, while the body of Brown is identified by Cybel as "Man!" "How d'yuh spell it?" asks the police captain.

(d) *Lazarus Laughed*, 1928

This play shows the search in conjunction with faith. When Lazarus was brought back from the dead, he laughed. This was his answer to those who asked what lay beyond the grave (the meaning in life): "There is only laughter!" For those who follow him in life, there is laughter, the symbol of knowledge. At the end of the play, Lazarus is burned at the stake by Caligula and answers questions as to what is beyond life with laughter: "Fear not, Caligula! There is no death!" At first Caligula laughs, too; then he changes and boasts that he has killed Lazarus, proving that there is death; but he is finally made humble: "Fool! Madman! Forgive me, Lazarus! Men forget!" Men will search for meaning, O'Neill seems to say, and be defeated because they cannot learn from others or the past. "Men forget!" Each must make his own discovery. Yet here a partial success in the search is attained, and the play looks toward *Days Without End*.

(e) *Dynamo*, 1929

The theme of this play, in O'Neill's words, is "the death of an old God and the failure of science and materialism to give a satisfactory new one for the surviving primitive religious instinct to find a meaning for life in and to comfort its fears of death with." The play describes the search of Reuben Light for a god, for meaning in life. His father, a devout but cowardly minister, is one force. Another is the atheist next door who taunts Reuben, and whose daughter, Ada, Reuben loves. Conflicts cause Reuben to reject his faith and leave home, becoming a hardened cynic and worshiper of science in the form of a dynamo. But a conflict still exists, as Reuben, symbolic of modern man for O'Neill, finds the need for a cold intellectual father-god as well as a warm emotional mother-god. The dynamo suggests both science and, with its dual commutators, woman; and in his attempt to worship it, Reuben is destroyed by its electrical force. Again, man is defeated in his search for meaning through the internal forces which make him what he is.

3. THE SEARCH ENDING IN FAITH

In *Days Without End* (1934), O'Neill dramatizes a search for meaning which leads clearly to Christianity. It is, according to O'Neill, "primarily a psychological study. . . . revealing a man's search for truth amid the conflicting doctrines of the modern world and his return to his old religious faith." The struggle between John and Loving, two aspects of John Loving, is dramatized through a novel that John is writing. The theme of the novel—Can a man who has sinned against his wife be forgiven?—is, of course, the problem in which John is personally involved. Loving, whom nobody sees or hears, answers the question with "No!" Aided by Father Baird who tries to make John repent, John finally becomes conscious of his soul and starts for the church; his wife forgives him; and Loving dies at the foot of the Cross, as John shouts, "Life laughs with God's love again." With love, one's search for truth ends in a meaningful faith.

4. THE SEARCH AND MAN'S ILLUSION

After a single burst of optimism following a period in which damnation seemed a part of life, O'Neill stopped publishing his plays until *The Iceman Cometh* appeared in 1946 (copyright, 1940). Here and in following plays his attitude toward a search for meaning focuses on illusions in life. Man may seem to find value in self-deception rather than in self-analysis, O'Neill admits, but in a life of illusion there is neither truth nor happiness—only sickness and stagnation.

(a) *The Iceman Cometh*, 1940

A motley group of has-beens wait in Harry Hope's saloon for the annual visit of Hickey, a happy salesman who jokes about his wife being home with the iceman. The men are all failures: Harry hasn't been out of the bar for twenty years; a Harvard-trained lawyer got frightened, took to drink, and now only dreams of his potential; Jimmy Tomorrow is always waiting for tomorrow to act; an anarchist talks of the worthlessness of life as he tries to forget his past; and so on. But when Hickey arrives, he is changed. He insists now upon facing the truth, and he tries to make each bum accept himself for what he is and see life truthfully. Reluctantly, all do as he says. But they are not happy, and Hickey can't understand this development. Unnerved by his failure, he confesses to having killed his wife; she lived in a dream, and he killed her to prove the dream. The men are stunned and can reach only one conclusion—Hickey is crazy! If this is so, of course, all of his talk has been insane, and they can return to their old lives, their old illusions, and safety. Only the anarchist has learned. Having preached suicide but now a convert to Hickey's truth, he realizes his own failure because he is too weak to take his own life. Long ago O'Neill had abandoned Hickey's philosophy; here he shows the inadequacy of the life illusion.

(b) *A Touch of the Poet* (1941), 1957

Part of the cycle entitled *A Tale of Possessors Self-Dispossessed, A Touch of the Poet* suggests the spiritually desolate life of those who would live by illusions. Con Melody, his wife, and his daughter, Sara, run a tavern near Boston. A prideful, would-be aristocrat, Major Melody lives in his past glories as a soldier and rides a thoroughbred mare in spite of approaching poverty. The crisis comes when Sara falls in love with a wealthy young Bostonian, Simon Harford, who was taken sick at the inn. When the Harfords try to interfere with the young lovers and even attempt to bribe Con, he is infuriated by the snub. Dressed in his officer's uniform, he goes to Boston to challenge Mr. Harford to a duel and is beaten by his servants. His pride destroyed, Con returns home, shoots his mare and relapses into a thick Irish brogue. Sara, meanwhile, has seduced Simon so that he will marry her. She, too, has lost pride but become more understanding of her mother's love for her father. The illusion of aristocracy lost, Con resorts to another life, equally inadequate. Although Sara may face life happily, sustained by love alone, she has not escaped reality nor found peace and understanding, as *More Stately Mansions*, O'Neill's later play, so effectively dramatizes.

D. O'Neill's Contribution to American Drama

It is tempting to assert O'Neill's Promethean characteristics, especially since the lack of much substantial criticism of his contemporaries before World War II simply enhances the outstanding quality of his work. In many ways, of course, O'Neill *is* Promethean. To the American drama, he brought a knowledge of the theater and a creative desire to examine its potentials when America most urgently needed his talents. His knowledge of past dramatic literature and his interest in modern philosophy and psychology made him appeal to the literary critics and scholars. Essentially, he was the first American dramatist who gained the respect of both theater people and literary scholars.

It is also true that his understanding qualities may be exaggerated, especially when compared with the work of his contemporaries. His language has been criticized for its weakness. His plots have been shown to be melodramatic. There is no doubt that he built his plays on his own tensions, attacking cherished values and beliefs in American society and creating mainly a pessimistic view of life. *But*, he had, as John Gassner points out in *Theatre at the Crossroads,* "the courage of his discontent." When he does portray, as in *Long Day's Journey into Night*, "a stranger who never feels at home, who does not really want and is not really wanted, who can never belong," he is expressing a basic modern conflict, a struggle which places him with Herman Melville, Thomas Mann, and Albert Camus. Quite in spite of his many weaknesses, his contribution is in his meaningful ideas, expressed frequently with great emotional, if uneven, power and in a manner which is exceptionally effective on the stage. Sean O'Casey notes: "Of course, he's left an impact on the Theater of today as Shaw has: neither the English nor the American Theaters can ever be quite the same since these giants leaped onto the stage. . . ." This is high praise and indicative of the international reputation which O'Neill brought to America.

It is, perhaps, useless to list particularly worthy O'Neill plays, but the following are a distinguished part of his contribution to American drama: *Desire Under the Elms* (1924), a naturalistic New England tragedy of adultery, murder, and pride, which employs classical comparisons, attacks on religion, and a theme of loneliness with conflicting greed and sense of freedom; *Mourning Becomes Electra* (1931), a modern psychological version of Aeschylus' *Oresteia*, and *Long Day's Journey into Night* (1941, 1956), a dramatization of the torments, horrors, and struggles within the O'Neill family.

III. LET FREEDOM REIGN: REALISM TO POETRY

The sense of freedom that O'Neill stimulated was immediately reflected in the plays of the 1920's. In both idea and technique, this new decade of American drama is distinctive. Critics were enthusiastic about the new realism, and Alexander Woollcott joyfully announced the "waning tyranny of the happy ending," that "fine, bosom to bosom, lip to lip finale." In their enthusiasm to portray life truthfully, playwrights like Maxwell Anderson and Sidney Howard proved to be shocking (but enjoyable), while those who experimented in form—Elmer Rice, John Howard Lawson—brought gasps from their audiences with their interpretations of German Expressionism. Throughout the decade, numerous dramatists commented on society's shortcomings, employing mainly the ideas of social melodrama adopted by Eugene Walter earlier in the century. One of these writers, Sidney Howard, provided a key for the decade with his thesis: "They knew what they wanted." It was a decade in which the independence of the individual was a byword. This sense of freedom also allowed dramatists greater scope in the kind of plays they wrote. Although these plays were part of a transformation which had been building since the early part of the century, writers of folk drama, pageant drama, and poetic drama found new energy in the 1920's.

A. Insurgent Realism

No plays suggest the change in realism more than *What Price Glory?* and *They Knew What They Wanted.* Produced the same year, 1924, they suggest the robust and liberal characteristics of the time. Just previously, 1923, Owen Davis had shown his talent for a lesser realism in the Pulitzer Prize winning *Icebound.* Both he and Susan Glaspell—the other major dramatist, with O'Neill, of the Provincetown Players—have lost the reputations they enjoyed in the Twenties. A seriously undervalued playwright, Susan Glaspell provided not a violent or controversial realism, but a truthful portrayal of life that indicates the insight of the emotionally and intellectually mature. Numerous other dramatists, of course, contributed to this new realism.

1. TWO STARTLING PLAYS

Both *What Price Glory?* and *They Knew What They Wanted* are essentially comic-melodrama, but they are vivid theater—one through its realistic action and language, the other through its "new" morality.

(a) *What Price Glory?*, 1924

This war play by Laurence Stallings and Maxwell Anderson takes place in a French village during World War I and tells mainly of the rivalry of Sgt. Quirt and Capt. Flagg, two tough regular army fellows, for Charmaine de la Cognac. From many adventures together in the past, they hate but respect each other, and when Quirt steals Charmaine during

Flagg's absence and gets into trouble with her father, Pete Cognac, Flagg is tempted to make Quirt marry the girl. Then orders for an advance come, and Flagg backs down rather than leave Quirt in jail for refusing to obey his order. In the action, both Quirt and Flagg show their courage, but Quirt is hit in the leg and hospitalized until he escapes to Pete's place to see Charmaine. There he meets Flagg. Both drunk, they have a violent battle over Charmaine until orders come for a return to the front, and Flagg rushes out followed by Quirt—"Hey Flagg, wait for baby!"

(b) *They Knew What They Wanted*, 1924
In this play, Sidney Howard tells how Tony, a lonely and wealthy old Italian winegrower in California, had wooed and won a girl, Amy, by writing letters to her and sending the picture of a young radical friend of his, Joe. On the day Amy arrives at Tony's home, Tony breaks both legs in a car wreck, while Amy, a footsore waitress who wants security, is shocked to discover that it is the old but goodhearted Tony that she is to marry rather than the more physically attractive Joe. Tempted to leave, she reconsiders and stays. A colorful marriage takes place, and Tony is very generous with his gifts. Physically and emotionally exhausted, however, Amy is drawn to Joe that first night. Three months later, Amy and Tony are getting along well, but she knows that she is pregnant with Joe's child. Realizing her unworthiness and now loving Tony, she prepares to leave, after telling Tony of her baby. At first he is furious; then he, too, reconsiders. Amy has not been with Joe since that first night, and Joe, a radical, is interested only in wandering through life. Amy wants security and love; Tony, too old to father a child, wants a baby. They know what they want, and they accept the happiness which they now have.

2. OWEN DAVIS: MELODRAMATIC REALISM

The author of over one hundred successful romantic and violent melodramas, Owen Davis (1874–1956) stopped writing that kind of play with *The Family Cupboard* (1913) and created a Pulitzer Prize play ten years later with *Icebound*. An earlier experiment in realism, *Detour* (1921), takes place in New England. Helen Hardy has finally gotten $1000 to take her daughter, Kate, to New York where she can study art. At this time, however, a next door neighbor, Tom Lane, is about to be dispossessed because his gas station failed when the detour rerouted traffic. Land happy and land poor, Steve Hardy wants to buy Tom's land and orders Helen and Kate out when they refuse to give him their money. When, by chance, a visiting art critic tells Kate that she has no talent, Kate is hurt but decides to give the money to her father and marry Tom. Helen must now save her money and her illusions for her grandchildren.

Icebound (1923) tells a similar tale of lost illusions and barren life in New England. The Jordans are a greedy family, who wait only for their mother to die and will them her money. The mother loved best her youngest but dissipated son, Ben; a young cousin, Jane, who tended the sick mother also loves Ben. When Jane inherits the Jordan money, she signs it all over to Ben, who then realizes his love for his mother and for Jane. Jane, however, has no illusions about the sincerity of his attitude; she has only her love, the knowledge that she is doing what she thinks is right, and the bitterness of the rest of the Jordans.

3. SUSAN GLASPELL: MATURE REALIST

With her husband, George Cram (Jig) Cook, Susan Glaspell (1882–1948) was a distinct force within the Provincetown Players and wrote several short but theatrically effective and intellectually stimulating plays. She was clearly much closer to O'Neill in her concern for intense, meaningful drama than any of her contemporaries. Slight but effective, *Suppressed Desires* (1914) is a witty satire on the theory of complete freedom in self-expression. *Bernice* (1919) shows the insight that only a woman would have. A little too conversational perhaps, and contrived, it shows how a dead woman brings a change for the better in her philandering husband by having him told (falsely) that she killed herself. The *Inheritors* (1921) dramatizes the different views which succeeding generations have toward the administration of a college founded by a liberal ancestor. It is in *The Verge* (1921), however, that she reveals her closeness to the emotional struggles of Eugene O'Neill. A woman on the verge of insanity is searching for the answer to life in her attempt to create new forms of life and to understand her own soul. But she can only reach the "verge." Something eludes her. Rich in language and idea, this play unfortunately lacks the theatrical quality that O'Neill might have supplied. The problems of the Provincetown Players proved a source of disappointment to Susan and George Cook in the 1920's, and after her husband's death, she spent part of her time in Europe. Then in 1930, Susan Glaspell wrote *Alison's House*, in which she created a thought-provoking and beautifully expressed, if sentimental, play based on an interpretation of Emily Dickinson's life.

4. OTHER EXPRESSIONS OF REALISM

The urge to find realism everywhere struck many critics of this time. Even a play like Philip Dunning and George Abbott's *Broadway* (1926)—a melodrama about a chorus girl who learns which guy is right for her, after a murder, a certain roughness and some risqué language—was called realistic. A better play and more deserving of being called realistic is Zona Gale's (1874–1938) Pulitzer Prize winning dramatization of her own novel, *Miss Lulu Bett* (1920), the story of a strong woman who leaves a taunting brother-in-law and her sister to marry a man who has not divorced a previous wife. Lewis Beach's melodrama, *The Goose Hangs High* (1924), describes in some realistic detail the economic problems of a mother and father whose grown children finally discover that they can be more thoughtful toward their parents. *The Front Page* (1928) by Charles MacArthur and Ben Hecht is a satiric farce of newspaper life; realistic only in language, description, and general vulgarity, it was very effective theater. A more serious play on an old theme is Samson Raphaelson's *Young Love* (1928), which tells of two young people who stay together for a night, show no faith in the institution of marriage, and become increasingly cynical as they are involved in mate swapping with a young married couple. Realism, therefore, appeared in many guises.

B. Expressionism in the Twenties

One reaction to realism in the theater would be expressionism, whose use is consistent with the experimental attitude of the Twenties. Coming to America from Europe, expressionism in art was defined by Sheldon Cheney in *The Primer of Modern Art* as "that movement in art which transfers the emphasis from technical display and imitated surface aspects of nature to creative form; from descriptive and representative truth to intensified emotional expressionism; from objective to subjective and abstract formal qualities." Expressionism in the theater came mainly from Germany, but the closeness of art and theater art is clear. According to Ludwig Lewisohn in a review of *The Adding Machine* (*Nation*, April 4, 1923), "expressionism has two chief aims: to fling the inner life of the dramatic figures immediately upon the stage; to synthesize, instead of describing, their world and their universe into symbolic visions that shall sum up whole histories, moralities, cosmogonies in a brief minute and a fleeting scene." O'Neill's use of expressionism is well known, but there were others who employed expressionism with great effect.

1. ELMER RICE: *THE ADDING MACHINE*, 1923

Using numbers instead of people, Rice satirizes a mechanical world and the inept quality of all who succumb to this loss of humanity. The story is told quite simply in seven scenes. In a long soliloquy, Mrs. Zero explains her dissatisfaction with life, condemning Mr. Zero for his ineffectiveness. The next day on the job as a clerk, Zero is fired; and in anger and frustration, he kills his boss, is arrested, tried, and executed. In Heaven, he learns to operate a large adding machine and is soon sent back to earth, while his willingness to return causes only laughter from the guards in Heaven. Expressionism in the play is shown in the devices which reveal Mr. Zero's emotions. For example, the Boss fires Zero: "His voice is drowned by the music [of a merry-go-round]. The platform is revolving rapidly now. Zero and the Boss face each other. They are entirely motionless save for the Boss's jaws, which open and close incessantly. But the words are inaudible. The music swells and swells."

2. GEORGE S. KAUFMAN AND MARC CONNELLY: *BEGGAR ON HORSEBACK*, 1924

Showing an artist's revolt against middle-class family ties, this play uses a dream expressionism very effectively. Neil, a would-be artist, really loves Cynthia but does not realize it and is being urged to marry the daughter of a wealthy businessman, Gladys Cady, who wants him to inherit her father's business. In a dream, he marries Gladys, goes to work for her father, where he has a chaotic time trying to get a pencil before he is put in the proper cell from which he is to produce, at a particular time and in a particular way, a work of art. When he awakens, he calls off his engagement with Gladys, who really is not bothered, and goes to Cynthia.

3. JOHN HOWARD LAWSON: *PROCESSIONAL*, 1925

Best known for plays which show his commitment to Marxism, John Howard Lawson also wrote the earliest American expressionistic play in *Roger Bloomer* (1923), which with its various anti-realistic devices and Freudian psychology reveals the hero's mind as he searches, in much the same way as Thomas Wolfe's Eugene Gant, for knowledge of self. Howard explained his second expressionistic play, *Processional* (1925), as a "jazz symphony of American life." With its thesis of class war, the play dramatizes a strike in which the proletarian hero, Dynamite Jim, is abused by anti-Marxist forces in America, until the workers finally revolt and win. Although Howard called his technique neither realism nor expressionism but "essentially vaudevillesque in character," his episodic approach uses many expressionistic devices to create a panoramic view of American life.

C. Sidney Howard and Social Drama of the Twenties

The tendency of dramatists to present "a serious study of contemporary social problems"—a tendency which Clayton Hamilton, the drama critic, deeply resented in

1911—took on added meaning in the 1920's. In the past, social comment had been mainly superficial; dramatists of the Twenties were more alert to the psychological approach. Into this stream of American drama, Sidney Howard launched his plays, adding an imagination and a talent which, guided by a new sense of realism, gave social drama a new dignity in the eyes of audiences and critics, both in America and abroad. He was not alone, but he stood preeminent in employing a form of drama which was to be used by those of various intellectual persuasions during the years before World War II. And in his particular approach, he caught the spirit of the social drama of the Twenties.

1. A VARIETY OF SOCIAL PLAYS

One of the lesser playwrights of this period was Zoë Akins (1886–1958) whose *Déclassée* (1919) commented on difficulties of the divorcee. In *Daddy's Gone A-Hunting* (1921), Zoë Akins displayed a bitter view of the world—"a very unsafe place," full of "shifting sands and changing minds"—where a conventional woman is married to a morally irresponsible artist whose ego and sense of personal freedom make a normal life impossible. *Ambush* (1921), by Arthur Richman, describes a family which has become morally and spiritually bankrupt. Learning that his daughter is deceitful and sexually promiscuous and that his wife is contemptuous of him, the father degrades himself further by accepting these aspects of life which wait in ambush for man. George Abbott and James Gleason's *The Fall Guy* (1924) is a melodrama which shows that economic problems might force a man into crime, but for the alert conniving of the dramatist. Plays treating the problems of married life include Frank Craven's *The First Year* (1920), Maxwell Anderson's *Saturday's Children* (1927), and Gilbert Emery's *The Hero* (1921) which dramatizes the effect of the war hero on the wife whose husband stayed home.

2. SIDNEY HOWARD: FIRST MAJOR WRITER OF SOCIAL DRAMA

Not a profound or original playwright by his own admission, Sidney Howard (1891–1939) knew how to mix comedy, realism, and melodrama in expertly contrived scenes of fast-moving action and rapid emotional change. His own background, as a radical reporter and writer for Hearst newspapers, perhaps made his concern for social problems inevitable. He was not, however, an experimenter in the drama but followed the tradition of the "satisfactory" play. In this type of play, his major interest was in character portrayal—witness the titles of his plays. Literary critics have also pointed out his mastery of dramatic irony of situation and his concern for ideas. A major theme in his plays is the idea of self in society—distinguishing those who accept freedom with responsibility from those who are merely selfish and therefore damned. During a decade in which O'Neill's achievements eclipsed all playwrights, Sidney Howard escapes notice as the first major writer of social drama in modern America.

(a) Strong Characters: They Know What They Want

After several plays—including a poetic drama, *Swords* (1921), about the Guelphs and Ghibellines; and a pageant, *Lexington* (1924)—Howard wrote *They Knew What They Wanted* (1924). From that point on, his best plays are built around strong characters. Sam in *Lucky Sam McCarver* (1925) uses people to get ahead, even his wife, and becomes a hardened, cynical man who can never love, lucky in only an ironic sense. Carrie, *Ned McCobb's Daughter* (1926), shows her determination and the superiority of her character as she overcomes a weak husband, a conniving brother-in-law, and even bandits, to get what she wants. Doc Haggett in *The Late Christopher Bean* (1932) thinks he knows what he wants when he tries to take advantage of a servant girl; the wife of Christopher Bean whose paintings become collector's items; but he changes in time. The liberal heroine of *Alien Corn* (1933) chooses a romantic escape to freedom but definitely knows her mind.

(b) *The Silver Cord* (1926): Social Thesis Drama

With its well-drawn characters, sharp irony, emotion-packed action, and Freudian emphasis, *The Silver Cord* is one of the best social thesis plays in American drama. Mrs.

Phelps has raised her two sons alone—David and Robert. When the play opens, David has just returned from abroad with a wife, Christina, and Robert is engaged to Hester. Facing this situation, Mrs. Phelps must fight to maintain possession of her sons. With diabolical cunning, she breaks the engagement and would destroy the marriage but for Chris' expected baby, which proves—though barely—a stronger tie for David than his mother's "unselfish love." The thesis probes the distinction between "life and self"—between living in responsible freedom and being destroyed by self-love.

(c) A Key to the Decade

The title of Howard's first successful play provides a key to character portrayals in most of the social plays of the 1920's: *They Knew What They Wanted.* Jane in Davis's *Icebound* knows and gets what she wants. Maxwell Anderson's *Saturday's Children* are less successful, as is Abe McCrannie in Paul Green's *In Abraham's Bosom* (1926), but they knew what they wanted. S. N. Behrman's hero in *The Second Man* (1927) knows what he wants and keeps it. So does Mary Hutton in Philip Barry's *Paris Bound* (1927) and Lissa in his earlier *In A Garden* (1925).

D. Modern Folk Drama

"If you draw the locality with which you are most familiar, and interpret it faithfully, it will show you the way to the universal," so wrote Fred Koch, director of the Carolina Playmakers at the University of North Carolina, a center for folk drama in America. Few would disagree with Professor Koch's premise, but folk plays (and the phrase is frequently synonymous with regional plays among modern critics), though successful on the stage, have rarely achieved universal significance. This problem of the folk dramatist— to strive for the limited historical spirit and raise his particulars to universal—has been solved with some success, mainly by Paul Green, one of Koch's students, who wrote about the South. Generally, however, the various geographical folk sections of America, as well as America's traditional myth characters, have been treated in plays. Through the efforts of Koch, Green, and others, folk drama achieved its

greatest popularity in America during the years between the
World Wars.

1. BACKGROUNDS OF MODERN FOLK DRAMA

Folk literature in America was given form by men and
women who sang of "Frankie and Johnny," "Picking Cotton," or "Pat Works on the Railroad." The beginnings of
American folk drama appeared early with the nineteenth century emphasis on sectional characters, such as the Yankee,
the Indian, and the Negro, and later interest in mythical
characters, like Paul Bunyan, and in local color stories.
Further stimulation appeared when the Abbey Players
visited America. Both John M. Synge and William Butler
Yeats had written plays for the Abbey Players based on Ireland's folklore. The suggestion was not missed, and the
growth of the American Little Theaters and Community Theaters re-emphasized an interest in the common man. Soon
the pecularities of custom, the superstition, the naïveté, and
the mixture of sentiment and realism which make up America
began to appear in plays. A few plays were very effective.
The danger was that the folk background would become—
as it frequently did—mere flavoring for melodrama.

2. THE REGIONS OF AMERICA

Representing the same geographical sections portrayed
in local color drama, folk plays were created about the West,
New England, and the South. Lynn Riggs wrote of the great
Southwest in *Roadside* (1930) and in *Green Grow the
Lilacs* (1931), which became the musical *Oklahoma!* John
Steinbeck dramatized *Of Mice and Men* (1937), using a
western background; *No More Frontier* (1929) by Talbot
Jennings tells of three generations of an Idaho pioneer family. Dan Totheroh's *Wild Birds* (1925) makes effective use
of the Middle West, although the story approaches both sensational and sentimental melodrama. Owen Davis represented New England well with *Detour* (1921), *Icebound*
(1923), and a dramatization, with his son, Donald, of Edith
Wharton's novel, *Ethan Frome* (1936). O'Neill also illustrated the pecularities of New England in *Desire Under the
Elms* (1924).

Some of the best folk plays, however, have portrayed the South, such as Hatcher Hughes' *Hell-Bent for Heaven* (1924), which employs feuding, supersitition, and religious fanaticism in a moving portrayal of North Carolina mountain people. Lula Vollmer's *Sun-up* (1923) tells how a mountain woman, after hearing that her son has been killed in the war, hides an army deserter, even though the boy's father killed her husband. The language, the peculiar customs, and the supernatural vision suggest folk characteristics. In 1927, Dorothy and DuBose Heyward wrote *Porgy*, which was later made into an opera, *Porgy and Bess*. The story of Porgy's love for Crown's Bess has many folk aspects—the saucer funeral, the ominous bird which will bring disaster wherever it lands, the bleeding corpse, and the conjuring for Bess. One of the best-known folk dramas is Marc Connelly's *Green Pastures* (1930). Explaining the Bible in terms of Negro life, this play humanizes God as a country preacher who watches over and loves his people. "De Lawd" attends a fish fry in Heaven and with a spectacular flurry creates the world and man. The first half of the play ends with the Flood: "I only hope it's goin' to work out all right," says God. The second part dramatizes the stories of Moses and Joshua and shows God's anger at his people—"I repent of dese people I have made"—ending with the advent of Jesus.

3. THE SOUTH AND PAUL GREEN

In *The Drama* for October, 1930, Paul Green (1894–   ) wrote an essay entitled, "Needed—A Native American Theatre," in which he contended that thus far no American dramatist had spoken for his country. He might have added that more than other playwrights, he approached his ideal. His powers of observation, his poetic sensitivity, and his philosophic turn of mind are enlivened by his years of living in North Carolina—years that have provided the basis for much of his writing. Although he had written protest plays and made an art of the outdoor pageant much of his best work has been his dramas of Southern life in which he shows instinctive understanding of the Negro and white problems. Emphasizing the folk elements of his characters, Green shows an idealism and a feeling for America's past which make him a distinctively American dramatist.

(a) One-Act Plays

Many of Green's one-act plays combine his basic interest in folk characteristics with his equally strong concern for social justice. *The Last of the Lowries* (1920) is strongly imitative of Synge's *Riders to the Sea* as it dramatizes a mother's reaction to the killing of her last son, who with his brothers and father comprised an outlaw gang. *White Dresses* (1926) portrays in poignant and bitter sentiment the story of a mulatto girl who feels doomed to live with Negroes. The white dress which the landlord's son gives to Mary is burned by her grandmother along with another one, presumably given to Mary's mother by her real father, a white man. *In the Valley* (1928) is concerned with the unfair treatment of Negroes in society.

(b) Longer Plays and the White South

Much of the strength of Green's plays comes from his insight into the conditions and problems of the Southern white as well as the Negro. His insight and imagination, however, sometimes suggest a universal note as his work transcends the regional particulars on which his plays are built. Hardy Gilchrist in *The Field God* (1927) is proud of his successful farm, while his sickly but fanatically religious wife, Etta, questions this pride. When Rhoda, young and pretty, arrives from the city to help on the farm, the love that springs up between her and Hardy is inevitable, but, when confessed, causes Etta's death. Later, married, Hardy and Rhoda have constant trouble—the farm animals sicken, their son dies—until, their pride gone, they appeal to God and find their salvation in Him and love. *The House of Connelly* (1931) again treats the southern white plantation class. Will Connelly realizes that his mother and sisters live in the past, but he is too weak to do anything about the problem until he must thwart their desires to marry him to a wealthy aristocrat who would save them from poverty. Instead, he marries, for love, the daughter of a tenant family. The past must be buried and a new life begun. *Shroud My Body Down* (1935) is a fascinating play of the control which superstition and religious fanaticism exert on the uneducated southern white.

(c) A Pulitzer Prize: *In Abraham's Bosom*, 1926

Here, in this play, presented with courage and understanding, is the tragic struggle of the idealist, who is defeated by environmental forces and by the very people he is trying to help. The working songs of Negroes in the turpentine woods, the rhythm of their speech, and the use of supernatural visions enhance the folk quality of the play. Abraham McCrannie, idealistic, stubborn, and furiously ambitious, wants to learn and to be a teacher of his people. His white father, old Colonel Mack, finally persuades the school board to let Abe teach, but the Negroes are reluctant pupils. Abe's own son turns against his father, and the school closes when old Mack dies. Taunted and frustrated, and beaten by white men when he tries to reopen his school, Abe kills Lonnie, his white half-brother, and is lynched.

4. MYTH CHARACTERS: TRUE FOLK DRAMA

The terms folk and regional drama are generally confused, although, strictly speaking folk drama should be built upon American myths. E. P. Conkle is the best of the playwrights who have made use of mythic material. He writes of *Bill and the Widowmaker*, a story of Pecos Bill, his great purple stallion, and his argument with Don Coyote, the last of the cowboys; *Paul and the Blue Ox*, which tells of Paul Bunyan's problems with logging bosses; *The Delectable Judge*, a tale of the prejudiced and intolerant Judge Roy Bean; and *Johnny Appleseed* (all published in 1947). Other playwrights have written folk-myth plays—*John Henry* (1940) by Roark Bradford, *Paul Bunyan* (1932) by Richard L. Stokes, and *Missouri Legend* (1938), a story of Jessie James by Guthrie McClintoc.

E. Pageant Drama

Modern American pageantry began in 1905 with the Louis Evan Shipman (Augustus) *Saint Gaudens Masque* for which Percy MacKaye, a major figure in American pageantry, wrote the prologue. Essentially, the pageant is a healthy expression of the democratic and community spirit and can be loosely defined as a festival, in episodes, of thanksgiving,

worship, or history. Types of pageants include the processional, which is the oldest type; the historical, concerned with
ideas or institutions and employing dialogue, pantomine,
music, and dance; and the masque, which includes allegory and
spectacle. Pageantry in America progressed with greater activity
than is frequently realized, until it has reached a contemporary
zenith in the work of Paul Green.

1. VARIED BEGINNINGS

Pageants celebrated a variety of events and institutions.
The Boston Normal School produced *The Pageant of Educa-
tion* in 1908; Thomas Wood Stevens wrote the *Pageant of
Illinois* (1909), showing the history of the region from the
coming of Christianity to the Blackhawk War of 1832; George
Pierce Baker celebrated the American musician, Edward
MacDowell, in *The Peterborough Pageant* (1910); a propa-
ganda pageant called the *Suffrage Allegory* was given in
Washington in 1913, the same year that John Reed pro-
duced the *Pageant of the Paterson Strike* in New York's
Madison Square Garden. Enacted by 1,000 strikers, this last
pageant was extremely effective propaganda.

2. PERCY MACKAYE AND AMERICAN PAGEANTS

The author of several books—*Community Drama: Its
Motive and Method of Neighborliness* (1917)—on community theater, MacKaye wrote a number of pageants: *The
Roll Call* (1918), requested by the American Red Cross;
The Will of Song (1919), experimenting with community
singing; *Wakefield* (1932), an attempt to dramatize the contribution of "the Folk-Spirit of America" to American
freedom. Perhaps his most interesting pageant is *Caliban, By
the Yellow Sands* (1916) produced on the 300th anniversary
of Shakespeare's death. "The theme of the Masque—Caliban
seeking to learn the art of Prospero—is, of course," Mac-
Kaye wrote, "the slow education of mankind through the influences of cooperative art, that is, of the art of the theatre
in its full social scope." Presenting his pageant on three stage
levels, MacKaye interposed his attempt to humanize Caliban
with various scenes from Shakespeare's plays. The symbolism

was obscure, but the effect of the play with a cast of 2500 was spectacular.

3. PAUL GREEN: THE SYMPHONIC DRAMA

Pageants continued in varied form. An interesting one for students of American drama was *The Masque of American Drama* (1917) by Albert E. Trombly. And there were numerous historical pageants: Frederick Koch's *A Pageant of the Northwest* (1914), George Pierce Baker's *The Pilgrim Spirit* (1921), and the *Yorktown Sesquicentennial Pageants* (1931) written by Thomas Wood Stevens. Then came Paul Green's *The Lost Colony* (1937) and a reawakened popular interest in pageantry that remains active today.

(a) *The Lost Colony*, 1937

Using music, dance, a procession, dramatic action, and dialogue, Green wrote this historical pageant at the request of the Roanoke Island Historical Society to honor the 350th anniversary of Raleigh's Colony. Performed at the Waterside Theater on Roanoke Island, it tells the story of the people who sailed from England in 1587 and, led by Governor White, came to the previously established but then razed Raleigh settlement on Roanoke Island. There, before White returned to England later that year, the settlers were befriended by the Indian, Manteo, and Eleanor Dare gave birth to Virginia, the first child born of English parents in the New World. In England, Governor White found difficulties —the Spanish Armada was defeated in 1588—and when he returned to Roanoke Island in 1590, he found only desolation and the word CROATOAN carved on a tree. By prearranged signal, the settlers had said that, if forced to, they would leave Roanoke Island and carve their destination on a tree. The pageant-play ends as the settlers leave their fort for a new location, singing "Oh God that madest earth and sky." Despite numerous theories, no one has been able to determine where this "lost colony" went.

(b) Other Pageants by Paul Green

The Highland Call (1939) was written to commemorate the Scots settlement in the Cape Fear River Valley of

North Carolina. *The Common Glory* (1947) dramatizes the contribution of Jefferson and the State of Virginia to America, treating the years 1775–1782. For the following period (1783–1799), Green wrote *Faith of Our Fathers* (1950) to celebrate Washington's life and career. *The Founders* (1957) dramatizes the Jamestown Colony.

4. GROWING POPULARITY OF THE PAGEANT

Numerous pageants are now performed yearly for summer visitors to historic places or are written for particular celebrations. For the Mountainside Theater in Cherokee, North Carolina, Kermit Hunter told the story of Conquistador De Soto and the Cherokee Indians in *Unto These Hills* (1950). *Forever This Land* (1952) presents Lincoln's life in New Salem from 1831 to 1837. And pageants are yearly performed from Plymouth in New England to Paul Bunyan land and to the southern shores of California.

F. Poetic Drama between the Wars

A cyclical movement in American poetic drama is nearing the completion of its first full turn. From the Colonial period to the middle of the nineteenth century in America, any dramatist who considered himself a serious writer wrote poetic drama. This drama obviously had severe limitations, but even with its imitative style and weak poetry, it presented the major themes of this period. From the Civil War of 1900, poetry and poetic drama suffered in conflict with the Rise of Realism in literature and the theater. Not until the decade before World War I did the influences of European dramatists stimulate in America a slight interest in poetic drama. As an emerging critical body discovered weaknesses of language in American plays between the World Wars, poetic drama gained some status as a challenge to poets and dramatists. In the 1920's and 1930's, Edna St. Vincent Millay, Maxwell Anderson, and Archibald MacLeish enjoyed some success in this difficult form. Although their efforts have seldom been great triumphs, a direction, of which contemporary dramatists are increasingly aware, seems to have been indicated.

1. IN THE DISTANT PAST—THEN THE PRESENT

For many writers of poetic drama a definite fear of the present is manifest. Even the more successful poetic dramatists generally set their stories in the distant past, and this is clearly true of the early, lesser writers of poetic plays: Edwin Milton Royle, *Lancelot and Elaine* (1921); Arthur Goodrich, *Caponsacchi* (1923); Alfred Kreymborg, *Rocking Chairs* (1921). Not until Marc Blitzstein wrote *The Cradle Will Rock* (1937) did dramatists indicate another view of poetic drama—as an emotional impact for propaganda plays. Archibald MacLeish also saw the value of intense emotion in the contemporary themes of his radio plays. Others followed: Delmore Schwartz, *Shenandoah* (1939) concerned with the naming of a child; N. R. Nusbaum (N. Richard Nash), *Parting at Imsdorf* (1940), a war play.

2. WALLACE STEVENS: *THREE TRAVELERS WATCH A SUNRISE*, 1916

Explaining his intention in this play to Harriet Monroe (quoted in the Introduction to *Opus Posthumous*, 1957), Stevens, a major figure in modern American poetry, wrote: "The play is simply intended to demonstrate that just as objects in nature affect us, . . . we affect objects in nature by projecting our moods, emotions, etc." "On a hilltop in eastern Pennsylvania" three very cultured Chinese talk about wisdom and art while waiting for the sunrise. They are joined by two Negroes. Soon there is revealed the body of a man hanging from a tree beneath which sits a girl. The poor Italian farmer and the girl were in love but were not allowed to marry, and in despair he hanged himself in front of her. The philosophic discussion of the Chinese indicates that love and wisdom appear in art only by the "invasion of humanity." The strong symbolism of the play enhances its poetry if not its theatrical effectiveness.

3. EDNA ST. VINCENT MILLAY OF THE PROVINCETOWN

Known as "the beautiful young actress of the Provincetown," Edna Millay became the popular poet of the 1920's, who burned her candle at both ends. An excellent poet of strong emotions with a fair sense of the dramatic, she wrote several poetic plays—a moral farce called *Two Slatterns and a King* (1916), the slight but bright romantic play *The Princess Marries the Page* (1918), the more conventional romantic story of *The Lamp and the Bell* (1921), and *The King's Henchman* (1926), a play built along the Tristram-Isolde pattern for which Deems Taylor supplied music.

Her most successful play was *Aria da Capo* (1919), a blank-verse satire which Harriet Monroe, editor of *Poetry Magazine* called "a masterpiece of irony, sharp as Toledo steel." Onto a stage set for a harlequinade, Cothurnus, the mask of tragedy, thrusts two shepherds who are to enact a tragedy. Prompted by Cothurnus, they finally arouse each other's sense of human greed and kill each other. Cothurnus then shuts his prompt book and the harlequin characters return to the set but are disturbed by the bodies of the shepherds. To their complaints, Cothurnus tells them to hide the bodies: "The audience will forget." They agree and start to repeat the routine with which they began the play. The poetry is effective as well as beautiful, and the satire and power of the play are hard to forget.

4. MAXWELL ANDERSON: POET-DRAMATIST

A controversial figure, Maxwell Anderson (1888–1959) has been praised as second only to Eugene O'Neill in American drama and condemned as a fourth-rate poet and confused thinker. A poet-dramatist who believed that it is "incumbent on the dramatist to be a poet," he was also concerned with political and social issues which sometimes served as a framework for his philosophical probing. During his lifetime he wrote over thirty plays, but his best work and most of his original plays appeared before World War II. Not a first-rate poet, he seriously and with considerable talent attacked a difficult problem in modern drama—that of combining meaningful language, effective theater, and significant ideas. His attempt in his poetry, however, to depend upon poetic traditions rather than to follow the more flexible forms of modern poetry makes it impossible for some critics to consider him as a writer of poetic drama.

(a) A Theory of Drama

In *Off Broadway* Anderson collected a number of his essays concerned with dramatic theory, including "Poetry in the Theater," which reveals clearly his idealism, his belief that "dramatic poetry is man's greatest achievement," and that the theater should be "essentially a cathedral of the spirit." To Anderson, prose was "the language of information and poetry the language of emotion." Believing that man must feel in order to endure and live fully and that such enduring could be created artistically only in the theater, he felt that the serious dramatist must write in poetry. The serious dramatist must also believe in the strength and freedom of individual man, thus according him a singular dignity in his essentially tragic destiny. In arriving at this conclusion Anderson relies heavily on Aristotle's *Poetics*, particularly the theory of Recognition and Reversal. In an essay on "The Essence of Tragedy" he phrases his main point in this way: "a play should lead up to and away from a central crisis, and this crisis should consist in a discovery by the leading character which has an indelible effect on his thought and emotion and completely alters his course of action." The person who makes the discovery must have a tragic fault and must suffer as a consequence of an experience which makes him aware of his fault. Whether he dies, as in a tragedy, or not, the essential point is the spiritual awakening or regeneration of the person.

(b) Historical Poetic Drama

After the failure of his first poetic play, *White Desert* (1923), a tragedy of loneliness in North Dakota, Anderson decided that a contemporary theme could not be meaningful in poetic tragedy. During the 1930's, therefore, he concentrated on historical poetic plays—with one notable exception. *Elizabeth the Queen* (1930) dramatizes the love of Elizabeth and Essex as it conflicts with their individual desires for power. *Night Over Taos* (1923) tells of the stubborn last stand of one of the large landholders in the Southwest of 1847 before the passing of the old Spanish feudal regime. In *Mary of Scotland* (1933), a popular success, Anderson shows Queen Elizabeth's persecution of the Catholic Mary, who is finally executed in the Tower because she will not release her right to the throne. *Valley Forge* (1934) is a weak attempt to dramatize that cold, desperate winter as it and Congress presented serious challenges to General Washington. In *The Wingless Victory* (1936) he describes the hypocrisy and intolerance of the Puritans toward a Malayan princess who is brought to New England as the wife of a sailing master. After World War II, his historical plays include *Joan of Lorraine* (1946) and *Anne of the Thousand Days* (1948).

(c) *Winterset*, 1935, and the Contemporary Scene

Anderson wrote several prose but few poetic plays in which he treated the contemporary scene and contemporary problems. In one poetic drama, however, *Key Largo* (1939), which fits very well into his theory of tragedy, he portrayed a man who, having refused to die with his comrades in the Spanish Civil War, goes to Key Largo to see the family of one of those who did die, and is spiritually awakened when he discovers something worth dying for. A much better poetic play with a more significant contemporary issue is *Winterset* (1935).

(*Plot*) In the spirit of revenge, Mio Romagna is searching for someone who can identify a murderer in whose place his father was executed. In a New York tenement district, he meets and falls in love with Miriamne, whose brother, Garth, witnessed the murder. Not realizing who Garth is, Mio stays in the neighborhood, where there soon appear Trock, the murderer, who, with TB and only six months to live, wants Garth's continued silence, and Judge Gaunt, the murder trial judge who, having questioned the possibility that justice was not served, has become mentally deranged. Eventually, after a mock trial over which Judge Gaunt presides, Mio learns the truth about Garth. But with the love of Miriamne he now realizes something greater than revenge, something for which he can die, undefeated.

(*Discussion*) Basically, this play is an attempt to put modern tragedy into the pattern of the past with the themes of revenge and truth and justice as meaningful issues. Mio at the beginning is defiant, bitter, and cynical, filled with a desire for revenge; but under the pressure of love, he changes and makes a discovery which causes his spiritual awakening. Like Job he accepts a Christian resignation. Although the dialogue in the play sounds at times artificial, several passages display considerable poetic power. There remains, however, much to question in this play—the contrived gathering of the people, the relationship of the action to the language, the weak imitation of the past.

5. ARCHIBALD MACLEISH: POET-DRAMATIST WITH POTENTIAL

Although he wrote mainly poetic plays for radio during the period under discussion, Archibald MacLeish showed the potential in both poetry and theory which has since become one of the more exciting aspects of contemporary drama. In an introductory statement to *Panic* (1935) and in an essay entitled "A Stage for Poetry" (from *A Time to Speak*, 1941), he has made significant statements on the theory of poetic drama. Convinced that true poetic drama could be more realistic than prose, MacLeish declared that verse should be an integral part of the verse drama rather than an ornament. He favors the precedence of "the word-excited imagination" over experimentation in staging, which, of course, is one reason for the success of his radio plays. Contrary to the theories of past writers of poetic drama in America, he finds blank verse completely ineffective in expressing modern speech. "The classical rhythm equivalent to American speech," he writes, "would be more nearly the trochee or dactyl than the iamb of blank verse." Sensing a special connection in subject, form, and language, he has attempted to restore the importance of word and rhythm to poetic drama. His work of the 1930's shows his efforts to carry out his theories.

(a) MacLeish's Radio Plays

Panic (1935) describes a time in America when banks were closing and businesses failing; its theme is the consuming power of fear. *The Fall of the City* (1937), suggesting that people invent their oppressors, was described as "thirty minutes of the finest verbal music of its time." The City is thrown into confusion by a dead woman who comes from her tomb with a message: "The City of masterless men will take a master." When a messenger arrives to tell of an approaching conqueror, the words of the Priest and the General are not heard by the terrified people. Finally, the conqueror appears in armour, and the people bow down before him. But the armour is empty! *Air Raid* (1938) is less effective as it shows any city in the grip of terror, yet the accents of American speech were thought successful.

IV. FROM LEFT TO RIGHT: PROPAGANDA TO HIGH COMEDY

Underlying a great portion of modern American drama is a social-realistic tradition—a concern for society, its faults and foibles, expressed mainly in a realistic fashion. The scope of these plays runs from blatant propaganda to detached and sophisticated high comedy. In between are a great number of plays which vary in their objective from bitter denunciation to a concerned comment on social, economic, and moral problems, from a more intellectual and psychological interest in conditions, to a light comic approach to the idiosyncracies of life. This panoramic view includes a discussion of all major dramatists of the 1930's and dips back into the 1920's for those plays which show the beginnings of trends which reached their heights in the Depression Decade.

With this approach, observations concerning the relationship of the drama to the major literary figures of the day in poetry and fiction are interesting. Generally, the novelists were able to infuse more universal significance into their work than the dramatists of this period can boast, and the major novelists wrote with greater imagination from similar concerns and interests. A number of the novelists, in fact, wrote plays, though seldom very good ones: F. Scott Fitzgerald, *The Vegetable* (1923), a satire on man; Sinclair Lewis, *It Can't Happen Here* (1936), an attack on fascism; Jack Kirkland and Erskine Caldwell, *Tobacco Road* (1933), almost a classic with its vigorous language and seven-and-a-half-year run in New York; John Steinbeck, *Of Mice and Men* (1937); John Dos Passos, *The Garbage Man* (1926). Among the poets, too, there were those who considered the same economic, social, and political problems which bothered the dramatists—Archibald MacLeish, Robinson Jeffers, Carl Sandburg, Robert Frost, Edna St. Vincent Millay. The finest drama of this period reflects the ideas and interests of the best literature being written in America at this time, and a number of the plays achieve a literary significance altogether noteworthy. These were the products of playwrights who searched for answers in the social environment.

A. Art as a Weapon

The use of art for persuasive purposes was not new in America. Around the turn of this century, America had a number of protest writers—Thorstein Veblen, Henry George, Lincoln Steffens, Upton Sinclair—and there had been propaganda playwrights during the Revolutionary War. Drama, however, did not become a particular genre for protest until stimulated by the Marxists in America, who found meaning in the Russian Revolution as well as in the American Depression. With their various Five Year Plans the Russians attempted to regiment both art and the theater—art as a weapon—to serve political purposes. Such Russian playwrights as Alexander Afinogenov with *Far Taiga*, a study of the psychological importance of the people in Siberia, and Nikolai Pogodin with *Tempo*, which contrasts the new regime with the old regime, indicated their efforts to persuade through the theater.

In America, Leftist or Radical theater groups comprised a major part of the theater in the 1930's. Capitalism presumably failed in 1929, and Communism was considered the logical answer by many people. Idealistic dramatists frequently espoused Communist philosophy, attacked social conditions, and wrote about opposing ideologies and the conflicts of labor and capital. Generally, their plays were artistically weak but compensated for this by recourse to violent or radical action and a particularly unsubtle political dogma. Their themes centered on strikes, evictions, unemployment, penal institutions, and the oppressed and persecuted among common man. Drama as a weapon in America is one of the more vivid although brief trends in modern theater.

1. "THEATER IS A WEAPON"

The Communist Party established its own theaters very early in the Thirties and later tried with some success to use other theater groups, such as the Theatre Guild and the Group Theatre.

(a) Communist Theater Groups

Working through the German speaking Proletbuehne, the Communist party in America first established the Workers' Laboratory Theatre. From 1932 to 1934, the Communists' League of Workers' Theatre attempted to destroy the bourgeois theater. Rarely producing good plays, however, it advised: "Make the plays short and concise and make a thorough study of the Communist Party platform before writing them." In 1935, lasting until 1941, the Communists' New Theatre League attempted to establish a Soviet America with plays of "highest artistic and social level." But Communist theater in America failed to control amateur theaters and failed to get good repertory mainly because of the more varied fruits of capitalism. Good dramatists found the scope of Communist material very confining both intellectually and imaginatively. Broadway offered greater freedom—and money.

(b) The Labor Stage

Many non-Communist amateur theater groups produced left-wing plays. One of the best and most active of these groups was the recreational theater program of the International Ladies Garment Workers' Union. Established with the purpose of creating a balance of humor and propaganda, the sketch-revue called *Pins and Needles* was started in 1936 and, more or less frequently revived, closed in 1940 after 1100 performances in New York. In one *Pins and Needles* skit, Charles Foster's late nineteenth-century heroine in *Bertha, the Sewing Machine Girl* was rescued by a union man. In another, the D.A.R. was flayed in song as "filled to the brim with bigotry." Always maintaining a topicality, *Pins and Needles* once burlesqued a Mussolini Handicap, featuring as Public Enemy #1 the woman who could have only one child.

2. AGITPROP

The agitprop (agitation propaganda) provided a direct means of teaching Marxism. In its simplest form it could be produced in any place—a street corner or a factory gate. *Vote Communist*, for example, shows a capitalist with a top hat and a large dollar sign over his heart being heckled by actors in the audience. Each time he tries to masquerade as a Republican, or a Democrat, or a Socialist by placing cards with the appropriate word over his heart, the card is torn away to reveal again the dollar sign. Another typical agitprop was John Bonn's *15 Minute Red Review* (1932) which extolled the excellencies of Soviet Russia and ended with a promise to fight "For the Soviet Union." The objective of agitprop was action for the cause, and the effect of slogans was not underestimated. Plays like *Dimitroff* (1934) by Art Smith and Elia Kazan are filled with Communist slogans and songs—hence the necessity for the playwright to keep abreast of the Communist platform. Clifford Odets' *Waiting for Lefty* (1935) is basically an agitprop, a very effective one with considerably more than the usual artistry.

3. THE LIVING NEWSPAPER

A contribution of the Federal Theatre to American drama, the Living Newspaper drama simply analyzed and commented on particular events or situations. A number of the best plays were composed by Arthur Arent and a staff of writers. Not always very different from agitprop, the Living Newspaper used a variety of means to present well-documented facts and liberal opinions rather directly to an audience. In *Triple-A Plowed Under* (1936), the Voice of the Living Newspaper announces the twenty-six scenes which trace agricultural depression from World War I through foreclosure of farm mortgages, farm auctions, deliberate destruction of crops, droughts, to the creation of the Agriculture Adjustment Administration (AAA), and its termination as the Supreme Court declares it unconstitutional. The Communists approved of this play and this type of theater. Other living newspapers include *One-Third of a Nation* (1938), commenting on the housing problem in New York City, and the rather daring and more imaginative *Spirochete*, which traces the history of syphilis in the world.

4. A VARIETY OF PROTEST PLAYS

The purpose of this section is to suggest briefly the variety of subject matter among the protest plays. Each play is a particular protest, and according to William Koslenko in his Introduction to *The Best Short Plays of the Social Theatre* (1939), "no art can *serve* a loftier purpose." One of the most effective among full-length propaganda plays was George Sklar and Paul Peters' *Stevedore* (1934). From a seemingly insignificant event in which an outspoken Negro is involved, the authors build their thesis of Negro persecution to a mob scene of murder and rioting in which the Negro dock workers are joined in their fight against the white mob by the stevedores in the Union, thus cleverly linking race prejudice and economics. That same year, 1934, John Wexley effectively dramatized the Scottsboro case in *They Shall Not Die*. Another play with a Southern scene, *Let Freedom Ring* (1935) by Albert Bein, portrayed a strike in a North Carolina mill town.

Albert Maltz' *Black Pit* (1935) is called a Marxian tragedy; a union miner, forced to work as a company spy, betrays his fellow workers, and is ostracized. Another Maltz play, *Private Hicks* (1936), shows the victory of one soldier in a National Guard outfit who refuses to act as a strikebreaker. Paul Green's *Hymn to the Rising Sun* (1936) condemns the cruelties of the Negro convict road gang in the South. One of the most successful protest plays against war is Irwin Shaw's *Bury the Dead* (1936), the satiric tale of the refusal of dead soldiers to be buried. Marc Blitzstein's poetic musical, *The Cradle Will Rock* (1938), attacks capitalism through a bitter satire on its paid adherents—Rev. Salvation, Editor Daily, President Prexy, and Doctor Specialist. All do what Mr. Mister, the boss, demands; but when the wind blows, the cradle will rock.

5. JOHN HOWARD LAWSON: DRAMATIST OF COMMITMENT

A true member of the Lost Generation who spent time with the American ambulance service in France during World War I and marched in protest against the government's treatment of Sacco and Vanzetti, Lawson (1895–   ) became the most zealous convert to communism among American dramatists. From an idealistic searching during which he showed considerable talent in dramatic expressionism, he progressed to the forthright position regarding society and government which brought him a prison term after an appearance before the Un-American Activities Committee. In his plays there is a remarkable vitality, supported by an integrity and a personal commitment that is distinctive in American drama.

(a) A Lashing Out

For ten years after his first major play, *Roger Bloomer* (1923), Lawson displayed both his idealism and his bitterness against aspects of humanity. He was clearly searching for something in which he could believe. In *Loud Speaker* (1927), he followed Coolidge's advice to "look well to the hearthstone, therein all hope for America lies," but all he discovered were problems of persecution and injustice. In particular, he saw the political manipulation of the American people and the worship of success. Like *Processional* (1925), which used a strike to dramatize class war, *International* (1928) is an experimental mixture of Freud and Marx in which love actually conquers. The Communist press had been pleased by *Processional* and *Loud Speaker*; but, although Lawson had stressed loyalty to a cause in *International* and had castigated capitalism and commented on prejudice and economic persecution, the press was bothered by the play's bourgeois sentiment and by an obvious indecision on Lawson's part. A later play, *Success Story* (1932), was even less pleasing to Communist reviewers. Although Lawson attacked capitalism in this play, his theme—money does not bring happiness—was not widely accepted by a Communist press which found Lawson more interested in an individual than a class struggle.

(b) The Regimented "Bourgeois Hamlet of Our Time"

Lawson's 1934 production of *Gentlewoman* dramatized a dying class but made the personal embodiment of that class quite admirable. Reviewing the play in *New Masses*, "A Bourgeois Hamlet of Our Time," Mike Gold, the chief literary spokesman for the Party, attacked Lawson severely as confused and without direction. Quite unexpectedly, Lawson was contrite; he underwent an "intensive re-evaluation" of his work in terms of Marxist orthodoxy, and joined the Communist Party. Now convinced that the dramatist must

take sides, he began to write dramatic criticism and theory—
Theory and Techniques of Playwriting (1936)—and, in
1937, wrote his final play, *Marching Song*, which was to be
a model for revolutionary drama. The play does have a collective hero but a recognizable plot and much melodramatic
—though politically clear—action. To protest a blacklisted
worker's eviction, the Auto Worker's Union goes on a strike,
which is followed by a bombing, strikebreakers, guns, and
tear gas. Finally, the union men win by capturing the power
station. Politically oriented, however, they keep the power
going at the hospital. Certainly the Communist critics could
not complain. After writing this play, however, Lawson went
to Hollywood, where he became less effective in dramatic
circles.

6. ELMER RICE: A TOUCH OF MARXISM

Elmer Rice (1892–   ) presents a problem for the
drama historian because his career, starting in 1914 with *On
Trial*, still continues and includes protest plays, social commentary plays, and light comedies. (Mainly, his work will
be discussed under "Troubled Playwrights.")

(a) Marxist Ideals but Not Marxist Methods
The Communist press was not pleased with *We the
People* (1933), because although Rice had written a bitter
attack on Depression times, he had not insisted on the Marxist solution. Protesting quite properly, he showed the disintegration of the proletarian family—father loses his job, his
health, his house; a son is falsely accused of murder and
executed—and the ending of the play is agitprop. The action
it calls for, however, is a return to democratic ideals rather
than Marxist revolution. *Judgment Day* (1934) was little better from the Communist view. In this attack upon Nazi fascism, Rice re-emphasized his belief that art could serve a
useful social function. Based on the trial of Georgi Dimitroff
by the Nazis, Rice melodramatically manipulated his material
to bring about the destruction of his Hitler character. In *Between Two Worlds* (1934), Rice contrasted the Social-politi-
cal system of America with that of Russia, emphasizing an
awareness of social purpose and a concern for humanity.

Although the Communists saw value in this play and potential for its author in the Party, Rice was sufficiently disturbed by the Broadway reviews that he announced his retirement from the theater. Not until four years passed did he return to Broadway with *American Landscape* (1938), a play which presented not only American traditions but Rice's inclination to be a liberal rather than a Communist.

7. CLIFFORD ODETS: AGGRESSIVE MARXIST

The year Clifford Odets died (1906–1963) he complained that critics remembered him only as a playwright of the Thirties. With some reason, his fear was real, and some day the year 1935 may hold all of Odets that is interesting to the drama historian—the year he had four plays on Broadway: *Waiting for Lefty, Till the Day I Die, Awake and Sing,* and *Paradise Lost.* Born of working Jewish parents, he became an actor and was a charter member of the Group Theatre in 1930. In 1934, he joined the Communist Party, leaving it in mid-1935 because "I am a liberal, not a Communist." After his year of tremendous success in which he was hailed as the most exciting dramatist since the emergence of O'Neill, he continued to write plays, but left for Hollywood and money in 1936. The change was dramatic and a bit traumatic for some. The remark by Frank Nugent of *The New York Times* after viewing Odets' movie adaptation of *The General Died at Dawn* seemed an apt critical summary at the time: "Odets, where is thy sting?" Although he wrote three plays after World War II, he never reached his earlier success in the theater.

(a) "That Wonderful Year, 1935"

Odets was superior to other Marxist writers because he believed not only that a play should be "immediately and dynamically useful" but that it should also be "psychologically profound." He had joined the Communist Party in the "honest and real belief" that it was a way out of the dilemma he saw in society, and his plays in 1935 show typically Marxist characteristics. *Waiting for Lefty* is the best, of course, with its agitprop ending. The closing lines in the other plays suggest Odets' liberal idealism which permeated even his post World War II plays. *Till the Day I Die* tells of a Communist agent working underground in Nazi Germany who is caught by the Nazis, tortured and released, only to be thereafter suspect by members of his cell. Even his brother does not trust him, and he can regain their confidence only by killing himself. *Awake and Sing* dramatizes the agony, the argument, and the disintegration of the Berger family. Life is frustration: life is "printed on dollar bills"; the entire picture is one of spiritual death. Finally, a real death in the family resurrects the individual spirits, and they decide to "look on the world" and crusade for a better future. *Paradise Lost* presents a similar degradation of the middle-class Gordon family until they also feel that one can "fight" for a better world with those who understand—more of a Marxist solution.

(i) Waiting for Lefty

Awarded a prize by *New Masses* and *New Theatre* magazines, this militant agitprop represents protest drama in America. Its impact was so great in 1935 that the actors were arrested in Boston, and a producer of the play in Hollywood was beaten by thugs. Odets once said that the theater is at its best when the plight expressed by the stage action is at one with the plight of the audience. In this play he was successful in that the problems and the collective action suggested were meaningful to audiences in 1935. As one character says, "The world is supposed to be for all of us!" Using a minstrel show technique and a union meeting in which a group of taxi drivers wait for their leader, Lefty, before discussing a proposed strike, Odets dramatizes five scenes showing (1) the poverty of a taxi driver and his wife, (2) a lab assistant who is asked to spy on his superiors, (3) a young cab driver who can't get married for economic reasons, (4) a labor spy in the meeting, and (5) prejudice against a Jewish doctor. Finally, the news comes that Lefty has been killed and the union leaders are confronted with the compelling force of the workers' decision: Strike!

B. Troubled Playwrights

The twenty-odd years between the two World Wars were a time of concern for the thoughtful man. The pace of the social life that characterized the Twenties suggested a greed—live all you can, get all you can, forget all you can—

that was a part of the moral, economic, and political life. Inflationary in many aspects, the joy ride of the Twenties seemed feverishly unhealthy. When the stock market crashed in 1929 and government control with welfare state characteristics appeared in F.D.R.'s administration, individualistic-minded people saw difficulties. Another source of worry was the small but frequently violent propaganda of the Communist Party and left-wing organizations.

In poetry, novel, and drama, the creative world reacted to the problems that it saw or foresaw. Some dramatists protested vigorously—having espoused a philosophy that preached revolution. Other dramatists, equally concerned but more liberal, commented seriously on various social and political problems: they may be called "Troubled Playwrights." The main ones were Elmer Rice, Maxwell Anderson, S. N. Behrman, Robert Sherwood, and Sidney Kingsley—all meaningful social critics in their best plays.

1. ELMER RICE: A DEHUMANIZED SOCIETY

Elmer Rice's (1892–   ) career in the theater started in 1914 with *On Trial*, an experimental play in which a courtroom scene served as a basis for flashbacks into aspects of the crime being tried. Born in New York, graduating from law school before deciding to become a writer, Rice (Reizenstein) has made use of his legal acumen in several plays and in various theater disputes in which he has been involved. He is a fearless and talented man, who has spoken with forthrightness and wisdom on subjects popular and unpopular. Uneven and varied, his plays range from slight comedy —*Cock Robin* (1928) with Philip Barry, *Dream Girl* (1945)—to realistic social drama. It was in the Twenties, however, that his plays became most meaningful in the development of modern American drama. Troubled by the growing victimization and dehumanization of man, his efforts to arouse the public became more serious in intent until he questioned the validity of the theater as a means of realistic social comment. During the Thirties he tried his version of Marxist drama and became somewhat disillusioned with the commercial theater. A lover of the theater, however, he was never so disturbed that he could not write more plays— either as protest or pure entertainment. Mainly, he has been a troubled liberal, a temporarily disillusioned playwright, and a passionate debater, who has spoken out against all manner of social injustice and in support of the democratic traditions of America.

(a) Victims of Society

Rice made his first real success in *The Adding Machine* (1923). In this and in two other plays in this decade—*The Subway* (1929) and *Street Scene* (1929)—he effectively dramatized his concern for man, crushed and victimized by society. Mr. Zero, representative of man, from *The Adding Machine*, is condemned as a "waste product" and a "slave to a contraption of steel and iron." Not only is he dehumanized while alive, but even after death his existence is that of a spiritless slave. *The Subway* shows man again as a victim of civilization. When scientists of the distant future dig in America, they will find the symbols of our society—bones, a glass eye, false teeth, blackened coins, and a key for a safe deposit box—the things that suggest our falseness and materialism, "all that remains of Western Civilization." In *Street Scene*, the theme is expressed again: "Everywhere you look," says a character, "oppression and cruelty!" It is important to note that throughout these plays, man is unable to be close to nature; it was a cruelty of humanity not nature that troubled Rice.

(i) Street Scene, 1929

(*Plot*) As people representing many aspects of slum life gather on the steps of an apartment house in New York's tenement district to discuss the day and their feelings, everyone knows that Mrs. Maurrant from upstairs and Mr. Sankey, the milk collector, are having an affair. When Mr. Maurrant comes home, his daughter Rose, who has some understanding of her mother's love of beauty and romance, begs him to move the family out of New York, but he refuses. The next day when Maurrant must be out of town, Sankey visits Mrs. Maurrant. But Maurrant returns, his suspicions having been earlier aroused; and before the lovers can be warned, he kills his wife. After the police capture him, he tries to explain to Rose his love, his desire for law and order; but his ineffectiveness is symbolic of the situation. As the slum area returns to normal, Rose prepares to leave with her younger brother.

(*Discussion*) Mrs. Maurrant is a sensitive person with hopes and dreams; Mr. Maurrant is hard working, has good ideas, and believes in law and order. But how does one attain happiness? What are the choices—promiscuity, waiting and hoping, being a kept woman, Marxism? In a "street scene"—a cross section of slum life where kids play games, the gossip has a vulgar daughter, a family is evicted, a baby is born—shouldn't everyone have a chance? At the end of the play, however, nothing is changed. There is no better understanding; there is no solution.

(b) From Marx to American Traditions

With the bitterness that Rice preached in *Street Scene*, there was perhaps good reason for him to become disillusioned with the effectiveness of Broadway as a reform media and to begin a slight flirtation with the radicals. In the early Thirties, he wrote *We, the People* (1933), *Judgment Day* (1934), *Between Two Worlds* (1934). But he did not find his answer with the radicals. He saw, realistically, that the theater was in the hands of business and real estate operators (as it continues to be); the drama was a "bond maiden of commerce." *Not for Children* (1935) condemns the theater as "unrelated to reality." But this discovery did not stop him from writing plays. Perhaps re-evaluating his own desires in the theater (certainly showing the inconsistency which is a part of Rice's work) or perhaps being influenced by the cloud of approaching war, he wrote *American Landscape* in 1938. Here he emphasized, as he had suggested before, the basic values of American traditions—"a tradition of freedom and the common rights of humanity." Still a troubled playwright, he now linked his interest in social evils and all dehumanizing aspects of society to a belief in the American democratic tradition.

2. MAXWELL ANDERSON: SOCIAL AND POLITICAL ANARCHY

In all of Anderson's (1888–1959) plays, there is a concern for individual freedom, while the social or political institutions which inhibit this freedom are criticized as evil. Although criticism of specific social institutions is avoided in many of his plays, his impassioned conviction that the individual is victimized in a socio-political state suggests the anarchy of his themes. This distrust of social and political institutions, evident in his early prose plays, turns to rather bitter satire in *Gods of the Lightning* and *Both Your Houses*. In the Thirties, he became interested in government—the inhuman institution which the struggle for power promotes—and the corruption which he found coexistent with all government. Finally, he reached the conclusion that some government is necessary and that democracy is best, although the sensitive individual who prizes his freedom may still be a victim.

(a) A Basic Independence

Even in *What Price Glory?* (1924), there is beneath the military order a basic independence of spirit which distinguishes Flagg and Quirt, satirizes visiting Congressmen, and damns the authorities for useless killing. *First Flight* (1925), written with Laurence Stallings, dramatizes the independent attitude of the backwoodsmen who finally persuade Andy Jackson that not only are the rights of the state more meaningful than the rights of a federal government but that the individual should oppose any kind of government. Another play with Stallings, *The Buccaneer* (1925), dramatizes aspects of the life of Captain Henry Morgan who tells government representatives that men are "all robbers and thieves," that government means dishonesty. It is only the individual who counts. An adaptation of Jim Tully's *Beggars of Life*, Anderson's *Outside Looking In* (1925) burlesques the injustices of society's trial by jury and shows the hoboes' proper contempt for authority. *Saturday's Children* (1927) tells of a girl who beguiles her sweetheart into marriage only to find that the institution of marriage lacks the romance and sense of living that she wants. Her final solution, which shows her independence, is unconventional and critical but only slightly rebellious. In all of these plays, however, Anderson asserts a basic independence.

Anderson takes a more violent view of government in *Gods of the Lightning* (1928), written with Harold Hickerson, a rather liberal interpretation of the Sacco and Vanzetti trial in the 1920's. Bitter against the administration of biased justice, Anderson finds the government "rotten"; even the

District Attorney in the play is wary of government. Anderson's Pulitzer Prize play, *Both Your Houses* (1933), satirizes men of both houses of Congress for their stupidity and their dishonesty. One congressman admits that "the sole business of government is graft, special privilege and corruption—with a by-product of order." A new congressman, Alan McLean, is shocked by such corruption; yet by keeping his hero idealistic, Anderson indicates an attitude toward democracy on which he will build later. For the moment, he is concerned with the growing powers of a government that preys on individual freedom.

(b) Corruption by Power (Poetic Plays)

"It rots a man's brain to be in power," says a character in *Valley Forge* (1934). This idea is basic in a number of his poetic dramas, although in *Valley Forge* Anderson had to resort to a little double talk in order to make Washington a rebel-idealist rather than the kind of triumphant dictator whom Anderson detested. Elizabeth must value power over love in *Elizabeth the Queen* (1930), and she must assent to the cruelty that is power to protect her throne in *Mary of Scotland* (1933). In *High Tor* (1937), the individualist who wants freedom from the power of government must simply leave; that is his only means of escape. Rudolf in *The Masque of Kings* (1937) also dislikes authority, but when the logic of power is explained to him, he realizes that for the idealist escape comes only in suicide, that even an idealistic revolution would fail when the revolutionists became corrupted, as they inevitably would. Anderson's theme again and again is social pessimism: men cannot unit justice and power. The theme is repeated in *The Feast of Ortolans* (1937) and *Second Overture* (1938). In man's struggle for his individual integrity and freedom in a world of socio-political power, he can accept his defeat as Essex does, or become corrupt like Elizabeth, or escape through suicide, or run away, or die for an ideal as the hero does in *Key Largo* (1939). In any event, power corrupts.

(c) Compromise through Democracy

In *Night Over Taos* (1932) and *Both Your Houses* (1933), Anderson had suggested that some government was necessary and that democracy seemed the best method. In *Knickerbocker Holiday* (1938), that rousing satire of the New Deal and F.D.R. with music by Kurt Weill, he blasted the philosophy of benevolent despotism but finally concluded in some seriousness: "Let's keep the government small and funny, and maybe it'll give us less discipline and more entertainment." The individual was still uppermost in his mind, however, as he allowed the heroine of *Candle in the Wind* (1941) to voluntarily give her life for love and freedom. "A tyrant is a tyrant, beneficient or maleficent," he wrote in his "Thoughts about the Critics." But the soldiers in *The Eve of St. Mark* (1942) died for freedom and a democratic government, while Socrates in *Barefoot in Athens* (1951) defended democracy. When the king asks: "What do you trust?" Socrates (and seemingly Anderson) answered: "The Citizens—the voters."

3. S. N. BEHRMAN: COMEDY WITHOUT DETACHMENT

Whenever S. N. Behrman's (1893–   ) reputation in modern American drama is established, he will probably be recognized mainly for his few plays which contribute to high comedy. Most of his plays, however, although they are witty in dialogue and sophisticated in idea, lack the degree of detachment necessary for comedy of manners. The various aspects of the social and political life, which Behrman treated with considerable urbanity, frequently touched the marrow of his emotions. His interest in power-mad fanatics and all tyranny became in the Thirties a major aspect of his plays, until he seriously questioned the possibility or the value of detachment in the theater. Essentially, he was a troubled playwright who, nevertheless, did not completely abandon the comic spirit when he presented his view on some of the social issues of his day.

(a) The Fascist World

Early in his career, Behrman presented some of the characters and ideas which he obviously found distasteful. It became immediately clear that he was not opposed to commenting, but that he was generally subtle in dramatizing the defeat of hated forces. Raphael Lord in *Meteor* (1929), for example, is a success in the business world because he is ruthless, and he is made to suffer for his inhumanity. A number of people in an English country house provide generally divergent ideas in *Rain from Heaven* (1934). Opposed to one another are Hobart, an Anglo-American fascist-capitalist, and Hugo, a German-Jewish refugee. Hugo, by far the most appealing character, will return to Germany to fight Nazism, while Hobart, made to see himself more clearly, can only sulk. In *End of Summer* (1936), Behrman labels one character "the enemy," a fraudulent psychiatrist named Dr. Rice, who cynically woos the heroine of the story in order to get her money for his fascist cause. Behrman defeats him in high comic splendor.

(b) "No Time for Comedy"

In 1939, Behrman wrote a play called *No Time for Comedy* in which he attempted to justify the writing of comedy in a world threatened by war. His playwright hero feels that he should leave his successful genre of comedy for serious drama, but he fails in his attempt and returns to his forte. Perhaps one should laugh in the face of danger, but how can one laugh when people are not even allowed to live? Behrman's troubled view is seen as he questions the value of detached comedy in a world in which detachment is almost impossible. The previous year he had commented vigorously in *Wine of Choice* (1938) on a proletarian writer whose hatred had warped his sense of humanity, and he had opposed this revolutionary fanatic with a person who upheld the traditional values. In his usual way he had shown the radical defeated; but in *The Talley Method* (1941), he revealed a new position. The Talley Method, that of detachment, cuts off the sense of humanity. This, Behrman also finds intolerable; he cannot leave his writer-hero in this play a victim of an animal world. He became, therefore, a playwright of social issues.

4. SIDNEY KINGSLEY: DETAILED DESPAIR IN MELODRAMA

A newcomer to the theater in the Depression Decade, Sidney Kingsley (1906–   ) indulged in realistic studies which, though melodramatic in action and conception, present a vivid picture of aspects of life. While he has not been a prolific playwright, he has written some stirring and successful plays—*Dead End* (1935), his most effective social drama; and *Men in White* (1933), a Pulitzer Prize winner about a young doctor's life in a hospital, replete with overwhelming hospital details, an agonizing love triangle, and the maturing of the doctor. Kingsley seems seriously interested in dramatizing a detailed social life, and it is in the accuracy of his detail that he is effective. His "troubled" concern for social issues, however, is seriously weakened by his use of controlled melodrama for theatrical effect, although he did write a serious protest against war and munitions makers in *Ten Million Ghosts* (1936). Its failure perhaps led him back to realistic social melodrama, in which he excells.

(a) *Dead End*, 1935

(*Plot*) Into a squalid East River scene where several boys swim in the filth-covered river comes a wanted criminal, "Baby Face" Martin, to see his mother and his first sweetheart. To his shocked surprise, his mother has only contempt for him, while his sweetheart has become an obviously diseased prostitute. Life in the slums is a struggle. The gang of boys, led by Tommy, indoctrinate a new boy, fight with the Second Avenue gang, and steal the watch of a rich kid living in a nearby hotel. When the kid's father tries to catch the boys, Tommy cuts him with a knife and the police are called. There is also love in the slums. Drina, Tommy's sister, constantly tries to take care of him. Gimpty, a crippled young architect, and Kay are in love, but she fears his poverty and chooses to be the mistress of a rich man. Finally, Martin is killed by G-men on a tip from Gimpty, and the police catch Tommy, who seems destined for a life of crime although the reward money will be used for a lawyer. And the slum life continues.

(*Discussion*) These are the conditions in New York slums. Brooks Atkinson, drama critic, called the play a "public social document." Gimpty, the intellectual, says to Tommy's sister: "Yeah, Drina, the place you live is awfully important. It can give you a chance to grow, or it can twist—like that." Although the play was infused with melodrama, the realistic scene, dialogue, and bits of action produced a rather shocking drama. In sensation rather than lesson, it can be compared with Rice's *Street Scene*, and from its characters it produced another Americanism—"the Dead End Kids."

5. ROBERT SHERWOOD: TROUBLED WARRIOR

Robert Sherwood's (1896–1955) rather uneven contribution to American drama includes a few plays marked by distinct insight and a number of plays of more limited view and dogmatic approach. These last plays classify Sherwood as a "troubled playwright." After serving in France in World War I, he developed a hatred of war that became the theme of several of his plays. As the Thirties moved on, however, and war became a definite threat to civilization once more, Sherwood's attitude changed. His concern for the individual was as strong as ever; but in terms of a greater humanity, which he had discovered in his more thought-provoking plays of the Thirties, he realized a concept of man and freedom greater than the mere fulfillment of the individual. Again he had an answer—obviously an appealing one, since two of these war plays were awarded Pulitzer Prizes—but his tendency to control and dominate his action with his beliefs distracts from the general value of these plays.

(a) War Condemned: "The Human Equation"

The Road to Rome (1927) shows Sherwood's early satire on war. The scene is Rome: Fabius has just been made dictator when Hannibal's army appears outside of the gates. Feigning a return to her family home, Fabius' Greek-born wife, Amytis, goes to Hannibal's camp, is captured, condemned, but saved by Hannibal, whom she then beguiles. Questioning him about his interest in war, she explains the force which leads him to war as "the voice of the shopkeepers in Carthage," and tells him of the "human equation" which is "so much more beautiful than war." The next morning Hannibal decides to retreat, and Amytis is returned to Fabius, who pompously stated that Hannibal has been overcome by the moral force of Rome. The play is slight with a great deal of farce and burlesque about it, but Sherwood's statement has force. In *Idiot's Delight* (1935), Sherwood restated his belief that war is completely irrational. At the outbreak

of a war, a varied group of people react to the tragedy as
they share a small hotel near the Italian border. Above the
frightened banter of the individuals, the execution of the
Communist, and the sentimental love of Harry Van and
Irene, there is Sherwood's voice damning the munitions
makers—the league of "Krupp, Skoda, and Vickers, and du
Pont. The league of death"—and the stupidity of war.

(b) The Question of War: A Time to Fight

There Shall Be No Night (1940) was Sherwood's violent reaction to Russia's invasion of Finland. A renowned Finnish
scientist, Dr. Kaarlo Valkonen, cannot understand the reasons
for war until Russia attacks, his son is killed, and invasion
seems imminent. Throwing aside his experiments, he joins the
medical corps and is killed. In his neurological research, he
had been trying to defeat the "degeneration of the human
race," but, he now concludes, "This is a war for everybody."
The point was clear—made in emotional, melodramatic
terms. A troubled playwright forced his way out of a dilemma
at an appropriate time.

6. "THE TROUBLES I'VE SEEN"

It has been noted that in the typical modern play the
chief cause of conflict is not man, nor Fate, nor universal
law, but a social condition in which the dramatist sees some
possibility of adjustment. The best playwrights who were conscious of various social troubles in life have been discussed,
but there were many more. For this period in American
drama, this topic is the most inclusive. The following headings and listed plays will suggest additional activity and diversity.

(a) Economic and Political Issues

Mainly, these issues have been adequately presented in
plays by Anderson and Behrman. One might also mention
Beggar on Horseback (1924) by George S. Kaufman and
Marc Connelly, *Holiday* (1928) by Philip Barry, *Having
Wonderful Time* (1937) by Arthur Kober, and *The Land
is Bright* (1941) by Kaufman and Edna Ferber.

(b) Social and Personal Issues

Social and personal problems are the basis of most plays by Behrman, Philip Barry, George Kelly, and Rachel Crothers. A brief list would include *Expressing Willie* (1924) by Rachel Crothers, *In a Garden* (1925) by Philip Barry, *Brief Moment* (1931) by S. N. Behrman, *Wednesday's Child* (1934) by Leopold Atlas, *Reflected Glory* (1936) by George Kelly, *The Women* (1936) by Clare Boothe, and *Claudia* (1941) by Rose Franken.

(c) War and Crime

Many of Robert Sherwood's plays would be included here. Other plays would be Clare Boothe's anti-Nazi play, *Margin for Error* (1939); Paul Green's war play, *Johnny Johnson* (1936); and crime plays, such as Elmer Rice's *Counsellor-at-Law* (1931) and Irwin Shaw's *The Gentle People* (1938).

(d) Religious and Moral Issues

Plays inviting moral comment include such diverse issues as prohibition, *The Old Soak* (1922) by Don Marquis; free love, *The Vinegar Tree* (1930) by Paul Osborn; and academic freedom, *The Male Animal* (1940) by James Thurber and Elliott Nugent. The extensive part that religion has in numerous dramas suggests the unfailing interest of American playwrights: *Susan and God* (1937) by Rachel Crothers; *The Fool* (1923), in which a Christian minister practices Christ-like living and loses his job and the respect of his fellow men; and *The Enemy* (1925) by Channing Pollock; *Bride of the Lamb* (1926) by William Hurlbut; *The Green Pastures* (1930) by Marc Connelly; *The Criminal Code* (1929) by Martin Flavin; *Shroud My Body Down* (1934) by Paul Green; *Hotel Universe* (1930) and *Here Come the Clowns* (1938) by Philip Barry; and numerous plays by Eugene O'Neill and Maxwell Anderson.

(e) Race and Prejudice

Those plays listed among the folk drama and the protest plays frequently showed race prejudice. Prejudice toward Orientals appears in John Colton's *The Shanghai Gesture* (1926) and *The Color Line* (1928) by Irene Taylor Mac-

Nair; Negro prejudice is frequent in *Judge Lynch* (1924) by
William R. Rogers, Jr., DuBose Heyward's *Brass Ankle*
(1931) which tells of those who pass for white but have
enough colored blood to bear colored children, and plays by
Paul Green. Maxwell Anderson's *The Wingless Victory*
(1936) concerns New England prejudice toward a Malayan
woman.

C. The Heightened Problem

Although the socio-political condition of America provided the conflicts for most of the plays during the Twenties
and the Thirties, the treatment of those conflicts varied with
each dramatist. Frequently, troubled dramatists were sufficiently talented to express their concern effectively, but playing upon specific emotions during a time when emotions were
rarely hidden indicates dated melodrama. Such, of course,
was frequently the essence of success in the theater. Few
dramatists had the imagination and the craft to raise a particular issue to a suggestion of universal significance. These
few, however, might be termed writers of social or thesis
drama. Their limitations are significant, if one is speaking in
terms of great drama, but they did more than simply comment on social issues, while still not involving themselves in
a profound search for meaning in life. Essentially, they are
all moralists, all careful analysts of society, all realists who
have not been interested in experimentation in form. Reflecting the attitudes of some American novelists and following a
trend started by Susan Glaspell's *The Verge* and John Howard Lawson's *Roger Bloomer*, they have shown certain psychological insight into both character and situation, and they
have had both the intelligence and the imagination to express themselves with significant effect in a few plays—Robert Sherwood (in *The Petrified Forest*), George Kelly, and
Lillian Hellman.

These writers were not concerned specifically with satire
or social commentary, nor were they interested in the spiritual or psychical struggle of man. They saw him rather as a
social animal, and they dramatized his reactions to society.
Historically, their work shows a dependence upon the writings of Auguste Comte, the Father of modern sociology, and
the psychology of William James.

1. ROBERT SHERWOOD: *THE PETRIFIED FOREST*, 1935

Robert Sherwood (1896–1955) was both intellectually and emotionally concerned with the conditions of man. When his emotions were in the ascendance, he wrote satiric war melodrama. He could be more detached, however, as in *Reunion in Vienna* (1931), in which he portrayed, with psychological insight and clever dialogue, a woman's reaction to her own past. He could also write a very human and moving play about a man's struggle to live a life he enjoyed and at the same time take a dignified stand for what he believed—*Abe Lincoln in Illinois* (1938). And in *The Petrified Forest*, he could create a thought-provoking play which epitomized the romantic "lostness" of a generation. Unfortunately, in all of these plays, melodramatic tendencies detract from the thought of the play and the frequently effective use of language.

(a) *The Petrified Forest*, 1935

(*Plot*) The Black Mesa Filling Station and Bar-B-Q in eastern Arizona is run by the Maples—old Gramp, Jason, and his daughter Gabby—and Boze, a dull football player who wants Gabby. All show their dissatisfaction with life, even Squier, a newly arrived traveler, who had artistic talent until he married a rich wife and forgot his ambitions. Before he leaves, however, Gabby shares her romantic dreams of going to France and her taste for Villon's poetry with Squier, who understands her love of beauty because he also had illusions once. Then Duke Mantee, a hunted criminal, arrives with part of his gang to wait in this appointed place for his girl. Squier returns, and the desperate situation of the people becomes as revealing as it is uncomfortable. Squier, drawing an analogy between himself and Mantee as frustrated individualists, makes out his insurance policy to Gabby so that she can go to France and then arranges for Duke to kill him. When the manhunt for Mantee closes in, Duke kills Squier as he promised. Perhaps in Gabby some of Squier's ambitions and dreams will be realized. The issue remains in doubt, but she at least has ideals.

(*Discussion*) Sherwood presents a group of people who have become dissatisfied with life because man has lost his ideals, has given up his illusions. The intellectuals failed to conquer Nature, and people have become neurotic rather than express their real emotions. As a consequence, the world has changed; and man now lives in a petrified forest, a "world of outmoded ideas." Squier suffers the "lostness" of the sensitive individual, and both he and Mantee, romantically linked as Poet and Gunman, are condemned in this world as romantic idealists. In making the point that modern man should keep his illusions and escape from the petrified forest, Sherwood and Squier find hope in Gabby. The solution to the problem, then, becomes that of the romantic idealists.

2. GEORGE KELLY: MORAL LESSONS

George Kelly's (1887–   ) career in the theater goes back to the second decade of this century when he wrote vaudeville skits. A definite person, bent on satisfying himself in his plays, he wrote several fine ones in the Twenties, among which *Craig's Wife* (1925) was awarded a Pulitzer Prize. The critical response to most of his plays, however, discouraged him; and since the failure of *Philip Goes Forth* (1931), he has written for the movies but created only four dramas. Essentially a realistic and moral man, he is concerned with the self-condemning weakness of the individual in society. Montrose J. Moses, an historian of the drama, has noted that Kelly "is a simple moralist using the theatre for simple moral purposes." Such a criticism is an over-simplification, but Kelly does base his judgments on a few essential moral principles: be honest, be pure, be truthful, be true. He believes that people control their own lives, and he judges them for their failures, blaming neither heredity nor social forces. His insistence upon judging, however, sometimes detracts from the value of his plays, although it is his purpose to make the lesson more universally applicable than the situation dramatized. In this, he has attained only partial success.

His technique throughout his work has been that of the well-made play. His mastery of this form and his conscious interest in the details of straightforward realism have suggested to some critics that he has created puppet characters and a photographic exactness which has led to caricature.

Kelly, however, has not strayed from his formula, and the authenticity of his scene and dialogue and the force of his characterization are often memorable. Consequently, his format is both his strength and his weakness, as it allows his logic to appear with considerable force at the same time that it limits and detracts from the living and more universal quality of his plays.

(a) Social Problems and Individual Weaknesses

Although he has attacked various social ills, Kelly is mainly concerned with human weaknesses. Not society itself but the reactions of the individual in a society which makes happiness impossible interest him. In *The Torchbearers* (1922), Kelly attacked the absurdities of the Little Theatre Movement and the ridiculous affectations of the people involved, but he did it through a revelation of individual weaknesses. The plot of *Philip Goes Forth* (1931) concerns a man who is persuaded to go to New York to write when it is obvious that he belongs where he is as a businessman. Kelly, however, soft pedals a criticism of the society which makes the choice so appealing and emphasizes the weakness of the man who allowed himself to be persuaded when he knew what his position in life should be. An unpublished play, *Can Two Walk Together,* dramatizes "the tragic rushing into marriage," but finds the fault in the hero's inability to distinguish between reason and passion. Kelly, then, may treat social disorders, but his judgments fall upon individuals. Only in *The Show-Off* (1924), in which a braggart and liar is blessed far beyond his deserts, did he dramatize a conflict between an individual and society, but the play is situation farce and cannot be taken seriously as social criticism.

(b) The Damned

Those whom Kelly does find willfully corrupt among a weak and vacillating humanity, he damns with a Puritan conviction. *Craig's Wife* (1925) tells of Mrs. Craig's determination not only to be independent but to control. She is a cold and quarrelsome person, who alienates her neighbors, accuses her aunt of snooping, tries to ruin a niece's life, and distrusts her husband. She wants independent security; and at the end of the play, Kelly gives her just that—with the loss of friends and husband—because he believes that she acted willfully. Likewise in *Behold the Bridegroom* (1927), he judges a wanton woman and condemns her for the choices in life which she has made. When Antionette Lyle finally meets someone she loves, the guilt she feels makes her reveal her past, but she finds that she is too late in her discovery. There will be no marriage. In *Daisy Mayme* (1926), a well-made plot brings a happy ending for the hero and Daisy Mayme, while her antagonist, a conniving and vicious woman, loses everything. Throughout these plays, Kelly shows a discriminating insight into character, an attention to truthful detail, and a conviction for judgment which distinguish him among his contemporary writers of the social problem play.

3. LILLIAN HELLMAN: "I AM A MORAL WRITER"

During the period between the Wars, Lillian Hellman (1905–   ) wrote only four plays, but their promise has been happily displayed in some of the more thought-provoking plays at mid-century. Her output has not been voluminous but has included war plays, adaptations, and plays emphasizing the South, in which she spent a good part of her youth. In a preface to a collection of four of her plays, she wrote: "I am a moral writer, often too moral a writer, and I cannot avoid, it seems, that last summing up." This determination to make her point clear, plus her reliance upon violent action, has brought charges of "melodrama" and "sensationalism" from critics. Miss Hellman has argued, however, the effectiveness of violent action for a purpose, and no one could mistake her craftsmanship. Her concern for social problems is clearly evident in her plays; and with considerable force, she has attacked evils in society as well as the power of fascism. Combining her interests, she has produced tales of horror dealing with Lesbianism, unnatural greed, and human degeneracy—tales in which she has imposed certain criticism against gossip, racial problems, and Southern prejudices. Her morals have been obvious: do not fool around with human lives; do something about degenerate greed. Using both comedic and melodramatic techniques, Lillian Hellman has exposed the selfishness and the cruelty of man with a penetrating clarity and a highly theatrical, if sometimes melodramatic, effectiveness. Generally, her objectives are no different from many writers of the Thirties; but with superior artistry and more intense and controlled imagination, she has succeeded in suggesting a universality in her works.

(a) Social Anger

Victorian writers extolled the moral strength of woman. The moral view of an aroused and talented woman playwright constituted a powerful force in the theater. *The Children's Hour* (1934), ironically taking its title from Longfellow's poem, dramatizes an evil quality in people. To satisfy her own distorted desire for excitement, Mary Tilford, a student in a girls' school run by Martha Dobie and Karen Wright, invents a story suggesting an unnatural affection between the two teachers and petulantly tells it to her grandmother when she is punished for misbehaving at school. The grandmother is incensed; the story is spread around; and although the teachers try to defend themselves, they are ostracized by the community and forced to close their school. Later, a despairing Martha becomes morbidly concerned with her own actions and commits suicide, fearing that she may be preventing Karen's happiness in her approaching marriage to a young doctor. Then the grandmother understands and reveals the truth. It is too late for Martha, but Karen can try to find a future for herself. Brooks Atkinson called the play a story of "two people . . . defeated by the malignance of an aroused public opinion."

Lillian Hellman's second play, *Days to Come* (1936), sided with labor in a strikebreaking episode. *Watch on the Rhine* (1941) was a forceful anti-Nazi play. With sentiment, intrigue, and violent action, she dramatized a conflict between two Germans—a Nazi agent and an anti-Fascist undercover worker—which takes place in a Washington, D. C., home.

(b) The Degeneracy of Greed: *The Little Foxes*, 1939

(*Plot*) To increase their fortunes, the Southern Hubbards are negotiating a partnership with a Chicago industrialist. Ben is the older brother in the Hubbard family—crafty, unscrupulous, with pretensions toward aristocracy. It was he who forced his cruel and cowardly brother, Oscar, to marry Birdie, a naïve but tender woman, cruelly used, whose family estate the Hubbards now control. Regina, the greedy sister, unloving and unloved, is married to Horace Giddens, who is now recuperating from a heart condition at Johns Hopkins. To get her third of the money necessary for the proposed partnership, Regina sends her daughter, Alexandra, for Horace. In the meantime, Leo, Birdie and Oscar's weak son who works in Horace's bank, has revealed that Horace's safe deposit box contains some bonds worth $88,000. When Ben realizes that Horace will not give Regina any money, he has Oscar "borrow" the bonds and go to Chicago. Horace discovers the theft when he remakes his will in favor of Alexandra, but without stopping the thieves, wills the bonds to Regina. Furious, Regina causes Horace to have a heart attack and then coldly watches him break a medicine bottle in his excitement and die in an attempt to get another bottle. Now Regina forces Ben to give her the greater part of the new business, but he suspects her. Her greedy satisfaction is also marred by Alexandra's new understanding of the family degeneracy.

(*Discussion*) Basically, this romantic and realistic study of greed is a horror melodrama and a social warning. Very carefully designed theater, the action of this play rises and falls with excellent suspense and sensation. There are the bonds, the medicine, and the overwhelming cruelty set against well-drawn characters. The Hubbard family, in its greed and suggestion of incestual idiocy, presents a dramatic contrast to Birdie. As usual in a Hellman play, the moral which is both the horror and the warning is clear: "There are people who eat the earth and eat all the people on it like in the Bible with the locusts. Then there are people who stand around and watch them eat it. Sometimes I think it ain't right to stand and watch them do it."

D. Satire on the Stage

Satire as a technique of comedy and a means for social comment is one of the oldest traditions in the theater. In America, it dates back to the plays of Mercy Warren during the Revolution and Royall Tyler's *The Contrast* (1787). Mainly as a part of farce-comedy, it continued in the Yankee plays, in the social comedies about New York City, and through the works of Charles Hoyt and George Ade to World War I. Between the wars, the bitter protests against aspects of society were almost always satiric, and a good number of the plays already mentioned include some satire. O'Neill, Anderson, Sherwood,

Howard, Kelly, Rice—all were satirists. Particular emphasis, however, must be given to the plays of George S. Kaufman and Moss Hart. The purpose of this section will be to suggest concentration upon particular objects of satire.

The means for satire is the ridicule, sophisticated or blunt, of institutions or aspects of human behavior. Its objective is to reform, although the degree of seriousness involved varies with the playwright. There is also a variation in the degree of detachment which the dramatist exercises. The dramatist, however, does have a preconceived end, and whether one laughs or grimaces, the final appeal, stimulated through emotion or intellect, is for the audience's positive response.

1. CAPITALISM AND MATERIALISM

A representative list of plays satirizing capitalism and materialism would include the following: *Dulcy* (1921) by George S. Kaufman and Marc Connelly, a satire on business, made delightful by a lovingly scatterbrained wife; *The Adding Machine* (1923) by Elmer Rice, an expressionistic satire on America's machine society with Mr. Zero as a symbol of the whitecollar slave; *Beggar on Horseback* (1924) by George S. Kaufman and Marc Connelly, another expressionistic satire on the American commercial spirit which confines and regulates the work of the greatest living novelist, poet, painter, and composer; *Marco Millions* (1927) by Eugene O'Neill, "the sourest and most magnificent poke in the jaw that American business and the American businessman have ever got," according to George Jean Nathan, the drama critic; S. N. Behrman's picture of a businessman in *Meteor* (1929); Sidney Howard's dramatization of Sinclair Lewis' satire on the American businessman, *Dodsworth* (1934); *High Tor* (1937), Maxwell Anderson's condemnation of greedy capitalism; *The Little Foxes* (1939), a picture of materialistic greed by Lillian Hellman.

2. POLITICS AND POLITICIANS

Politics and politicians have always provided good material for the satirist: Maxwell Anderson's bitter satire of justice in the Sacco-Vanzetti trial in *Gods of the Lightning* (1928) and his picture of the corruption and "pork-barrelling" in Congress in *Both Your Houses* (1933); the riotous musical-drama,

Of Thee I Sing (1931) by Kaufman and Morrie Ryskind, which ridicules the manner in which a president is nominated, his platform (which is "love"), his campaigning, and the way he and his wife view the affairs of the nation; Kaufman and Katharine Dayton's *First Lady* (1935), a satire of such a "politically-minded somebody as Alice Longworth Roosevelt might have been"; another satire of the Roosevelt Administration, *I'd Rather Be Right* (1937) by Kaufman and Moss Hart; Maxwell Anderson's satire of tyrannical government, *Knickerbocker Holiday* (1938); *Washington Jitters* (1938) by John Boruff and Walter Hart, a satire on congressional activities and the language of government.

3. THE MOTION PICTURE INDUSTRY

Once the movie industry got under way, its idiosyncracies provided excellent material for the satirist: *Merton of the Movies* (1922) by Kaufman and Connelly, a spoof of the movie-struck clerk who cannot act; *Once in a Lifetime* (1930) by Kaufman and Moss Hart, an hilarious burlesque of movie making through the activities of three vaudeville performers who decide to teach the silent movie stars how to talk; Lawrence Riley's *Personal Appearance* (1934), the problems of a star and her public; *Boy Meets Girl* (1935) by Bella and Samuel Spewack, a satire on writing and casting a movie; *Kiss the Boys Good-bye* (1938), a satire on Hollywood's search for talent by Clare Boothe.

4. WAR AND VIOLENCE

Robert Sherwood's early attacks on war were satirical in nature: *The Road to Rome* (1927) and *Idiot's Delight* (1935). One might also list Reginald Lawrence's *Men Must Fight* (1931), John Haynes Holmes' *If This Be Treason* (1935), Irwin Shaw's *Bury the Dead* (1935), and Maxwell Anderson's *Feast of the Ortolans* (1937).

5. LIFE, LIVING, AND SOCIETY

Other than those which can be expressed under particular headings, a number of aspects of life have been ridiculed in the theater. Social life is always a good target—*Dinner at Eight*

(1932) by Kaufman and Edna Ferber. Theater life may be represented by Kaufman and Ferber's *The Royal Family* (1927), suggestive of the Barrymore family, and George Kelly's *The Torch-Bearers* (1922), a satire on the Little Theater Movement. *The Front Page* (1928) by Ben Hecht and Charles MacArthur satirizes reporters, editors, politics, police corruption, psychology, and schools of journalism. Social responsibility is treated in Sinclair Lewis and John C. Moffitt's anti-Fascist play, *It Can't Happen Here* (1936). Clare Boothe's *The Women* (1936) is a pointed satire on women who, according to the author, "deserve to be smacked across the head with a meat ax." Occasionally, the satiric view slips into something more serious than the play's first act suggests. *Merrily We Roll Along* (1934) by Kaufman and Hart develops from a burlesque of Hollywood activities to the serious choice facing the artist—the dilemma between one's idealism and his compulsion for financial reward. *The Male Animal* (1940) by James Thurber and Elliott Nugent satirizes the absurdities which can only be found in a college or university. The play becomes more serious when the social and romantic problem changes to the personal problem of surrendering to "prejudice and dictation." In satire the iron fist is frequently within the minstrel's white glove, and many of America's best playwrights of this period used satire.

E. Light Comedy

The spirit of the Thirties was not particularly conducive to light comedy. S. N. Behrman had, in fact, tried to argue this point in a play called *No Time for Comedy*. With the stock market crash, the Depression, the concern for Fascism, the problems in Europe, the dissatisfaction with the "New Deal," and the approach of World War II, the attitude of playwrights was generally not best expressed in light comedy, as the majority of plays indicate. And frequently, those plays which did approach light comedy carried a sting of seriousness in some poignant satire. The prime exponent of this type of drama was George S. Kaufman, who, with various collaborators, created some of the liveliest nights in the theatrical years between the Wars. There were other good light comedies written in this period, but they were scattered and few. Too many playwrights, Kaufman included, tumbled into farce.

1. OUTSTANDING LIGHT COMEDIES

Farce and light comedy tread closely to one another, but they can be distinguished. Whereas in farce the world is irrational or frivolous, the action coincidental or absurd, and the characters simple and manipulated, in comedy one is drawn into the realm of meaningfulness where attention is focused on wit and irony by well-developed characters who determine the action. Farce characteristics, however, are frequently found in comedy, and critics may differ as to what constitutes the point of domination.

(a) *Ah, Wilderness!* by Eugene O'Neill, 1933

Many have regretted that O'Neill wrote only one comedy. Sean O'Casey, Irish playwright, noted: "I've one reproach only to make of him—that he didn't use his gift for comedy oftener, as shown in 'Ah, Wilderness!' " Written just before the hiatus in O'Neill's career, this play indicated something of the romantic and positive values that he wanted to find, while fitting clearly into his search for meaning—this time through the quite serious maturing of Richard Miller, a typical O'Neill poet and the central figure in the play. Filled with easy and effective dialogue and with a quite haunting nostalgia as well as some acute insights into humanity, the play has the reality and wit of comedy at its best.

(*Plot*) The serenity of the Miller household on the Fourth of July is disturbed by Mr. Macomber, who has come to accuse Richard Miller, aged sixteen, of writing nasty poetry to his daughter, Muriel. Discontented with himself and the world, Richard denies Macomber's charges to his father, who has recognized Swinburne's poetry, and asks to be alone. Another lonely person is Sid, Mrs. Miller's brother, who would like to marry Mr. Miller's sister. Pathetically, she can't marry a man who drinks, and he can't stop drinking. Reacting from his disappointment with Muriel, that night Richard goes to a bar with an older boy who has a "couple of swift babies," finally gets into a fight and is tossed out of the bar. In a dishevelled and drunken condition, he returns home. Trying to discover what to do about Richard occupies the thoughts of Mr. and Mrs. Miller, as an experienced Sid nurses Richard the next day. A letter from Muriel helps Richard, and that night in adolescent wonder and awe they declare their love. The difficulties which face maturing youth are many, but for parents and children the curtain falls on happiness.

(b) *Abie's Irish Rose* by Anne Nichols, 1937

Having one of the longest runs in Broadway history, *Abie's Irish Rose* is a situation comedy which is distinguished by its witty and effective dialogue. When Abraham Levy falls in love with Rose Mary Murphy and secretly marries her, he expects difficulties in the family circle and therefore introduces her to his father as Rose Mary Murpheski. But his father is so impressed with the girl that he urges Abie to propose marriage. At the wedding, Rose Mary's father is late and they are married by a Rabbi before he comes in with a Catholic priest and both families discover what is happening. Amid the uproar, the priest marries them for the third time, but a year later the fathers are still unreconciled. Then there is to be a baby—more difficulty. Murphy will leave the baby his money if it is a girl, and Levy will do the same if it is a boy. Fortunately, the "baby" turns out to be twins—Patrick Joseph and Rebecca—and both sets of in-laws are finally delighted.

(c) *Having Wonderful Time* by Arthur Kober, 1937

This is a play about young people in New York who ride to work every day in the subway thinking of "those two weeks of vacation-paradise which are accepted as handsome recompense for fifty weeks of drudgery." The scene is an adult vacation camp, which, with its penny-pinching owner and waiters who double as gigolos, is not what the heroine, "Teddy" Stern, expected. Chick, an unemployed lawyer, is interesting, but he feels too poor to ask her to marry him. Then a party at which a "wolf" tries to get Teddy drunk preparatory to seduction stimulates Chick to anger and makes Teddy decide that perhaps he is the one. At her instigation he says "yes," and she will keep her job. The satire in the play provides a gloomy if compassionate seriousness to the farce-comic episodes.

(d) *Life With Father* by Howard Lindsay and Russel Crouse, 1939

This play ran for 3,216 consecutive performances (1939–1947), breaking all New York records. It gracefully combines the humor of the father and his attempts to run his family with a great deal of information about American upper-class life during the later nineteenth century. Although the plot is negligible, the thread that goes through the entire play is Vinnie's (the mother) constant attempt to get Father baptized, an event which seems imminent at the end of the play. A reviewer called it "a series of tableaux rather than an orthodox dramatic work." During an hilarious evening, however, the audience learns of Father's response to all exigencies ("Damn!"), the effect that Father's suit has upon young Clarence (it will not let him kneel in church), young John's success in selling "Bartlett's Beneficent Balm," and Vinnie's conniving to get father baptized.

(e) *The Male Animal* by James Thurber and Elliott Nugent, 1940

This is the story of an English professor's decision to read Vanzetti's declaration of faith to an English class. The reaction of the trustees and all alumni-conscious university people provides a serious issue. But the action takes place on the day of the *big* football game, and the professor's self-centered wife provokes him into defending his manhood against a former football-playing sweetheart of hers. This becomes comedy, but as one critic commented, "There is more than meets the funny bone in this scrawled lampoon on the civilized male at bay."

2. GEORGE S. KAUFMAN AND COMPANY

George Freedley, an historian of modern drama, calls Kaufman (1889–1962) "one of the best representatives of the highly competent craftsmen in playwriting in America." His thorough knowledge of the theater, in fact, earned him the title of "play doctor." But he was more than this. Although early critics tended to regard him mainly as a gay, irrepressible spoofer, he provided a depth of insight in the sanity and satire beneath his mirth that revealed much of the absurdity and pretense in life. Essentially, he gave the audience what it wanted and at the same time stung them in ways that his pervasive wit made palatable. A born collaborator, he demanded much of those who worked with him, while contributing an imagination and originality which make his light, satiric comedies distinctive in a history of American drama and theater. With a number of

collaborators—Morrie Ryskind, (*Of Thee I Sing*, 1932, a satire on politics), Ring Lardner (*June Moon*, 1929, a spoof of
Tin Pan Alley), Katharine Dayton (*First Lady,* 1935), Marc
Connelly, Edna Ferber, and Moss Hart—Kaufman managed
to provoke comedy from many aspects of life: movies, theater,
politics, high society, businessmen, love, and various individuals.

(a) Kaufman and Marc Connelly

After some unsuccessful attempts at playwriting, Kaufman
teamed with Marc Connelly (*The Green Pastures,* 1930) to the
delight of thousands of people. Their first attempt, *Dulcy*
(1921), based on a Franklin P. Adams character, celebrated
the small-brained but well-meaning wife whose stupidity almost
ruins but actually helps her husband's business career. Next
came *To The Ladies* (1922), a view of the bright wife who
saves the job of the dull husband. As the heroine says, "Nearly
all of the great men have been married; it can't be merely a
coincidence." *Merton of the Movies* (1922) burlesqued the
Hollywood actor. Their most successful collaboration, however,
was *Beggar on Horseback* (1924), which attacked a society
that attempted to mechanize its artistry.

(b) Kaufman and Edna Ferber

The author of the memorable *Show Boat* and Kaufman
were successful in three of their playwriting ventures: *The
Royal Family* (1927), *Dinner at Eight* (1932), and *Stage Door*
(1936), which toyed with the young actress breaking into
Broadway big time and gave her the additional problem of
choosing between the movies and the stage.

(c) Kaufman and Moss Hart

Through this combination America received some of its
best light farce-comedies. Hart was an intense but warm and
emotional man whose wit and humanity is perhaps summed up
in one of the many quotable lines from his autobiography, *Act
One*: "Playwriting, like begging in India, is an honorable profession." Starting with one of the touring companies of Augustus Pitou, Jr., "King of the One Night Stands," Hart reached
success first with Kaufman in *Once in a Lifetime* and later
wrote several successful plays by himself; *Lady in the Dark*
(1941) is a good example of his work. His sense of humanity,

as well as his love of large and complex scenes with numerous characters, is evident in his work with Kaufman.

Their beginning with *Once in a Lifetime* (1930) remains the outstanding burlesque of Hollywood absurdity. *You Can't Take It With You* was a Pulitzer winner in 1936. They were less successful in other plays—one about the theater, *The Fabulous Invalid* (1938); a very patriotic play called *The American Way* (1939); and *George Washington Slept Here* (1940), built on their own adventures in restoring an old house. But in *The Man Who Came to Dinner* (1939), based ostensibly on the successful lecture tours of the drama critic, Alexander Woollcott, they reached their heights in light farce-comedy.

(i) *The Man Who Came to Dinner*, 1939

The main plot line is quite simple. A lecturer, Sheridan Whiteside, supposedly breaks a hip in a certain town and is forced to stay with a family whom he happily and bitterly torments through the guests he receives, the advice he gives the children, and his numerous acid comments. Then he discovers that his prize secretary is falling in love with the town's newspaperman. What had once been fun for "Sherry," now becomes serious. To break up their happiness he does everything possible—which is considerable.

The play is essentially episodic and cluttered, but very witty and fast moving. In true farce style, embarrassment is used for the sake of embarrassment and for the pleasure of Whiteside and the audience. Each device is exploited for humor: telegraph, telephone, letters, the penguins, the incompetent village doctor, the Christmas radio program, the convicts, the impersonation, the mummy case. But the play is not pure farce. Love is taken seriously in the final scenes, and Whiteside has a speck of humanity. A major problem in this kind of play is the ending. Having written at a tremendous speed for three acts, what does a dramatist do? In this play, however, a broken hip is an effective answer.

F. High Comedy

Whereas "drama as a weapon" involved the utmost commitment to a cause on the part of the dramatist, high comedy or a sophisticated comedy of manners demands the author's sense of detachment. As one might expect, detachment was far from a keynote of American drama of the Twenties and Thirties. Writers of propaganda, social commentary, problem plays, and satire could not be detached. The point is well made in S. N. Behrman's *Biography* in which Marion Froude has lived an irregular life of enjoyment and satisfaction. Richard Kurt, the committed young radical in the play, reacts toward Marion in a mixture of anger and love: "God, how I hate detachment," he says. A corollary to the necessary detachment in a high comedy is the characters' dependence on expediency as a basis for decisions. Generally, the writer of high comedy must have a sophisticated attitude toward life and be able to portray a fashionable society with wit and imagination.

America has produced very little high comedy. One has to go back to the Restoration and eighteenth-century England and the works of Congreve and Sheridan to find excellent examples. Those in America who have most nearly approximated high comedy are S. N. Behrman and Philip Barry, and neither one could fully concentrate his efforts in this genre. Behrman found himself protesting with the other dramatists of the Thirties, and Barry became involved in a philosophical search for truth. It is a difficult genre, and critics have either employed the term indiscriminately or, refusing to be put on the defensive, have purposefully used it in a vague manner.

Barrett Clark's ("Some Broadway Plays Pass in Review," *Drama Magazine,* XXI, 1931, p. 14) criticism of Paul Osborn's *The Vinegar Tree* as a "high comedy, bordering on both farce and tragedy," indicates the vague use of the term. As a drama in which a man is pressured first by a girl who wants "experience in life" in order to meet one of her fiancé's demands, and second by the girl's mother who is feeling the pangs of middle age, the play has high comedy potential. But its conventional ending lacks both the expediency and detachment of high comedy. Another near miss is Mark Reed's *Yes, My Darling Daughter* (1937). The daughter of a once rebellious freethinking mother and a conservative father, Ellen forces her mother to agree to her spending a weekend with her boy-friend who is leaving for Europe. Afterwards, the father is furious and wants to force a marriage, which the boy will accept but which Ellen refuses as old-fashioned moral coercion. Finally, she agrees when she sees how silly it is to refuse on principle the man she loves.

1. S. N. BEHRMAN: WIT, INTELLIGENCE, AND SOPHISTICATION

S. N. Behrman (1893–   ) studied with George Pierce Baker and worked as book reviewer, press agent, and play-reader before writing a successful play for Broadway. Soon he was faced with a dilemma which he dramatized in *No Time for Comedy* (1939). In that play, a character advises the playwright protagonist: "Your genius is for comedy; stand with it." In life, however, Behrman was unable to do this consistently. In most of his plays, even those which show his fine wit, his talent for clever dialogue, and his particular skill in dramatizing a sophisticated situation, he allows his emotions to become involved. It is too abundantly clear, for example, that he is opposed to political totalitarianism, that he believes in the civilized individual, that he distrusts fanaticism and hates fascism. Such feelings, however, cannot be allowed to control the action and thought in high comedy.

When Behrman avoids emotional involvment, he approaches high comedy. Leonie Frothingham from *End of Summer* (1936) is a fine character for high comedy; so is Lady Wyngate in *Rain from Heaven* (1934). But Behrman does not confine his attitudes and those of his characters to high comedy. Only *The Second Man* (1927) and *Biography* (1932) approach this sophisticated genre.

(a) *The Second Man*, 1927

(*Plot*) Clark Storey, a cynical, fourth-rate writer, "lives" in reasonable happiness with Mrs. Kendall Frayne, a widow who enjoys supporting him. His comfort is interrupted, however, when he is pursued by young and eager Monica Grey, who is in turn jealously adored by a brilliant chemist but a bumbling lover named Austin Lowe. When it seems that Storey may finally marry Kendall, Monica desperately tries everything, including the invented news that she carries Storey's baby. Storey is interested and Austin is infuriated, but the big problem is whether Storey can exchange comfort for love. When he makes a date to meet Kendall in Europe, his decision has been made.

(*Discussion*) There is the "second man" for Storey: "For, together with, and as it were behind, so much pleasurable emotion, there is always that other strange second man in me, calm, critical, observant, unmoved, blasé, odious." The play is marred by some melodramatic heroics, but the good dialogue, the detachment by which the hero lives, and the expediency of his final decision suggest the characteristics of high comedy.

(b) *Biography*, 1932

(*Plot*) Marion Froude is a second- or third-rate artist who has received much publicity for her paintings of and affairs with notable people. Newly arrived in New York, she is visited by a rather staid and naïve Leander Nolan, presumably her first lover and still interested in her. When, however, Marion tells him that Richard Kurt, a sensitive young man who hides behind a brash and cynical attitude, has asked her to write her biography for his magazine, Nolan, a candidate for the U. S. Senate, fears that his political life will suffer from her revelations. Immediately, he appeals to his backer, Orin Kinnicott, father of his fiancée, Slade. But when Marion charms Kinnicott, and Slade is fascinated both by Kurt and by "the woman" from Nolan's past, Nolan leaves in disgust. By this time, Marion and Kurt realize that they are in love; yet when Marion tells Kurt that she has decided not to do the biography, he is furious. His fanaticism makes it impossible for him to understand the tolerant person. Marion knows now that they would not be good for one another, and when she is called to do a portrait of a Hollywood celebrity, she happily departs.

(*Discussion*) The dominance of Marion makes this play high comedy. Her detachment and sense of expediency indicates the author's control of his materials. She has an inescapable wit and an ability to throw people off balance, while she remains in command of her emotions. Behrman, as usual, may resort to melodrama to rescue a character or a plot, but the sophisticated action, dialogue, and characters show that relationship between emotion and intellect which is high comedy.

2. PHILIP BARRY: "THE LIGHTNING BUG"

A critic once described Philip Barry (1896–1949) as "the lightning bug"—now he lights up, now he doesn't. The quip suggests insight. Barry was a serious-minded man with a quick wit and a talent for sophisticated comedy, but he wanted to write profoundly about life. When he tried to plumb the meaning of life (*Hotel Universe, Here Come the Clowns*), he failed in the theater; when he exploited his comic touch, (*Paris Bound, The Animal Kingdom*), he was very successful—the lightning bug!

Like many of his characters, Barry was a worldly person. He lived on Park Avenue, on the French Rivièra, in London and Paris. His observations made him aware of the restlessness and the stuffiness of society, and a note of concern and sadness always penetrated even the bright life of his comedies. As a playwright, he was a meticulous craftsman and a stylist in language, who expressed only contempt for critics and continued to try to satisfy his audiences with sparkling comedies and himself with his determined search for meaning in life. His comedies are in the tradition of Clyde Fitch, Rachel Crothers, and Sidney Howard, yet superior to all in wit, intellect, and imagination. Like his predecessors, he was occasionally prone to preachment, but mainly he showed the necessary disciplined detachment. This control of viewpoint, plus polished dialogue and a sense of unity of effect, distinguish Barry as America's foremost writer of high comedy.

(a) Discovery—Intelligently Used

In a lecture on high comedy, April 4, 1904, George Pierce Baker, the Harvard professor who stimulated interest in drama and playwriting, said: "You see a certain number of people, and you see the difference between what each of these persons is and what he thinks he is. Now, if you can represent that for your particular public, you can write high comedy" (*George Pierce Baker and the American Theatre,* p. 99). Barry did this and more, as a good writer of high comedy should. Introducing appropriate sophistication, he allowed the person to see the difference himself and to act upon his knowledge with the proper mixture of emotion and intelligence. In *You and I* (1923), he posed a question: Shall the hero get married or go to Paris and study architecture? The father of the hero once chose marriage. When the hero does the same, the father gives up his business in order to paint, only to discover that he lacks real talent. He has, however, realized something else and decides to send both son and girl to Paris after they are married. The hero in *Holiday* (1928) makes an expedient decision after his discovery. Tracy Lord discovered the truth about herself in *The Philadelphia Story* (1939) and reacts in an intelligent manner. Accused of lacking love and understanding by her first husband, she is forced to see the truth. Expediently, she begins again. Generally dealing with problems of marriage, Barry's comedies enjoy that quality of sophisticated discovery from which truthful and expedient choices are made—the whole producing excellent high comedy.

(b) *Paris Bound*, 1929

(*Plot*) On Jim and Mary Hutton's wedding day, the only sour note is the presence of Jim's divorced parents—divorced because the father was unfaithful and the mother could not agree with his reasoning that the spiritual side of marriage was more important than the physical. Mary shares her father-in-law's views, but her real test comes six years later when she learns that Jim has been seen with an old girl friend on his business trips to Europe. Immediately jumping toward divorce, she discovers to her own surprise that her own friendship with a young ballet composer could develop into an affair, and she accepts her husband without a question.

(*Discussion*) A tendency toward preachment may be found in the elder Mr. Hutton, but there is sustaining wit in the dialogue, excellent change of pace, and a remarkable unity throughout. The ballet cleverly accentuates the idea in the play.

(c) *The Animal Kingdom*, 1932

(*Plot*) Tom Collier is a rebel. A bachelor, he publishes good books which do not make money and has an artist, Daisy, as his mistress. Then he marries the ambitious Cecelia Henry, who immediately campaigns for changes—abandonment of his friends, merger with a big publisher, reconciliation with his father, who frowns on Tom's way of life. When Tom occasionally does what she wants, she rewards him with herself; otherwise, she locks the bedroom door. Finally, he makes a decision and leaves the locked door to go to Daisy, who is more truly his soul mate.

(*Discussion*) In this play Barry presents an unorthodox but expedient and honest conclusion. He forces nothing but allows his free and expedient characters to act as their natures incline. Again, unity of effect and careful dialogue show his craftsmanship.

V. "TOWNHALL TONIGHT"

Melodrama & Farce

There is always melodrama and farce, and a good part of American drama written between the World Wars fits into one of these categories or has some of the characteristics of one. The terms melodrama and farce are frequently used in a derogatory fashion to suggest that a playwright attempted tragedy or comedy and failed to achieve the necessary insight of character development, and although the criticisms may be just, the condescending tone may be damaging to two perfectly fine dramatic genres. Eugene O'Neill, for example, has been dealt with disparagingly as a writer of first-rate melodrama, while Lillian Hellman is sometimes criticized for her use of melodramatic techniques to achieve the thrilling climaxes in her plays. Most of the protest and social commentary plays employ some of the characteristics of melodrama, and many American comedies have the contrived action and controlled confusion of farce. This does not mean, however, that the dramatists completely lacked insight or their plays character development, although it does suggest the great difficulty of writing tragedy or fine comedy. The terms melodrama and farce, then, describe kinds of drama; they may be accurately employed to suggest dramatic techniques in plays and perhaps to note some discrepancy between a dramatist's objective and his achievement.

Melodrama and farce as genres, however, make definite demands upon the dramatist. Melodrama lacks psychological insight and well-rounded character development but depends on fast-moving and suspenseful action to fulfill its objective, which is to thrill. The concept of time, which the dramatist must unashamedly manipulate, is also important in melodrama. Farce uses one-dimensional characters whose actions are determined by cleverly contrived plot movements, and it reaches its objectives of laughter by the creation of confusing and embarrassing situations through an abundance of incongruous misunderstandings. Few American dramatists have mastered the requirements with any great success. This section emphasizes those purposefully written melodramas and farces that are always a delight for the people who come at eight.

A. Modern Melodrama

The melodrama of Augustin Daly and Owen Davis is dead. Frank Rahill, writing in *Theatre Arts* ["Melodrama," XVI (April, 1932), 293] complained that "what passes for melodrama today is really a degenerate offspring"; the "sacred dogmas have become a joke," and instead of being thrilled, people simply laugh. The criticism is a little severe, but it is true that, by and large, sensational melodrama has been replaced by other kinds of melodrama. The most successful kind is probably the mystery or crime melodrama that the movies and television now so expediently control. Other melodrama is rather difficult to classify. Its aim is, as always, to thrill—and it does this through an exciting adventure, an heroic act, or a heart-touching ordeal. It differs from the older American melodrama in the modern dramatist's attempt to be more subtle, more realistic, and perhaps more truthful.

1. MELODRAMA OF MYSTERY AND CRIME

Mystery and melodrama go together in many plays, but the few outstanding mystery melodramas are easy to list: *The Bat* (1920) by Mary Roberts Rinehart and Avery Hopwood; *Broadway* (1926) by Philip Dunning and George Abbott; and *Arsenic and Old Lace* (1941) by Joseph O. Kesselring. Others include Sidney Howard's *Ned McCobb's Daughter* (1926); Bartlett Cormack's *The Racket* (1927); and Howard Lindsay and Damon Runyon's *A Slight Case of Murder* (1935). Of all dramas, the complicated plot of the melodrama is the most difficult to summarize.

(a) *The Bat,* 1920

Miss Cornelia Van Gorder has leased an old country house, where she lives with her maid and a young woman named Dale Ogden. Recently, however, the local bank has failed and a cashier named Jack Bailey has disappeared; also, someone has tried to enter the house, and a criminal called The Bat is at large. The action begins as Brooks (actually Bailey, who is engaged to Dale) arrives, supposedly hired to be a gardener; and a detective appears, employed by the women for protection. Dr. Wells drops by and acts suspiciously by trying to persuade Cornelia to leave. As Jack and Dale secretly discuss their difficulties, Jack remembers hearing that the old house has a secret room and, expecting to find the missing bank money in that room, he calls Dick Fleming, son of the bank president who owns the house, to come over that night. The house blueprints are found, but Dick is mysteriously shot and killed. Immediately, Dr. Wells tries to get the blueprints from Dale, who is suspected of Dick's murder by the detective. There is more mystery and more suspense when the detective is found tied up, an unknown man faints at the door of the room in which the women stay—and a black bat is tacked on the door. In the final act, the secret room is discovered along with the bank president's body. The doctor is revealed as being part of the conspiracy, and the unknown man is identified as a detective. When the Bat, who had been masquerading as the hired detective throughout the action, sets the garage on fire to get the people out of the house where the money is hidden, the real detective captures him—ending a fast moving and exciting drama.

(b) *Broadway,* 1926

Barrett Clark called *Broadway* "a first-rate specimen of the peppy melodrama, jazzed up with girls, a couple of murders, wise cracks, light repartee, and music." Brooks Atkinson commented on it as "exhilarating, madly colored melodrama, a kaleidoscope, spattered with the bright pigments of local color." The scene is the Paradise Night Club in New York. Roy, a poor but nice night club performer, loves a very naïve but sweet chorine named Billie. But Billie is being rushed by Steve, a liquor peddling gangster who shoots his chief competitor in the back. Justice is served, however, as the dead gangster's girl friend—and a very nice girl—shoots Steve, leaving Billie with some second thoughts which eventually turn her to Roy and marriage.

(c) *Arsenic and Old Lace*, 1941

The two sweet old Brewster ladies, Martha and Abby, are really sentimental and senile murderers, who give poisoned wine to lonely old men whom they wish only to make happy. They have killed twelve men whom their insane nephew, who thinks he is Teddy Roosevelt, buries in the basement under the delusion that he is digging locks for the Panama Canal and burying yellow fever victims. Mortimer Brewster is horrified when he discovers this particular idiosyncrasy of his aunts, and his understandably disturbed activities irritate his girl friend, Elaine. He has been trying to get Teddy committed to an institution; now he sees other obligations. To complicate matters, Jonathan, a brother of Martha and Abby, having escaped from a Prison for the Criminal Insane, arrives with a friend and a body of their own to dispose of, a Mr. Spenalzo. After an interesting evening full of well-timed suspense, the police finally arrest Jonathan, and Mr. Witherspoon from the rest home arrives to take not only Teddy but Martha and Abby, who have decided that they will commit themselves, having told Mortimer that he actually cannot sign for them because he is not really a Brewster. Everyone thrills to Mortimer's joyous shout, "I'm a bastard!" and Elaine "leaps into his illegitimate arms," as the old ladies, having discovered that Mr. Witherspoon is lonely, serve him some of the poisoned elderberry wine.

2. MORE SUBTLE MELODRAMA

The material for melodrama is unlimited. It is necessary only that the dramatist find excitement and thrill in the life he pictures. That life could be almost anything, but the writer of modern melodrama is less dependent upon the spectacular achievements of the stage carpenter than his brother of the late nineteenth century had been. Owen Davis, a master of the old melodrama, suggested the change in style in *The*

Nervous Wreck (1923) and numerous other plays. Don Marquis, best known for his poetry writing cockroach in *archy and mehitabel*, wrote a sentimental melodrama about an old drunkard who took the blame for his son's misdoings and finally brought happiness to everyone in *The Old Soak* (1922). A very fine writer of melodrama was Sidney Howard, whose serious themes sometimes subverted melodrama into social drama. His play about Walter Reed's discovery of the yellow fever mosquito, *Yellow Jack* (1934), is a good example of adventure melodrama. More successful in the theater were Preston Sturges' melodramatic farce, *Strictly Dishonorable* (1929), and the sophisticated musical melodrama, *Lady in the Dark* by Moss Hart, lyrics by Ira Gershwin and music by Kurt Weill.

(a) *Lady in the Dark*, 1941

At the pinnacle of her success as editor of *Allure* fashion magazine, Liza Elliott is having a nervous breakdown. Depressed, filled with terror, unable to sleep, she goes to a psychiatrist who discovers, through a song that she sings when she is depressed and a dream she tells him, that she is afraid to be herself and a woman. She lives with Mr. Nesbitt, publisher of the magazine, whose wife has thus far not given him a divorce. Slowly her character is revealed through well-designed and suspenseful action. She wants to be beautiful, but she dresses in a severe manner. She seemingly dislikes one of the men in her office named Charlie, who, in one of Liza's dreams, tells her that she is afraid to be the woman she wants to be. When Nesbitt tells her that he is getting a divorce, she is frantic with fear. Through her dreams, her song, her talks with the psychiatrist, she gradually learns about herself and discovers that she can find happiness with Charlie.

B. Same Old Farce

The professed writers of farce during this period between the wars were far fewer than those who actually wrote farce. Not only did the protest plays exist on contrived situations and unmotivated embarrassments, but writers of comedy and social drama more than occasionally forced a point, a character, or an effect. Most of the burlesques about Hollywood abound in farce—Kaufman and Hart's *Once in a Lifetime*, the Spewacks' *Boy Meets Girl*. Kaufman, in fact, dealt liberally in farce as his original play about theatrical life, *The Butter and Egg Man* (1925) clearly shows. Another good farce involving theater people is John Emerson and Anita Loos' *The Whole Town's Talking* (1924). To make his daughter, Ethel, interested in marrying his business partner, Chester, Mr. Simons invents a tale of Chester's affair with Letty Lythe, a movie star. The scheme works until Letty comes to town with a very jealous boy friend, but eventually both Chester and the truth triumph. As with melodrama, a large number of the plays written at this time have some of the characteristics of farce; many farces were written and have been well forgotten; and a few good farces remain.

1. A PERIOD OF FARCE

The spectrum of drama in the Thirties was both wide and colorful. Beginning about the middle of this decade and extending into the war years, farce became quite popular. In 1933, Howard Lindsay's *She Loves Me Not* explored the farcical problems that two Princeton boys would have if they tried to hide a chorus girl in their rooms. Frances Swann's *Out of the Frying Pan* (1941) tells how a group of young theater enthusiasts try, among other ways, to work their way into a director's heart by way of his stomach. *Room Service* (1937) by J. Murray and A. Boretz again deals with the theater, a man's attempt to produce a play. Two frequently repeated farces of youthful absurdities are J. Monks and F. J. Finklehoffe's *Brother Rat* (1936), which describes life in a military prep school, and *What a Life!* (1938) by Clifford Goldsmith, which dramatizes the exploits of none other than Henry Aldrich. By 1940, war conditions were everywhere. In *My Sister Eileen* (1940), Joseph Fields and Jerome Chodorov showed small-town girls living in New York—their troubles with their friends and their apartment (since a prostitute lived there before them) and additional episodes involving jobs, jail, and the Brazilian navy.

(a) *Three Men on a Horse*, 1935

George Abbott as a director of plays and musicals has shown a magic touch in production. Here with John Cecil

Holm he wrote a successful farce about a poet named Erwin who worked for a greeting card company, but entertained himself while riding to and from work on a bus by his uncanny ability to pick winners in horse races. He never bets, but he also never misses. His talent is recognized, however, when he is captured by gamblers who hold him in a hotel room while he supplies winners. There are absurd situations and incongruous disagreements among the gamblers. Finally, a four horse parley becomes the big bet, and Erwin is forced to bet, too. The gamblers think they have lost everything until a disqualification shows Erwin to be right. Now, however, having bet, Erwin can no longer figure out the winners.

VI. SEARCHERS AND FINDERS

The major figure in American drama between World War I and World War II is Eugene O'Neill, much of whose reputation rests upon his intellectual and imaginative search through both theme and form for an understanding of life—a search for meaning. The "haunted heroes" of his plays and his life—who propelled him on his mystical search—suggest the psychological and philosophical probings in which he indulged. Because O'Neill overwhelmed audiences and critics, a general impression remains that he was the only playwright of the period interested in ideas, but this is not so. Although not as mystical in their approaches, four other dramatists were similarly concerned, trying to present in their plays a meaningful interpretation of life: Maxwell Anderson, Philip Barry, Thornton Wilder, and William Saroyan.

Maxwell Anderson in both essays and dramas attempted to play the philosopher—and had some measure of success. Lacking a psychoanalytical interest in man, he was still bothered by the problem of evil, mainly as a day-to-day reality rather than as a philosophical concept; but he arrived at a satisfactory conclusion in which he combined a strong individualism with Aristotelian views on tragedy. Philip Barry did not suffer the personal agonies of O'Neill, but he followed O'Neill's investigation of mysticism and life illusion. He ended his career, however, not on a note of despair but with an emphasis on love. Thornton Wilder, on the other hand, met no serious problems in his search for meaning. His solid Christian background provided an answer in which he found peace and security rather than agony and frustration. Another "finder," or perhaps one who does not need to find anything, is William Saroyan. Like Wilder, he writes fables which suggest epic proportions. Like Barry, Anderson, and O'Neill, he tries to discover basic truths, but he is perfectly satisfied to disappear in a cloud of fantasy and simple faith, which is both disconcerting and enjoyable to his audiences. All of these dramatists have seriously experimented in dramatic form; all have been searchers for truth.

A. Maxwell Anderson: Prophet, Dreamer, and Interpreter

During his lifetime, Maxwell Anderson (1888–1959) was called an historical dramatist, a romantic, and a protest playwright—all names equally distasteful to him. Although not the best of poets nor the deepest of thinkers, he seemed interested in becoming a philosopher poet-dramatist; nor is he wholly undeserving of that title. In an essay entitled "Whatever Hope We Have," he concerned himself with ideas effectively, and the force with which he attacked aspects of society in his plays shows him to be a man of definite convictions. Through the particular to the abstract, he displayed his faith in the unrestricted freedom of the individual mind to the degree of its own strength and desire. He was, of course, an idealist, not of the ivory tower, but as a thoughtful writer who saw the potential of man seemingly marred beyond correction by his baser aspects. Yet Anderson found a faith in which his idealism could attain satisfaction. He was a searcher, less demanding than some, who made a reconciling discovery. Concerning the direction of his search, he had this to say: "It is incumbent on the dramatist to be a poet, and incumbent on the poet to be prophet, dreamer, and interpreter of the racial dream."

1. A CONCERNED IDEALIST

As an idealist who believed in individual freedom, he was forced to see evil as a part of that freedom. In a frequently repeated image in which rats represent the evil in man, he shows the struggle between good and evil, a struggle in which evil predominates. In *Elizabeth the Queen* (1930), he complained that "the rats inherit the earth." In *Key Largo* (1939), a character bitterly refers to "the rats that ate my country to the bone." By the time he wrote *Anne of the Thousand Days* (1949), Anderson had become more reconciled to the "mask and tongue" of man, "the hog behind the eyes, the rat behind the tongue, . . . Man, woman, and child, you have obeyed them always, and I have." (II, 4) Man is not perfect and never will be. His corruption makes absolutes impossible, as Anderson noted in *Winterset*: Esdras says, "You're young enough to see the truth, and there is no truth." Justice on earth is man made and therefore relative: "The truth is what the judges will find, what the king will decide." (*Anne of the Thousand Days*, III, 2) Recognizing evil as a part of man, the idealist must keep searching.

2. "NONE BUT THE LONELY. . . ."

Anderson's most significant early plays are about strong and searching individuals who suffer from feelings of lostness and loneliness. Their fate is that of the sensitive individual in modern society—a loneliness which approaches the agony of O'Neill or the lostness of Thomas Wolfe's Eugene Gant and Albert Camus' Stranger. Mio (*Winterset*) feels himself an "Outcast of the world, snake in the streets"; Oparre (*The Wingless Victory*) says, "I've never known you, and I'm alone"; Mary Stuart (*Mary of Scotland*) "We are alone, always alone"; Pablo Montoya (*Night Over Taos*) remembers that "always I've known too late that I was alone"; Elizabeth (*Elizabeth the Queen*): "The years are long living among strangers." This recognition of the lonely state of man in a society in which evil is a dominant force propelled Anderson toward his final philosophical step.

3. A FAITH IN MAN

In an essay entitled "Poetry in the Theater," Anderson expressed a belief "that the theater is essentially a cathedral of the spirit, devoted to the exaltation of men." "The artist's faith," he wrote in another essay ("Whatever Hope We Have"), "is simply a faith in the human race and its gradual acquisition of wisdom." Without "a personal, a national, and a racial faith," men become "dry bones in a death valley, waiting for the word that will bring us life." The search exists, and it is the artist with a faith—even if it is "only a faith that men will have a faith"—expressing living emotions in the language of poetry, who may be able to bring that wisdom and exaltation. This faith, though a rather vaguely conceived cornerstone of Anderson's philosophy, is the basis of a search in which he sees man as finding meaning. The rats may inherit the earth, man may suffer loneliness, and justice may not exist, but man can find his soul. He has that freedom. This belief or faith in man is the basis of Anderson's "Essence of Tragedy" which gives man a strength and a dignity seldom accorded him since Shakespeare's time.

B. Philip Barry: "Looking for an Answer"

The serious side of Philip Barry's (1896–1949) drama is seldom discussed. Mainly, those plays were theater failures and have not attracted thoughtful criticism. Although the bright comedies of manners brought him both success and money, it was in the serious plays that he sought personal satisfaction, and carried on the philosophical probings which he was capable of understanding and imagining. Obviously, he was bothered by some of the same basic problems that disturbed O'Neill, but although he took some of the steps that O'Neill had found meaningful, he was far removed from this great playwright at the end of his career. Both were Irish Catholics, but Barry remained one, and therein lies a difference.

Quite distinctly alternating between successful high comedies and the heavier, less dramatic thematic plays, Barry started asking questions about the nature of man in *In a Garden* (1925). Here he probed with some psychological insight into a man's experimentation with human life, only to show that man understands very little. In *White Wings* (1926), a satire on the changing world, he dramatized a romance between Archie Inch, the son of a street cleaner, who depended upon horses as a necessity of his profession, and Mary Todd, whose father invented the automobile which was rapidly replacing horses. But here again Barry is probing the nature of man and his conflicts—his struggle to progress and his inability to absorb change. *Hotel Universe* (1930) shows Barry's attempt to use a mystical approach to solve his problems, as O'Neill had done in *Desire Under the Elms* and *Mourning Becomes Electra*. In *Here Come the Clowns* (1938), he seems to rest upon the necessity of illusion in life, a play which suggests O'Neill's *The Iceman Cometh* (1946). But whereas O'Neill became more pessimistic and more concerned with illusion in later plays, Barry went back to an answer that O'Neill had already (*Days Without End*) found unsatisfactory. The answer that he looked for in *Hotel Universe*, he found in *Second Threshold* (1949–51)—Christian love. Unfortunately, it was not a convincingly portrayed answer.

1. *HOTEL UNIVERSE*, 1930: INCONCLUSIVE BUT HOPEFUL

(*Plot*) A group of Ann Field's friends are visiting at her French Riviéra home. All are unhappy and torture themselves over the recent suicide of a young man who simply jumped off a cliff into the Mediterranean shouting, "I'm off for Africa." Pat Farley, for example, cannot return Ann's love because of the suicide of a girl he once loved. Norman Rose, a Jew, is afraid to declare his love for Alice Kendall, whose emotional aimlessness is a key to her unhappiness. Pat plans a suicide; Lily Malone, a repressed actress bothered by an Electra complex, has already tried it; none of the group would avoid death. Then Ann's father, Stephen, a scientist who seems to have strange powers, makes each relive his past and become purged of his emotional problems. Stephen finally dies, but with this suggestion of hope: "Wherever there is an end—from it the beginning springs."

(*Discussion*) The play was dismissed by critics as "hackneyed," "sentimental," and filled with "second-rate mysticism," but it suggests well Barry's sense of despair. Typical of the Lost Generation, it shows a Fitzgerald scene with a

Hemingway regret: "It's a rotten feeling, knowing your youth is gone—knowing that all the brave things you once dreamed of doing somehow just won't get done"; "Nothing matters a damn anyway." Unfortunately, the use of Freud is a bit heavy-handed, and the mysticism is rather artificially imposed. The play also lacks action. The concluding note of hope, however, is characteristic of Barry's search.

2. *HERE COME THE CLOWNS*, 1938: ILLUSION AND TRUTH

(*Plot*) In the back room of Ma Speedy's cafe where the theater performers gather, the talk is of Clancy, an actor who wandered on the stage that evening after a year's absence, apparently looking for someone. When Clancy enters, Max Pabst, who calls himself an illusionist, asks if Clancy had been looking for him: "I am interested only in truth. But truth is so often an illusion I must, you see, in truth call myself an illusionist." Clancy then reveals that he is searching for God, and Pabst ("Truth would prepare the way for Him, would it not?") proceeds to tell some of those present the truth about themselves in order to sweep away their illusions. Clancy, himself, discovers that his wife, Nora, had been pregnant by another man when she left him, and he questions Mr. Concannon, the owner of the Globe Theater, about evil and suffering. His answer is a question: "There must be persecution, must there not—to fortify man's faith in heaven?" Then one of the actors tries to shoot Pabst because he told him the truth and kills Clancy instead. Clancy dies without regret, but not before he gives Barry's hopeful answer to the confusion of truth and lies that man has made: "The free will of man . . . can as easily be turned to Good as to Bad. . . . It can rise over anything, anything!"

(*Discussion*) A confusing play and not well unified, it reveals Barry's hopeful search for meaning in life. In *Hotel Universe* he had no answer, only hope. Here he suggests the agonies that men suffer because they lack truth. The "illusionist" is the necessary man in life, but he is badly misunderstood. Although Barry says that the free will of man can bring truth, only Clancy, who dies, realizes this. There must be another step, philosophically speaking.

3. *SECOND THRESHOLD*, 1949: LOVE

(*Plot*) Josiah Bolton, "a man of 42 at the end of his soul's rope, recovering from [an] attempt at suicide," has been a successful lawyer while making a mess of his life: his wife has divorced him; his son, Jock, has disappointed him; and his daughter, Miranda, is about to marry a middle-aged bachelor. Then Miranda learns that Bolton's various accidents of late have been half-hearted attempts at suicide. Immediately, she tries to do things to make him interested in life, but the arranging is obvious and unsuccessful. Finally, she confronts him and, opening her heart to him, says that although she loves life, she'll kill herself if he commits suicide. Suddenly they both discover that genuine love was all that he needed and wanted.

(*Discussion*) Given the disillusionment of *Hotel Universe* and the suffering of *Here Come the Clowns*, what makes life worth living? Barry's answer involves the threshold of the room separating life from death. Step over the first threshold into this room. Perhaps it is so long that you can't see the end of it; perhaps it is a stuffy alcove. Each person determines the position of the second threshold. The answer to the question, for which there was no answer in *Hotel Universe*, is love. In some ways, particularly in its dialogue and over-all unity, *Second Threshold* is nearer to Barry's comedies in effect, and it was much more successful on the stage than the other two plays discussed. Although he had worked on the play off and on for eleven years, Barry did not live to see it produced, and Robert Sherwood made some revisions before its production. It dramatized, however, the answer for which Barry had searched.

C. Thornton Wilder: Man Will Prevail

Having written a Pulitzer winning novel, *The Bridge of San Luis Rey* (1927) and several one-act plays, Thornton Wilder (1897–   ) started his professional career in the theater with the Pulitzer Prize winning *Our Town* (1938). Wilder's original dramatic output has been slight in quantity but impressive. A humanist whose experiments in dramatic

form suggest some influence from the German expression-
ists, Wilder has a strong and substantially based approach to
life. (His brother, Amos Wilder, a theologian, has written
effectively on religion and literature.) The themes which he
uses in his plays reveal no agonizing search for absolutes because he has already accepted an answer which Barry worked
toward for years and which O'Neill found unsatisfactory—
love. There is good and there is evil, but there is no frustrating dilemma: there is only life. Men can best be happy on
this earth by loving one another and, one might add, by
espousing Wilder's faith in a cyclical life and a Christian
God. As the stage manager in *Our Town* says, "The cottage,
the go-cart, the Sunday afternoon drives in the Ford, the
first rheumatism, the grandchildren, the second rheumatism,
the death bed, the reading of the will.—Once in a thousand
times it's interesting."

1. A THEORY OF PLAYWRITING

In an essay entitled "Some Thoughts on Playwriting,"
Wilder explained some of his experimentation in the theater.
The stage, he noted, is "fundamental pretense" which
thrives on a "multiplication of additional pretenses." Rebelling from a past emphasis on realism, he believed that a primary objective in drama was to stimulate the spectators'
imagination. Therefore, through bare stage realism, imaginary
scenery, and colloquial but strongly suggestive speech, he intended that the events of the play be raised from the specific
to the general. This experimental release from realistic conventions, together with his concern for a literary style and
thought-provoking ideas, has made Wilder's work very attractive both to theater and literary critics.

2. ONE-ACT EXPERIMENTATION

The Angel That Troubled the Waters (1928) consists
of sixteen three-minute sketches in which three actors discussed problems of morality and religion. In technique, these
sketches suggested some of the experiments of German expressionism. Later, in 1931, Wilder published *The Long
Christmas Dinner and Other Plays in One Act*. The title play

showed his interest in experimental stage devices and his interpretation of the cyclical and fleeting nature of man. Distorting time, *The Long Christmas Dinner* condenses ninety years of Christmas dinners into a one-act play. With a long dining table, chairs, and two doorways, one wreathed in flowers and the other draped in black, Wilder suggests birth and death, sadness and humor, as people come, sit down, eat, live, and leave. People are pretty much the same. On a stage, bare except for strategically placed chairs, another play shows a family taking a "happy journey to Trenton and Camden." In both idea and form these earlier one-act plays suggest the nature of his later work.

3. THE CYCLE OF LIFE

Wilder's best commentary on life appears in *Our Town* (1938) and *The Skin of Our Teeth* (1942). In a deceptively simple manner, he interweaves what seems to be important with casual day by day activities; but in his view of life, the seemingly inconsequential is the meaningful. One must live each day as he thinks best. Truth will persist; man will prevail. There is no cause to worry or wonder—this is life! In that view in which man is part of that energy which comes from the Creator, the here and now is only an aspect of the larger cycle of things in which one considers, philosophically, time, space, and motion. In this sense, Wilder is one of our most modern of playwrights, although his techniques suggest the traditional literary epic and allegory, and his humanistic approach springs from a strong Christian optimism.

(a) *Our Town*, 1938: Our Living and Our Dying

(*Plot*) The Webbs and the Gibbses live side by side in a small town, Grover's Corners, New Hampshire. George Gibbs and Emily Webb share childhood and school, fall in love, and marry. Later, Emily dies in childbirth but has an opportunity to return to earth for one day. Although warned by the dead not to return, she chooses her twelfth birthday and is shocked and very disturbed by the lack of perception and understanding on the part of the living. Back in the graveyard she is happy as the play ends.

(*Discussion*) The complete lack of scenery and props,

except for a couple of chairs and stepladders and the use of a stage manager to introduce and comment on the action of the play, indicates Wilder's expressionism. The play is disarmingly simple with its folk approach—language, customs, superstitions, and homey characters—and sentimental idealism. But the simplicity evokes thought-provoking ideas about man's relationship to man—the strangeness, the frustration. In this life, man never reveals himself completely. Emily pleads: "Let's look at one another!" But the thesis is not the perhaps pessimistic idea of the stage manager that only "Saints and poets maybe!" can appreciate life. Rather, it is that man is like that; it is acceptance rather than frustration.

(b) *The Skin of Our Teeth*, 1942: The Story of Civilization

(*Plot*) George Antrobus of Excelsior, New Jersey, lives with his wife, a daughter, and two sons, one of whom, Henry (Cain), killed his brother—"a boyish impulse," because he is only 4000 years old. Sabrina appears as maid, temptress, and camp-follower, sometimes leaving her character to comment on the play action to the audience. In Act I, the family anxiously awaits the return of Mr. Antrobus, who has just finished inventing the wheel and the alphabet, as a sheet of ice is beginning to cover the entire continent. The Antrobuses try to maintain their fire, and people crowd around to keep from freezing to death. Sabrina finally appeals to the audience: "Pass up your chairs, everybody. Save the human race."

Act II takes place at a convention of the Ancient and Honorable Order of Mammals, Subdivision Humans, in Atlantic City. Antrobus is elected president with the help of his wife, and Sabrina has become a temptress trying to seduce George. But she fails, and as a storm and the floods approach, Antrobus saves his family and Sabrina by taking them into an ark along with the animals, two by two. After a war (Act III) in which Henry has fought on the wrong side, Mr. Antrobus' conflict with Henry becomes so real that the play has to be stopped. There seems to be no way to change Henry, and Sabrina, a maid once more, speaks the words which opened the play and tells the audience: "We have to go on for ages and ages yet. You go home. The end of this play isn't written yet. . . . Their [Mr. and Mrs. Antrobus] heads are full of plans and they're as confident as the first day they began—and they told me to tell you: good night."

(*Discussion*) Following the general movement of Ice Age, Flood, and War, the play suggests a perpetual life cycle of progress. The play ends as it begins; man recovers from chaos, sees evil as a part of life, and learning "that all the objects of my desire and fear were in themselves nothing good or bad save insofar as the mind was affected by them," determines to search out "something truly good and communicable to man." It is the never ending but stubborn struggle of man to survive by the skin of his teeth; and with man's pressing needs, his family, and great books, he will succeed. The theme is serious and the comic treatment is successful only because Wilder is certain of his theological and philosophical position. Concerning his technique, Wilder has admitted debts to James Joyce's *Finnegans Wake* and *Hellzapoppin'* with vaudevillians Olson and Johnson. The combination of the serious and the comic is a consistent and meaningful approach for Wilder.

D. William Saroyan: "The Beautiful People"

William Saroyan (b. 1908) has an unbounded faith in the goodness of man and his ability to overcome all evil; but unlike Wilder, he seems to have absolutely no reason for believing as he does. In the preface to *Don't Go Away Mad* (1949), he writes: "I seem to insist that people are good, that living is good, that decency is right, that good is not only achievable but inevitable—and there does not appear to be any justification for this." Saroyan becomes a mythmaker, an epic fabler. As Wilder wanted to present scenes which required for their complete effect the audience's imagination, Saroyan presents characters which, to become real, must stimulate an audience's imagination. With both artists, theater is a cooperative experience among dramatists, actors, and audiences. As a searcher, however, Saroyan makes no pretense to being a philosopher. He simply believes in "the beautiful people" who are basically sweet and kind and good. Life is, he knows, sadly beautiful, but in his plays, he insists that the beauty dominate the sadness. And if he disturbs people with this view and makes them think, he only emphasizes another part of the human myth which needs retelling.

1. VAUDEVILLE AND DREAMS

Saroyan's major plays before World War II were *My Heart's in the Highlands* (1939), *The Time of Your Life* (1939), *Love's Old Sweet Song* (1940), and *The Beautiful People* (1941). In all of these plays, there are strong suggestions of vaudeville in action and characters. In an typical Saroyan play, for example, the plot is so sketchy and improbable that its insignificance becomes a basic, if false, assumption, and the characters are as strange an assortment of people as ever appeared on the RKO Keith vaudeville circuit. In *The Time of Your Life*, one confronts a Kit Carson storyteller, a dancer, a pinball machine act, a comic monologuist of the Joe Cook variety, a prostitute, and a free-spending hero who does anything he can for anybody. The scene is a San Francisco honky-tonk and people come to perform, to complain, and to dream. No act on vaudeville is much better than Mr. MacGregor's bugle playing in *My Heart's in the Highlands*, and the poet's son, Johnny, is a master at conning Mr. Kosak out of more groceries. When a large family of Oklahoma migratory workers decides to camp on a lady's lawn in Bakersfield, California, until one of them gives birth to a child, the audience watches an extraordinary scene (*Love's Old Sweet Song*). Both the happenings and the people in Saroyan's plays are rambling, sketch-like, and unexpected, like a series of disconnected acts on a vaudeville stage.

But the people all have dreams; in fact, the plays are held together by their dreams. In *The Time of Your Life,* Joe says: "I believe in dreams sooner than statistics." Of course, Joe and the others know that there is evil in the world. Johnny, the poet's son in *My Heart's in the Highlands*, comments on the situation he finds: "I'm not mentioning any names, Pa, but something's wrong somewhere." Mainly, however, Saroyan's characters let it rest at that, because at this same time "There will always be poets in the world." Sometimes they act—Kit Carson kills the mean Blick in *The Time of Your Life* and then dreams are resumed—

but usually Saroyan's people accept their misfortune as part of life and believe that things will come out all right finally. And, interestingly enough, in Saroyan's plays dreams frequently come true.

2. LIVE AND LOVE

In spite of Saroyan's sense of humor and use of vaudevillian fantasy, he is a serious playwright with a feeling for experimentation and a significant and positive approach to life. A believer in dreams and a maker of myths, he is not bothered by most of the conflicting evils and problems that have frustrated other writers. Barry worked hard to arrive at his conclusion in *Second Threshold*. Wilder has a strong Christian faith to help him; but Saroyan sings happily as he walks along and believes. His conclusions do not seem profound because they are so simply revealed, but they are very stimulating in the theater. Clearly, he plays upon the emotions, and he believes in honest sentiment. But there is more to his art.

Essentially, Saroyan talks about living and loving. Love is not only possible; it is the only way in the modern world. And why wait to live! "In the time of your life," he says, "live—so that in that good time there shall be no ugliness or death for yourself or for any life your life touches, so that in that wondrous time you shall not add to the misery and sorrow of the world, but shall smile to the infinite delight and mystery of it." Now is "the time of your life"! As Joe tells Tom in the play: "Go ahead. Correct the errors of the world." And Tom is capable of the attempt, because he is capable of love. In *My Heart's in the Highlands*, it is an impulsive love of beauty which controls man and what little plot exists. Love conquers all at the end of *Love's Old Sweet Song*. If this approach seems overly sentimental or optimistic, it probably is.

(a) *My Heart's in the Highlands,* 1939

Johnny, a nine-year-old boy; his father, an unsuccessful poet; and Johnny's grandmother live in poverty in an old house in Fresno, California. One day, old Jasper MacGregor, who has run away from an old folk's home, appears and plays the bugle so beautifully that neighbors bring food, but soon he is returned to the old folks' home and Johnny must try to get food from Mr. Kosak, the grocer. Then the real estate man tells Johnny's father that they are being evicted. MacGregor returns, having run away again, and dies while playing his version of King Lear. The new tenants arrive, and Johnny, his father, and grandmother leave. "My heart's in the highlands, my heart is not here. My heart's in the highlands a-chasing the deer." (Robert Burns)

VII. CRITICISM: AN EMERGING TRADITION

With the production of a more sophisticated and penetrating drama after World War I, there emerged a more cosmopolitan and educated criticism. Until the late nineteenth century, dramatic criticism had been mainly that of the "paid puffer." Some scholarly criticism began to appear before the turn of the century in the writings of W. D. Howells, Henry James, and Brander Matthews, but most of the criticism of plays still remained in the hands of newspaper reporters who were frequently neither competent nor interested in their work. It was, then, an achievement in criticism when theatrical performances were regularly criticized by those who professed some knowledge of theater and drama, and were concerned with their development in America. J. Rankin Touse, William Winter, and John Corbin, in spite of distinct limitations as critics, were among the best journalistic drama critics before World War I; James G. Huneker was outstanding. With experimentation in the American theater stimulated by the various little theater movements in Europe, and increased interest in the drama as a means of conveying meaning as well as enjoyment, the drama critic faced a growing challenge. And he responded.

In the period between the Wars, the drama critic achieved new status, and the results of his more enlightened work suggested the faint beginnings of a criticism competent to cope with modern drama. Academic critics were beginning to awake to the pleasures and achievements of the drama, while newspapers and magazines were coming to attach more significance to theater reporting and to select their drama critics with greater attention to the talents of the person involved. Generally, however, criticism remained a body of theater reviews with reference to the particular performance. It became clear, as William Hawkins, drama critic for the New York *Telegram and Sun*, has suggested (*Theatre Annual,* XIV, 1956), "that the bulk of the Critics' readers are interested in a simple, blanket opinion which makes clear the subject of the show and its over-all quality. They do not want their limited reading time cluttered up with complex or erudite explanations or comparisons." Although some books were being written about American drama, the scholarly critic with a perspective of the drama as literature as well as theater had appeared rarely. American drama in particular did not make a strong appeal to the literary scholar, and the tradition of criticism of American drama remained largely journalistic rather than academic or scholarly. A literary tradition was emerging—yet very slowly.

A. Rise of the Educated Critic

Just after the turn of the century, a number of university professors began to teach, lecture, and publish their ideas about drama and theater. Brander Matthews of Columbia University and George Pierce Baker have been mentioned. Richard Burton of the University of Minnesota published *The New American Drama* in 1913, the same year that Archibald Henderson of the University of North Carolina wrote *European Dramatists*. Thomas H. Dickinson from the University of Wisconsin wrote *The Case of American Drama*, and Ludwig Lewisohn, Ohio State University, published *The Modern Drama* in 1915. A rising young critic at this time was Barrett H. Clark, a prolific writer, who served as editor for plays published by Samuel French, Inc. from 1918 to 1936, was drama editor of *Drama Magazine* during the 1920's, a biographer of Eugene O'Neill, a compiler of *America's Lost Plays* (20 volumes), and with George Freedley author of *A History of Modern Drama* (1947). Two critics who were mainly interested in American drama and who have reputations as historians of American drama were Arthur Hobson Quinn and Montrose J. Moses.

B. Guide Lines by the Journalists

As American theater became a more creative and imaginative institution and American drama became intellectually and emotionally challenging as well as enjoyable, the status of the drama critic improved and his number increased. The following list will simply include some of the better-known critics whose reputations were established during the Twenties and the Thirties. Brooks Atkinson started his long career as drama critic for *The New York Times* in 1925. John Mason Brown was drama critic for the *Theatre Arts Monthly* for four years before his 1929–1941 tenure in the same job for the New York *Evening Post*. Richard Watts, Jr. started working for the New York *Herald Tribune* in 1924 and became its drama editor twelve years later. Burns Mantle was drama critic for the New York *Daily News* from 1922 to 1943; his volumes of *Best Plays* provide some continuity in the study of American drama. Robert Benchley is remembered most clearly for his writing in *The New Yorker*, whose staff he joined in 1929. For nine years previous to that move, he had been drama editor of the old *Life* magazine.

Other critics whose writings have some significance during this period are Walter Prichard Eaton, Gilbert Seldes, Kenneth MacGowan, John Anderson, Percy Hammond, Joseph Mersand, and John Gassner. These are only a few of the people who served as guides for those interested in attending the theater in New York.

C. Cosmopolitan Tastes

Three outstanding columnists and theater critics during the Twenties and Thirties were George Jean Nathan, Alexander Woollcott, and Stark Young. Edith J. R. Isaacs, a fine critic in her own right and editor of the *Theatre Arts Monthly*, labeled them as follows: Nathan, "Critic as Showman"; Woollcott, "Critic as Actor"; and Young, "Critic as Critic" [*Theatre Arts Monthly*, XXVI (February, March, April, 1942)]. Whatever their sophistication, however, they were interested in the theater as an evening's entertainment rather than with drama as literature.

1. GEORGE JEAN NATHAN: FORTHRIGHT CRITIC

A person of considerable mind and wit and only a modicum of heart, Nathan (1882–1958) acted as drama critic or drama editor for several magazines and newspapers, in particular *Smart Set, Vanity Fair, The American Mercury,* and the New York *Journal-American.* During the early years of his career, he enjoyed shocking people with rather irreverent attacks on American character and institutions—attacks which gained him a reputation as an incisive critic and iconoclast. He was one of the first to recognize the stature of O'Neill and Saroyan, and his books on the theater appeared with remarkable consistency after *Another Book on the Theatre* (1916).

2. ALEXANDER WOOLLCOTT: "THE MAN WHO CAME TO DINNER"

The source of inspiration for Kaufman and Hart's *The Man Who Came to Dinner,* Woollcott (1887–1943) assumed an attitude toward this play which is characteristic of his criticism. He toured with the play, acting himself, as Sheridan Whiteside—but without the success of Monty Woolley. As a critic who loved the theater and fitted well into the F. Scott Fitzgerald circle, he reported for *The New York Times,* the *Herald,* and the *World.* His published volumes of criticisms, such as *Enchanted Aisles* (1924), gained him a popular audience, but he contributed mainly himself, his wit, and his enjoyment of theater gossip. Unlike Nathan who could criticize with perspective and art as well as wit, Woollcott added nothing but a little glitter to American dramatic criticism. But he did that very well.

3. STARK YOUNG: ACADEMIC CRITIC

Tending to be more intellectual than emotional in his criticism, Young (1881–1963) taught English on the university level before becoming an associate editor of *Theatre Arts Monthly.* He had an appreciation of art and literature which gave his criticisms a distinctive tone. Although among such contemporaries as Nathan and Woollcott he was a somber companion, his opinions are more valuable in a history of American drama.

D. Marxist Criticism

It should be clear that in the 1930's the Communist attempt to create and control theaters had to be accompanied not only by committed playwrights but by committed critics. *New Masses* and *The Daily Worker*, of course, could be expected to promote Marxist causes; Mike Gold was the prominent spokesman for Communist party lines. *New Theatre* was another magazine with a Marxist slant, and its editor, Ben Blake, provided it with Leftist direction. Some playwrights of the Left-Wing theater also wrote vigorous dramatic criticism; John Howard Lawson is an excellent example. A Left-leaning critic of sufficient seriousness to present her criticisms in book form was Eleanor Flexner, *American Playwrights, 1918–1938* (1938).

E. Critical Books and Magazines

One criterion of a developing and serious criticism of the drama is the number of publications dealing with the subject. Some of the books published during the decade between the Wars remain primary sources in American drama and theater research. The three existing histories of American drama were written in this period: Montrose J. Moses, *The American Dramatist* (rev. 1925); Margaret Mayorga, *A Short History of the American Drama* (1932); Arthur H. Quinn, *A History of the American Drama from the Beginning to the Civil War* (1923, rev. 1943) and *A History of the American Drama from the Civil War to the Present Day* (1927, rev., 1936).

Other books include John Anderson, *The American Theatre* (1938); Barrett H. Clark, *An Hour of American Drama* (1930); Thomas H. Dickinson, *Playwrights of the New American Theater* (1925); Eleanor Flexner, *American Playwrights, 1918–1938* (1938); Joseph Wood Krutch, *The American Drama Since 1918* (rev. 1957); Oliver M. Sayler,

Our American Theatre (1923); the yearly volumes of Burns Mantle and George Jean Nathan.

Among the theater magazines, the *Theatre Arts Monthly,* founded in 1916 by Sheldon Cheney, stands supreme. During much of this period, however, it was edited by Edith J. R. Isaacs, assisted by Rosamond Gilder. *Theatre Magazine* ran from 1900 to 1931. *The Little Theatre Monthly* combined with *The Drama* which, started before World War I and continued under various names until 1931, was particularly effective during the Twenties with Barrett H. Clark as drama editor. Suggestive of magazine activity in the 1930's was the *New Theatre* magazine, which started in 1931 as *Workers Theatre*, became *New Theatre* in 1934, and appeared for two issues in 1937 as *New Theatre & Film*.

VIII. ACHIEVEMENT IN THEATER

The history of American theater from 1915 to 1941 is the story of change and achievement. During the second decade of the century, several influences brought distinct innovations in theater production which were translated into mature achievements in the Twenties. Then two events—the talking movie and the stock market crash—had their effect upon theater attendance. Various producing organizations, however, stimulated theater activity during the Thirties; and by the beginning of World War II, the quality of American theater productions, helped by new and imaginative playwrights and designers, had reached a new height.

A. Approaching Maturity

Spurred on by influences from Europe and by imaginative Americans, the theater during the second decade in this century assessed and organized itself in ways that had never before been attempted. Much of this activity has been mentioned earlier in this chapter: the foreign influence of the Moscow Art Theater and the Abbey Players, the work of university people like George Pierce Baker, the interest of Percy MacKaye in civic theater, the growth of the Little Theater Movement.

Such activity had its consequences. Foreign influence was clearly healthy for American theater. An illustration of German expressionism appeared in New York in Max Reinhardt's *Sumurûn* in 1912. In 1915, the English producer-drama critic, Granville Barker, showed English stage techniques with a series of plays he produced at Wallack's Theatre in New York. Two years later, Jacques Copeau and his Vieux Colombier brought the French version of the new staging to New York. Baker's teaching in Harvard's 47 Workshop affected the theater through several of the prominent dramatists of the Twenties. Little Theaters also produced significant results. The Provincetown Players supported the talent of Eugene O'Neill; and the Theatre Guild, founded in December of 1918, grew from the desires of the Washington Square Players. Other organizations started about this time were the Drama League of America, 1910, which with its magazine, *The Drama Quarterly*, aimed to support good drama, and the Dramatists' Guild, started in 1912 as a division of the Authors' League of America.

One particular incident during this second decade showed the actor's growth in maturity and power. For 150 years, he had been notoriously disorganized and had reached an absurd position of indignity under the Theatrical Syndicate. The arch individualism, the self-importance exhibited by actors, had always been a major problem, but in 1919 a new era was started. For six years, actors, through Actors' Equity Association (established in 1913), had tried to work out a contract with managers involving fair wages, travel compensation, eight performances a week, etc., but they had failed. In the summer of 1919, the actors, or most of them, went out on strike—and, four weeks later, won their cause. After the first actors' strike in American theater history, the first Equity contract was signed on September 6, 1919.

By 1920, American theaters and actors enjoyed a strong position. Realism in the theater prevailed, although it was being challenged. There was some threat posed by the movies and the popularity of the radio, but otherwise the outlook was bright.

B. Theater in the Twenties: Prosperity

In 1920, there were 150 plays produced on Broadway; in 1927–28, 280 plays were produced in New York's eighty theaters for stage plays. There was also a significant activity throughout America, as Kenneth MacGowan reported in *Footlights Across America* (1929). The Theatre Guild was very active, bringing many foreign plays to America and stimulating work by native playwrights. Even repertory was revived with a modicum of success, when in 1926 Eva Le Gallienne opened the Civic Repertory Theatre for six seasons. It was definitely a period of prosperity for the American theater.

O'Neill dominated the decade, and expressionism was the innovation in theater staging. Besides introducing a number of new American playwrights, this decade showed the developing artistry of several stage designers—Joseph Urban, Robert Edmund Jones, Lee Simonson, and Norman Bel Geddes. Unfortunately, the decade ended on a low note. The first full-length talking movie, *The Jazz Singer,* was released in 1927; and in 1929, *Variety* magazine reported the stock market crash—"Wall St. Lays an Egg." The Depression had begun.

C. Theater in the Thirties: Struggle

Across the country in 1920 theaters for stage plays numbered nearly 1500; ten years later, that number had been reduced to about 500. In New York during the 1930–31 season, there were about 190 plays produced; by the 1939–40 season, there were only eighty. The struggle in this decade is also marked by the activity of various producing organizations, including the Left-Wing theaters (which have been discussed earlier in this chapter). One bright development in the struggling theater was the increased delight in musicals. By 1940, the movies had become more than a threat to the stage, but, although fewer plays were being produced, quality was sustained. Soon war would bring drastic changes.

1. PRODUCING ORGANIZATIONS

The best-known experiments in theater production are the Group Theatre, the Federal Theatre, and the Playwrights' Company. With Communist theaters, the Mercury Theatre of John Houseman and Orson Welles, and the Theatre Guild which had been producing plays since its formation in 1918 and had subsidized the Group Theatre, these varied producing organizations make the Thirties one of the more interesting decades in American theater history.

(a) The Group Theatre

Three employees of the Theatre Guild—Harold Clurman, Cheryl Crawford, and Lee Strasberg—were responsible for starting the Group Theatre in 1931. Their objective was to produce plays concerned with contemporary moral and social problems and to develop serious playwrights for a permanent acting company. They were also united in their approach to acting—a training method involving improvisation and the Stanislavsky system. Before the Group Theatre was dissolved in 1941, it offered twenty-three productions, of which thirteen emphasized social and economic problems. Too often the Group is remembered mainly for some Left-Wing productions, although it was clearly not Communist controlled. Rather its significance should be measured in terms of the more serious playwriting that it stimulated and for its influence on the development of American acting—ideas now carried on by Lee Strasberg's Actors' Studio. Finally, however, a number of difficulties brought about the end of the Group Theatre—little money, poor plays, and temperamental actors.

(b) The Federal Theatre

America's only attempt at nationally sponsored theater was the Works Progress Administration's Federal Theatre. Initiated to help unemployment among theater artists, the Federal Theatre enjoyed an appropriation of over six million dollars and the effective leadership of Hallie Flanagan, its national director. Starting in 1935, Mrs. Flanagan saw her objectives as providing relief for the unemployed, incentive for developing native plays and theatrical skills, and experimentation in a variety of theater forms. Until this project of the WPA was killed by Congress on June 30, 1939, many of her objectives were fulfilled, while she ran the project with an efficiency and patience which have been rarely duplicated in government. Among the Federal Theatre's more memorable accomplishments were the Living Newspaper productions and its simultaneous presentation at twenty-one theaters across the nation of *It Can't Happen Here,* October 27, 1936, by Sinclair Lewis and John C. Moffitt. Like the Group Theatre, however, the Federal Theatre was accused of Communist infiltration. Although it did produce a few Marxist plays, it was never Communist controlled, and the Theatre's social plays were (according to Hallie Flanagan, *Arena,* 1940, p. 183–4) to depict "the struggle of many different kinds of people to understand the natural, social and economic forces around them and to achieve through these forces a better life for more people." Generally, the scope of the Federal Theatre productions in both theme and form is to be admired.

(c) The Playwrights' Company

During the spring of 1938, five dramatists—Maxwell Anderson, S. N. Behrman, Sidney Howard, Elmer Rice, and Robert Sherwood—decided that the best way to produce their plays was to form an organization, the Playwrights' Company. The implied emphasis was a step forward for dramatists who now asserted an independence which they had failed to get in the Dramatists' Guild, formed in 1912. All of the original members were established dramatists, and their early productions, some of them presented in conjunction with the Theatre Guild, were among the most successful in the American theater.

2. THE MUSICAL THEATER

American musical comedy is not modern. William Dunlap, the Father of American Drama, wrote a musical play called *The Archers; or, Mountaineers of Switzerland* in 1796, and his was not the first. Many nineteenth-century plays, in fact, made use of music and song; and frequently, an actor with a good voice could insert a song in a play. For most critics, however, *The Black Crook* (1866) by Charles M. Barras is recognized as the ancestor of modern musical comedy. With ballet, song, and sensation, *The Black Crook* played for sixteen months. Its sensational aspects, however, seemed most attractive to audiences, and other such plays appeared. Eventually, legs usurped the legitimate aspects of these musicals, and burlesque became popular. Musicals continued, however, in revues, follies, minstrels, vaudeville, and some plays.

(a) Successful Experimentation between the Wars

Before World War I, two major writers of musical drama —Victor Herbert with *Babes in Toyland* (1903) and *Sweethearts* (1913); George M. Cohan with numerous musicals, such as *Forty-five Minutes from Broadway* (1906)—suggested the two trends that modern musicals would take: the romantic operetta and the fast-moving comedy. The writers who followed them during the period of experimentation between the Wars were Rudolf Friml (*Rose-Marie*, 1924; *The Vagabond King*, 1925), Sigmund Romberg (*Blossom Time*, 1921; *The Student Prince*, 1924), and Vincent Youmans (*No, No, Nanette*, 1925; *Hit the Deck*, 1927). Jerome Kern gave Marilyn Miller a memorable role in *Sunny* (1925), created the very successful *Show Boat* (1927) from Edna Ferber's novel, and wrote *The Cat and the Fiddle* (1931) with Otto Harbach. George and Ira Gershwin started writing together in 1918 but became particularly successful with *Lady, Be Good!* (1924) and *Strike Up the Band* (1930). They joined the Heywards for *Porgy and Bess* (1935) after creating a lively political satire with Kaufman and Ryskind in *Of Thee I Sing* (1931). Other political satires include Richard Rodgers and Lorenz Hart's *I'd Rather Be Right* (1937) and Maxwell Anderson and Kurt Weill's *Knickerbocker Holiday* (1938). The musical revue of the Thirties is well represented by Arthur Schwartz, Howard Dietz, and Kaufman's *The Band Wagon* (1931) and the songs ("A Pretty Girl Is Like a Melody") and the revues (*As Thousands Cheer*, 1933) of Irving Berlin.

(b) Approaching Maturity

The stage had been set. The music and songs of Irving Berlin, Jerome Kern, George Gershwin, and Cole Porter (*Fifty Million Frenchmen*, 1929, with Herbert Fields; *Anything Goes*, 1934, with Guy Bolton and P. G. Wodehouse) had established a popular entertainment which would only grow. The deaths of George Gershwin in 1937 and Jerome Kern in 1945 thinned ranks which were quickly filled by Richard Rodgers and Lorenz Hart (*The Boys from Syracuse*,

1938; *Pal Joey,* 1940) and Oscar Hammerstein II. George Abbott became a director with a magic touch for musical comedy which was beginning to reach a form in which the score and the lyrics were unified into an artistic whole. When *Oklahoma!* (1943) by Rodgers and Hammerstein was produced, the artistry of modern American musical comedy and its position in world theater were unquestioned.

IX. SUMMARY

This period in American drama began in some confusion and ended with a sense of achievement and distinction that the drama in America had never before experienced. Recently emerging from a commercial theater monopoly that produced few plays which were more than a satisfying mediocrity, dramatists and theater artists alike reacted enthusiastically to foreign influences. These stimulating forces for the drama appeared before World War I, but America needed creative and rebellious spirits in both the drama and the theater. In Eugene O'Neill, the Little Theater Movement, the Theatre Guild, and the strength that these forces in American drama and theater supplied to others, America began to build a significant modern drama. Various threads of its own past were happily cut, while others were woven into the skein of modern drama in ways once thought impossible.

The Twenties were a period of happiness and prosperity in the theater. The sense of freedom and individuality which pervaded the decade also characterized the drama. As a consequence of increased emphasis on the drama in universities and communities, the prosperity of the stage in general, and the heightened status of the playwright among literary people and critics, a new group of dramatists appeared—Sidney Howard, Maxwell Anderson, Philip Barry, Paul Green, among others. Their training was generally quite different from that of the dramatists at the turn of the century, and the effect was a refreshing variety in theme and form. The experimentation in form (particularly expressionism), the range of ideas, and, quite simply, the quality of the plays distinguished the Twenties from past American drama.

The Thirties were a vital and moving period in the history of American drama and theater. The range of play themes continued, but a great majority of the plays were generally what might be called social drama. Certainly, they contributed to the dominant social theater of this decade in a major or a lesser fashion. From Left to Right serves as a guiding principle for studying many of the plays written during these years—from propaganda drama of the Left-Wing theater through social thesis plays, social melodramas, and social satires to light or domestic comedies and comedies of manners. It was a period of theater growth and turmoil in which the playwrights whose reputations had been started in the previous decade were joined primarily by social dramatists. At the close of this decade, World War II had begun, and a different atmosphere surrounded both playwrights and the theater.

Perhaps the most significant aspect of American drama between the World Wars is the concern of the dramatist for ideas of a spiritual and universal import. Although it is true that a social consciousness dominated or was infused into most of the plays of this period, it is also true that an awareness of the spiritual side of life and a questioning of man and his values constituted a strong interest of the best playwrights— O'Neill, Anderson, Barry, Thornton Wilder, and William Saroyan. Their plays indicate in both craftsmanship and depth of thought that American drama from its early imitation through its growth to a profession and an art, had finally reached a position of challenging importance in world drama.

SELECTED BIBLIOGRAPHY

Broussard, Louis, *American Drama Contemporary Allegory from Eugene O'Neill to Tennessee Williams.* Norman, Oklahoma: University of Oklahoma Press, 1962.

Bucks, Dorothy Sims, *The American Drama of Ideas from 1890 to 1929.* Unpublished dissertation, Northwestern University, 1944.

Clark, Barrett H., and George Freedley, *A History of Modern Drama.* New York: D. Appleton-Century Co., 1947.

Deutch, Helen, and Stella Hannau, *The Provincetown.* New York: Farrar & Rinehart, Inc., 1931.

Dickinson, Thomas H., *Playwrights of the New American Theater.* New York: The Macmillan Company, 1925.

Downer, Alan S., *Fifty Years of American Drama 1900–1950*. Chicago: Henry Regnery Company, 1951.

Dusenbury, Winifred L., *The Theme of Loneliness in Modern American Drama*. Gainesville, Florida: University of Florida Press, 1960.

Falk, Doris, *Eugene O'Neill and the Tragic Tension*. New Brunswick, New Jersey: Rutgers University Press, 1958.

Flanagan, Hallie, *Arena*. New York: Duell, Sloan, and Pearce, 1940.

Flexner, Eleanor, *American Playwrights, 1918–1938*. New York: Simon and Schuster, 1938.

Hewitt, Barnard, *Theatre U.S.A. 1665–1957*. New York: McGraw-Hill Book Company, Inc., 1959.

Himelstein, Morgan Y., *Drama Was A Weapon*. New Brunswick, New Jersey: Rutgers University Press, 1963.

Kinne, Wisner P., *George Pierce Baker and the American Theatre*. Cambridge, Massachusetts: Harvard University Press, 1954.

Krutch, Joseph Wood, *The American Drama Since 1918*. New York: George Braziller, Inc., rev. 1957.

Macgowan, Kenneth, *Footlights Across America*. New York: Harcourt, Brace and Company, 1929.

Miller, Jordan Y., *American Dramatic Literature*. New York: McGraw-Hill Book Company, Inc., 1961.

Modern Drama, VI, (December, 1963).

Quinn, Arthur H., *A History of the American Drama from the Civil War to the Present Day*. New York: Appleton-Century-Crofts, Inc., rev. 1936.

Rabkin, Gerald, *Drama and Commitment*. Bloomington, Indiana: Indiana University Press, 1964.

CHAPTER V

American Drama at Mid-Twentieth Century

From 1941 to the Present

In *Mid-Century Drama,* the English drama critic Laurence Kitchin entitled his essay on drama in the United States "The Potent Intruder." The intrusion, of course, began 150 years ago, but its potency has been seriously questioned during most of the intervening years. By the end of the Thirties, however, American drama had assumed a position of some stature in world drama. At mid-century, it became a recognized force.

The study of contemporary American drama is a study of this force—as it reaches its potential, and as it fails. During the war years of the Forties, American plays largely reflected the agony and anger of an aroused people; the major distinguishing feature was a psychological interest in man's emotional reaction to war. The quality of the earlier plays by Eugene O'Neill, Maxwell Anderson, Thornton Wilder, Lillian Hellman, William Saroyan, and Philip Barry, which had attracted international interest was continued mainly in the later dramas of O'Neill and in the work of two newcomers: Arthur Miller and Tennessee Williams. In a manner unequalled by past performance in American drama, Miller and Williams captured the attention of an international audience and criticism. For many of the dramatists writing before World War II, the gap provided by the war years marked an end to their most creative art, and the years since 1945 have recorded mainly the artistic decline and/or the deaths of the active playwrights of the Thirties.

The major part of American drama since World War II has been a continuation of the social drama, satire, comedy, and melodrama that was popular in the theater between the wars, although attempts to write poetic drama have become more numerous and in a few instances have gained both commercial and artistic success. A rather traditional American concern for sentiment was bonded with a post-war interest in violence and sex to produce a distinctly commercial art. And in the modern Broadway theater, controlled so coldly by big business, the mark of success is SRO (Standing Room Only). An alternative success, now more highly regarded than ever before by playwrights, is measured by production in the increasingly active off-Broadway theaters, the municipal playhouses, university theaters, and in summer stock for the tourist trade. The central conflict in the American theater world, therefore, has become a more intensified New York vs. All Others. Meanwhile, commerce is served, while critics are slowly but increasingly concerned with art.

Lady Gregory, the Irish playwright and director of the Abbey Theatre, once noted that the Abbey directors had early in the life of the theater made the mistake of confusing theatrics with literary values. The difficulties consequent to such a confusion will probably always exist in all theaters. Certainly, the exception is noticeably rare. One way to avoid confusing literature and theater, however, is to avoid the question—an effort remarkably illustrated by the commercial success of American musical comedy and some drama of the Absurd. On the contemporary scene in world theater, the force of American drama is most effectively observed in the plays of O'Neill, Miller, and Williams, while Broadway and off-Broadway subsist mainly on light comedies, musical drama, and, lately, Absurdist plays.

I. AMERICAN DRAMA AND WORLD WAR II

In the past, the theater has responded with varying amounts of vigor to wars in which America was involved. During the Revolution, Mrs. Mercy Warren's partisan war satires were a vital part of the War of the Belle Lettres, and the naval battles of the War of 1812 stimulated spectacular theater entertainment. The mid-nineteenth-century war with Mexico and the Spanish-American War sparked only minor interest among playwrights, but numerous writers dramatized romantic and exciting adventures which they associated with the Civil War. Hardly any of these plays, however, dramatized a serious war issue: the object was entertainment. Plays concerned with World War I did little to change this view of wartime drama; vaudeville and musical comedy were interspersed with such plays as James Forbes' *The Famous Mrs. Fair* (1919), Gilbert Emery's *The Hero* (1921), and the successful *What Price Glory?* (1924) by Anderson and Stallings. World War II, however, stimulated dramatists to treat more searching issues. Amid the light comedies, the musicals, and the heroic melodramas, some plays appeared which dealt seriously with the problems that war engenders.

A. Melodrama and Propaganda

Wartime adventures slip easily into the demands of melodrama, and wartime passions frequently arouse prejudices that are expressed as propaganda. For some writers, the Spanish Civil War had already aroused both principles and passions. Ernest Hemingway had written a slight play about counter-espionage and girls in *The Fifth Column* (1940), and Maxwell Anderson had posed a more serious question in *Key Largo* (1939). John Steinbeck described the heroism of the Norwegians against Nazi occupation in *The Moon Is Down* (1942). As American dramatists of the Thirties directed their thoughts toward the war, they were joined by others.

1. STRONG OPINIONS BY HELLMAN AND SHERWOOD

Both Lillian Hellman and Robert Sherwood reacted vigorously to the war in Europe. With her superior control of melodramatic action, Lillian Hellman wrote a powerful antifascist play in *Watch on the Rhine* (1941). She made an even more serious comment as she ridiculed the previous twenty years of American foreign policy in *The Searching Wind* (1944). By 1940, Sherwood had abandoned his satiric approach to war in

There Shall Be No Night, a straightforward and bitter denunciation of totalitarianism. In *The Rugged Path* (1945), he presented a biased argument in favor of intervention as opposed to isolation and in some patriotic splendor found nobility and meaning for his cause.

2. *COMMAND DECISION*, 1947, BY WILLIAM W. HAINES

Building its action on the decision of an air base commander to order certain long-range bombing, *Command Decision* manages to include the right ingredients for a successful war melodrama. There is suspense in the waiting for the planes to return, sentiment in a pilot's death contrasted with the birth of his son, satire on congressmen and stupid Congressional pressure, humor to ease the tension, propaganda for the patriotic, and the overall impression that war exhibits no heroes—only heroic men who won the peace for a grateful country despite incomprehensible blunders by its government officials.

B. A More Serious Tone

The best drama during World War II revealed some psychological concern for the individual and for the social problems which war entails. Maxwell Anderson's *The Eve of Saint Mark* (1942) suggested the change in a soldier's life as the challenge of battle and his thoughts of home and his girl friend gave him a power in which he could find meaning in his own death. *Tomorrow the World* (1943) by James Gow and Arnaud d'Usseau pictured a Nazi war orphan brought to America and the seemingly impossible task of reshaping people once controlled by Nazi ideals.

As the fighting stopped, more dramatists became interested in the results of war. Philip Barry's *Foolish Notion* (1945) contrasts the actual homecoming of a soldier with the expectations of four people intimately concerned with him. *Home of the Brave* (1945), Arthur Laurents' first play, is a penetrating dramatization of the shock treatment necessary to make a Jewish soldier aware of his ethnic sensitivity and his guilt complex which have left him paralyzed after an initial ecstasy because a companion was killed in battle. Another play concerned with race prejudice and war psychology is Arnaud d'Usseau's *Deep Are the Roots* (1945), in which a Southern white girl, grateful for a Negro friend's efforts in the war, offers to marry him when he returns a hero.

C. War Farce and Comedy

As a balance to the attacks on war, some dramatists appealed to a broader view in numerous farces and sentimental comedies. Conditions in Washington prompted *The Doughgirls* (1942) by Joseph Fields, as military and civilian personnel bumped heads and rubbed shoulders. *Dear Ruth* (1944) by Norman Krasna is a sentimental comedy of a young girl who involves her older sister with a soldier by writing amorous letters to him over her sister's name. John Patrick's sentimental story of *The Hasty Heart* (1945) tells of a Scottish soldier dying in a hospital in an unfriendly atmosphere. Perhaps the most popular of war comedies, however, was Joshua Logan's *Mister Roberts* (1948), an adaptation of Thomas Heggen's novel. By this time, the war was over and everyone could laugh more easily at the G.I.'s complaints and his rebellion against an unbending authority.

II. INTERNATIONAL AMERICAN DRAMATISTS

Although American drama at mid-century is a recognized force in world theater, it is unfortunately true that American dramatists with international reputations are but a small handful. The few plays of Thornton Wilder are still produced on the Continent; O'Neill's work is treated with respect; but the only post-war playwrights receiving continuous attention are Arthur Miller and Tennessee Williams. No other contemporary American playwrights have written sufficiently substantial plays or shown sufficient insight in their work to warrant serious critical discussion. The best dramatists present a philosophy, and it is significant that Miller and Williams are distinct in their individual views of man. The one upholds the dignity of man; the other denies it. One concerns himself with man's soul, the other (with a few exceptions) with man's organs. One searches for meaning; the other assumes a void and creates sensation to compensate for man's sorrowful loss. One tries to find man in a real world; the other sees man as part of a romantic vision. With such divergence of approach, their positions as America's foremost playwrights since World War II suggest the scope of the American mind, the growing liberalism of the American theater, and a maturity in American criticism.

A. Arthur Miller and the Dignity of Man

In the tradition of the great playwrights of the past, Arthur Miller (1915–　　) is concerned with truth and man's unrelenting yet doomed search for recognition as a human being. Although his success as a writer of tragic drama is seriously questioned, Miller has written a body of criticism presenting his views on tragedy and modern drama and has created a handful of plays which, with varying effect, illustrate his ideas. Because he is a man of philosophic temperament concerned with an explication or defense of drama, he has been condemned for displaying argument rather than theater in both his essays and his plays. In the eyes of such critics, he has failed to dramatize effectively the meaningful ideas which bother him. Despite a limited amount of creative work, however, he has also aroused considerable enthusiasm, popular and critical, both for his ideas and his techniques. His concern for dramatic theory, his effective combination of the realistic and the expressionistic in his plays, and his basic interest in the dignity of man link Miller with the best traditions of the past and combine to make him America's outstanding dramatist at mid-century.

1. A THEORY OF THE DRAMA

Miller has written a number of essays on the drama, the most significant being his very important Introduction to his *Collected Plays* (1957); "The Family in Modern Drama," (*Atlantic Monthly,* April, 1956); and "On Social Plays," an Introduction to *A View from the Bridge* (1955). With Ibsen, he believes that *idea* is important in a play; like Robert Frost, he believes that his purpose is to state a truth that is known but not really known. In discussing the possibility of tragedy, he contends that, Aristotle notwithstanding, the common man is a fit hero—and that more important than social status is the intensity of the passion dramatized and the discovery of a conflict or challenge that a man can neither resist nor deny. In these ways a playwright approaches tragedy.

A major hypothesis in Miller's writing is that the dramatist must concern himself with men and the nature of man. Until the dramatist accounts for the total condition of man, he will not produce great art. With an almost Emersonian emphasis, Miller believes in dramatizing the whole man—as he is part of a family and as he is part of a society. To do this it is necessary to combine theatrical techniques of realism and expressionism which he equates representationally with family and society. In his essays, Miller is an idealist who recognizes the limitations of the theater only in the imaginations of dramatists and theater people. His theories describe his own efforts to a considerable extent; his challenge is a drama that extends itself to "ultimate causes," engaging its "relevancy for the race," and emphasizing a balance which is "all" in great drama.

2. PERSONAL DIGNITY: NAME VS. ANIMAL

"The tragic feeling," Miller writes, "is evoked in us when we are in the presence of a character who is ready to lay down his life, if need be, to secure one thing—his sense of personal dignity." It is Miller's concern for the dignity of man which sets him apart from other modern dramatists—a concern which he dramatizes as a person's concern for his name. Without this name or dignity, man becomes an animal; and it is a conflict between retaining one's name or being called an animal that is the culminating crisis in his plays. Although he does not always win or even know how to win, Man always fights for his name. In *All My Sons* (1947), Chris condemns his father at the end of Act II for being "not even an animal," and the last act dramatizes the father's vain attempt to salvage some dignity from the situation. Biff, the truthsayer in *Death of a Salesman* (1949) having complained that "we're all animals," remarks that his father, Willy Loman, did not know who he was. Striving desperately, wildly, for a dignity that he did not understand, Willy was doomed to destroy himself. The point is made more explicitly in *The Crucible* (1953) as Proctor, in contrast to the "dogs" he sees around him, refuses to let his confession be used to influence others: "How may I live without my name? I have given you my soul; leave me my name!" The climax of *A View from the Bridge* (1957) occurs when the informer, Eddie Carbone, encounters the vengeful Marco. As Eddie half pleads and half demands to be given his "name," Marco can utter only the word "animal." In *After the Fall* (1964), the question "In whose name?" is asked and then answered in such a way as to suggest the imponderable significance of personal dignity: "Always in your own blood-covered name you turn your back!"

3. LIMITED PRODUCTIVITY BUT SIGNIFICANT ACHIEVEMENT

Miller's reputation in the theater rests upon a very few plays. His first play for the New York stage, *The Man Who Had All the Luck* (1944), failed. Three years later, *All My Sons* won three awards, and *Death of A Salesman* (1949) received a Pulitzer Prize. *The Crucible* (1953) was followed in 1955 by two short plays: *A View from the Bridge* (later expanded to two acts) and *A Memory of Two Mondays*. In 1950, Miller had adapted Ibsen's *An Enemy of the People;* and in 1960, he again strayed from original stage drama to write *The Misfits,* a screen play. He returned to the theater in 1964 with *After the Fall,* a painful explanation of his own life (particularly that part during which he was married to Marilyn Monroe) in which he attempts to regain an innocence but mainly succeeds in slipping into the same abyss of self-torment and passion which weakened the last work of O'Neill. In general, Miller's plays are marked by a concern for truth that is sometimes proclaimed too broadly. More than other modern American dramatists, however, he has asked meaningful questions about the relationship of man to his society, his family, and his own fulfillment.

(a) *All My Sons,* 1947

During the war, Joe Keller was a businessman who not only caused soldiers to die by shipping out faulty cylinder heads for airplanes but allowed his partner to go to prison for the deed. Misguided by his desire to make money for his family and not wholly aware of the falseness of his position, he is finally driven to suicide by his son who forces upon him a larger consciousness of responsibility.

(b) *Death of A Salesman*, 1949

Illustrating Miller's theory of the tragedy of the common man as well as his technique of mixing realism and expressionism, this play is perhaps the most controversial of modern American drama. Intended to dramatize "the process of Willy Loman's way of mind," *Death of A Salesman* portrays a man with "the wrong dreams," who is never able to see the truth or accept the world as it is. Frustrated by his own weaknesses, desperately disappointed in his sons, victimized by a twisted view of social and personal values, Willy is a misplaced man, without "a thing in the ground," who will give up his life before giving up his false ideas. Victim and hero, his suicide is an ironic comment on man's concern for personal dignity.

(c) *The Crucible*, 1953

Stimulated by the "witch-hunt" tactics of Senator Joseph McCarthy, Miller drew his scene from the Salem witch trials. The accusations of witchcraft against John and Elizabeth Proctor and the subsequent trial showing John's personal integrity and power are set, first, against the mass hysteria of a village overwhelmed by superstitious fears; and, secondly, against the impassioned change in the Reverend Hale who, sent to help exorcise the Devil, finally denounces the proceedings of the court. When Proctor, in the face of death, first confesses witchcraft and then refuses to allow his name to be used to influence others to a confession which he knows is false, he becomes ennobled and reaches a personal dignity to which death brings a sense of tragedy.

B. Tennessee Williams: Master of Compassion

Reared in a family where his father's strong and violent approach to life was in dramatic contrast to the gentler, protective view of his mother, Thomas Lanier (Tennessee) Williams (1914–   ) has fused two seemingly paradoxical approaches to life. A lover of beauty, he is also frighteningly aware of the ugliness of man. The questions he has asked in his art, however, ("Is there no mercy left in the world anymore?")

have propelled him toward an overwhelming compassion for man in all of his weaknesses. Frequently seeing man as a Christ figure crucified for his acts, Williams has symbolically played God and tried to free man, realizing fully that there is no escape. Because of this knowledge (and perhaps aided by the personal problems which have kept him close to his analyst), he has remained a romanticist, one who admittedly "feels" more than he "thinks." The resulting dramas have been frequently sensational and satisfying theater, excellent social commentaries which have stopped short of the psychologically probing insight that is tragedy. Williams has always felt it necessary to express the violent and the vulgar but only as a means to approaching truth. It is at this point, however, that his compassion for man intrudes upon his insight, and his plays do not reach the scope and universality that would seem to be the potential of his art. A master of playwriting in which the realistic scene and the symbolic act are fused, Williams is extremely successful in dramatizing emotion and writing about people—bizarre though most of them may be—who are trying to live.

1. THE INESCAPABLE LONELINESS OF MAN

When *A Streetcar Named Desire* (1947) was produced in Austria, it was called *Loneliness, the Last Step*. Loneliness and its consequent fears dominated *The Glass Menagerie* (1945); and in *Camino Real* (1953), the word *lonely* is repeated as a prelude to death, while the word *brother* may not be spoken. Williams instinctively understands the loneliness of man—his constant and desperate attempt to escape the reality that is his loneliness, and his subsequent failure to do so. In *The Glass Menagerie*, for example, Tom tries to run away, the mother tries to escape into the past, while Laura becomes a part of her collection of glass figurines. The South becomes a symbol of escape in this play as it does for Blanch (*Streetcar*) who, failing to retreat successfully into the South, can escape the reality of loneliness only through insanity. The price of admission to "the way of life" (*Camino Real*) is "desperation," and for humanity which cannot bear much reality there is no escape: "A dream is nothing to live in." The cannibalism in *Suddenly Last Summer* (1958) symbolizes the self-destruction that man inevitably brings upon himself in his loneliness. Alone-ness is the secret of Shannon's problems in *The Night of the Iguana* (1961): "the need to believe in something or in some-one—almost anyone—almost anything . . . . something." And for him, there will be nothing. He, like all the others, is the "fugitive kind"—those who will lose out!

(a) *The Glass Menagerie*, 1945

Tom lives with his mother and his sister, Laura. A sensi-tive and poetic soul, he revolts from his routine job in a shoe factory and from his mother's insistence that he bring home a young man who might be interested in Laura, a crippled and excessively shy girl. Finally, he brings a boy who, ironically, is engaged to be married. The mother's anger drives Tom to roam, but in this "memory play" he can never forget Laura.

(b) *Camino Real*, 1953

In sixteen blocks, or scenes, on the Camino Real, Don Quixote dreams a pageant of old and new meanings in which Kilroy, the all-American boy with a solid gold heart, meets the corruption of life, is seduced by fraud, becomes a patsy, and finally is chosen the fit companion of Don Quixote, dreamer.

2. THE VIOLENCE AND THE VICTIM

Loneliness is a truthful aspect of life; so is violence. Al-though in *The Night of the Iguana*, Shannon, the defrocked minister who is a guide for Blake Tours, cannot understand why he feels that he must explain the filth of life, the compul-sion is there. And it is a compulsion with Williams. Sensa-tionalism and violence have filled his plays since *The Glass Menagerie* (which many critics still consider his best): rape in *Streetcar*; homosexuality in *Cat on a Hot Tin Roof* (1955); a man torn apart by dogs in *Orpheus Descending* (1957); castra-tion in *Sweet Bird of Youth* (1958); cannibalism in *Suddenly Last Summer* (1958); a comment on people eating undigested food particles from a dung pile in *The Night of the Iguana* (1961). These are means to an end, however, with Williams. Whether symbolically or realistically, he describes man as self-destructive or corrupted by society. In *Orpheus Descending*, he explains the corruption by telling a story about a legless bird that remains pure because it need never alight on earth and become contaminated by its corruption. Man is simply made this way, a victim of "the earth's obscene, corrupting love," as the thematic poem in *The Night of the Iguana* states.

3. COMPASSION FOR MAN

For this victim, this man who is trying to live, Williams feels tremendous sympathy: lonely and sensitive man cannot stand reality, nor can he escape. Man does not want pity or even understanding, as Chance Wayne explains in *Sweet Bird of Youth*. In particular, man should not pity himself; he must simply try to live. As Kilroy says, "the deal is rugged"; "God shows a savage face to people" (*Suddenly Last Summer*). One needs to avoid mendacity (*Cat on a Hot Tin Roof*), to say "Brother," to believe in "something." Knowing that these are impossible acts, Williams clearly manifests his great compassion for man, struggling as he is destroyed.

III. PRE-WAR DRAMATISTS

For its post-war entertainment, America has been looking toward new dramatists. In the main, those who had been actively writing in the Twenties and Thirties became less effective in the Fifties. Some died, some wrote fewer plays, others simply faded from the scene. Although O'Neill's plays continued to appear, all were written before the War. Few of the pre-war playwrights enhanced their reputations, although Elmer Rice, Maxwell Anderson, and S. N. Behrman continued to write plays with some of the characteristics which had made their pre-war efforts effective, and Clifford Odets returned to the theater. Of those writing fifteen years after mid-century, better work might be expected only from Lillian Hellman, Thornton Wilder, and William Saroyan—all of whom are limited by their particular approaches to the drama.

A. The Posthumous Eugene O'Neill

O'Neill died in 1953, but he had written his last play in 1941–42. This play, *A Moon for the Misbegotten,* and *The Iceman Cometh* were produced in 1947 and 1946 respectively, but without much success. It was not until the late Fifties that

O'Neill enthusiasts began again to gather in the wings. In 1956, a successful revival of *The Iceman Cometh* was followed by *Long Day's Journey into Night,* a play concerned with O'Neill's family and often acclaimed as one of his best. *A Moon for the Misbegotten* appeared again in 1957, the same year that *A Touch of the Poet* was produced in Sweden before being brought to America. Critics observed that O'Neill's faults were as damning as ever, but they still recognized him as America's major playwright. To date he has not been replaced, and with the exception of Miller and Williams his competition has not proved very worthy.

1. THE CONTINUING IDEA OF ILLUSION

O'Neill's attitude toward illusion has been discussed in the previous chapter with reference to *The Iceman Cometh* (written in 1939, published in 1946) and *A Touch of the Poet* (written in 1936, published in 1957). *A Moon for the Misbegotten* (written in 1941–42, published in 1952) dramatizes a similar thesis as the characters live behind pretension and psychic masks—without success. For O'Neill, there is both value and condemnation in illusion.

2. THE CYCLE: A TALE OF POSSESSORS SELF-DISPOSSESSED

Although never quite sure of the number of plays that his cycle would include, O'Neill (according to Donald Gallup in his Introduction to *More Stately Mansions,* 1964) wrote drafts of the first four plays of this cycle which was to trace the fortunes of the Harford family and the corrupting effect of material things upon it. On February 21, 1943, in despair at world conditions, he burned the first two plays of the cycle—*Greed of the Meek* and *Give Me Death.* The third play was *A Touch of the Poet. More Stately Mansions,* the fourth play, was begun in 1935 and published (after being produced in Sweden) in 1964 in a version less than one-half the length of O'Neill's manuscript (shortened by Karl Ragnar Gierow and edited by Donald Gallup).

(a) *More Stately Mansions,* 1964

O'Neill's later plays turn desperately upon himself. He sees greed and corruption engulfing man, and his despair toward life allows him to see man's end only in terms of illusion or insanity. Once the illusion has been stripped away, there is only corruption and cruelty. Simon Harford, now married to Sara, once wanted to be a poet, but has now, as a rich merchant, become consumed by "the possession of power as the only freedom." Oliver Wendell Holmes' poem from which the title of the play is taken is quoted by Simon with "a mocking irony tinged with a bitter, tragic sadness." His life is consumed by his desire to dominate in business and to be dominated by his wife and his mother, whose bitter fight with one another for control of Simon is the central action of the play. His cruelty toward them is climaxed by his suggestion that they murder each other. Yet he thinks often of escape to insanity, which finally comes to him and, although violently opposed by Sara, also to his mother, leaving him as a child to Sara, who swears with "a fierce, passionate, possessive tenderness" to be all he will "ever need in life." As always, O'Neill's sensitive poet is defeated. The play is not pleasant, however, as O'Neill tortures himself with his views of corrupt and weak man, condemned by greed and controlled beyond escape by a female god.

B. Fading Slowly Away

The decade of the Forties was primarily one of war—anxiety, violence, and rehabilitation. Most of the dramatists who had established reputations in the Thirties continued to write; but, with few exceptions, their plays did not approach the quality that had previously distinguished their work. Slowly, the excitement which their plays had once stimulated faded away. There were, of course, exceptions, but mainly America after the War looked toward its new playwrights.

1. ELMER RICE (1892–   )

A dramatist whose career started before World War I, Rice has written several plays since 1940, although with little success. (His book, *The Living Theatre,* 1959, has the value of his long experience in the theater.) Only *Dream Girl* (1945), an expressionistic comedy which dramatized a girl's many dreams, achieved a popular and critical success. A musical version of *Street Scene* (1947) with Kurt Weill and Langston

Hughes did not last in the theater. Three later plays have done nothing for his reputation—*The Grand Tour* (1951) in which a school teacher and an embezzler find romance in Europe; *The Winner* (1954), a crime melodrama which once more makes use of Rice's early legal training; and *Cue for Passion* (1958), a weak story of a California Hamlet whose Horatio is a criminal psychologist.

2. GEORGE KELLY (1887–   )

Coming to Broadway via the vaudeville circuit where he produced his own skits, Kelly forged his reputation in the Twenties. In *The Deep Mrs. Sykes* (1945), Kelly portrayed a blindly egotistical woman who is damned by her own suspicious and crafty nature and thereby joins the Kelly gallery of unpleasant women. *The Fatal Weakness* (1946) comments in somewhat outdated fashion on marriage. Neither play was successful, although they preserve the hallmarks of Kelly's dramatic talent—a concern for "the satanic female race" and a lack of detachment in picturing it. His latest work is unpublished and unproduced: *Can Two Walk Together,* concerned with "the tragic rushing into marriage," and *When All Else Fails,* a satiric comedy about a recent and reluctant widow. Kelly is now a rare visitor to the theater.

3. MAXWELL ANDERSON (1888–1959)

During the final twenty years of his life, Anderson wrote a dozen plays, most of which show a decline in his dramatic powers. *Candle in the Wind* (1941), concerned with an American actress' efforts to get her fiancé released from a Nazi prison, was followed by two mediocre war plays—*The Eve of St. Mark* (1942) and *Storm Operation* (1944). Several of his last plays were adaptations of novels—*Lost in the Stars* (1949), a musical dramatization of Alan Paton's *Cry the Beloved Country; The Bad Seed* (1954), the melodramatic story of a child criminal by William March; *The Day the Money Stopped* (1958) a co-authored adaptation of Brendan Gill's novel.

Three of his post-war plays, however, are substantial dramas which continue the serious thought and dramaturgy of his earlier work. In *Joan of Lorraine* (1946), Anderson presented a rehearsal of a Joan of Arc play in which the leading actress and the director argue over interpretation—whether beliefs should be compromised. Joan's and Anderson's answer is that one cannot live without belief. *Anne of the Thousand Days* (1948) tells of one of the wives of Henry VIII, a weak return to the theme of *Elizabeth the Queen* and *Mary of Scotland* but repeating a bitter attitude toward mankind and his concern for power. Although not a carefully written play of ideas, *Barefoot in Athens* (1951) becomes a climax to Anderson's writing. Using Socrates' trial in ancient Greece as his scene, Anderson answers two questions that have always bothered him: democracy is the only acceptable form of government; truth is the only guide for freedom and life.

4. S. N. BEHRMAN (1893–   )

Although Behrman has been the most consistently active of those dramatists who made their reputations before World War II, his recent plays have been mainly adapted or derived from existing stories or plays. He has never returned to the high comedy of his early playwriting years. Instead, he has taken the strong, egotistical characters from his plays of the late Thirties and created sentimental comedies. Occasionally, the old Behrman wit is recognizable, but his reputation remains that of a dramatist of the period between the Wars.

His best post-war plays are *Dunnigan's Daughter* (1945), the story of a determined woman who controls her circumstances; *Jane* (1952), another eccentric but capable woman borrowed from a Somerset Maugham story; *Lord Pengo* (1962) the story of an art dealer (taken from Behrman's "The Days of Duveen") who is typical of Behrman's characters of the Thirties in his eccentricity, egotism, charm, and single-minded concern for the material things, but is distinguished from those earlier characters by being allowed to learn and to change his ways. As World War II approached, Behrman abandoned sophisticated detachment in favor of honest conviction—*No Time for Comedy* (1939). Since the war, he has shown more interest in light sentiment.

Other Behrman plays include *Jacobowsky and the Colonel* (1944), a farce comedy with suspense and a war setting, adapted from a play by Franz Werfel; *I Know My Love*

(1949), a Lunt and Fontaine comedy adapted from Marcel Achard's *Aupres de Ma Blonde; Fanny* (1954), a musical with a sentimental love story in which Joshusa Logan was co-author, adapted from Marcel Pagnol's trilogy, *Marius, César,* and *Fanny*; *The Cold Wind and the Warm* (1958), based on Behrman's memoirs, *The Worcester Account* (1954).

5. GEORGE S. KAUFMAN (1889–1962)

After spectacular success in the Thirties, Kaufman had great difficulty catching the comic spirit after the War. With Edna Ferber, he wrote *Bravo!* (1948); for *The Small Hours* (1951) and *Fancy Meeting You Again* (1952), he worked with Leueen MacGrath. Only with Howard Teichmann in *The Solid Gold Cadillac* (1953), a play which exploited the comic situation of a little old lady taking over the leadership of a large corporation, did he recover his old form and success.

6. MOSS HART (1904–1961)

Kaufman's main collaborator in the Thirties, Hart wrote three plays and a fascinating autobiography, *Act One* (1959). *Christopher Blake* (1946) is a drama about a divorce hearing; *Light up the Sky* (1948) toyed with types of theater people but without success. In *The Climate of Eden* (1952), Hart tried unsuccessfully to dramatize Edgar Mittelhölzer's *Shadows Move among Them,* a strange and serious tale of spiritual growth and burdens of guilt set in British Guiana.

7. PHILIP BARRY (1896–1949)

Barry's immediate reaction to the war was a protest play called *Liberty Jones* (1941), which dramatized a fascism vs. democracy theme. *Without Love* (1942), a romantic comedy, made use of Ireland's role in the war. After *Foolish Notion* (1945), a psychological study of a soldier's homecoming, Barry returned to the problem of man's search for meaning and found his answer in love, dramatized in *Second Threshold* (1949), which was revised slightly by Robert Sherwood before a posthumous production on Broadway in 1951.

AN OUTLINE HISTORY OF AMERICAN DRAMA

8. ROBERT SHERWOOD (1896–1955)

After the early war years, Sherwood became more involved in FDR's administration and less interested in writing plays. *The Rugged Path* (1945) is a propaganda play for victory in the war. After collaborating with Irving Berlin and Moss Hart on the musical *Miss Liberty* (1949), he wrote a final play, *Small War on Murray Hill* (performed posthumously, 1957), in which he used the flirtatious wife of a Tory sympathizer to ridicule the efforts of the British during the New York battles of the American Revolution.

9. CLIFFORD ODETS (1906–1963)

Odets never returned to Broadway with the force of his initial debut in the Thirties. *Clash by Night* (1941) was a failure in spite of Odet's intensity in treating love and social forces. After the war he wrote only three plays—*The Big Knife* (1949), the story of a successful actor who bargains his soul for fame and finally commits suicide; *The Country Girl* (1950), a dramatization of the psychological problems of an aging, alcoholic, and insecure actor and his wife who are redeemed by his success in a play; *The Flowering Peach* (1954), an interesting and modern retelling of Noah and the Ark in which the symbol of regeneration for a corrupt world is the family.

10. SIDNEY KINGSLEY (1906–   )

Although he will probably maintain a place in the history of American drama only for *Dead End* (1935), Kingsley's meager dramatic output has been increased by five plays since the 1930's. In *The Patriots* (1943), he explored the differences that separated Alexander Hamilton and Thomas Jefferson but wisely emphasized for a wartime audience that they shared the same ideals for their country. After the war, Kingsley pictured a conscientious police detective whose emotional involvement in a particular case drove him to sadistic action in *Detective Story* (1949). His adaptation of Arthur Koestler's novel *Darkness at Noon* (1951) dramatized the trial of a once hard core Russian Communist who found that he could not follow the Party philosophy. A slight farce, *Lunatics and Lovers* (1954), was followed eight years later by *Night Life* (1962), a melodrama about a murder in a key-club with overtones of labor and power politics.

C. A Past *and* a Future

Of the dramatists whose reputations were established before World War II, there are only three whose activity fifteen years past mid-century promises greater achievement: Thornton Wilder, William Saroyan, and Lillian Hellman. For quite different reasons, these dramatists demand close critical attention for post-war efforts.

1. THORNTON WILDER (1897–)

Wilder's reputation rests on only a handful of plays, most of them in one act. His search for the essence of life, however, plus his mastery of experimental dramaturgy and his strong humanism, make it impossible for the drama critic to treat him lightly. It is true, of course, that in the past twenty years he has written little—*Our Century* (1947); a translation of Sartre's *The Victors* (1949); *A Life in the Sun* (1955), which was based on the Alcestis legend; and a brief portrayal of a time Apollo got the Fates drunk in *The Drunken Sisters* (1957). His best work was a revision of *The Merchant of Yonkers* (1938) entitled *The Matchmaker* (1954), an amusing and stylized farce-comedy in which just about everyone gets what he or she wants. But the final criticism of Thornton Wilder cannot yet be written.

2. WILLIAM SAROYAN (1908–)

Saroyan is an honest eccentric whose view of life is startling, exciting, and penetrating in its abrupt simplicity. At a time when optimism and innocence are suspect in society, he has created a brave new world without much else. As he continues to write plays, he continues to philosophize in an unorthodox but frequently amusing manner that reflects modern confusions in society as simply and straightforwardly as it shows his interest in the good life. Frequently as impressive as it is erratic, Saroyan's work is not yet completed.

Since the war, Saroyan has written a number of short plays and several long ones. In 1949, he published *Don't Go Away Mad*, a play of Saroyan optimism set in a hospital for incurable diseases; and *Sam Ego's House*, which represents life in the United States. *The Slaughter of the Innocents* (1952) dramatizes the idea that man is the victim of his own acts. Saroyan's one Broadway play, *The Cave Dwellers* (1957), tells of people with virtues of royal proportions who live in a theater that is the world and find that all is good. More recent play titles include *The Paris Comedy, or The Secret of Life; The Moscow Comedy, or No One in His Right Mind;* and *The London Comedy, or Sam the Highest Jumper of Them All*.

3. LILLIAN HELLMAN (1905–   )

Still a moralist with a tendency to emphasize melodramatic techniques, Lillian Hellman continues to write the type of play which gained her a reputation in the Thirties. Her productivity for Broadway has not been remarkable—including a war play (*The Searching Wind*, 1944); work on the musical *Candide* (1956); two adaptations (Jean Anouilh's *The Lark*, 1955; Emanuel Roblès' *Montserrat*, 1949); and the almost absurd *My Mother, My Father and Me* (1963) based on Burt Blechman's novel *How Much?*—but she has written three strong plays, the last of which shows the compassion and artistry which make her one of the better dramatists of the contemporary theater.

Another Part of the Forest (1946) shows the Hubbard family in a period before *The Little Foxes* and dramatizes Ben Hubbard's unscrupulous way of gaining control of the family. The South is also the scene of *The Autumn Garden* (1951) which, in a rather Chekovian tradition, portrays some of the cruelties of man as well as the agony of age: "at any given moment you're only the sum of your life up to then." In *Toys in the Attic* (1960), Lillian Hellman created a penetrating picture of life, warning man of the innocent who falls in love with truth.

IV. ART AND ENTERTAINMENT

"The purpose of Art is to raise doubt; the purpose of entertainment is to reassure," wrote John Whiting, a modern English dramatist ["From My Diary," *The Twentieth Century*, CLXIX (February, 1961), 200]. The distinction made is an interesting one, even if the critic assumes that in the best entertainment there is evidence of art. In the Broadway theaters there is no doubt that people want to be reassured and that light entertainment is the best means to this end. Plays that have stayed on Broadway—that is, those that have made money for the owners of the theaters—have been melodramas, comedies, or musicals. As drama critic Murray Schumach noted (Kansas City *Star*, Oct. 4, 1964): "Broadway's angels are mainly on the side of the cynics who cater to the matinee ladies and the tired businessmen." And in the contemporary American theater, as in the theater of the past, money controls. Although each year a few serious plays —that is, plays that show some insight concerning man— have appeared on Broadway, they have seldom been outstanding. Other than Williams and Miller, contemporary American drama can boast no dramatist who has evidenced sustained excellence in the theater. Instead, there are many plays by numerous playwrights. Certain Absurdists have asserted themselves with some originality, but their work lacks maturity. Poetic dramatists are still learning that poetry "must serve the theater before it can again rule there," as the Irish playwright, Lady Gregory, once warned. With only an occasional nod to "art," contemporary American theater is a business designed to help people enjoy themselves.

A. Seriousness and Entertainment

A number of plays, with varying success, suggest the serious ambitions of dramatists. Many of these plays may be grouped under the heading of psychological dramas; other plays point to some social problem; still others—such as William Archibald's *The Innocents* (1950), an adaptation of Henry James' *The Turn of the Screw*; and Louis O. Coxe and Robert Chapman's adaptation of Herman Melville's short story, *Billy Budd* (1951)—bring to the stage some of the serious thoughts of American literary men. The only dramatists who present a body of work which pretends to deal seriously with life are William Inge, Arthur Laurents, and Paddy Chayefsky. In general, however, even their plays emphasize a psychological approach which flatters the audience's passions and intellect rather than presenting an insight that challenges. Entertainment is still the key.

1. THREE DRAMATISTS OF SKILL AND AMBITION

William Inge (1913–   ) has managed to mingle successfully sex and sentiment and to present lonely people whose problems are solved, for good or for ill, by love. There is a certain formula to his work which suggests a subservience to both Broadway and Hollywood commercialism. Although his characters are conceived with some insight and skill, his psychologically oriented solution to life's problems frequently seems superficial. His late plays—*A Loss of Roses* (1960) concerning the growth from youth to maturity; and *Natural Affections* (1963), a poorly constructed melodrama of unnatural affections of a mother and a son—have been particularly weak. His earlier and better plays, on the other hand, include *Come Back, Little Sheba* (1950), the story of a slovenly romantic woman and her alcoholic husband as they are made to face the reality that is their life; *Picnic* (1953), a portrayal of women revealed by their passion and driven to a bleak future; *Bus Stop* (1955), a sketchy presentation of various people in a bus stop and their attitudes toward love; *The Dark at the Top of the Stairs* (1957), a psychological study of the need for love and understanding within a family and among all people. Superior craftsmanship is his hallmark.

Arthur Laurents (1918–   ) has shown a strong social consciousness in all of his plays. Starting his playwriting career with the war play, *Home of the Brave* (1945), Laurents has also written movie scenarios and stories for musicals—*West Side Story* (1957) and *Gypsy* (1959). Although sometimes inclined to sentiment and melodrama, Laurents suggests his potential in drama with his honest concern for the dignity of the individual in society, his insight in revealing character, and his imaginative experimentation in form. *The Bird Cage* (1950) describes a world of tyranny as it is mirrored in the activity of a night club owner who is defied by an heroic chorus girl. In *The Time of the Cuckoo* (1952) a sentimental spinster touring Europe learns a good deal about life and herself during a stay in Venice. The theme of loneliness is imaginatively portrayed in *A Clearing in the Woods* (1957), where three characters are used to show aspects of the heroine's past and to help her reconcile herself to a world where she can find love. *Invitation to a March* (1960) is a comic fantasy which dramatizes the individual's choice either to follow his own bent or the desires of others.

Paddy Chayefsky (1923–   ) is a playwright whose literary skill and fine touch of humor combine well with thought-provoking themes. His professional career started with television (*Marty*), and his first Broadway play, *The Middle of the Night* (1956), was developed from a television script. In *The Tenth Man* (1959) Chayefsky shows a group of Jews exorcising a dybbuk from a demented girl who is finally taken from the synagogue by the "tenth" man. The presumption that she will be cured by this man's love is sentimental and romantic to extreme, but the humor is a delight. A more thoughtful play, but one also marked by clever humor and good writing, is *Gideon* (1961). Chosen by God to deliver his people, a reluctant Gideon becomes prideful and, when rebuked by God, angry: "O God! I cannot believe in you! If you love me, let me believe at least in mine own self!" And the Angel is humanized: "I love you, Gideon!" With a mixture of humor and insight, Chayefsky shows some potential in American drama.

2. SOCIAL DRAMA

This category is vague, but it is intended to include plays of more thoughtful than comic purpose which build, sometimes in a melodramatic fashion, upon a social issue. Alfred Hayes' *The Girl on the Via Flaminia* (1954) is such a play, as it portrays the wartime love of an American soldier for an Italian girl, their desire for independence yet their dependence upon one another, and the attitudes of society. So is Ketti Frings' dramatization of Thomas Wolfe's *Look Home-*

ward, Angel (1957) and Carson McCullers' Broadway version of *The Member of the Wedding* (1950). The outstanding writer of a more conventional social drama is Lorraine Hansberry, whose *A Raisin in the Sun* (1959) dramatizes the decision of a Negro family to move into a white neighborhood. Her dramatic virtues of humor, intellectual insight, and compassion for man are also evident in *The Sign in Sidney Brustein's Window* (1964).

Two other plays which present meaningful social ideas based on personal experiences are Dore Schary's *Sunrise at Campobello* (1958), concerned with FDR, and William Gibson's *The Miracle Worker* (1959), the story of young Helen Keller.

B. Contemporary Melodrama

Modern drama being what it is, the dramatist's concern for producing a thrill or a chill or a tug at the heart is almost primary. Melodrama, then, is a strong ingredient of most contemporary American plays, whether the approach to the material be social or psychological.

1. PSYCHOLOGICAL MELODRAMA

A good number of dramatists who have some pretension to serious comment emphasize a psychological approach to their material. Joseph Kramm's *The Shrike* (1952) is a good illustration. Waking up in the psychological ward of a city hospital, an attempted suicide, separated from his wife, learns that in the eyes of the authorities he is a potential criminal and that he can be released only if he subdues all normal emotions and places himself under the control of his wife. Michael V. Gazzo's *A Hatful of Rain* (1955) deals with the problems of a dope addict. Herman Wouk created a fine courtroom psychological melodrama from his own novel in *The Caine Mutiny Court Martial* (1954). *The Diary of Anne Frank* (1955) by Frances Goodrich and Albert Hackett is essentially a psychological drama showing a young girl's perceptive reactions to the cruelties of war. Morton Wishengrad's *The Rope Dancers* (1959) is the best among plays of this type. A woman conceives from her drunken husband, and their child has six fingers on one hand. Fearful and guilty, the mother calls the hand evil, a curse, and makes the child wear a mitten until a doctor convinces her that "we all wear a glove over something." When the doctor removes the finger, however, the girl dies. In a manner close to Nathaniel Hawthorne's "The Birthmark," Wishengrad talks about God and good and evil.

2. CRIME MELODRAMA

Crime melodramas are here to stay. *A Case of Libel* (1963), a play by Henry Denker based on Louis Nizer's *My Life in Court*, makes its point for an honest lawyer, while bringing all the crudities and niceties of a libel suit in court. One of the best of crime dramas is Joseph Hayes' *The Desperate Hours* (1955). A convict has escaped from prison and is returning to a city to kill the sheriff who sent him away. Waiting for his chance, the killer and his two pals commandeer a house and family, and amid great excitement and suspense are finally killed.

C. Contemporary Comedy

All too frequently on Broadway, the only alternative to giving the audiences a thrill seems to be to make them laugh. In comedy, the range is great; but a number of playwrights have found success with sentimental, light, or satirical comedy.

1. SENTIMENTAL COMEDY: ROBERT ANDERSON

Sentiment has long been a marketable item on Broadway, although some playwrights manifest more finesse in its dissemination than others. Jerome Chodorov and Joseph Fields made sentiment predominant in their treatment of sex and marriage problems in *Anniversary Waltz* (1954) and *The Ponder Heart* (1956). William Gibson's *Two for the Seesaw* (1958) effectively infuses sentiment in a modern psychological comedy. Joshua Logan's version of *The Cherry Orchard*, called *The Wisteria Trees* (1950), capitalized on a traditional sentimentalism of society; while John Patrick's *The Teahouse of the August Moon* (1953), an adaptation of

Vern Sneider's novel, creates a comic sentimentalism on the romantic island of Okinawa.

The most successful among the writers of sentimental comedy and melodrama is Robert Anderson (1917–   ). Building his plays largely on a theme of sentimental loneliness, Anderson shows his skill and sensitivity in the atmosphere and the people he creates. On the other hand, the slow movement in his plays and his unrelenting emphasis on sweetness, sentiment, and illicit sex as a solution to man's problems, detract from his over-all effectiveness. After writing several plays that never got to New York, Anderson in *Tea and Sympathy* (1953) treated a lonely and sensitive student at a New England boy's school whose problems in trying to prove his manhood are solved by his housemaster's wife whose sympathy knows no limits. Having the "right" amounts of sex and sentiment, the play was a Broadway hit. *All Summer Long* (1954), dramatizing the actual flooding of a family house by a river and the symbolic erosion of the family foundations, was less than successful on the stage. *Silent Night, Lonely Night* (1959) describes a lonely Christmas Eve vigil by a husband and wife, not married to each other, who find during this brief night in their lives an understanding which each needed and a strength to face the life ahead.

2. LIGHT COMEDY

A commonplace observation among theater people is that tired businessmen and the ladies who attend matinees enjoy a bright, witty, fast-moving comedy that requires practically no thought. The subject matter is not extremely important. Marriage and sex, of course, are always good for laughs or titters, as George Axelrod's *The Seven Year Itch* (1952) and *Will Success Spoil Rock Hunter?* (1955) show. Neil Simon is also an effective writer of this type of comedy, with *Come Blow Your Horn* (1961) and *Barefoot in the Park* (1963); both plays capitalize on fast repartee and farce situation. Norman Krasna's *John Loves Mary* (1947) shows girl-boy post-war problems; *Sabrina Fair* (1953) by Samuel Taylor brings a romantic Cinderella theme to mid-twentieth century circumstance. For those who want excellent light comedy and have no preference concerning theme, there is Mary Ellen Chase's play about Elwood P. Dowd's six-foot rabbit, *Harvey* (1944). *Auntie Mame* (1956), an adaptation of Patrick Dennis' novel by Jerome Lawrence and Robert E. Lee, dramatizes another quite fantastic character. Other light comedies are Anita Loos' *Happy Birthday* (1946), Harry Kurnitz' *Reclining Figure* (1954), Ira Levin's *No Time for Sergeants* (1955), Jean Kerr's *Mary, Mary* (1961). All of these plays reassure the tired businessman and the matinee ladies.

3. SATIRIC COMEDY

Almost all American comedy attempts to satirize or ridicule something or somebody—from suburbia in *Auntie Mame* to the army in *The Teahouse of the August Moon*. For example, Garson Kanin's *Born Yesterday* (1946) satirizes business and politics, while exploring the comic possibility of a millionaire junkman and the ex-chorus girl who lives with him. More definite political satire is Howard Lindsay and Russel Crouse's *State of the Union* (1945), which dramatizes the personal and public problems of a Presidential candidate. Gore Vidal satirized war in *Visit to a Small Planet* (1956) and politics in *The Best Man* (1960).

D. Drama in Poetry

Without becoming involved in an argument over terms—poetic drama, verse drama, or mood drama—it is possible to note a slowly increasing post-war interest in plays written in poetry. The problem of uniting good poetry and good drama simultaneously—of creating poetry which serves the theater—still exists, but it has been adjoined by a growing awareness of the necessity for a poetic drama and of its potential in the theater. This concern for a poetic language in the theater is seen in the plays of Arthur Miller and Tennessee Williams; however, in general, attempts to write poetic drama have come from poets rather than dramatists—Robert Frost, Robinson Jeffers, William Carlos Williams, E. E. Cummings, Archibald MacLeish, Langston Hughes, and Richard Eberhart.

1. DRAMATISTS WRITING IN POETRY

Of the dramatists who used poetry, Maxwell Anderson is the best example. After World War II, however, he continued his writing of poetic drama only in *Anne of the Thousand Days* (1949), which, although it continued a thesis he had used in previous plays, reached his pre-war achievements in neither poetry nor drama. N. Richard Nash was markedly unsuccessful with a pretentious romantic tragedy, *See the Jaguar* (1952), and later, in *The Rainmaker* (1954), showed that his talent is for prose comedy. Equally poor was Arch Oboler's *Night of the Auk* (1956), a space-age melodrama in which the dramatist's confused approach to language is illustrated by his inability to describe his medium in his Preface.

2. POETS WRITING DRAMA

Practicing poets wrote much better poetry than the playwrights, although their plays are marred by poorly created and motivated characters and a serious lack of dramatic conflict and action. E. E. Cummings pits Death (knowledge) against Santa Claus (understanding) in a discursive thesis play, *Santa Claus* (1946). Robinson Jeffers adapted *Medea* (1947), slightly revised an earlier dramatic narrative called *The Tower Beyond Tragedy* (1950), and wrote *The Cretan Woman* (1954), a forceful and stage-worthy play on the Phaedra-Hippolytus theme. Among his published plays, William Carlos Williams' *Many Loves* (1959), concerned with the writing of a verse play, showed in production the difficulties that an abstract poet must overcome to write an actable play. *The Visionary Farms* (1952) by Richard Eberhart, however, dramatizes the modern paradox of progress and commercial corruption in a manner which shows promise for American poetic drama. But the outstanding poetic dramatist since World War II is Archibald MacLeish, although *This Music Crept by Me on the Water* (1953) is more the creation of mood than a drama, as two people react to the magic of the moon. With *J.B.* (1958), a modern version of the Job story, MacLeish showed that he could write drama that was both good poetry and effective on the stage—"an imitation of an action."

3. PRODUCTION AND RECEPTION

With varying degrees of success, the above mentioned plays have been performed on Broadway, off-Broadway, or by a professional acting group. This fact in itself suggests a change in attitude toward poetic drama. Although this genre has not become the province of the serious dramatist as it was 150 years ago, the use of language has become a major concern of the serious dramatist. Moreover, the growing interest of a commercial theater in poetic drama indicates an awareness of a change in audience tastes.

E. Musical Comedy

Having gained considerable momentum during the Thirties, American musical comedy after World War II attained a popularity and an artistic achievement that indicate its superiority in the world of musical comedy. Although some musicals are clearly commercially analyzed patchwork products, the best musical comedies—such as Alan Jay Lerner and Frederick Loewe's *My Fair Lady* (1956), based on G. B. Shaw's *Pygmalion,* and Frank Loesser's *The Most Happy Fella* (1956), modelled on Sidney Howard's *They Knew What They Wanted*—present well-developed characters, and plot conflicts which are supported by the music and the songs. Mainly, the musicals are light and gay, but occasionally, as in the Romeo-Juliet theme of Leonard Bernstein's *West Side Story* (1957), with Arthur Laurents and Stephen Sondheim, the appeal is to emotions of sadness and despair. Love, however, is invariably the issue which the composer, the lyricists, and the story writer surround with sweetness and sentiment, fast-moving comedy, perhaps some light ridiculing or a bit of moralizing, and hopefully a good story. Although revues, such as Harold Rome's *Call Me Mister* (1946), have tended to disappear in recent years, and another kind of musical play exemplified by Gian-Carlo Menotti's *The Medium* (1947) has appeared, the form of the musical comedy still varies considerably within the limits of these two extremes.

On the imaginative artistry of those writing in this broad area, however, rests America's reputation as creator of the world's best in musical comedy.

As the names of the composers of the Twenties and the Thirties slip away, new names quickly take their places, and specialists become a part of an entertainment requiring the integrated efforts of several people. In his Foreword to Stanley Green's *The World of Musical Comedy* (1960), Deems Taylor tells this story: when a man backstage at a theater greeted a composer friend with "I hope your show goes well tonight, old man," fourteen men answered "Thanks." Thus a composer may have two or three people work with him on story or lyrics. Two old-timers after World War II were Irving Berlin (*Annie Get Your Gun*, 1946, book by Herbert and Dorothy Fields; *Call Me Madam*, 1956, book by Howard Lindsay and Russel Crouse) and Cole Porter, whose only big hit after the war was a musical treatment of *The Taming of the Shrew* called *Kiss Me, Kate* (1948), with book by Sam and Bella Spewack. Richard Rodgers and Oscar Hammerstein continued their *Oklahoma!* (1943) success with *South Pacific* (1949) and *The King and I* (1951).

The best of post-war composers and musicals would include Lerner and Loewe (*Brigadoon*, 1947; *My Fair Lady*, 1956); Jule Styne (*Gentlemen Prefer Blondes*, 1949; *Gypsy*, 1959); Frank Loesser (*Guys and Dolls*, 1950; *How to Succeed in Business Without Really Trying*, 1961), Leonard Bernstein (*West Side Story*, 1957); Richard Adler and Jerry Ross (*The Pajama Game*, 1954; *Damn Yankees*, 1955); and Meredith Willson (*The Music Man*, 1957). In the production of these many musicals, the work of George Abbott, the director with the "magic touch" for musicals, must not be forgotten.

F. Absurdists in America

Theater of the absurd is a post-war phenomenon in which the dramatists, in despair and anxiety, show their sense of the senselessness of the human condition in a world in which man is deprived of certainties. Expressing their convictions concerning the impossibility of communication among men and the inadequacy of a rational approach to life, absurd dramatists discuss in their distinctive fashion the *noth-*

ingness which is their approach to reality. "Nothing is more real than nothing," Martin Esslin (*The Theatre of the Absurd,* 1961) quotes Democritus. Abandoning conceptual thinking and logical language, the absurd dramatist deals in paradoxes, illogical behavior, and absurd situations, while attempting to create meaningful insights into the human condition. Samuel Beckett (*Waiting for Godot,* 1953) and Eugène Ionesco (*The Bald Soprano,* 1950) stimulated the writing of absurd drama and are still the outstanding dramatists in the movement.

In America some of the followers of Beckett and Ionesco have so abused their dramatic innovations as to produce contrived pieces of showmanship that have no meaningful relationship with life, absurd or not. Generally, the so-called new American playwrights lack the finesse and sophistication of their European contemporaries and are more willing to emasculate and condemn man than to provide insight into the human condition. Frequently, the dramatist's emasculating attacks suggest a degenerate society and a depraved mankind, while the hero of his play becomes "homo" or "homosexual" (the homosexual in Gelber's *The Apple* represents *Christ*), rather than "homo sapient." More specifically, a few Americans have achieved some significance in this genre, mainly off-Broadway, since Jack Gelber's *The Connection* was produced in 1959—Edward Albee, Jack Richardson, and Arthur Kopit, whose reputation rests on *Oh Dad, Poor Dad, Mamma's Hung You in the Closet and I'm Feelin' So Sad* (1961), an hilarious burlesquing of absurd drama, which ends with the question that probably stimulated Kopit in the beginning: "What is the meaning of this?"

1. JACK GELBER (1926–   )

Techniques among writers of absurd drama differ radically. Gelber denies the illusion of the stage and merges the actors and the audience to create a reality in which pretense is presumably unnecessary. *The Connection* (1959), the audience is told, presents real dope addicts who ad lib a plotless evening for which their payment will be a "fix." This artifically inspired realism is promoted by a jazz accompaniment and by panhandlers working the lobby between the acts. In *The Apple* (1961), Gelber makes the theater a coffee shop and brings on his characters—a Negro, a Jew, a homosexual, a whore, a spastic, and a drunk. The series of improvised scenes, however, symbolically dramatizes a theme of mankind which is both interesting and promising in terms of Gelber's potential.

2. EDWARD ALBEE (1927–   )

Albee attacks with a vitriolic vigor the human condition. With wit and some skill in creating concise dialogue, he dramatizes a hatred for social and personal complacency, false values, and the "American Dream." Although he takes his cue from Ionesco and enjoys a cynically intellectual approach to life, he lacks the compassion and the concern for man's dignity which distinguishes the works of major playwrights. Since the 1960 performance of *The Zoo Story* (1959), in New York, however, newspaper critics have considered him a major writer among American dramatists.

Mainly, he has written one-act plays. *The Zoo Story* (1959) dramatizes the meeting of two strangers, one of whom tells the other his life problems, goads him to anger, and finally forces him to be the means of his suicide. *The Death of Bessie Smith* (1960) uses the auto accident of blues singer Bessie Smith, and the refusal of two white hospitals to admit her, to illustrate hate and violence as seen in America. Both *The Sandbox* (1960) and *The American Dream* (1961) show the emptiness of the American dream; in the second play Albee presents a grotesque caricature, suggestive of Ionesco. His full-length plays are *Who's Afraid of Virginia Woolf?* (1962), in which a man and his wife, with malice and ingenuity, destroy one another; an adaptation of Carson McCullers' *The Ballad of the Sad Café* (1963); and *Tiny Alice* (1964).

3. JACK RICHARDSON (1935–   )

Richardson, a dramatist of quite penetrating intellect, is concerned with the victimization of man by various social forces. In *The Prodigal* (1960), he retells the story of Orestes (the Greek Oresteia legend), making him a modern cynic who wishes to remain detached from society but is forced to abandon his position. *Gallows Humor* (1961) contrasts a condemned man with his executioner and shows the greater "freedom" of the former. *Lorenzo* (1963) uses a group of players in Renaissance Italy to suggest the value of illusion over reality.

V. SUMMARY

Just three hundred years ago, the first recorded play written in English in America, *Ye Bare and Ye Cubb,* was performed in Accomac County, Virginia. During the intervening years, the advance of American drama to a position of world significance has been slow and painful. It took America a hundred years to produce an imitative romantic tragedy, *The Prince of Parthia,* another seventy-five years to build a society and provide a dramatist who could caricature American *Fashion*, and nearly fifty more years to stimulate the imagination that created *Margaret Fleming*, a play that American audiences could not then accept. The story of this labored progress is the history of an American drama and theater which, comparatively speaking, moved rapidly and with some vigor from James Herne to Eugene O'Neill. It was the period between the World Wars, however, that made America a world force in the drama.

By 1941, American dramatists had suggested their potential in the world theater, leaving to their followers the problem of more abundant and sophisticated evidence of excellence. Since this time, the progress of American drama has again been slow. During the past twenty-five years, most of the pre-World War II dramatists have ceased to write, and only two new dramatists have appeared who have possessed the imagination and talent to press the challenge of American drama upon the world. In the meantime, the great mass of plays on Broadway are psychological or sentimental melodramas, while the demands of the commercial interests have given more and more theaters to the increasingly popular musical comedies.

In one sense, the demands of the commercial theater in New York are proving to be a great boon to American theater and drama. Never before has the off-Broadway theater been so significantly productive, particularly with the work of playwrights of some reputation. While the establishment of the theater in the Lincoln Center has interested many people, the work of the Tyrone Guthrie Theater in Minneapolis and the increased number of workshop theaters and summer stock companies in various American cities are equally impressive. College and university theaters now attract professional actors and actresses, who work with students in creating productions of taste and excellence. If there is a contemporary theater movement at all, it is obviously designed to spread theater throughout America. And if the commercial demands of Broadway encourage this movement, the life of the theater will be enhanced.

The writing of more challenging dramatic criticism is a distinct advance in the history of American drama. Some of the respected older journalistic critics still write—John Mason Brown, Walter Kerr, Brooks Atkinson, Richard Watts, Jr.—and they are now supported by such critics as Henry Hewes and William Glover, and academic critics like Robert Brustein and Gerald Weales. The establishment of scholarly journals—*Tulane Drama Review, Modern Drama, Drama Survey*—and the interest of university presses in publishing scholarly research in American drama has recently stimulated an atmosphere conducive to a tradition of literary criticism for American drama. In essence, criticism of American drama, though progressing slowly from the turn of the century, is now reaching a significant level of achievement.

With his customary flash of insight, G. B. Shaw once declared that the theater is always at a low ebb; that, generally speaking, things always look bad for contemporary drama. In any safe and sensible view, of course, a perspective of a hundred-odd years is always necessary for one to assess a drama accurately. If America has not produced the number of contemporary dramatists of world significance that by World War II seemed its obvious potential, the condition of American drama is still not one of despair. Let the historians and critics of the distant future draw that conclusion if they must. American drama has become a force in world drama, and its promise remains rich for a more dominant role in the future.

SELECTED BIBLIOGRAPHY

Cahalan, Thomas L., and Paul A. Doyle, *Modern American Drama.* Boston, Massachusetts: Student Outlines Company, 1960.

Donoghue, Denis, *The Third Voice Modern British and American Verse Drama.* Princeton, New Jersey: Princeton University Press, 1959.

Downer, Alan S., *Recent American Drama.* Minneapolis, Minnesota: University of Minnesota Press, 1961.

Gassner, John, *Theatre at the Crossroads.* New York: Holt, Rinehart and Winston, 1960.

Kitchin, Laurence, *Mid-Century Drama.* London: Faber and Faber, 1960.

Lewis, Allan, *American Plays and Playwrights of the Contemporary Theatre.* New York: Crown Publishers, Inc., 1965.

Melchinger, Siegfried, *The Concise Encyclopedia of Modern Drama.* New York: Horizon Press, 1964.

Nelson, Benjamin, *Tennessee Williams, the Man and his Work.* New York: Obolensky, 1961.

Weales, Gerald, *American Drama Since World War II.* New York: Harcourt, Brace & World, Inc., 1962.

Welland, Dennis S. R., *Arthur Miller.* Edinburgh: Oliver and Boyd, 1961.

Wellwarth, George E., *The Theater of Protest and Paradox.* New York: New York University Press, 1964.

INDEX